Suffer Little Children

Reginald C. Longman

Published by

MELROSE BOOKS

An Imprint of Melrose Press Limited
St Thomas Place, Ely
Cambridgeshire
CB7 4GG, UK
www.melrosebooks.com

FIRST EDITION

Copyright © Reg Longman 2012

The Author asserts his moral right to
be identified as the author of this work

Cover designed by Jeremy Kay

ISBN 978-1-907732-58-4

All rights reserved. No part of this publication may be reproduced, stored in a retrieval system, or transmitted, in any form or by any means electronic, mechanical, photocopying, recording or otherwise, without the prior permission of the publishers.

This book is sold subject to the condition that it shall not, by way of trade or otherwise, be lent, re-sold, hired out or otherwise circulated without the publisher's prior consent in any form of binding or cover other than that in which it is published and without a similar condition including this condition being imposed on the subsequent purchaser.

Printed and bound in Great Britain by:
Mimeo Ltd, Huntingdon, Cambridgeshire

FSC
www.fsc.org
MIX
Paper from
responsible sources
FSC® C019549

RATIONALE

A compassionate and understanding philosopher, or even the figmented Silas Ratslinger, may well have said of orphans forced into workhouses, dressed in rags and begging in the streets, or perhaps having to stoop to prostitution to survive:

"Judge not the orphans whose destiny was caused by wars, crime, disease, and even society, for the plight in their lives, their lack of understanding of love, and their rejection of authority.

But better, blame the generations before them, for theirs is the legacy they leave the World, and remember those frightening words of John Bradford (1510–1555) upon seeing an evil-doer hanged by his so called 'betters:'"

"THERE,
BUT FOR THE GRACE OF GOD,
GO I."

Reg Longman

SUFFER LITTLE CHILDREN

by

Reginald Charles Longman

This is the story of a Dr Barnardo boy, who was raised in the 'Homes' during the Second World War and until 1950. Whether the upbringing was an ordeal or a nurtured success, the reader will decide, and of course, is free to form his or her own conclusion.

~o~o~

The characters, good, bad, or otherwise, are or were real people. At the time of my writing this book, there are/were others who can/could bear witness to the facts mentioned.

~o~o~

SUFFER LITTLE CHILDREN

DEDICATION

My eldest son, Dr Shane Longman, not having any 'Longman' grandparents or otherwise any knowledge of the Longman side of our family, has asked me on several occasions to write the story of my childhood and youth.

As well, Donna, my wife for the past forty-eight years, is, of course, aware that my parents had died many years ago, but until I actually wrote this book she had little knowledge of the orphanage system in which I was raised. My childhood and adolescent years has been a subject that I seldom ever talked about in any detail either with her, or any of our sons.

Now, having written the story of my early life, I realise that as well as the sad and sometimes violent, even brutal times I endured as a child, I also had a happy and memorable childhood, as one will discover upon reading my story.

I have found as well that the writing of this book has been very therapeutic and somewhat satisfying because now, even though I may be getting on in years, I can, with perhaps a wry smile, put behind me for whatever time I have left on this earth the somewhat turbulent upbringing I received as an orphaned child.

With the completion of my book, I trust now that Donna, having put up with the character that I am, can, together with our sons Shane, Mark, Cory and Brynley, better understand a little more about her husband, and they, their father, and as well, a little about the Longman family.

With much pride and love, I dedicate this book to all of you.

∼o∼o∼

SUFFER LITTLE CHILDREN

ACKNOWLEDGEMENT

To my dear Donna

Anyone who has written a book of any size, type or otherwise, knows just how much work is involved prior to its being submitted to a publisher for its appraisal.

Besides the actual writing of the book, which took in excess of six years, comes the editing, which you, Donna, and I did together. This we did, over and over again, at least five, perhaps even six times. As well, there is the research into the size of the book, font type, formatting, book binding type and several other details involved, all of which we did prior to the professional publishers (Melrose) becoming involved.

Without your diligent help, persistence, constant reading, checking of detail, and patience with me, this book would never have been completed, and its objective realised.

I shall forever remember you, Donna, toiling away, sometimes at two in the morning, your tearstained glasses fogging your vision. You were brilliant!

Thanks for all your help, Don; without it this book would never have been finished. God bless you, my dear, and thank you for marrying that little boy in my story.

With all my love for eternity,

Your ever-loving 'rotten little sod'

∼o∼o∼

SUFFER LITTLE CHILDREN

PREFACE

Mine is the story of a World War II soldier's son who, orphaned at the age of five (my mother having died earlier, when I was just three years old) was subsequently brought up in the world-famous British institution: Dr Barnardo's Homes.

For more than a century Dr Barnardo's Homes was, in all likelihood, the largest orphanage institution in the world.

My story is primarily about its author, from infancy and until I reached the age of sixteen and a half years old and left Dr Barnardo's Homes, to join the 'outsiders' world'.

As a child I looked beyond the orphanage system I was being raised in, and saw the rest of the world as being perhaps a gentler place – a place which we institutionalised children referred to as the 'outsiders' world.

However, as well as the basic hardships of the harsh, institutional way of life, there were, as well, the masters and matrons, with their idealistic yet unqualified ideas of discipline, who beat the children in their charge.

There were times and orphanages that were very difficult for me to endure, but, as well, there were, of course, many, many other youngsters who suffered the same, or even worse, physical abuse than I did. Most of us survived, however, with no lasting damage to our beings, minds, or bodies.

Fortunately there were many who, being our caregivers, were sympathetic, caring, and compassionate people, with an understanding for those hapless ones in their keeping.

With these thoughtful caregivers, who through their kindness helped provide many, many memorable and happy times for us young impressionable boys, our lives were far more bearable.

Under those happy, or even unhappy conditions, boys often became very close friends – closer even than many, if not most, natural-born brothers.

SUFFER LITTLE CHILDREN

Unfortunately however, many children and young people left their orphanage institutions traumatically affected, which in some instances resulted in them needing psychiatric or otherwise therapeutic treatment. Some even committed suicide. Others, on the other hand, fared well and lived, relatively speaking, normal and successful lives. I believe I was one of the fortunate ones.

Of course, others, orphans or not, could and have written their story of being raised in an orphanage institution, their stories being quite different to mine. But as I have mentioned, for better or worse, for the good and bad times, this is my story and how I must write it.

~o~o~

Dr Barnardo's Homes was founded and established in London, England in 1870, primarily to give safe harbour to the orphans or waifs and strays, from the slums of east London.

My (and over six hundred thousand other people's) benefactor, Dr Thomas John Barnardo, the founder of Dr Barnardo's Homes, was born in Dublin, Ireland in 1845.

It had been Dr Barnardo's original intention to become a medical missionary in China, but due to circumstances he, while studying in London in 1866, decided to help the poverty-stricken children there instead.

So intense was his dedication towards helping the poor, the destitute and orphaned children from the East End of London he ran into many difficulties. His enthusiastic desire to help the unfortunates, including even, the kidnapping of child prostitutes for their own protection, and as well being a doctor, resulted in Dr Barnardo coming under suspicion of being the infamous 'Jack the Ripper'.

Needless to say, any and all charges were quickly dismissed and Thomas Barnardo continued on with his now famous charitable work.

Dr Thomas John Barnardo died on 19 September 1905.

A few brief facts concerning Dr Thomas Barnardo and Dr Barnardo's Homes can be found further on in my story.

CONTENTS

Rationale iii
Dedication vii
Acknowledgement ix
Preface xi
List of Photographs xiv

Chapter
1	Primary Memories	1
2	The Beginning of a Turbulent Childhood	13
3	Dr Barnardo's Homes	24
4	On the Move Again	42
5	Tamworth – Foster Home	56
6	Happy Days at Meriden	72
7	Bayfordbury – Part 1	85
8	Bayfordbury – Part 2	110
9	Bayfordbury – Part 3	127
10	Bayfordbury – Part 4	149
11	Bayfordbury – Part 5	176
12	Bayfordbury – Part 6	202
13	Bayfordbury – Part 7	224
14	Bayfordbury – Part 8	239
15	Churchill House – Part 1	253
16	Churchill House – Part 2	271
17	Churchill House – Part 3	294
18	Churchill House – Part 4	306
19	Goldings – Part 1	337
20	Goldings – Part 2	367
21	Goldings – Part 3	387
22	Goldings – Part 4	402
23	Goldings – Part 5	439
24	Goldings – Part 6	464
25	Goldings – Part 7	482
26	Dr Barnardo's Homes – Revisited	495

Conclusion 513
Postscript 514
Chapter Index 515
Aftermath 524
In Retrospect 525

SUFFER LITTLE CHILDREN
LIST OF PHOTOGRAPHS

Reginald Charles Longman	Frontispiece
My Parents and Grandparents	9 / 12
Thomas John Barnardo	28
The Girls' Village Home, Barkingside	29
Admitted into Dr Barnardo's Homes	30
Boys Garden City, Woodford Bridge	30
Bayfordbury Mansion	87 / 88
Bayford Church	122
Bayford Village	122
Reg, sitting on a stone	175
My sister Barbara and I visit Gran	230
Mr Scougall's Gravestone	247
Churchill House, Eastbourne	255
Boy Scouts Jamboree	265
Torquay	303
The 'Bigger' Family	314
Fred Dyos	328
William Baker Technical School 'Goldings'	365
Mr Wheatley with Princess Margaret	366
Rev. Corbett	366
Mr Wheatley 'Pinhead'	366
'Snowy', 'Tech' White	366
Longman, Foley and Goodger	388
Sgt. Reg (Silver Bugler), Corp. Goodg	437
'Baggy', 'Flappers', Reg – Aged 15	437
Army Cadet Bugle Band, Goldings	438
Wimbledon, Goldings 'Ball Boys'	468
Goldings School 'Honours' Crest	482

1

PRIMARY MEMORIES

~o~o~ Longman – My Father's Family ~o~o~

Fortunately, having surpassed my allotted biblical lifespan of three score and ten and, by all accounts, being fit physically, with a good memory recall and a continuing long life expectancy, I feel ready to write my memoirs as an orphaned child. They include the good and bad, the very happy and yet sometimes sad times of my quite interesting childhood.

What I am about to reveal, is primarily about my upbringing in the well-known British institution of Dr Barnardo's Homes.

My story begins from my birth and continues up to the point when I reach the age of sixteen and a half. The remainder of my life to this point is, I believe, quite interesting but not the subject of this book.

Having been orphaned at the early age of four and a half, I have very little recollection or direct knowledge of my infancy. Much of the information I am endeavouring to write about regarding my infancy is as was told to me by my paternal grandmother Maud Longman, and in later years by my older sister Carol.

My grandparents, Reginald and Maud Longman, lived much of their lives in the market town of Taunton, in the county of Somerset, England. They had six children – four sons and two daughters: Reg, Albert, Jack, Harry, and the two girls Molly and Rose. My father Albert (Bert, as he was known) was the second eldest, and was born in the tiny village of North Curry, Somerset in 1903.

My grandmother Maud was, to me, a dear and kindly old lady during the period of time that I knew her. She was a lively soul who talked a lot and had little sayings, which in later years I would adopt and pass on to my wife and children. Such sayings were:

> "*A little of what you fancy does you good*", and
> "*He who doesn't care comes to a sticky end.*"

SUFFER LITTLE CHILDREN

These, to quote just a couple, have stayed with me all of my life and, at times, bring back the lovely memories I have of her.

I will always remember the way that after she had turned on the big old radio in the parlour early in the mornings, she would reply to the radio announcer's pleasantries. The announcer would start the morning news with:

> "*Good morning, this is the BBC Home Service, and this is the seven o'clock news...*"

and she would always reply in a chirpy voice: "Good morning", as though the announcer was talking to her personally.

Gran would mutter comments to my grandfather, and if a little annoyed with him would say quietly, without even looking at him, "Silly old sod."

My grandfather, generally speaking, was perhaps more stern. He had started his working life as a boy 'in service' grooming horses, and later, as a young man, worked as a horse-drawn carriage driver to a wealthy family in the Somerset countryside. Later still, he was to 'better himself', as the saying goes, and own and operate one of the first automobile garages in Taunton.

He did not communicate well with me, though he wasn't in any way whatsoever unfriendly. He probably was not known as a 'children's man', and was not as patient with me as maybe he could have been.

My grandfather was known to be a strong willed man, a staunch supporter of the Conservative Party and very stubborn in his beliefs. Amongst other things, he was certainly well respected by his peers. I liked him; he was my granddad.

During the years that I knew my grandparents, they lived at 99 Winchester Street in Taunton, Taunton being the county seat of Somerset.

Number 99 was a colourful, bustling house, with people coming and going much of the day. It was the centre of the Longman family. At Christmas time, in fact any time I was there, it seemed that the house was always very busy, with family members and friends just dropping in at any time during the day.

SUFFER LITTLE CHILDREN

Together, my grandparents were a happy couple, and both lived to ages in excess of ninety years. At the time of their deaths I was living in Canada. I still think of them, particularly my grandmother, from time to time, and only have kind thoughts of both of them.

I wasn't to meet or know my father's siblings, or my grandparents either, until I had reached the age of about ten and a half, when I first visited my grandparents in Taunton for three weeks during the summer of 1944. I will write more about this later in my story.

As I recall, I visited them only on one more occasion, in 1946, for a further three weeks, spending my summer holidays once again with them. These were the only times I actually stayed away from the orphanages. The rest of my early years, from the age of five until I was almost seventeen (with the exception of a short period of time, when I was fostered, or 'boarded out', by a family in Tamworth), I lived and was raised as a ward of Dr Barnardo's Homes, and lived consistently in an orphanage.

My father was rather a good-looking man, with dark wavy, black hair. He wasn't very tall and was of medium build. Upon leaving school he was apprenticed as a carpenter, and apparently was quite accomplished at his trade.

He joined the Army, enrolling in the RAMC (Royal Army Medical Corps) shortly after the great depression of 1929, and remained in the Army until he was killed in 1939, shortly after World War II had broken out. He had the unfortunate distinction of being the seventh British soldier killed after the declaration of the war.

~o~o~ Pinfold – My Mother's Family ~o~o~

My mother, Florence Violet Longman, (nee Pinfold) was born in Camberwell, London, in 1908. My sister Carol, even though only at the age of between seven and eight when our mother died, remembers her as being a gentle, loving person, which in turn probably accounts for Carol's own gentle and quiet personality.

Our sister Barbara, being just six years old at the time of our mother's demise, has, like myself, very little, if any, recollection of our mother.

I have just a few photos of my parents, in which my mother looks like

SUFFER LITTLE CHILDREN

a pleasant, patient woman, who I would describe as looking handsome, rather than pretty. I think I would have liked her, or even loved her of course, given the chance.

Carol, being eight years old when our father died and therefore becoming an orphan, would have missed our parents' passing far more than did Barbara and I.

Unfortunately, Carol doesn't remember a great deal about our mother, but does remember the trip by sea with her sister Barbara and our mother to Hong Kong and back.

Being less than seven years old at the time of her trip to Hong Kong Carol, understandably, remembers just a few major events and incidents that happened in China, the biggest event being the birth of her and Barbara's baby brother.

Florence Violet was one of fourteen children. Actually, there were even more than fourteen, but one or two died at birth or were miscarried. Neither my sisters nor I have ever met, or even heard from any of my mother's siblings. This in itself was, and still is, one of the most disturbing factors of my life.

Of the possible fourteen surviving siblings, not one of my mother's family could find it in their hearts to 'take in' just one, if not all, of their sister's children after the eventual death of both of my parents. Neither could my mother's own parents.

By such actions, or lack of, they allowed all three of us small children to be sent to orphanages to spend our entire childhood. I find this fact unreasonably selfish. As the result of this heartlessness, I am not particularly proud of being from such a heritage, or the Pinfold family.

~o~o~

Of Florence's parents – my grandparents on my mother's side – I, as previously mentioned, know almost nothing about. They were fairly 'well off' in the monetary sense. He was a builder in the Camberwell area of London, and apparently did very well at his profession.

When eventually their daughter (my mother) died in 1937 at the early age of twenty-eight they, to the best of my knowledge, made no effort to make contact with us, their grandchildren.

SUFFER LITTLE CHILDREN

Even though my grandparents Pinfold lived to be more than eighty-five years old, or until I was about fourteen or fifteen years of age, I never did, as far as I know, ever see them. Never, during my entire childhood while being brought up in orphanages, did they ever show any compassion for my sisters or myself. They never came to see us, write, or even send any of us a Christmas card. To the entire Pinfold family, it seems that we simply never existed.

From time to time during my early years, these troubling thoughts crossed my child's mind, and to this day I still can't understand their rationale regarding us: their daughter's parentless children.

As it is, I know almost nothing of my mother's rather large family, except for perhaps two of my cousins on my mother's side, and even then I'm not absolutely sure who or where they fit in on the Pinfold side.

One of the cousins I refer to is Queenie Eastland, but again I must say that I'm not quite sure how she is related to me or to my mother. I believe she was perhaps a daughter of one of my mother's siblings.

~o~o~ Queenie Eastland (Pinfold) ~o~o~

I don't have much to write about Queenie, except to say that in 1982 she was on holiday in Canada from England and contacted me. Apparently she was visiting a ninety-year-old uncle of hers in Merrickville, Ontario, which was about a hundred miles from our farm in Moose Creek, Ontario.

One day, shortly after arriving in Merrickville, Queenie phoned me quite unexpectedly and introduced herself. She informed me that she was related to me on my mother's side and that she would like to visit us at our farm, so that she could meet my family and myself. The uncle she was visiting was in some way related to us, but I have no idea how and to what extent. I never did meet him.

How Queenie found out about my whereabouts, I'm not sure, but I can only surmise that my sister Carol must have made contact with her in some way or another. Regardless, I was quite pleased that she phoned us and that I was to meet someone from the Pinfold family at last. I was already well over forty-five years old when Queenie contacted me.

SUFFER LITTLE CHILDREN

Having made contact with someone from my mother's family was quite exciting, and so I drove the hundred miles to Merrickville and brought Queenie back to our farm. I found Queenie to be about twenty years older than me, and a rather nice lady.

However, after meeting her I was only slightly more enlightened by her regarding the Pinfold family. She gave me a photo of herself holding hands with my sister Carol. Queenie, who was about eighteen in the photo, was much taller and several years older than Carol. Carol was about four years old in the photograph.

The only information I have about my mother and the Pinfold family, other than what I have mentioned, came mostly from Queenie, which still isn't very much.

~o~o~ Carol Muir – (Pinfold) ~o~o~

There is one other person related to the Pinfold family who I did hear from – in 1998 or thereabouts. She is Carol Muir, who in some distant way is related to me on my mother's side of the family.

I believe Carol Muir, who lives in the Camberwell area of London, is of the same generation as my own children, but again, I am not sure, as I didn't actually meet her or discuss our family connection in any great detail with her. My contact with Carol happened absolutely by chance.

As it was, my wife and I had decided to obtain British passports for our sons several years ago, when they were in their twenties. In applying to the British Passport Registry Office, we found it was necessary to obtain copies of my mother's birth certificate, as well as my parents' marriage certificate.

Having no idea where or when my parents were married, and not having a copy of my mother's birth certificate or any details of her birth or family, I had a serious and problematic obstacle.

To compound the problem, there was no one in the Longman family of my parent's generation still alive. So, 'grasping at straws', I wrote to Queenie Eastland to find out if she could be of any help.

Queenie couldn't help personally, but was able to contact Carol Muir, who is, I believe, a great granddaughter of one of my mother's many siblings and therefore a very distant relative of mine.

SUFFER LITTLE CHILDREN

Carol was a great help to me, and researched the necessary record office in London (St Catherine's House) and eventually, with some difficulty, managed to obtain the required documents, for which I will be always grateful.

Carol Muir also informed me that the house in Camberwell where my mother's family had lived, and where my mother had been born, had been demolished many years ago. Even the street's name had been changed.

After corresponding with Carol Muir a few times, I became aware of several interesting pieces of information about my infancy.

Carol mentioned in her letters that my sisters and I were discussed at her parents' and relatives' homes from time to time, and that there were some sympathetic comments made regarding us.

Apparently my grandmother Pinfold was a very religious person. Even so, and though she and my grandfather Pinfold lived financially well, and into their eighties, it was thought to be heartless that they couldn't, in some way, have helped us: their grandchildren or otherwise their daughter's orphaned children.

After a few letters over a short period of time, and having exhausted our mutual interests, we had no further contact. Even so, and with the brief contact I had with Carol, I'm still not exactly sure how Carol fitted in relative to her connection to the Pinfold family. She didn't mention her mother or much about the Pinfold family structure generally.

As it was, Carol Muir and Queenie Eastland were the only members of the Pinfold family that I was ever in contact with, and Queenie was the only member of the Pinfold family that I ever did actually meet in person.

The Pinfold family is still a great mystery to me. I don't know if my mother's siblings ever really knew what happened to my sisters and myself, or even if we were still alive.

Everything was, and still is, very vague to me regarding the Pinfolds, to the point that I will probably never know the current extent or fortunes of my mother's family or where I might even find them, if in fact I was even remotely interested in knowing their whereabouts, or anything further about them.

Actually the only immediate family interest I ever had shown to me,

SUFFER LITTLE CHILDREN

much to my dear mother's disappointment no doubt (if there is 'a life hereafter' so to speak, and she was aware of her own family's callousness) was by my father's (the Longman) side of the family, and even this interest (in their son Albert's children), didn't come about until several years in the future.

SUFFER LITTLE CHILDREN

My Mother
Florence Violet Longman (Pinfold)
Died 1937 – Age 28

SUFFER LITTLE CHILDREN

My Father
Albert Ernest Longman
Died 1940 – Age 34

SUFFER LITTLE CHILDREN

*My Gran
Maud Longman*

SUFFER LITTLE CHILDREN

*My Granddad
Reginald Longman*

2

THE BEGINNING OF A TURBULENT CHILDHOOD

~o~o~ Arrival in Hong Kong ~o~o~

I was born in the British Victoria Hospital in Hong Kong on the 28th of December, 1933, and christened Reginald Charles Longman. Reginald is derived from my grandfather Longman's Christian name, and Charles from my mother's father's Christian name.

The details of my birth are taken from records, which include my birth certificate and a letter from the British War Office, which I received in 1964.

My father, Private Albert Ernest Longman, was serving in the Royal Army Medical Corps and stationed in Hong Kong (a British protectorate) at the time of my birth.

Being born within a declared British protectorate is exactly the same as being born on British soil.

My mother Florence Violet (nee Pinfold) and my two sisters (Carol, aged four and Barbara, two) had travelled by ship to Hong Kong, to live in married quarters at the military barracks there with my father, as was, and still is, customary on such overseas postings.

Three or four months after my birth, my mother and my two sisters returned to England with me – her with her new son and they with their new baby brother. My father was to return a short while later with his regiment.

In 1937 my mother, I was given to understand, was to die of pneumonia. My grandmother (Longman) did, when I was about eighteen years old, give me a 'memorial card' indicating that my mother had died in 1937 at the age of twenty-eight and was buried in Camberwell, London. I have never seen a death certificate or confirmation of the cause of death.

I can only surmise that my father, still serving in the British army at the time of my mother's death, must have had a great deal of difficulty with the prospect of bringing up three small children and serving in the

SUFFER LITTLE CHILDREN

Army at the same time. Subsequently we were put into an orphanage. I would have been a little over three years old.

There would be no doubt that life would have been far more stressful for my sister Carol, her being a little older than Barbara and me, knowing her mother had died, and not being able to live with or see her father in what is considered the normal family way, him being in the Army and, to make things even worse, knowing she was now living in a pitiful institution called an orphanage.

Carol, who would have been about seven years old, remembers much of the turbulence of those early years, and remembers in particular the poor treatment we received at the 'church' orphanage we had been placed in.

Even as a child, much like the gentle woman she is today, Carol was a quiet, unassuming, soft-spoken little girl and very shy. She was, like the rest of the Longman family, small in stature.

It seems rather pitiful to realise that at such a young age and with all of the trauma going on in Carol's life, she was made to help look after many of the needs of both Barbara and myself, as well as those of the other orphans, in the orphanage.

So, Carol was unfortunately the hapless child who, besides having to live her own stressful life, was also working for the church orphanage.

My sister Barbara, being a year and a half younger than Carol, would not have understood our predicament in the same way as Carol did.

Sadly, Barbara would be without her mother or father but could not, of course, really understand why. She may not, being a little under six years old, have fully understood that she was in an orphanage. Even so, life would have been very difficult for Barbara too, and it would have been very hard for her to comprehend what was going on.

It would have been at this time, when I was about three years old, that I developed severe ear trouble and had to go into a hospital in London to have a mastoid operation on my left ear.

Such an operation involved surgically cutting behind the ear, rolling back the ear, and then scraping the infection from the mastoid bone.

The operation, though not so complicated today, would in all probability not even have been necessary nowadays: the infection merely being treated with an antibiotic. The result of the operation, though it cleared

SUFFER LITTLE CHILDREN

up the infection, left me ninety per cent deaf in my left ear. I was, according to Carol, in hospital for several months following the operation.

I have vague memories of the ordeal with my ear, and also remember my father and his new wife – my stepmother Beat – coming to get me from the hospital and taking me home. I recall too, my then baby half-sister Betty being with them.

~o~o~ Stepmother, Beatrice Snell ~o~o~

It was something like a year after my mother had died, that my father remarried. He married Beatrice (nee Snell) of Taunton. 'Beat', as she was called, had three brothers, who later were to become high-ranking policemen in the Taunton Police Constabulary, one of them being Chief Inspector Fred Snell.

It's possible, and quite reasonable, to believe that my father married Beat for the convenience of her having to look after his children, but I don't really know if this is correct. No one ever mentioned it, and the subject was never talked about in my grandparents' (Longman) house.

However, neither my sisters nor I had anything to do with the Snell family. It doesn't seem to me that my grandparents liked my stepmother or the Snell family very much. After my father's eventual demise, Beat was never invited to my grandparents' house.

A short while after my father remarried, he retrieved us from the church orphanage, and we all went to live in Taunton for a short time, except for poor Carol.

Carol was sent to live with my grandmother Longman's married brother in Nottingham. Carol wasn't to see us, or us her, again for at least another six or seven years. She would also never see her father again.

However sad and difficult it was for Barbara and myself, it must have been so much worse for Carol. Her life was in constant turmoil and, to make things worse, she was old enough to realise and understand what was going on in her life.

I remember living in Taunton for a while, in perhaps 1937, and have vague memories of learning to tie up my shoelaces; and being stung on the back of my hand by a big bumble bee, and my father and stepmother laughing.

SUFFER LITTLE CHILDREN

On another occasion, I rode some other child's tricycle home to our house from a nursery school I was attending, and I remember the police coming to get the tricycle back. I don't think anyone got into any trouble over the incident but nevertheless there was enough commotion and fuss made, to the extent that I can still remember the occasion. My sister Barbara, too, remembers this incident. This, I would suppose, was my first act of 'larceny', and me being no more than about four years old.

Another memory of that time in my life in Taunton was the fun of pushing our fingers through the cardboard caps on the milk bottles, and licking the cream off our fingers. The milkman would have left the bottles on the front doorsteps of most people's houses, early in the mornings.

On one occasion, a chap came out of his house just in time to see me putting my finger in his milk. He called after me as I was running away, shouting that next time he saw me he would catch me, and "skin you alive". He must have been an older man as he didn't try to chase me but, instead, he put the fear of God into me.

The thought of being skinned alive, which I would have taken literally at that time of my life, must have really frightened me, because I never forgot his frightening threat, though I must admit that in later years we still continued doing that disgusting prank. Apparently this was a common act of mischief, and many kids did it.

We left Taunton shortly after a plastered ceiling fell down in our council house. Barbara, who had been sent to bed for something she had done wrong, remembers the occasion quite well, just as I do to a certain extent.

A large patch of the heavy plastered ceiling came falling down onto the bed beside her, just missing her. This may well have resulted in a serious accident had the heavy plaster actually landed on her. She would have been a little over six at the time.

~o~o~ The Millbank Barracks, London ~o~o~

My father had in all probability just been 'posted' (army term for moved) to London and the ceiling falling down was just coincidental. It would have been about late 1937, the time when the Germans were starting their rampage through Europe.

SUFFER LITTLE CHILDREN

My next memories are of us living in the Millbank Barracks in Westminster, London. Married quarters for soldiers with no rank must have been somewhat disgraceful during those times; the Millbank Barracks' living conditions were not much better than the reputed slums of London. The barracks were old and in need of much repair. Soldiers' pay was poor, and commonly, soldiers in peacetime were 'looked down on', so to speak, by society in general.

~o~o~

I recall that we had separate gas and electric meters in our quarters. The method of paying for our electricity (and gas) was to put a shilling into a meter, which would last for a couple of hours or more, depending on how much of the gas or electricity was consumed.

When the shilling ran out, or the time paid for expired, the electricity (or gas) would shut off. Our meter would constantly run out of money, and so our stepmother would send me to 'borrow' a shilling from the neighbours. We were often, it seems, running out of electricity as well as gas, both of which were provided by the same payment process.

I wouldn't like to think that I am maligning my sister, but I think that Barbara, realising this was an easy way to make a 'bob', would simply get me to ask the neighbours for a shilling for either the gas or the electric meters. Then we would take the shilling and run to the sweet shop to buy liquorice or other sweets.

We, in all likelihood, would never have had money to buy sweets with. A shilling was a lot of money in those days, and would buy quite a lot of sweets.

Naturally the neighbours would ask our stepmother for the shilling back and, of course, she would not have known what was going on. So she would, as would be expected, punish us by hitting or spanking us. Barbara remembers, though I can't say that I do, those punishments, and never did forgive our stepmother.

Barbara believes she remembers our stepmother pulling her up the stairs by her hair, and locking us in the cupboard under the stairs and other abusive treatment like that. She also said she remembers our being beaten and bruised, and that our father would come home and

SUFFER LITTLE CHILDREN

then beat our stepmother because of the way she treated us. Of course, anything was possible but I, being too young, have no memory of such treatment.

One particularly nice thing I remember of that time was my stepmother making rabbit pie. Rabbit was a very cheap meal, and often eaten by those with low incomes.

My stepmother's rabbit pie, as I recall, was just marvellous. After the rabbit was skinned, dressed, and prepared, she would put almost all of the rabbit into the pie. The part I remember liking most were the kidneys. The pastry I believe, was just a top, rather thick, pastry. The bottom side of the pastry was soft and sagged into the savoury pie filling. In all probability, the pastry just wasn't cooked enough. Regardless, we thought her rabbit pie, and particularly the pastry, was just delicious.

I don't remember my stepmother making cakes or buying them, or us getting any other treats. Those were just exciting luxuries we didn't think about.

I can't say that I remember very much about our half-sister Betty, her being so small and just a baby. In fact, the only thing I do remember about her was that Barbara and I would take Betty, who was hardly a year old, for walks on the barracks parade ground – her in her high baby carriage.

The asphalt parade ground was quite undulated. Barbara and I would push the big-wheeled pram, with baby Betty in it, and then at the top of a slope, let the pram go. The pram would run free, down the slight declines, with us running after it. As I recall, it was all great fun. We were just fortunate the pram didn't tip over or crash into anything.

~○~○~ Feeding the Birds and Us ~○~○~

We, as a soldier's family, were, as I have indicated, no doubt quite poor. I remember one of our neighbours, probably another soldier's wife in the Millbank Barracks, bringing us back a stick of 'Blackpool rock'. It would have been such a great treat for Barbara and me, as we would never have gone on holiday at all, let alone to Blackpool, which was known as the 'playground of England'.

Sometimes Barbara and I would go to a nearby park. It was a small

SUFFER LITTLE CHILDREN

public park with formal gardens, as I recall. People would go there to feed the pigeons.

They would break up buns and chunks of bread and throw them for the pigeons and the other types of birds in the park. Barbara and I, being as hungry as the birds, would wait until the people threw their bread, and then run and pick up the crusts of bread before the birds could get them. With absolutely no concern for what the other people around us may think, we would sit on one of the benches in the park to eat the crusts or anything we could get. I can well imagine what those people may have thought about us scruffy little urchins, and how critical they may have been of us.

~o~o~

I remember too, in the evenings, my father would make us children be quiet so that he could listen to the BBC news on the big cabinet radio – the monotone voice of the radio announcer telling of the German army and their savage attack of Poland and eventually, in 1939, Britain's ultimatum to Germany to stop their aggression against Poland, and shortly after, Chamberlain's declaration of war against Germany.

Needless to say, Barbara and I didn't understand the seriousness of what was going on in the world, but there was a tone and an atmosphere in our lives, and the lives of the other people around us in the Millbank Barracks, which indicated to us that something was wrong, in a very serious way.

~o~o~ World War II – Evacuation to Brighton ~o~o~

Shortly after the declaration of war, the British parliament required all children in the London area to be evacuated out of London and other major industrial cities and moved into the country, or to other safer locations around Britain.

I remember well the flurry of excitement on the day Barbara and I were to leave the Millbank Barracks. We, apparently, were among the first children to be evacuated, the Barracks being located in Westminster, the heart of London.

SUFFER LITTLE CHILDREN

On the day of the evacuation, or perhaps I should say the day that Barbara and I were to be evacuated, we were taken to the railway station, where we were given a half-pint bottle of milk each and a small tin of corned beef.

With our little suitcases (they must have been small or we could not have carried them), our tin of corned beef and bottle of milk, we boarded a train with hundreds of other London kids.

Our destination was to be Brighton, Sussex, which is located on the south coast of England. When viewed on the map, Brighton doesn't look much like a safe haven for evacuees when one considers that this is where the German invasion of England could well have begun.

France, which was less than thirty to forty miles away, was, although not occupied by the Germans at the time, very vulnerable to invasion by our mutual enemy. However, anywhere out of London was thought to be safer than being in London itself in those troublesome times.

Upon arrival at the Brighton railway station, we were put on open lorries, much like a dump truck. There were benches both sides of the lorries, and about ten to twelve kids were helped onto each lorry.

I remember too, how we were driven along a street and the driver, or otherwise an official-looking person, would get out of the lorry, knock on the door of the first house in the street, and ask how many people lived in the house.

Depending on the answers, two, four, or even six kids were sent into the house, and that is where they were to be temporarily billeted.

This major evacuation of children out of London was a national emergency and the people all over Britain, with few exceptions, responded well to it.

Barbara and I were sent into a house with about four other kids. It seemed that the people in the house were expecting us. It's quite possible that they had even registered their ability to temporarily take in evacuees. We wouldn't know, but it's all quite possible.

In the house we were temporarily billeted in, there was just one old couple living there. As was required, we gave them our bottles of milk and tins of corned beef.

The dear old souls sat all six of us kids around the fire in their living room, in a half circle. I must have been on the end of the half circle and

SUFFER LITTLE CHILDREN

closest to the fire, because I recall the fire was so hot that I could smell the scorching varnish on the wooden arms of the chair I was sitting on.

We spent that night, and perhaps the following night as well, sleeping on the floor in front of the fire.

The next day, or the day after, my sister and I were picked up by some person of authority, and relocated to another house in another street. It was part of a redistribution system.

To the best of my knowledge, Brighton was the first place where I attended a proper nursery school. It's hard to remember much about the school except that it was at least two storeys high, because it had a big winding staircase in it, and I remember sliding down the beautiful shiny wooden handrail.

Vaguely I remember too, that we were within walking distance from the 'front' (sea) and that we were not allowed on the beach. The pier had barriers in front of its entrance, and was now closed for the duration of the war.

~o~o~ The Big Red Rooster ~o~o~

In the house we were billeted in, the toilet or lavatory, as it was called, was in the back yard, which was quite normal at that time. Toilets in the towns were mostly flush toilets but, generally speaking, only the well-off people had their lavatories built inside their houses, and it was almost unheard of for ordinary working class people to have baths or showers in their homes at all.

The lavatories were usually built outside and adjacent to the house, and were unheated and cold. Beside the actual toilet bowl there would be a nail in the wall, and on the nail, torn up newspaper would be hanging, which one would use as toilet paper.

The national newspapers were called names like the *Evening Star*, the *Daily Express*, and the *Daily Mirror*.

The jokes of that day included: "Who is the tallest man in the world?" the answer being "He who wipes his bottom on the Evening Star".

Of course, the fastest man in the world was the man who did the same thing on The *Daily Express* (the daily express was also the name of a train), and so on. There were other such jokes about other such

SUFFER LITTLE CHILDREN

named newspapers, such as the *Daily Mirror* and the obvious risks of using it.

The people we were now billeted with kept a big rooster in the small back yard. There were no other chickens; just the one big red rooster, which, to me, seemed like it was three feet tall.

The rooster was very territorial, and so, of course, acted like it was his yard, and would attack anyone who came into it. To go to the toilet we had to put a big raincoat over our heads to protect ourselves, and then run like heck from the kitchen door, around the corner, and into the toilet; then afterwards, run past the rooster again to get back into the house.

The rooster would chase and attack any of us, any time we came into the yard. The others, including me when it wasn't my turn to have to go into the back yard, would watch each other from the back windows and laugh. But eventually, of course, we all had to go out there, as there wasn't any other toilet. Us being so small, the long raincoat protected Barbara and myself better than it did the others.

It seems funny now when thinking back and remembering the situation, but as I also remember, for me it was no joke and all rather frightening.

Then one day, probably a special day, or perhaps it was simply a Sunday, (Barbara and I weren't there for a Christmas) there in the centre of the dinner table was this lovely roasted chicken for dinner, with roasted potatoes around it. I can't believe that Barbara and I had ever seen a roasted chicken before.

~o~o~

With the exception of when I was in the nursery school, I was with Barbara all of the time. Barbara, who was only seven or eight years old herself, would look after me by seeing I was washed and bathed, and also, I believe, took me to nursery school.

We would walk down to the seashore, but we were not allowed on the beach because of the war. We would also wander around the town together, and probably get into mischief in some form or another.

I don't recollect much of what we did in Brighton, but I do remember

SUFFER LITTLE CHILDREN

that we weren't there very long before our lives were to be changed completely, for better or for worse – who is to say? – But certainly it was to be a dramatic change.

We didn't see our stepmother at all while we were in Brighton. Quite possibly she and Betty were billeted somewhere nearby. I don't remember seeing or expecting to see our father, or even wondering where he was. As it was, he was at the Millbank Barracks preparing for war and what would have seemed like the almost futile defence of Great Britain.

3

DR BARNARDO'S HOMES

~o~o~ Orphaned ~o~o~

My life, to this point had, compared with any standards, been somewhat disrupted to say the very least.

What with living "the wandering life of a soldier's family" as had one authority put it later, my mother having died, and our having to live in an orphanage for a while, my life was already beginning to become stressful. Then to add to the instability of my young life, I was hospitalised for over three months with an ear problem. As well, my father remarrying, and our continuing existence in "the wandering life of a soldier's family" would naturally have been very traumatic for my sister Barbara and me.

To further fragment or break up our family, our eldest sister Carol had been sent to live apart from us, in Nottingham. Then to top it off, World War II had broken out and Barbara and I had been evacuated with many, many thousands of children to Brighton, and also we were now separated from our stepmother and living with strangers.

At this point in my life, I being about five years old and Barbara just two years older, the turmoil wasn't about to end. Unbeknown to Barbara and myself, we were about to embark on a totally new phase of our very young lives.

We hadn't been living in Brighton for very long – just a month or two – when one day our stepmother came to the house where Barbara and I had been evacuated to, and took us back to London on the train with her. She had little Betty with her in the big pram – the pram I remembered from the Millbank Barracks.

At the time, I would think that Barbara and I might have thought we were going on an outing or something like that, which of course we weren't. We had never gone on an outing ever – our family just couldn't have afforded it, though we wouldn't really have been aware of that.

We might even have thought we were going to be somewhat secure

SUFFER LITTLE CHILDREN

again, and live with our stepmother, but this wasn't in the cards either.

This train ride was quite different from the train ride down to Brighton, when we were being evacuated with a bunch of other kids from London. On the way down to Brighton the train had been full of young as well as older children, laughing and shouting, and some even crying. Many of them would have been excited about travelling away from their homes for the first time, and were enjoying every minute of the adventure, while others would be feeling sad and lost, having been made to leave their parents and families.

This time though there was no laughter, no excitement, and somehow it didn't seem like fun.

Our stepmother was very quiet and didn't speak to us. Of course she would have been deep in thought; she had, just a few days earlier, received the same devastating news that she now had to relay to us.

No doubt she was contemplating what she was going to say to us, or how we were going to react to the bad news. We in turn would have had no idea why we were travelling on the train, or what exactly was in store for us. We certainly didn't know, or could comprehend, how much our lives were about to be changed, for ever.

I remember well that particular day and what happened, but I am not absolutely sure where exactly we were in London. Regardless, we were walking over a bridge, crossing the River Thames somewhere, possibly London Bridge even, when our stepmother told Barbara and me in what seemed like a matter of fact way, "Your father is dead!"

Whether it was her way of 'bearing up' or the simplest way she could put it to us, I couldn't say. There would have been no doubt that she would have been suffering emotionally herself.

I don't blame her for how or the way we were told about our father's death. However, that's the way it was, and that's how we received the terrible news.

I don't recall anything else that she said; only that "Your father is dead". There were no tears and nor was there any sympathy shown by her to us. She had told us of our father's death in what seemed like a rather obligatory and unemotional way.

I can't recall many other details of what would have been such devastating news. It all seemed rather 'matter of fact'. Strange as it may seem,

SUFFER LITTLE CHILDREN

Barbara and I weren't particularly upset by the news and nor was any fuss made by either of us, that I can remember. I can't believe even now that either Barbara or I could have realised the profound significance of what had just been told to us.

I have to believe that the bad news simply didn't register with us at all at that moment in time. We didn't cry, as would have been naturally expected in such circumstances. Nor did we ask questions.

I know now that my father had been killed as the result of an accident involving a big and probably primitive power saw in the Millbank Barracks. Carol believes he put himself in "harm's way", saving a fellow soldier when the saw 'kicked back'. She, being an incurable romantic, believes our father was a hero as such.

To some extent, Carol is not too far wrong. I have, in more recent years, seen a coroner's report relating to my father's death, but the report is somewhat conflicting. Nevertheless, it could be that my father did in fact die helping to save a fellow soldier.

Prior to, and in the mid-thirties, such circular power saws were huge and had no safety features. They were driven by webbing belts that ran off powerful steam engines, or even tractors, with saw blades as large as eighteen to twenty-four inches in diameter. As a result, if the wood being sawn jammed in the blade, because the engines were so powerful and because there were no safety features on the saw to shut it down, the engines would not stall. So the wood or timber would just splinter and fly, resulting in many serious accidents and deaths in those days.

Later in my childhood, and as a child having no idea how my father died, I would tell everyone and anyone interested enough to listen that he was a fighter pilot and that he had been shot down over France. It seemed plausible to mention too that he was one of the first casualties of the war, which, unbeknown to me at the time, he was. The fighter pilot bit sounded more exciting, and got more sympathy, than by 'just' being killed in an accident in an army barracks by a circular saw.

He was buried in the Colchester Military Cemetery, with full military honours for serving his country. Many, (sixty) years later, Carol and my half-sister Betty found his grave and paid their respects.

SUFFER LITTLE CHILDREN
~o~o~ Entering Dr Barnardo's Homes ~o~o~

I first remember being introduced to Dr Barnardo's Homes in early 1940. As I vaguely recall, it was a gloomy, rainy day. Our stepmother, pushing a baby carriage with our half-sister Betty in it, together with Barbara and I, was walking over London Bridge, I believe, and we were cold.

It wouldn't have been but a few minutes after our stepmother had told us that our father was dead, and while we were still walking across the bridge, that we met an institutionally organised column of children coming towards us in what, I was to find out, was called a 'crocodile walk'.

A crocodile walk is when children walk in an orderly column of pairs holding hands, under adult supervision, which is quite common in institutions. Usually there are twenty, thirty, forty, or even more children on such a walk, winding down city streets, around corners and along the country lanes, hence the term 'crocodile walk'.

All Dr Barnardo kids and the likes brought up in other institutions know what a crocodile walk is. It's not particularly enjoyable but it's absolutely necessary to be orderly, especially in London or in towns, cities or even along the narrow country lanes.

After my stepmother had spoken to the person in charge of the crocodile walk for just a few minutes, Barbara and I were told to hold hands and join the walk.

So, as children did, we obediently joined on at the end of the line of children, and walked with them to the orphanage.

As I have mentioned, I'm not exactly sure of where we were in London, only that we were crossing a big bridge, which I am assuming was crossing the River Thames.

And so, it could have been anywhere, even near Stepney Causeway – Dr Barnardo's Homes' headquarters – or perhaps one of the other Dr Barnardo's Homes or offices in London.

Our stepmother had quite possibly shown the person taking the kids on the walk a letter or some other document of identification, or may even have asked the way to Dr Barnardo's.

The person in charge may have basically suggested that we – Barbara and I – join the walk, and that my stepmother could go and register us officially with Dr Barnardo's at any time during the day.

SUFFER LITTLE CHILDREN

Thomas John Barnardo
1845 – 1905
Founder of Dr Barnardo's Homes in 1870
(REFER TO PAGE 32)

SUFFER LITTLE CHILDREN

*The Girls' Village Home
Barkingside, Ilford
where Barbara and I were first put into
Dr Barnardos Homes in 1940*

SUFFER LITTLE CHILDREN

This photo was taken for 'record purposes' on the day we were admitted into the Dr Barnardo's Homes system in 1940

Boys' Garden City, Woodford Bridge
Where I was placed after leaving Barbara three weeks after entering Dr Barnardo's Homes at the age of five

SUFFER LITTLE CHILDREN

Regardless of the formality, Barbara and I at that point had just entered the Dr Barnardo's Homes orphanage system.

It seems now, when thinking back on what happened that day, that our father had died several weeks or even a few months or so earlier, and that our being enrolled in Dr Barnardo's Homes had been pre-planned.

~o~o~ Goodbye Stepmother Beat and Half-sister Betty ~o~o~

It would have been about March or shortly after in 1940, when first I was to become aware of Dr Barnardo's Homes. That was the beginning of another world for my sister and me. A world which was no longer to be the normal family life, if what we had lived so far could remotely have been considered as being a 'normal family life'.

In reviewing the events of our being admitted into the Dr Barnardo's Homes orphanage system, as best I remember or as seen 'through my mind's eye', I feel we were a bit like Hansel and Gretel being led away into the forest by our 'wicked stepmother', never to be heard of again. You will see, as my story unfolds, how it was almost like that, but not quite.

~o~o~

I was not to see my stepmother again until I was about sixty years old and shortly before she died. She never wrote to Barbara or myself, not even once. Nor did she visit either of us in any of the many orphanages we were in. As a matter of fact, she never once ever contacted Carol or us in any way whatsoever.

All of the blame or heartlessness as to why we were 'dumped' into the orphanage system may not be solely the fault of our stepmother however, but she was a principal player in our lives; and for the longest time in my life, without due or fair consideration, I held her to some degree responsible for our family neglect.

My half-sister Betty was not part of my life either at that time. In fact, she didn't even know she had any half-sisters or a half-brother until many years later, when she was sixteen years old and I indirectly made contact with her.

SUFFER LITTLE CHILDREN

Betty's mother had never ever told her anything at all about Carol, Barbara and me. She (Beat) did, however, tell her about her father – our father – in such a way that Betty believed she was an only child.

~o~o~

The orphanage system I had just entered into could, like most orphanages no doubt, better be described as a sterile loveless institution; where every day was a routine consisting of discipline and order to the extreme; where all of us children had the privilege of being brothers and sisters in a romantic classification only, but where we lost our Christian names, and were known only by numbers or by the unfriendly identity of our surnames; and where the male adults were masters, always to be addressed as 'Sir' and where matrons demanded the same equal draconian respect.

With some bitterness I could say that the adults had all the authority required to act as our fathers and mothers, jailers and wardens. They were not seemingly required to show any affection, and most certainly not love. Many of the staff that were paid to look after us orphans had no understanding of what was expected of them in respect to compassionate and, in many cases, ordinary civilised standards.

On reflection I have no idea how these so-called headmasters, masters, matrons, and nurses would have qualified for their jobs. Needless to say, the war had a lot to do with it all, there being a shortage of qualified people for such a care-giving occupation.

~o~o~ Thomas Barnardo ~o~o~

In brief, and because there will be much mention of the orphanage system I was brought up in, in my story, I feel I should mention a little about Dr Barnardo's Homes and in particular its founder, Dr Thomas John Barnardo, my benefactor.

Dr Barnardo's Homes was originally established in 1870, when Dr Thomas Barnardo first brought a few destitute children to his 'Mission of Hope and Peace' in Stepney Causeway, London, for refuge from disease, poverty, child prostitution and deprivation, all of which ran

SUFFER LITTLE CHILDREN

rampant in London's East End.

Shortly after Dr Barnardo had helped several destitute children, a small boy nicknamed 'Carrots', asked if he could stay in Dr Barnardo's 'Mission' as well. Dr Barnardo fed the boy but then, to his regret, he turned the young boy away, telling him there was no more room in the Mission. The next morning 'Carrots' was found dead, the cause undoubtedly being malnutrition and exposure.

Being a rather wealthy man, Dr Barnardo determined he would never turn another child in need away again, and so established what he called his 'Ever Open Doors' policy for destitute children.

It has been said that Thomas Barnardo was probably one of the best-known Victorians of his time. His work with orphans and the destitutes living in the alleyways and slums of London's East End is part of the folk history of Victorian England.

It is interesting to know:

♦ *Thomas Barnardo was born in Dublin, Ireland on the 4th of July, 1845.*

♦ *He moved to London in 1866.*

♦ *In 1870, Thomas Barnardo opened his first mission church for orphaned and destitute children, in London's East End.*

♦ *In 1875, Thomas Barnardo set up and founded the 'Dr Barnardo's Homes' organisation in Stepney Causeway.*

♦ *Thomas Barnardo continued his studies and eventually graduated as a surgeon in 1876, at the Royal College of Surgeons in Edinburgh, Scotland. Because he graduated in Edinburgh, the Royal College of Physicians (in England) refused to recognise him as a doctor.*

♦ *In 1876 he also opened his first 'Home for Girls' at Barkingside.*

♦ *In 1882 Dr Barnardo started his 'Immigration of Children to Canada' programme. By the time his immigration policy was eventually discontinued, in excess of 30,000 children had been migrated to Canada and Australia "for a better chance in life". The last boy to be migrated was David Green – who in 1947, was migrated directly from Goldings to Canada. Interestingly, this occurred during the period of time I was enrolled at Goldings.*

SUFFER LITTLE CHILDREN

♦ *At the time of Dr Barnardo's death in 1905, Dr Barnardo's Homes was caring for 7,998 children.*

♦ *An estimate from a credible source has informed me that from the time Thomas Barnardo first opened a home for orphaned or otherwise destitute children in 1870, up to the time when it ceased to operate as an orphanage system in 1965, in excess of 600,000 children had passed through Dr Barnardo's Homes.*

During its peak, when Dr Barnardo's Homes was an institution for orphans and children in need, there were several hundred 'homes' or orphanages for boys and girls in existence throughout the British Isles, Canada and Australia.

It should be mentioned that Dr Thomas Barnardo's life was not without controversy. In his mission to help child prostitutes and young destitute vagrants, he was accused of regularly 'kidnapping' and abducting such children, and actually suffered prosecution in the courts.

It has been published that because he was well known for his nighttime sorties in rescuing homeless children in the East End of London, and his contact with child prostitutes, Dr Thomas Barnardo himself was among those suspected of being the so-called 'Jack the Ripper' murderer. This was further fuelled by a theory popular at the time that the murderer had medical knowledge.

Apparently, after one hundred and twelve witnesses came forward in Dr Barnardo's defence, all charges were dropped and he was heralded as one of the outstanding humanitarians of his time.

~o~o~

I should mention that Dr Barnardo's Homes was an orphanage for boys and girls of all colours and creeds. The age of the children living in the homes ranged from shortly after birth until they reached sixteen or seventeen. Dr Barnardo's Homes would continue to be their legal guardians until they reached the age of twenty-one.

Boys and girls lived in separate orphanages scattered all over the British Isles. The homes would be very big houses, huge mansions, and manors on big estates. Some would even be castles. Such estates would

SUFFER LITTLE CHILDREN

most commonly be located in the countryside.

In most of these homes there could be as many as two hundred and fifty boys (girls were never housed in such large numbers), or as few as forty or even twenty children living together.

During the war there were in excess of 60,000 children under Dr Barnardo's care. Many of them were not orphans, but simply children in need of care.

~o~o~ Goodbye Barbara ~o~o~

The Dr Barnardo's home called Barkingside was a village-like community located in Ilford, a short distance from the centre of London.

Barkingside consisted primarily of about twenty-five or more cottages, and was first and foremost a girl's orphanage, though very young boys would stay there for short periods of time. I was one of those very young boys.

A few days, or even a week after Barbara and I came to Barkingside, the so-called nurses packed up my bits and pieces and took me over to the Boys Garden City in Woodford Bridge, which is also very near London and just a few miles from Barkingside.

I don't recall saying goodbye to Barbara. I merely held some lady's hand and then we were off to my new orphanage.

I didn't see or hear anything more of Barbara from that day until seven or maybe eight years later, when we were to meet again at my Longman grandparents' house in Taunton.

As it was, Barbara and I had spent the first couple of days or so together in Dr Barnardo's Homes at Barkingside. These would be the last days we would ever live together as brother and sister, for what has turned out to be the rest of our lives.

~o~ The Boys Garden City – Woodford Bridge ~o~

Woodford Bridge, or the Boys Garden City – it was known by both names – was laid out much like Barkingside, where I had just come from and where Barbara was to remain for a while.

There were several houses or cottages, perhaps a total of ten or

SUFFER LITTLE CHILDREN

even fifteen – each housing maybe twelve to twenty boys of varying ages. There were roads and grassed areas throughout the Boys Garden City, and we even had our own private church. It was a rather large church, which was eventually – fifty or so years later – redesigned and transformed into part of a rather good class hotel, now called The Prince Regent Hotel.

At the Boys Garden City we ate our meals in a communal hall, possibly in shifts of about fifty to sixty boys, much like a workhouse as described in Charles Dickens's *Oliver Twist*, though certainly not quite as primitive as that.

As it turned out, many of my meals in most of the orphanages while in Dr Barnardo's Homes were to be eaten in dining rooms much like those at the Boys Garden City.

We would sit on wooden benches placed each side of long rows of wooden planked tables. The tables were white as the result of being scrubbed every few days with carbolic soap. They had no table coverings on them and the wooden seats, which were also scrubbed white, were very rough, causing splinters in our clothes and legs. I, like many other boys, often had many miserable visits to the nurse to have splinters removed.

'Grace' was always said before and after meals. Eventually we were made to sing the 'Grace'. The words and tune: I can still remember.

Be present at our table, Lord,
  Be here and everywhere adored,
    His name be blessed, his praise we sing,
      We thank thee Lord for everything.

There were several different verses of 'Grace', which we learned and said or sang. Many of them are well known, but the ones we sang were perhaps a little less known.

We were not allowed to talk during our meals and, understandably, we weren't allowed to leave the table for any reason without first putting up our hands and getting permission.

Everything put on our plates had to be eaten whether we liked it or not, even if it made us gag. At that time in our young lives we would not

SUFFER LITTLE CHILDREN

have understood that there was a war on, even though we were constantly being told, "You must eat it all up; there's a war on, you know."

I always remembered, and still do to this day, the terrible food at Woodford Bridge. The food in Dr Barnardo's Homes was, understandably, not very nice, particularly in those early days of my life. It was, after all, institutional food, and also there was a war on and therefore, it seemed, the food was not expected to be nice.

Everyone was required to 'make do' regarding rationing and food shortages. The food served to us was probably described as being nourishing and sustainable, thus, I would suppose, meeting our needs at that point in time.

But one vegetable served to us at Woodford Bridge was particularly horrible, even revolting. The vegetable I refer to was not cabbage, parsnips, or peas, or other such vegetables children frequently do not like at first – it was the humble POTATO.

This simple staple food, the most common of the vegetables and so easy to cook by any standards, was just horrible. The potatoes were boiled with their skins on and the eyes still in, which I didn't like at all.

But that wasn't the real problem with the potatoes; it was worse, far worse than that. The problem was, I believe, that the potatoes were boiled for perhaps an hour or more, thus unreasonably overcooked, and were also probably left soaking in the water that they had been boiled in, in order to keep them hot.

The problem may well have been simply the location the potatoes were grown in – maybe a swampy area of England. Anyway, the potatoes were a pale yellowish colour, and watery inside. They smelled and tasted swampy, but we still had to eat them. I can still remember well those horrible potatoes.

The need to conserve and not waste anything, particularly food, was paramount in Britain during the war. But all this was hard for us children to understand.

Being about six years old, I knew nothing else but wartime. Like most children of my age I too hadn't lived, or really been aware of any kind of life or routine, during peacetime.

For all we knew, if war was not the normal way of life, then what was meant by normal?

SUFFER LITTLE CHILDREN
~o~o~ Air Raids over London~o~o~

We slept in dormitories with eight to ten boys in each. If during the night the air raid warning sounded, we would be ushered from our warm beds and taken to the church for safety. To get to the church meant getting dressed and going outside into the drizzly rain or frosty night. If the air raid was particularly intense, then we would simply rush out of our dormitories, clad only in our nightshirts. We would all then settle down again and have to go to sleep on the wooden floors of the church, with only a single blanket over us.

The sound of the ack-ack (anti-aircraft) guns going constantly, fighting off the German bombers, combined with the roaring of the RAF fighter planes chasing the German bombers, was often deafening. Bombs, of course, would be exploding all around us.

If the air raid was particularly severe, and waves of German bombers were attacking London constantly, an air raid could go on for hours, which would keep many of us awake for much of the night.

Needless to say, it was all very noisy for everyone. For the Dr Barnardo's staff looking after us, particularly in London in the early years of the war, it was probably quite terrifying.

Because radar had not been invented in the early part of the war, there was no way to detect the German bombers coming over to attack British cities until they actually arrived. And so they had to be detected by 'spotters' either hearing or seeing them with the aid of searchlights, before the sirens were sounded, and the bombers could be driven off or shot down by the British fighter planes or anti-aircraft gunners. Most air raids, with some exceptions, would be carried out at night, under the cover of darkness.

Because we were so young and because we were unaware of the danger we were in, we weren't particularly afraid, even during the actual air raids.

From time to time, during the night a child, or sometimes two or three, would cry because, in all probability, the sound of the anti-aircraft guns and the continuous noise of the German bombs were so loud that the child couldn't sleep.

By far the hardest part for us, no doubt, was the disturbance it caused to our night's sleep, and our having to get out of our warm

SUFFER LITTLE CHILDREN

beds in the dead of night and walk outside in the cold winter air to the church; then, after the 'all clear' sounded, having to again go outside, and walk back to our cottages.

During the day, if there was an air raid we would be made to hurry to the church when the sirens sounded. We all quickly learned to recognise the difference between the siren announcing an 'air raid warning', and the 'all-clear' siren.

All of us children knew the sound of the air raid warning. It was a mournful, monotone pitch, whereas the all-clear siren was an up-and-down kind of pulsing sound. Certainly we could easily distinguish between the two of them.

The air raid siren for the most part did not frighten us children exactly as, again, we didn't really know the consequences of a disastrous air raid attack. It was more the disruption of our routine that we didn't like, particularly at night.

~○~○~Running Away ~○~○~

A vivid memory I have of those days in Woodford Bridge was the day I ran away from the orphanage. As it was, I ran away from our cottage in the Boys Garden City with a little black girl, who was about the same age as myself, both of us being no more than a little over six years old.

Contrary to my understanding, there must have been little girls at the Boys Garden City as well as boys. However, for the most part Barkingside was exclusively for girls, and the Boys Garden City was for boys.

It must have been that in the early days of the war the gender policy could have been relaxed a little for convenience, perhaps because of the influx of so many more children being admitted. I can't say that I know for sure.

I, like the other children, didn't know that black children were different in any way from white children; no attention was ever given to the distinction between them or us. The colour of one's skin just wasn't recognised in those days, or during the time I was in Dr Barnardo's care, until I was much older, but even then there was absolutely no racism in Dr Barnardo's Homes.

SUFFER LITTLE CHILDREN

Anyway, I ran away with this little girl. As I have mentioned, she was a black girl. Generally speaking there were not many coloured children in Dr Barnardo's Homes at all in those days, or black people in England either, for that matter.

The day we ran away it was raining. I remember well that a window on the ground floor of the cottage that we were living in was, for whatever reason, open. So we both climbed out onto the grass outside, which was just a couple of feet or so below the windowsill.

How or why we came to run away, or what prompted us to do so, I have absolutely no idea. It was simply an impulse, I believe; almost as though we were caged birds and that we flew out of the open window just to be free.

As it was, it was winter and raining, and we only had our indoor clothes on. We had no raincoats or other coats on. I remember that I was wearing a pair of bright red slippers with little woolly yellow ducks on top of each slipper.

The little ducks wobbled around as I walked. Unknown to me, and what would make me look like a little waif, was that I didn't have any socks on. I also had on cotton shorts with a single elastic band top to hold them up, and a short-sleeved cotton shirt. To top it off, as I have mentioned, it was absolutely pouring with rain. The little girl too, like me, would have been lightly dressed.

So off we went, running like somebody might be chasing us. Of course no one was, because nobody knew we were out of the orphanage. We ran down the road outside of the cottages, past the church and down the main street of Woodford Bridge.

I remember seeing people standing at a bus stop watching us. This lightly clad little white boy and, I would suppose, a similarly dressed little black girl, running as fast as they could in the rain, with no raincoat or any other rain protection on whatsoever. The jolly little yellow ducks were swaying from side to side on top of my soggy red slippers.

No one spoke to us or tried to stop us. I only remember them just looking at us. They seemed to be speaking and pointing at us. I remember too that they smiled at us, I suppose in amusement, as we ran by.

After we had run for what seemed to be several miles but what was possibly just a mile or so, we stopped.

SUFFER LITTLE CHILDREN

The little girl told me that she was going to Barkingside, where her older sister was. It never occurred to me that that was where my sister Barbara was; I purely thought that I was going to go with this little black girl, to wherever she was running to, and not really having any idea where I was going.

She then surprised me by telling me that I couldn't come to her sister's with her. This was no doubt, my earliest rejection by a girl – a little girl who was hardly six years old.

So off she went to Barkingside while I turned around, not quite understanding what was going on, and ran all the way back to the Boys Garden City, again passing all those people waiting in the rain to catch their bus. If they were the same people at the bus stop they would have noticed that I had lost my little black girl companion.

Now I would have certainly have looked like a pitiful little waif or stray. Unknown to them, a waif, or otherwise literally speaking, a 'stray' was exactly what I was at this point in time.

I remember that when I got back to the cottage I was, needless to say, soaking wet. They made me take off all my wet clothes and stand in the corner of the room. The other kids were eating something: perhaps we were given a snack at mid-morning, or it might even have been teatime, I'm not sure.

I don't recall being punished particularly, and I don't remember much more about that memorable escapade. Whatever happened to the little girl, I don't know. Actually I don't think that I ever even thought about her again.

~o~o~

I feel quite sure I didn't go to school at the time, although at about six years old, I believe I should have been. Dr Barnardo's Homes was a very religious organisation and in principle would certainly have had our welfare in mind, as schooling and prayers went hand in hand.

I remember us saying prayers every morning and having to go to church at least twice every Sunday. However, I don't recall my having to go to school while I was at Woodford Bridge. Maybe it was because I wasn't expected to be staying there long enough and, as it turned out, I didn't.

4.

ON THE MOVE AGAIN

~o~o~ Pillar to Post ~o~o~

About five or six weeks after arriving at the Boys Garden City, one of the so-called nurses (we called most of the women who looked after us 'nurse') told me I was moving to a new home. She packed a navy blue kitbag with all of my clothes in it. There would be no other belongings of mine, for I owned nothing: no toys, photos, letters, or anything personal at all.

My navy blue kitbag was a standard issue Dr Barnardo's Homes travelling bag. It was about two and a half to three feet long, and about fourteen inches in diameter. The clothes were simply stuffed into it, and drawstrings pulled together at one end and tied in a bow.

The kitbags were all the same. There were no suitcases, boxes, or other types of bags. If a child was migrated to Canada or Australia, they were moved with a sea trunk instead of a kitbag. Otherwise, we all had our own kitbag.

When one of us Dr Barnardo boys was travelling anywhere in Britain by train, 'tube', bus or other means, and being accompanied by an adult carrying a navy blue kitbag, one could be sure that most people would know that the child was in the custody of Dr Barnardo's Homes. These bags were almost trademarks, and we were easily identified by them.

I recall that being moved from one home to another always bewildered me, and I was to be moved several times during those early years. In fact I was moved to so many places for short periods of time that I can't remember all of them, or where some of them were. I only have extremely vague memories of them.

In many years to come, whilst I was retrieving my personal records from Dr Barnardo's Homes, I was to find out that even Dr Barnardo's head office had lost track of me at times, and didn't seem to know of all the places I had been sent to. There was some mention of a fire at sometime and that many of our records had been lost.

SUFFER LITTLE CHILDREN
~o~o~ Adventure ~o~o~

My memories of some of the very early orphanages in my life are to some extent quite vague, and I remember only incidents and little adventures that happened. But nevertheless, they are real though foggy memories, which in most instances are nice to remember now, though maybe not so nice at the time.

One such memory I have occurred at an orphanage I remember reasonably well, though I have no idea what it was called or even where it was. Nevertheless the memory remains clear to me.

Anyway, on this particular occasion another little boy and I ran away, or 'did a bunk', as it was called then, from an orphanage that was not a Dr Barnardo's home, but just another one of those private little orphanages.

The other little boy and I were perhaps a little over six years old, and we had decided to do a bunk from the orphanage for no particular reason that I can remember, but only to be free for a day.

On this particular occasion two major incidents occurred: one of these incidents being perhaps a little too dangerous for two small boys; the other, well, not so serious.

I remember it all very well. We were crossing a field, which had a herd of cows in it. As boys would, we were throwing cow cakes at each other and generally having great fun. While crossing the field we came upon a small pond measuring about fifty to sixty feet across.

We took off our shoes and socks and both waded ('paddled' as it was called) out towards the middle of the pond in our short trousers. The pond was just a few inches or so deep, sloping to about a foot deep in the middle.

The other boy was ahead of me by just a few feet. Without any warning, upon stepping into the centre of the pond, he simply dropped down a hole. Frighteningly enough, he went down right up to about his armpits.

Naturally we both panicked and shouted, obviously scared stiff. After what seemed like several minutes I finally got him up and out of the hole. Though it was raining and we were somewhat wet before we walked into the pond; now we were totally soaked through and through.

SUFFER LITTLE CHILDREN

Many years later I was to learn that farmers would dig or have holes dug in selected places in their fields so that water would percolate up from below to form ponds for watering their livestock. We had discovered this practice the hard way.

Following the ducking, we continued on our way and were passing through the farmer's farmyard, when our second escapade happened.

We were probably hungry as well as being soaked to the skin, and not enjoying our doing a bunk very much any more. I would think that at this point we wished we hadn't run away in the first place as we wouldn't have been as wet, cold or hungry as we were.

By now, it had been raining or drizzling for most of the day. The cows, like cows do, had made a deep muddy track through the farmyard. The ruts and foot holes from the cows' feet were probably eight to twelve inches deep, and full of muddy rainwater.

We must have been walking through the middle of the muddy farmyard, when one of my feet got stuck deep down in the thick gooey mud. While I was struggling to pull my foot out of the mud my shoe came off. At the same time as my shoe came off I staggered backwards, lost my balance, and fell over into the mud. I was now, besides being soaking wet, covered top to bottom in mud.

All of the hundreds and hundreds of mud holes had completely filled up with rainwater, and they all looked the same, and my shoe was at the bottom of one of them. We looked and looked, pushing our little arms down into the mud, but we just couldn't find my shoe.

The farmhouse was right beside the farmyard and so we went and knocked on the farmhouse door, and told the farmer that I had lost my shoe in his farmyard. The farmer came out with his pitchfork, and poked, and prodded the mud, but as much as he tried, he couldn't find my shoe anywhere.

The other little boy had stayed in the house while I went into the farmyard with the farmer to show him where I thought I had lost my shoe. I had come out into the yard with just my one shoe on, and a muddy sock on the other foot.

Following the farmer, I stepped into another deep hole in the mud, and after pulling my foot out of the mud, found I had lost my other shoe. Now I had lost both of my shoes.

SUFFER LITTLE CHILDREN

The farmer didn't look too concerned though, and came over to where I was to look for it. After searching the mud for a while, prodding each hole with his pitchfork, he gave up.

I'm sure the farmer would have tried very hard to find my shoes, as, like everything else, shoes also were rationed, and it would probably be rather difficult for me to get another pair.

The farmer and his wife must have been very nice people; they fed us and cleaned us up a bit. They knew where the orphanage was and so they took us back there in a cart pulled by a huge black horse. I don't suppose that we had actually travelled very far from the orphanage, though we probably thought we had travelled miles and miles during our little adventure.

Both of us, covered in mud from head to toe and soaking wet, and me with no shoes, would have looked a proper mess. In retrospect the staff at the orphanage, as well as the farmer and his wife, must have had a good chuckle at the sight of us, though they didn't let us see them.

We didn't seem to get into too much trouble that I can remember, or at least we were not badly punished. Kids remember punishment. In all probability we were just given a bath and sent to bed without any tea, which was a common punishment at that point in time.

~o~o~

Running away from a home (actually we called all orphanages "homes"), must have been, now that I think about it, quite troublesome for the people charged with looking after us. The police would usually have to be called after it was discovered that we were missing, and a search for us would be underway.

Some of the homes could have felt a personal disappointment because we had run away from their orphanage. They, many of them, would have done their best for us kids, but we still behaved badly in this regard.

Of course we wouldn't have realised the problems we were causing the orphanages by our thoughtlessness.

There were many orphanages run by churches, charitable organisations, and even private families. Some of these orphanages were

SUFFER LITTLE CHILDREN

financed by the British government, but not Dr Barnardo's Homes. Dr Barnardo's Homes did not receive any government assistance until 1948. Until then, Dr Barnardo's was financed strictly by commercial and industrial enterprises, the wealthy, and the public in general.

When we ran away, they would, no doubt, think we didn't like their home because of something they had done wrong, or that something else was making us unhappy.

Quite probably the worst thing the home would be concerned about would be that the police would keep records of us kids running away. Too many such incidents on police records could have looked bad for the home, though I don't recall anyone coming to question us as to why we would run away.

In many instances of us kids doing a bunk, the reason would purely be for adventure and not because of the orphanage, how they treated us, or the way they were looking after us at all. It wouldn't be until later years that we ran away for reasons related to a grievance.

Then it was quite a different matter. Most often, the police would find the kids and bring them back. We were commonly beaten with a stick on our backsides for running away. However, we knew what we were doing, and possibly expected to be caned when we were caught. This was our simple and almost unexplainable way of life.

In most situations (prior to Bayfordbury, which I will be writing about further on in my book) caning was not a brutal beating, but simply the 'capital' punishment of the time. At other times, in other orphanages, beatings were quite severe, and which, I believe, left permanent, deep emotional scars on many of our characters.

In later years I felt that I could rationalise that some of the poorly trained staff, who only worked for their pay and who lacked understanding of children, particularly the likes of us, would say we were merely ungrateful wretches and not worthy of the trouble of finding, when we ran away.

However, in defence of our so-called ungrateful acts like doing a bunk, it should be considered by the reader that we, the orphans, without professional counselling, could not understand why we had been dealt such a low blow at such an early stage of our lives, or why we, unlike ordinary 'outsider' kids (as we called those not in an orphanage) should be in an orphanage at all.

SUFFER LITTLE CHILDREN

Without breaking our hearts, it would be very difficult for anyone with feelings to explain to a child why they were in an orphanage, and that the child may well remain there for the duration of his or her childhood.

For the most part, it seemed to us as though we were simply under the care of people who only looked after us in a disciplinary way; and who showed us no love or affection, gave us no praise or encouragement, and punished us unreasonably at the slightest provocation.

It's hard to remember any of us kids, after running away from an orphanage, not being found, and I believe we were always found safely. To the best of my knowledge no 'outsider' adult ever interfered or physically assaulted any of us kids in those days or during these escapades, and there was never a concern that we might be.

~o~o~ A Village Orphanage ~o~o~

At another of these small private orphanages, somewhere in a little village in the countryside, there was a rather large pear tree on top of a hill, along a little country lane. There was also a church on top of the hill and so, fittingly, the hill was called Church Hill.

The pears were very small and very sweet. We called them 'pig pears'. I don't know if there really is a type of pear called a 'pig pear', but that was what we called those particular pears.

I have no idea where the orphanage was, but it's possible it was situated somewhere on a moor, because cows and sheep would come and wander at will through the village. The pear tree was a big attraction to the animals, and they would come to eat the windfall pears.

The small ripe pears would fall from the tree, and we would pick them up and eat them before the cows, sheep and perhaps the wild ponies even, could get them. Some of the pears would fall into the fresh cow 'cakes'.

These too, we would just wipe off and eat. We were not at all concerned about any disease, parasites, or other problems like tummy upsets that we could get from eating the pig pears. I certainly don't recall any of us kids getting sick as the result of eating them.

At that particular orphanage, I can still remember the staff having

SUFFER LITTLE CHILDREN

food so much better than ours. The home itself was much smaller than most of the other homes I had been in. Thinking back, I believe there were only about ten to twelve kids in this orphanage. I remember too, how we would have thin, yet lumpy porridge for breakfast, the lumps being as big as small dumplings. We had this gruel for breakfast almost every day, and that was it. There was nothing else except tea.

The porridge was always very hot and often smelt burnt. Slightly burnt porridge to us kids smelled nice and we would hope to get a little of the burnt porridge on our plates: it had more flavour than the normal sugarless, bland tasting lumpy porridge which we normally got.

The nurse, or person in charge of us, had her breakfast, which often consisted of a boiled egg or sometimes bacon and eggs, fried bread and occasionally mushrooms. I was the unfortunate child who sat next to the nurse on the wooden bench seat. After she had eaten her delicious smelling bacon and eggs, she would go and get a jar of marmalade with the 'golliwog' on it. I learned later that this would have been Robertson's marmalade. Then she would make delicious crunchy toast on the fire.

The only way bread could be toasted was on an open coal fire, in a fireplace. The bread was put on a toasting fork and held in front of the fire until toasted. While it was toasting it smelled so nice to us kids, even when it burnt a little.

Then the nurse, sitting next to me, would spread butter on her toast, making it make a delicious crunchy sound. With a small spoon she would, without any consideration given for us little kids with our mouths drooling, spread the Robertson's marmalade on the toast.

All us kids, from one end of the table to the other, would be watching her bite the crunchy toast with its sweet-smelling marmalade on it, our mouths opening with each bite she took, our teeth chomping down on, well, nothing! We could only imagine how nice it could have tasted. We never ever did get any toast and marmalade ourselves.

In retrospect, and giving due consideration to those caregivers, it would be impractical to think that they could have made toast for all of us kids. However callous it may sound by the way I have written about it, it really would have been too much trouble for them to have served us the same way. But in the same breath I would add that they need not have had their bacon, eggs, toast and marmalade in front of us.

SUFFER LITTLE CHILDREN

~o~o~ Frogspawn ~o~o~

A lovely memory I have of that time in my life, and while I was still at the same little country orphanage, was taking a jam jar down to a brook and getting frogspawn jelly.

Frogspawn is thick, slimy, gooey stuff, which would slide through our fingers. It floated near the edge of the ponds and brooks. In its early days, frogspawn is a transparent jelly with little black dots in it.

We would take the frogspawn back to the orphanage, and after a couple of days the little black dots in the frogspawn would hatch, and the little tadpoles would swim around in the jar. We would watch the little creatures develop. First, their back legs would appear and then their front ones would appear, their tails would disappear, and shortly after that they would become tiny frogs.

Most of the tadpoles in our jars would die before they matured, due to our not knowing enough to keep changing the river water, and the water would become too warm and lose its oxygen. Often we would just catch the tadpoles after they were well developed and keep them for a few days, before they jumped away to freedom.

We would also catch minnows in jars, by tying a string around the neck of the jar and putting a small piece of bread in it. When the minnows or sticklebacks went into the jar to get the bread, we would pull up the jar. These, too, were our pets, and we would devote time to them until they too died, for the same reasons usually as the tadpoles. We would also catch newts and lizards.

~o~o~ My Childish Wish ~o~o~

I remember one particular day, or rather, I should say, one late evening, while I was still at that same little orphanage, I went outside into the small fenced-in paddock. The paddock was just behind the rather big house that was temporarily being used as a small orphanage.

As would be the situation throughout the British Isles during the war, no lights of any kind, including gaslights, were allowed to be turned on during the evenings or nights, in the streets or anywhere.

This rule applied to all towns, cities, and even villages. No lights

SUFFER LITTLE CHILDREN

shone from the houses, churches, or pubs. There was a 'blackout' requirement throughout the British Isles.

On this particular night, a big full moon was shining high above me and I remember well that the night had a silvery glow to it. The silhouette of the church, with its proud steeple cock sharply outlined on Church Hill, together with the big old pig pear tree, was clearly visible against the clear night sky.

As well, I recall looking up and seeing the cloudless but very dark sky, with only the big silver moon looking down on me, from that clear evening sky.

The only other object, shining high above me, was one particularly big, shiny star, and like children do, I believed that on seeing 'the first star of the night', I was entitled to a wish.

All of my life I have always remembered that moment in my early childhood. I remember looking up into that starry night sky and I thought of my mother, whoever and wherever she was, and I 'wished' and asked her to help me be 'free'.

I remember as well that I had tears in my eyes and felt very sad for myself. I didn't really know what being free meant to me exactly. I just knew that I felt like I was a child in captivity.

~o~o~

I can't say that I really ever felt particularly sorry for myself during those early years of my life,. The life that I was living was the only life I knew, though I'm sure I would have known that mine was not the normal way a child should be brought up in the world.

In reality, and in all probability, nobody in the entire world really cared about me or how I felt. I could only go outside when I was told I could. I had no choices that I was allowed to make for myself. I could not choose what I ate, wore, said or where I went. I could be punished for things I didn't understand I had done wrong, or for things I did or didn't do, or for whatever the matrons, masters, or nurses may have thought I did.

Sometimes they would be right in their judgements of me or us, but often they were wrong. Either way, I simply tried to do as I was told,

SUFFER LITTLE CHILDREN

and lived the life of a strict routine, without the essential ingredients of love and understanding.

~o~o~ I'll Walk Beside You ~o~o~

One day there was a concert in the village hall. On such occasions people in the village would go onto the stage and recite a poem or sing a song. It was one of the ways people entertained themselves in the villages during the war years.

I can still see, when remembering back to those days, a soldier in his khaki uniform who was probably on leave, going up onto the stage and singing a song. I believe that it was a popular song in its day, and which today very few people know, but that I still remember very well.

The song was called 'I'll walk beside you'. I think I thought that the soldier, because while he was singing and glancing down at me from the stage, that he was singing the song just for me.

The song of course, was really a romantic love song for a lonely father, but for a motherless child it sounded warm and comforting in some way. The words went:

I'll walk beside you, through the world today,
While dreams and songs and flowers bless your way,
I'll look into your eyes and hold your hand,
I'll walk beside you through this golden land.

I'll walk beside you through the world tonight,
Beneath, the starry skies are blazed with light,
And in your heart, long stands the words I hide,
I'll walk beside you through the eventide.

Even though other memories may fade, I will always remember moments like these.

SUFFER LITTLE CHILDREN
~०~०~ The Soldier in Church ~०~०~

I still have many memories similar to that of the soldier on the stage, one of which made me feel very sad at that time in my life. This heartfelt memory is about a soldier in church one Sunday.

On this particular occasion, I was in church with the other kids from the orphanage. It happened during an ordinary Sunday morning service, typical of any Sunday in those days.

Our group of kids was sitting midway in the congregation and I was in the back row of our group. For no particular reason that I am aware of, something made me turn around and look at the people in the pews behind us. It was a very small church, typical of any small village church in England.

During the war the churches, even the village churches, would always be full.

There were many, many reasons for people to be in church in those troublesome years. Of those in the congregation would be men on leave from the armed services. There would be soldiers, sailors, and airmen, mostly dressed in their military uniforms. Wives would come alone or with friends. Often they would be together with their happy little carefree children, to pray for their husbands on active duty.

On this particular occasion, the one that I so well remember, a soldier a few rows behind us seemed to capture my attention. He was alone, kneeling down and praying. His hatless head was erect. His face looked gentle and kind and his eyes were closed as though he might be deep in prayer or thought. The rest of the congregation were sitting quietly in their seats.

Maybe the soldier was praying because he had just arrived at the church: some people did that. Or, just maybe, he was offering a personal prayer for the safety of the family that he would have to leave at home while he was on active service facing our foe.

The service hadn't quite started, but there was the usual hush in the church.

I remember looking, perhaps even staring, at the soldier for a rather long time. While I looked at him I had a strange, almost overwhelming feeling that this soldier might be my father, and that he was coming to

SUFFER LITTLE CHILDREN

take me home. I remember too that I had tears in my eyes just at the moment the soldier opened his eyes and looked straight at me.

As he looked at me, he smiled briefly and then looked down into his hymn book, and the moment passed. Reality returning, I turned around and buried my face in my hands, still with tears in my eyes, sadly thinking of what could be, and what happiness I was missing.

Naturally, it was all a deep yearning in my young life. All through those early years, if there were occasions when we were entitled to a wish, such as when you see the first star at night, or if you were lucky enough to get a wishbone (though we never saw such a thing), or if you said the same word at the same time as someone else, then you were allowed to wish. But you never told anyone your wish, or most certainly the wish wouldn't come true.

Our wish, the wish all of us kids in the orphanages wished for most of the time, was not for a bicycle, a toy, or a puppy. It was always the same. We would wish that:

I was not an orphan, that my mother or father were not dead, and that they would come and get me, and take me home.

My wish never came true, probably because we all told each other our wishes.

It takes a long time for a child orphan to realise he is an orphan, and that it will never change: that there never will be a mother or a father like the other kids had, and, sad as it may seem, that for most of us orphans, no one will ever come to take us home with them.

~o~o~ Sad Goodbyes ~o~o~

I was to find out several years in the future that many of the kids in the orphanage were not all orphans. In fact as many as seventy per cent of the children I lived with were not really orphans, the definition of an orphan being: 'one whose parents are both dead'.

Some of the children were only in the orphanages temporarily, due to many various reasons. Many were there as the result of being 'bombed out', or having mothers whose husbands had been 'killed in action' and

SUFFER LITTLE CHILDREN

many other such reasons resulting in mothers, and sometimes fathers, not being able to look after their children.

Several, though not many, of us kids' wishes did come true, as in the fortunate situation for a special little friend of mine at one orphanage in Meriden. I'll write more about him later in my story.

When a mother came to get her son she would have to make formal arrangements with Dr Barnardo's Homes. The headmaster would be informed that the boy's mother would be coming to take him away in a week or so. Soon the whole orphanage would be aware that the boy was leaving, and going home to a real home: a home we all dreamed of going to one day.

We would, needless for me to say, be so envious of the boy and for a day or so the fortunate child would be every other boy's 'best friend'. Even the staff would be particularly nice to him.

If the boy who was leaving was a particularly popular boy, then his leaving had a totally different impact on his friends – the friends who would be left behind at the orphanage. It would be like saying goodbye to a brother, or a special and dependable best friend. It was one of those often heart-wrenching sad times, which might even make us cry. The loss of such a friend was deeply felt.

There is a big emotional difference in the pain of losing a best friend, whether he is going home to his mother, or being transferred to another orphanage (which happened all too often) as compared to the pain of physical punishment, which we had to commonly endure.

It would be your best friend that would console you when you had received the pain of physical abuse from a master, or if you had to stand your ground against difficult odds or an overwhelming bully. But there would be no one to console us when we lost a 'best friend' for whatever reason. A best friend would be an orphan's only family.

I think now, when remembering those days, that the only consolation we may have had when a boy left the orphanage was that the 'going home boy's' good fortune might in some way rub off on us, the ones he left behind. That, and the thought that someone, some day, might just come to take us home.

Boys would bottle up their grief. Most boys would avoid letting another boy see him cry. If a boy was seen crying, other kids would

SUFFER LITTLE CHILDREN

call him a sissy, and that hurt in this world of 'dog eat dog'. Boys had to maintain their position of strength or pecking order amongst their peers, or they would be picked on or even bullied.

Sometimes after a beating from a master in front of the other kids, we would involuntarily cry and for the most part, all of us kids knew the ordeal the other child was going through. This was quite different.

We would often put on a show of 'crying' when we were being caned, in the hope that we would get less of a beating, though when we were younger I doubt that we could help crying.

Now I believe that it is quite possible that those masters who beat us liked to see us cry while being beaten. They would consider crying a form of submission or repentance and thus the beating was doing us good.

5

TAMWORTH – Foster Home

~o~o~ A Real Home ~o~o~

After moving to perhaps three or four different, smaller orphanages, I was again to be moved. As I have already mentioned, Dr Barnardo's have no positive record of some of these smaller orphanages, and I, only vague memories of.

This time the move was not to be to another orphanage, but to live with a real family, as part of their family.

During the war, people who could take children into their homes would notify a government organisation and let them know they were available to foster a child or two. I don't know much about the procedure for them to get a child to foster, but I'm sure it would not have been very difficult, bearing in mind the demand for such caring people to help, particularly in these troublesome times.

There were many, many children needing to be fostered as the result of them being from 'bombed out' family homes, or having widowed mothers unable to look after all of their children, or for several other reasons, no doubt.

There were also those mothers who simply needed temporary placements for their children into foster homes until they could take them back to look after them again themselves.

As well, there were many refugees still being moved around from place to place, for a variety of reasons. The very sad cases would be those children of fathers whose wives had been killed during an air raid, and who couldn't look after their children because of their having to return to their military units in order to serve their country in the various armed forces.

Many of these children came to Dr Barnardo's Homes, while others were fostered out by other governmental or church organisations.

The families who fostered children were paid a small amount of money to take maybe two or three children into their homes. It was all

SUFFER LITTLE CHILDREN

part of the 'war effort', which a boy of six or maybe seven years old, like I was, would have known little or nothing about.

Such was my good fortune that, for now, I was to be fostered out for a period of time even though, as it turned out, it was not for as long as I would have liked it to have been.

How kids were selected from an orphanage to go to a foster home, I wouldn't know, and could only guess.

It's quite possible that a child was evaluated by how well they were faring with regard to depression, social behaviour, temperament or for some other reason. I really have no idea. It may have been purely good luck, or simply one of my many wishes that I hadn't told anyone about, coming true.

However, I had been selected. My turn had come. I must have been very excited when I had been told I was to be fostered.

Someone at the orphanage packed my kitbag and I was ready to go. All of the other kids would have known I was going away, and I would have said my sad goodbyes to my friends, and probably promised, with good intent, to stay in touch with them, which for the most part we didn't or couldn't.

It would have been the time for all the staff who had been 'not so nice' to me, to be particularly nice to me now, hoping my child's mind would remember them as being only nice people.

The person in charge of me would take me to the train station and put me on the train, or accompany me. If there was a need for me to change trains, a porter would be looking for a little boy in grey flannel shorts (with his underpants hanging down below his trouser legs) and a grey coat. To top it off, I would be that unmistakable little urchin, dragging a navy blue kitbag off the train.

Most of the time when I was a child, the people in charge of moving us would quite often tie a luggage label on us, with our name, destination, and other particulars, informing anyone of who we were, and where we were going.

Generally speaking, almost everyone at that time, could recognise a Dr Barnardo boy by the clothes we wore. All the boys in Dr Barnardo's Homes, when dressed in their 'best clothes', wore grey flannel short trousers, a grey shirt, and long grey socks with green or red bands

SUFFER LITTLE CHILDREN

around the tops. As well, we always wore black boots, a grey jacket, and a Dr Barnardo's tie.

If we had kept ourselves tidy, I'm quite sure we would have looked reasonably smart in our institutional style clothes. However, regardless of any other identification, anyone could recognise a Dr Barnardo boy: we always seemed to look like well-clothed, but nevertheless, little scruffs.

As children we were made to wear braces (suspenders) to hold our short trousers up. Unfortunately, our underpants had cotton fabric loops at the top, which in turn, were looped around the braces. The braces were then fastened to the trousers by way of buttons. Often the fabric loops would break, or the buttons would come off our trousers. Then to our embarrassment, the unsupported leg of the underpants would sag below the legs of the short trousers. This made us little boys look like scruffy little imps and typical Dr Barnardo boys.

On this special day though, I would have been looking my very best. My destination was the little village of Wilnecote, near Tamworth. When I arrived at the family home I had been selected for, the lady – my new foster mother – was there to greet me, and take charge of me from my chaperon.

I would have noticed the smell of the home. It would have had homely smells, unlike the sterile smell of disinfectant, and the carbolic soap that was usually used throughout the institutions I was used to. It would also have been comparatively quiet, warm and welcoming, and so much different to the noisy, disciplined atmosphere of an orphanage.

~o~o~ Mrs Pownell, My Foster Mother ~o~o~

I can remember my foster mother fairly well, although I didn't until many years later find out that her name was Mrs Pownell. To me, she was probably, only, Mum. Calling her Mum would have been just marvellous. I could never have remembered calling anyone Mum before. We lived at 23 Quarry Hill in the little village of Wilnecote, just outside of Tamworth in Staffordshire.

Mrs Pownell was a big lady, who immediately made me feel welcome. Of course, everyone was big to me, and almost anyone outside of an

SUFFER LITTLE CHILDREN

orphanage would seem kind. I, being only about six going on seven years old, was particularly small for my age.

I remember what happened next, and never forgot. After my chaperon had left, the lady, Mrs Pownell, immediately picked me up and sat me on her forearm. Then, with me on her arm, she took me out of her back door and into her back yard and called over the fence to her next-door neighbour.

The lady next door came out of her house, and my new 'mother' showed me to her, like one might show off a cute little monkey. She meant no harm, of course, by her enthusiasm, and seemed pretty pleased with her new little 'pet'.

It was just as though I had been delivered, much like a gift. Mrs Pownell was obviously satisfied with my appearance, and was quite excited about having me. Now she had a new child in her house, and I could feel that she would do her best to make me happy.

All through my childhood and late into my teens, I was a very shy boy. What I didn't know at the time was that shyness is often appealing in a young child, and quite cute under certain circumstances.

All the time my foster mother was showing me to her next-door neighbour I was fully aware of what was going on around me, and remember thinking at the time, 'She hasn't got any idea of who I am or what I am like. I'll do my best to be good, but she's in for a handful'.

Young as I was, I remember thinking those thoughts so vividly. I knew that I immediately liked Mrs Pownell, my new mum.

Well, I was a handful to be sure. I know my foster parents were very good to me; they treated me like one of their own. There were two teenaged girls in the house, who were most probably their daughters.

Both of the girls were quite a few years older than me. They, like their parents, made me feel very welcome in their house and for the most part treated me like a little brother.

However, being about fifteen or sixteen years old, the girls didn't have an awful lot to do with this 'new little boy', but they were never anything but nice to me. In fact they even took me out with them from time to time.

There was, as well, a 'father' in the house, and he was to be my new foster dad. Why Mr Pownell wasn't in the armed forces, I don't know.

SUFFER LITTLE CHILDREN

There could be several reasons why he wasn't serving his country, such as him being an essential member in the working force, or a professional of some kind, who would be exempt from serving in the armed forces. He might possibly have had a physical problem, which could have prevented him from being called up. Nevertheless, Mr Pownell, like the rest of the family, was always pleasant.

The family was quite well off, I believe. We had nice food, like corned beef and tinned salmon (which they put vinegar in). The pressed corned beef came in tins about eight inches long and about four inches square. The father would slice the corned beef perfectly thin, and put it into our sandwiches at teatime. We also had sardines, which I have vivid memories of.

Theirs was the first place that I tasted 'fizzy' or effervescent pop – perhaps lemonade. It was the most wonderful drink that I had ever tasted in my young life and, like some things, very memorable.

~o~o~ Ration Books ~o~o~

Every man, woman and child throughout the British Isles had their own ration book during the war. All clothes, food, sweets (candies), and almost everything, was rationed. Whenever I was moved from orphanage to orphanage, and now to a foster home, my ration book would go with me, and this would be handed over to the new institution I was going to. It was now handed over to my new foster parents.

However, how the Pownell family managed to obtain such nice, almost luxurious food, I wouldn't know, but they certainly seemed to get the best of everything. At that time of my life I wouldn't have thought of how they could obtain such nice foods and things. But now that I give some thought to it, so many years later, I think perhaps Mr Pownell had contacts in the 'black market' which ran rampant during the war, though I cannot be certain whether he did or didn't. Whatever the reason, we never seemed to be short of meat, sugar, or anything that I can recall.

Rabbit and fish were the exception: I don't think they were on ration. People would go snaring rabbits to supplement their food rations. Fish as well was reasonably easy to come by, and cheap to buy. I don't believe

SUFFER LITTLE CHILDREN

that we received our fair food rations in the orphanages, particularly the smaller orphanages. In fact I don't recall that we ever had bacon or ham, biscuits, butter or any of the non-essential, nicer foods. We would have margarine instead of butter, though margarine was also rationed. The staff at the orphanages could easily take advantage of the rationing situation, and simply no one would ever have known.

Regardless of the rationing intent, all of the rationed items could be obtained at a price on the black market. However, if anyone was caught selling or buying rationed items on the black market, the punishment was quite severe.

~o~o~

The Pownell family had a large radio, which was the size of a large piece of furniture – about two feet six inches wide, two feet deep, and three feet high. This was how radios were built at the time. The radio was powered by two 6-volt batteries.

Each of the batteries were about a quarter of the size of a regular 12-volt car battery, as we know them today. The battery casings were made of glass and, like the automobile batteries of today, were filled with acid. As I recall, it was my chore to take the batteries to the local ironmongers' shop, which was just down the road, for recharging.

The batteries were put on a small cart and I would pull the cart down the street to the ironmongers. I don't remember this as being particularly hard work. The batteries weren't very heavy, though I don't think I could have carried them a great distance.

Radios, particularly for adults, were so very important during the war, the news being a daily priority to listen to. There were constant reports on air raids and the damage done and in what towns, as well as in the bigger cities like London, Coventry, Plymouth, Birmingham and others. There would be reports of aeroplane losses, sea battles, and the ships damaged and lives lost: both German and British.

The major portion of the news reporting was naturally about how the British Allies' 'counter- offensive fronts' were progressing in Europe, Africa, and other places throughout the world.

Our side: England, Scotland, Wales, Northern Ireland and the

SUFFER LITTLE CHILDREN

Commonwealth – Canada, Australia, New Zealand, India, and many other countries – were referred to as the 'Allied Forces'. They were a united front fighting the Germans – the 'Huns', as Winston Churchill called them, and also the Italians until they surrendered early in the war.

A few years later America, as the result of Pearl Harbor, came into the war on our side, and then they too were included as part of the 'Allied Forces'.

As well as the news, which of course I didn't understand, we would listen to classical music for the most part – something which I, being so young, didn't appreciate.

The most popular music of the day was that of Gracie Fields, George Formby, and several other entertainers, but Vera Lynn was the grown-up's favourite and was known throughout the British empire as 'The Forces Sweetheart'. Her songs were on everyone's lips. They seemed to give hope and brought enjoyment to all of us in different ways during those difficult years.

In our house in Wilnecote, the radio was on all of the time. In the evenings, before my bedtime, we all sat in the parlour and listened to the radio stories, and short half-hour comedy programmes.

I remember my foster parents' daughters, with their girlfriends, taking me to see a few pictures, (we called movies or films pictures in those days) or 'flicks' as they were sometimes called, and treating me like they would if I were their little brother. I know I enjoyed going to the pictures, even though many, if not most, of the pictures were 'silent pictures' with subtitles, which I would have had difficulty reading at that point in time.

Among my favourite pictures were those with characters like Laurel and Hardy and Joe E. Brown in them. My favourite out of all of them, was *Tarzan of the Apes*. This was a 'talkie' picture. Talkie pictures were marvellous, though I don't recall seeing many of them. They were all wonderful times with those girls, and as well, I was living with a 'real' family.

The girls, or perhaps it may have been my foster mother, took me to a couple of pantomimes. One of the pantomimes was *Puss in Boots*. I remember thinking that the huge black-and-white cat was a real cat. I also thought the cat was so friendly, particularly when it came down into the audience and talked with the people. Being able to speak,

SUFFER LITTLE CHILDREN

I probably thought the cat was pretty smart, too.

At all of the pantomimes that I was taken to there would be a theatre organist, and everyone would sing the popular war songs, lead by the cast. Some of the songs we sang were *The White Cliffs of Dover*, *We'll Meet Again*, and the song that I remember in particular: *Wish Me Luck as You Wave Me Goodbye*.

Many of these wartime songs, originating from both world wars, were very patriotic and very emotional. But generally speaking the pantomimes were all such boisterous fun, with lots of laughter and singing.

I vaguely remember going to school in Wilnecote, but not in too much detail, except for one particular problem which helped to change my life to some extent, no doubt. I'll come to that a little later in my story. It involved my finding a revolver.

~°~°~ A Good Old-Fashioned Spanking ~°~°~

Although my foster family were very good to me, I don't think I was so good to them. It was not that I did not like them: I'm absolutely sure I did. But at this point of my life I had not learned how to appreciate kindness, or how to respond to anyone or anything from adults that might be warm and friendly.

I didn't, nor did I have reason to, say anything to anyone in my foster family that would or could have be remotely considered as being unkind in any way, and nor was I cheeky. I didn't knowingly misbehave. I simply did some things wrong, as I will explain.

The memories of some of the things I did to my foster family, I remember well. They sound somewhat funny now, but must have been very trying for Mrs Pownell.

One day, after coming home from church, or perhaps it was Sunday school, I did something which made Mrs Pownell quite angry.

It was raining and I was dressed in my best Sunday clothes, which, quite possibly, Mrs Pownell had bought for me. Besides the money, the clothes would have required valuable clothes coupons in order to buy them.

I remember that on this particular occasion I was with another boy about my age, though I don't remember my foster mother being with us.

SUFFER LITTLE CHILDREN

The other boy and I were walking on the top of a muddy bank, located beside the road we were supposed to be walking on. The bank was probably five to six feet high, and the slope was pretty steep.

Dressed as we were, in our best Sunday clothes, we climbed to the top of the muddy bank and then slid down on our backsides. Then we climbed back up again and did the same thing. We probably did this several times, totally unaware of the mess we making of our best clothes.

My short trousers, new jacket and shirt would have been in a terrible state. My shoes, socks, and bare legs, as well as my face, would all have been covered in mud.

When I got home, my foster mum was, to say the least, very, very angry. She took off all my clothes and gave me a bath. There wouldn't have been any nice friendly talk, as was otherwise usual. To this point she hadn't, in all the time I had lived with the family, ever hit or even slapped me.

She must have been a fairly strong woman because after my bath she took me into the bedroom and, holding me up by one leg over the bed, gave me a darn good old-fashioned spanking.

Although it wasn't a brutal hiding, it was a 'darn good hiding' and what I would call, a classic 'good spanking' on my bare bottom, which I never forgot. I know I well deserved the hiding I got that day.

So much for that cute little child she was showing off to her neighbour when I was first delivered to her door.

I can't say though, that I didn't slide down any muddy banks again, though I'm quite sure I didn't while I lived with those kindly people in Wilnecote. But if I did, it was most certainly not in my Sunday clothes.

~o~o~ The Revolver ~o~o~

A short while later I did something that was really bad – something which I believe would quite possibly have got my foster parents into trouble with the law. It was, of course, all unintentional, but nevertheless quite mischievous of me.

I wouldn't have known or understood what an amnesty was, or what was meant by 'being prosecuted', but I was soon to find out.

SUFFER LITTLE CHILDREN

The ARP (Air Raid Patrol), or it could have been the Home Guard, put out a Notice of Amnesty on the BBC wireless (radio) and possibly in the newspapers, informing everyone who had come into possession of a revolver, rifle or firearm of any kind, including ammunition, grenades, incendiary bombs or any other such war weapons, that they had to hand them in to the authorities.

The offer of amnesty was to the effect that all such war paraphernalia or weapons must be surrendered or handed in to the ARP or the Home Guard by a certain date. The general public was also notified that this was clearly an amnesty, and that they would not be prosecuted provided they complied by the posted date.

The Notice of Amnesty might have been in effect for a week or two. After the amnesty date ran out, anyone caught in possession of such weapons was liable to be prosecuted under the National War Act.

Such weapons and ammunition became easily available as a result of soldiers bringing them home from the front lines as souvenirs.

One rather common source of such illegal items of war becoming available was from German, or even allied aircraft, being shot down. The first people who reached the site of the downed aircraft would get whatever could be useful, or might be considered as being souvenirs. Such items could be small arms, ammunition, or, if anyone was foolish enough to touch them, even bombs.

Weapons, it was widely thought, could be considered to be useful for one's personal self-defence if the German invasion of Britain came about, which at the time looked imminent. After all, Winston Churchill did say, "We will fight them in the streets" etc. But he didn't say with what!

Unfortunately perhaps, my foster father had acquired a revolver from somewhere. When the amnesty and the consequences for not surrendering weapons was announced, he, like many others, I suppose, wanted to keep his revolver, so he hid it in the Anderson shelter (air raid shelter) in our back yard.

One day I, not understanding the seriousness of the situation, went into the shelter and by chance found the revolver. It was a huge and heavy weapon. Thinking back, I don't think for a moment that it was loaded. Certainly I didn't fire it, though I'm sure I must have tried to.

SUFFER LITTLE CHILDREN

As one could easily imagine, a real revolver would be fascinating to almost any small boy. Quite innocently, I took the revolver to school to show the other kids. Other boys, just as boys would, showed lots of interest, to the point that one boy offered to swap his penknife for 'my' revolver.

The penknife was a small two-bladed knife, about two inches long at the most when it was closed. It had a Scottish plaid design on the sides, which was quite colourful. I believe that I knew I could not take the revolver back home to my house, so I agreed to swap the revolver for the penknife.

I don't think that I had the penknife for more than five minutes, before another boy offered me four pence for it.

Without hesitation, I took the four pence and went to the sweet shop with some other boys, and I remember buying some liquorice rope. I can't remember exactly what I spent the rest of the money on, but I remember the liquorice rope. And so, of course, we ate the liquorice.

It was then that the trouble started. As could be expected, the kid with the revolver got caught with it. The ARP or the Home Guard wanted to know where the boy had got the revolver. He said he had swapped his penknife for it, and naturally told them who he did his swapping with.

The Home Guard came to the school and questioned me, asking how I managed to come by the revolver.

Then the Home Guard came to my foster home, and had more than a few words with my foster parents and myself. My foster parents had some explaining to do, and it was all rather awkward for me too. The first thing the Home Guard wanted me to do was to give the penknife back, so I had to tell them I didn't have it and that I had sold it for four pence.

A few days later the Home Guard were back again, wanting the four pence back. I told them what I had done with the money and that I had eaten the liquorice.

I don't know just how much trouble, if any, my foster mum and dad got into, but I would expect they did. It was probably a fine. Either way, the Pownells weren't happy about the whole thing, and so they packed my kitbag and sent me back to Dr Barnardo's Homes.

I was probably very upset and in all probability cried about being sent back to the orphanage. I feel sure my foster mother was upset too.

SUFFER LITTLE CHILDREN

Even though I would certainly have hated the idea of going back to the orphanage, it's quite possible that I just took it all in my stride, along with all the other disappointments I had experienced in life so far. I probably had thought it was a fair punishment and simply accepted it. At least they didn't beat me, as might have been expected under the circumstances.

I'm sure I fretted or even pined somewhat for my foster parents because, for whatever the reason, I started having nightmares. They were quite intense and frightening at the time and I can still remember them vaguely. How long the nightmares went on for, I can't recall, but they certainly left an imprint in my memory.

~o~o~ Return to Mrs Pownell ~o~o~

Mrs Pownell must have missed me, because I know she and her family had liked me before I had got them into trouble of sorts. After all, she was like a mother to me and I seemed to fit in well with their family.

As it was, this dear soul asked for me to be returned to her. So, off I was to go again, kitbag in hand, to give them yet another dose of this 'rotten little sod'.

There were no repercussions regarding the revolver and my getting them into trouble. In fact I don't recall Mrs Pownell or anyone even talking about it again. I simply came back to a welcoming home, and a real family again. A couple of days later I returned to school.

~o~o~ The Big Fire ~o~o~

It seems to me now, when thinking back, that the small village of Wilnecote must have been just a few miles from the outskirts of Tamworth, as it wasn't a very busy area, and I seem to remember seeing lots of cows and other farm animals near where we lived.

My foster mother's mother, who I called Gran, was a wrinkled-faced old lady who I liked from the first day I met her. I can also recall that there were railway tracks crossing the main road near where we lived, and that my 'grandma' lived just down the road on the other side of the tracks.

SUFFER LITTLE CHILDREN

I would go and see my foster gran often. She would give me lemonade or a piece of cake if she was baking at the time, or a sweet, or maybe a halfpenny, or even a penny, almost every time I visited her.

She was a very friendly old lady who always seemed to be smiling. I knew that she was fond of me, just as I was of her. Such feelings are easily felt between a child and a grown-up. I spent many a Sunday at her house. I don't remember her having a husband. Maybe he had passed on, or was even in the war somewhere.

My gran's back garden, like all of the other gardens on her road, backed onto a field. There were quite a few – maybe fifteen or even twenty of these houses. Most of the people grew vegetables in their back gardens. They also had garden sheds as well as fences, to keep the rabbits out.

The gardens actually backed onto the field in such a way as to form the shape of a complete horseshoe. At one end there was quite a big opening into the field, which allowed vehicles like horses and carts, tractors or even lorries to get in and out. There was no gate.

It seemed as if the public were allowed to go into the field any time, if they so wished to. The area might even have been a common for the villagers use, and was often used by gypsies or didicois.

During the spring the common, or field, was probably left to go to hay if it wasn't getting sufficient use. After the hay had been taken off, we would be allowed to play in the field. I believe the local fair might have been held in this field too, if any fairs at all were in operation during the war.

~o~o~

The stove, or 'cooker', as it was usually called in England, in Mrs Pownell's kitchen was a gas unit. On the cooker, my foster mother always left matches for lighting the gas. There was no such thing as a pilot light in the cookers in those days. The type of matches Mrs Pownell used were like 'Swan Vesta' matches – the red-tipped type that could be scraped on anything abrasive to ignite them.

For the second time while living with my foster parents, I again did something very wrong, which I'm sure could possibly have got my foster parents, again, into plenty of trouble.

SUFFER LITTLE CHILDREN

Quite innocently, I believe, when no one was looking I took a couple of the matches off the cooker, and put them in my pocket. I can't believe that I actually planned the next mischief I got into. I, quite possibly, impulsively took the matches while I was just passing by the cooker on my way out of the back door to go to my foster gran's house, when it all started.

On this fateful day, another day that quite possibly changed my life's destiny yet again, I simply intended to go and visit my gran, like I so often did.

As was normal, when I went to visit my foster gran I went through the opening into the common, and headed towards my grandma's garden gate, which was on the other side of the field.

On my way through the field I nonchalantly made a little heap of grass in the long dry grass, struck one of the matches, and lit it.

The tall grass, which was just about ready for harvesting into hay, caught fire very easily and started to spread rather rapidly. I'm sure I wasn't too concerned about the extent of the fire until after I had taken off my jacket and, not realising my error, tried without success to put the flames out by swatting at them with my jacket.

The flames spread fast and the fire grew, and grew, and spread rapidly towards the perimeter of the field, and the people's back gardens.

Of course I had been doing absolutely the wrong thing by trying to put the fire out with my coat, and was really only fanning the flames and making it worse.

Now it was too late. Before long the fire was out of control and heading quickly towards the houses. Believe me, it became quite a big fire, and all I could do was stand in the middle of the field and watch it grow.

Well, all heck broke loose. The people, including my gran, came out of their houses with shovels and brooms, all trying to put the fire out. Eventually the fire engine came, and several water hoses were used to spray water on the field.

Eventually, after quite a large area of the field had been burnt, the fire was put out, leaving a smouldering, smoking hayfield, and lots of angry people, no doubt. But I didn't run away. In fact, I don't think it even occurred to me to try and run away.

It didn't take long for the people who had fought the fire to find out

SUFFER LITTLE CHILDREN

that this little kid, the one covered from head to toe in soot, was the cause of the fire and so, once again, I was sent back to Dr Barnardo's Homes.

Sadly, I never saw my foster mum or her family again and although over the years I thought of them from time to time, I couldn't get in touch with them as I didn't even remember their name, or exactly where they lived, although I knew it was somewhere near Tamworth. But I'm sure, for better or worse, they would have remembered me from time to time.

I lived with Mrs Pownell and her family for just about a year, and even though it was only for a year or so, it seemed a very long time in my early life. I have only the fondest of memories of them all.

~o~o~

It wasn't until very recently, in 2006, that a good friend of mine, Anne Newill, a senior social worker who worked for Barnardos Aftercare, traced my foster family and managed to obtain their names, and the address of where I was fostered.

~o~o~ One More Chance ~o~o~

But that wasn't quite the end of my being fostered.

So many unexpected things occur in a child's life which are hard to explain, particularly in that of an orphan's life.

A lady not too far from Mrs Pownell's village must surely have asked to foster me in particular, as opposed to just any child. If not, then it was quite a coincidence.

I really don't know the details, or how exactly it came about, that I would be fostered out again with a lady who lived so close to Mrs Pownell's village, and I was never to find out.

However, I was delivered to this new foster lady, who had a son a little younger than me. As well, my new foster mother had, shortly before I arrived, just given birth to a new baby.

The father, like my previous foster father, lived at home. I don't know much about him, but I do remember that he made model aeroplanes.

SUFFER LITTLE CHILDREN

Some of the model planes were hanging from strands of cotton from the ceiling in the living room.

My impression of my new foster mum was that she always seemed to be breastfeeding her baby. I could not have been at this new foster home for very long, because I don't recall much about anything in particular happening there. I didn't get into any trouble, either, that I can remember.

I knew that I was living near Mrs Pownell's village, though I was not living close enough to go to see her or my gran, and the rest of my old foster family. I didn't attend school at all. Perhaps it was because it was the school's summer holiday time, or perhaps I simply wasn't at my new foster home long enough.

After a short period of time, just six weeks even, I was sent back to Dr Barnardo's Homes, and that was the last time I was to be sent out of the orphanage to live in a 'real' family home.

6

HAPPY DAYS AT MERIDEN

~o~o~ My Friend Willy ~o~o~

After leaving the Wilnecote area, which was in 1942, I, being about eight years old, was sent to yet another one of those small private orphanages – one which, again, was not part of the Dr Barnardo's Homes system.

This one was in the little village of Meriden, near the village of Alspath, where the legendary Lady Godiva rode her horse while naked, through the village. I don't think I was there on the occasion that she was out riding, or most certainly I would be able to remember the occasion and be able to write more about it.

Meriden was, and still is, a beautiful little village, located between Birmingham and Coventry. It is claimed to be the 'centre of England'. In the centre of the village there is a moderately tall monument which is dedicated to the 'memory of the cyclists who were soldiers and who died in World War I'. Later, the monument also included the cyclists who gave their lives in World War II.

To get to the orphanage, one would have to travel through the little village to its outskirts, and then down a narrow, winding country lane.

Each side of the pretty little winding lane, which in itself is just wide enough for a single car to travel on, there were, and still are, hedges as much as eight to ten feet high.

The orphanage was a large house, or even a small manor, on an estate of about eight acres. Within the estate there was a small wood with a 'spinney' in it. A spinney is best described as an area of about half an acre to an acre or so in size, and where the ground is a 'hollow', with trees, ferns and shrubs down its banks.

At the bottom of the spinney there may well be stinging nettles and bramble bushes of various varieties. Rabbits are commonly known to live in a spinney, deep down in holes and burrows, which they dig in its grass and the weedy banks.

A man and his wife and one or two helpers ran the orphanage. The

SUFFER LITTLE CHILDREN

man, who was the 'headmaster', we called 'Sir'; and his wife would have been called 'Matron' or 'Miss'. Unfortunately, I cannot remember their surname.

There was also an upper and lower meadow, where the headmaster and his wife kept two ponies for their two small daughters, who were about our age.

In the spring the headmaster would deliberately set fire to the dead grass in the meadows, and burn off the previous year's old, dry grass. Us kids would help keep the fire under control. (Having had some experience of sorts in Wilnecote, I was probably better at spreading the fire than keeping it under control!)

There were only twelve to maybe fifteen of us young boys in the orphanage in Meriden, all of us about eight or nine years old.

The orphanage was run like a small farm, which accounts for why I knew a little about farm animals, or at least some of them, many years later in my life. The types of animals at Meriden included such animals as pigs, chickens, ducks, geese, about five or six sheep, two ponies, and a couple of goats.

I loved it there. I and another boy – his name was Willy – were best friends. We slept next to each other in the same little dormitory. There were only five or six of us in a dormitory at this orphanage.

Willy and I were just about the same age and size, and also we liked the same things. I don't remember us getting into too much trouble, but we fooled around a little more than the other kids did. We were known as always being together. I would suppose Willy was my first 'best friend'.

Willy's mother would send parcels in the post to him. He was one of the only boys who would receive any parcels at all. I remember he was a nice chap and always shared the little things his mother sent him with the other boys and myself. It was as the result of Willy's mother that I first tasted the little chocolate-covered, honeycombed biscuit type sweets called Maltesers, which have always been something of a favourite with me.

SUFFER LITTLE CHILDREN
~o~o~ Pinky and Belly ~o~o~

Among the other things Willy and I did together was to volunteer to look after the headmaster's two huge pigs. Their names were Pinky and Belly. The headmaster or someone else, maybe his daughters even, had named them. Willy's pig was Belly, and mine was Pinky.

The pigs were kept in a purposely built brick pigsty, which consisted of a small, eight-foot square brick house with an arched opening for its entry, and naturally it had a roof. The little pigsty was intended to give the pigs a place to get out of the sun or rain, and a place to sleep during the cold frosty nights.

There was also, attached to the pigsty, a twelve by twelve foot outside 'run' area with a three-foot high wall around it, which was also built of brick. There was a small door or gate to allow us to get into the pigpen. It was our job to feed and water the pigs, which we did, twice a day. We also had to keep the sty clean.

The feed was a type of powdery mash, which had a nice appetising smell. Every day the cook would boil up all the potato peelings and other vegetable waste. It would be our job to mash up the cooked vegetable waste, and add the powdery mash (probably ground oats) to the nice-smelling hot swill. Then we would carry the steaming pigswill from the kitchen, down to the pigsty.

Anyone who has had anything to do with pigs knows what a fight it is to be able to empty pigswill into a pig trough. The pigs aren't the best behaved. They jostle and push, and try to get at the swill before one has a chance to pour it into their trough.

Willy and I, both being rather small, were knocked off our feet many times, sometimes more than once at one feeding, because the concrete floor in the pigs' run would be covered with 'mess' and therefore quite slippery, particularly if it had been, or was, raining.

Especially on a rainy day, with the ground covered in pigs' mess, the state we would get ourselves in was no doubt disgusting. Even so, I remember well that we would laugh, and always enjoy ourselves in a devilish way.

The pigs were Willy's and my responsibility, and no one else's, it seemed. We really did enjoy the job of looking after them, and probably

SUFFER LITTLE CHILDREN

regarded them as our pets. We loved it: mess and all. Those were good times to remember, and never would I want to forget them.

But there were also other interesting animals at this orphanage which we were very aware of, but other boys looked after them.

There were several ducks that walked freely anywhere they wanted to, down the garden paths and in the gardens. A few of them nested and even hatched eggs.

The little ducklings would waddle behind their mother and look just wonderful to us little kids. Sadly, one by one, they disappeared. Each day, it seemed, there would be one less. We were told that the rats would kill them and drag them away at night. It all sounded terrible to us, but no one could do anything about it.

~o~o~ Parcels from Canada ~o~o~

Canada was a great ally of the British people, particularly during the war. Besides doing their part in fighting the 'Huns', long before America came to help, the Canadians also sent parcels of clothes through the Red Cross for the likes of us orphans and other unfortunates.

One day, the headmaster told us that a parcel or some parcels had arrived from Canada for us kids. We had no idea where Canada was. Canada, for all I knew, could well have been a small town in Scotland.

Although there was probably food as well, the parcels mostly contained clothes. We were told that among the clothes like gloves, socks and things, there were also a few lumberjackets but that, disappointingly, there were nowhere near enough of these jackets for everyone, and that only special and deserving boys would get one.

All of the lumberjackets were handed out, and one can only imagine our excitement when we found out that two of them were for Willy and me. Fortunately, both Willy and I received ours because we were the 'pig boys'. We were very proud of our lumberjackets. They were of a plaid design and made of heavy wool, with hoods attached. Typical, we thought, what lumberjacks wore, though I'm not sure we knew exactly what a lumberjack was.

SUFFER LITTLE CHILDREN

~ₒ~ₒ~ 'Giro the Germ' ~ₒ~ₒ~

The headmaster was also our teacher. He taught us all of our school subjects and was the only teacher. Our ages must have ranged from about eight to nine and, as I have mentioned, we were all boys.

On special occasions, the headmaster would show us cartoons on a very large, reel-to-reel projector. I believe he said that he had made the actual cartoons himself, but I'm not really sure. They were always about the same thing: cleanliness. The main character in the cartoon was 'Giro the Germ'. Giro was an ugly, yet comical little insect thing – a cartoon-type fly, or perhaps it was more like a mosquito.

Giro would be seen leaving its dirty little hand and footprints on the walls, floors and ceiling. Then there would be a broom and duster chasing it, eventually catching Giro, and putting it behind prison bars. We saw 'Giro the Germ' several times, and never tired of seeing him getting caught and ending up behind bars.

It was great fun for us to watch these cartoons. These were the only kind of pictures available to us kids in those days. Of course, we wouldn't have had the opportunity to go to the cinema and see pictures like *Tarzan of the Apes*, because at Meriden there was no one who would treat us, and even if there was, there wasn't a cinema in the village anyway.

~ₒ~ₒ~ 'How Do You Make Glass?' ~ₒ~ₒ~

Something else which left a lasting impression on me, was at one of the lessons (we sometimes called classes 'lessons') the headmaster was teaching us. He would stand in front of the class and say, "Ask me any question you like, about anything at all, and I will tell you the answer."

Some of the kids would ask questions, and he would certainly try to answer most of them as best he could. Undoubtedly we thought he knew the answers, and that anything he told us must be true!

I tried to ask him a question and couldn't get anywhere. So, I asked him the same question again several times.

"How do you make glass, Sir?" I would ask.

He would answer, "I don't make glass. Ask me again."

So, I would ask again, "How do you make glass, Sir?"

SUFFER LITTLE CHILDREN

Each time, his response was the same. "I don't make glass."

I simply couldn't understand his response. I must have asked the same question several times before I eventually understood what he was saying, and how he wanted me to ask the question, which was: "How is glass made?"

I suppose he did his best to explain how glass was made. Although I still have no idea how glass is made, he certainly taught me how to ask a question, the "silly old sod", as Grandma Longman would have said.

~o~o~ Chickenpox ~o~o~

I don't remember the headmaster at Meriden, or his wife, treating us badly, so everything must have been pretty nice there so far as an orphanage goes, though I must say that on at least one occasion I did get a 'darn good hiding', which I never forgot. But at the same time, I knew it was justified.

It all started when I came down with chickenpox. This was the only time that I recall getting a good hiding while I lived at Meriden, though I wouldn't say it was a brutal beating with a cane or anything like that.

Nevertheless, it was a 'good hiding', even though I didn't think it was a 'good' hiding for me at the time! But I know only too well that I had brought the wrath of the headmaster and his wife upon myself, and that I well deserved it.

As would be normal, being the only boy in the orphanage with chickenpox, I was put in a bedroom by myself, 'in isolation', as it was called, and away from all of the other kids. It was at Meriden that I first became aware of the terms: 'quarantine' and 'isolation'. I wasn't allowed to see or speak with anyone. No one could visit me, including my friend Willy.

Willy had to look after Belly and Pinky by himself, which would have been quite an undertaking for any small boy of our age, but Willy managed just fine, and no one else helped him.

Every day the headmaster's wife would come into my isolation room and dab a coloured liquid, probably calamine lotion, on all of my spots, which were all over my body.

I think the period of time they would have kept me in isolation was

SUFFER LITTLE CHILDREN

about two to three weeks, or perhaps even a little longer, which is a very long and boring time for any child to be kept away from everyone else, even though it was absolutely necessary.

I wasn't supposed to get out of bed, and so I ate my meals in bed on a beautiful, purposefully made mahogany bed tray.

The headmaster's wife would bring my meals to me and put them on this lovely tray, and I would sit up in bed to eat them.

There's no doubt that I would have spilt food on the bed and generally made a mess, like most children would. Without any noticeable fuss, my 'nurse', the headmaster's wife, would clean up the messes, wash and clean me up, and very conscientiously look after me.

Also I'm sure that I would have made a fuss about not being able to see anyone, and generally make a constant nuisance of myself, but I don't recall ever being chastised about any of that. However, that in itself wasn't the worst thing or the reason why I got that 'darn good hiding'.

One day, after about the second week, I must have become bored to death with being in quarantine, so I have to say that the 'rotten little sod' in me came out again.

The beautifully made mahogany bed tray that they brought me my meals on was an exceptionally well-made tray, with little turned legs and a rail, and designed so that cups and plates wouldn't slide off the tray and spill onto the bed. Also the legs on the tray were individually hinged, thereby allowing the tray to be folded up neatly.

The headmaster's wife had told me that it belonged to one of the villagers, or it might have even been her mother's or something like that. Regardless, it was something treasured by her.

On this particular day, the day the devil came out in me, I took the tray and broke all four of the legs completely off. Then I even broke a couple of the legs in half as well, I believe. I certainly made a terrible mess of the tray. None of my destructiveness was for any other reason whatsoever other than just boredom.

Needless to say, the headmaster's wife was, to say the least, quite annoyed with me and told me so in no uncertain terms. But that wasn't to be the end of it.

A few days later (perhaps they had both waited until I was completely better) they came into my isolation room together and,

SUFFER LITTLE CHILDREN

between them, they gave me a well-deserved good hiding, which I have never to this day ever forgotten.

I still don't think badly of the hiding I got. It wasn't a brutal beating like those often handed out in some orphanages: it was just a good old-fashioned spanking on my bare bottom, with their hands. But it still hurt, and I don't doubt that I screamed my head off.

They must have made it clear to me what a selfish and destructive thing I had done. I doubt that I thought well of my discipliners at the time, but in due course I understood why I received that 'good hiding'.

The next day I was let out of isolation and returned to my own dormitory and bed, and after a short time had passed, all was forgotten (so to speak) and it was never mentioned again. But I'll always remember my bout with chickenpox.

~o~o~ Gas Masks ~o~o~

Another thing I remember about Meriden was hearing the bombs falling on both Birmingham and Coventry. Meriden is located almost midway between these two big industrial cities.

Birmingham and Coventry were both major targets for the German planes. In the early part of the war, they would bomb them night after night. This constant bombing was known as 'the Blitz'. Stray bombs, as well as shot-down German planes, would fall quite near and around Meriden constantly, but still I don't remember myself or the other children ever being particularly afraid.

At some point in the early years of the war every man, woman and child throughout the British Isles was issued with a gas mask.

As I recall, the first gas mask that I was given was in Brighton. The mask was made to look like a funny face, like Mickey Mouse I believe. It was a colourful mask, and had a long flapping nose that vibrated when we blew inside the mask.

The Mickey Mouse gas mask must have been given to me, and to all of the other five-year-olds and younger kids, when first we arrived at Brighton after the big evacuation, or shortly after.

When I became a little older and bigger, I was issued with the standard black rubber gas mask with the green filter on the end.

SUFFER LITTLE CHILDREN

We would be made to go into a long portable caravan in order to test the gas masks for leaks. After being seated in the caravan, gas (I believe it was 'laughing gas') was pumped into the caravan, while we just sat in there. I don't recall anyone of us children actually laughing, so I must suppose that none of the masks leaked.

We never went anywhere without our brown cardboard box containing our gas masks. If the Home Guard or the Air Raid Police saw us without our gas masks, they would stop us and send us home to get them. Everybody: men, women, policeman, teachers, doctors, even German prisoners I presume (well, I don't know about Germans) in England, were required to take their gas masks everywhere they went.

At this time of my life, war, including gas masks, was the normal way of life, and we didn't know much of anything else.

~o~o~ Orchestral Concert Outings ~o~o~

If we were lucky, so we believed, and the headmaster or his wife decided it was our turn, we would be chosen and taken in the headmaster's car to Coventry. The headmaster's two young daughters would always go with us. Institutions such as ours, even the small ones, must have had petrol coupons provided for their cars.

Most often, as I recall, we would go to a big theatre or concert hall to listen to concerts or to hear an orchestra play classical music. Sometimes the so-called 'treat' would be for us to be taken to an opera, and because these treats would be rather 'classy' occasions, we would have to dress up in our best clothes.

Of course we would be expected to be on our best behaviour, and not talk through the performances. But unfortunately we were just young uneducated urchins, not cultured enough to understand or appreciate such beautiful music or operatic art. I remember Willy and me, not having the slightest interest in those dreary performances, giggling, and from time to time receiving severe or even threatening looks from the headmaster.

The performances would last well past our normal bedtimes, and it was hard just to keep awake.

Often we were so bored and fidgety during the performance that we

SUFFER LITTLE CHILDREN

could hardly wait until it was all over, and at times would actually fall asleep.

But the next time, if we were picked to go, we would again be so happy to be going out 'for a treat', and would forget exactly where we were going until after we got there, and that, too, would make us laugh.

While I was at Meriden, I'm quite sure everything possible was done to make us boys happy. We went on picnics, walks, and several other outings.

On one particular occasion, Willy and I, together with the rest of the orphanage, all went in a lorry to a pantomime somewhere in Birmingham.

It was spitting with rain most of the time and we were in an open-backed lorry all the way to Birmingham and so, naturally, we all got soaked to the skin. I can't remember much about the pantomime or even what was to be performed, because just as we were going into the concert hall, where the pantomime was to be held, the air raid siren sounded, and we had to vacate the place in a hurry and go to one of the local air raid shelters.

~o~o~ Goodbye Willy ~o~o~

One sad day – a day that I will always remember – was the day Willy and I had to say goodbye. It was one of the most upsetting days for me that I can remember.

Willy had been put into the orphanage by his mother, for what reason, I never knew. We kids didn't talk much about why or how we came to be in the homes. We just took each other for granted, assuming we were all simply 'orphans'. After all, we lived in an orphanage.

I vaguely remember Willy being told by the headmaster that his mother was coming to get him and that "he is going home for good".

~o~o~

From time to time Willy's mother had come to the orphanage and taken Willy out for the day, but as expected, she would bring him back again in the evening and say goodbye, always leaving Willy somewhat upset. Willy wouldn't see her again for perhaps a month or two.

SUFFER LITTLE CHILDREN

Willy's news, at first, seemed wonderful, Willy was going home to his mum, and not giving the situation enough thought, we were both excited about it. Then the reality set in, and it was very hard for me to take. Willy was like a brother to me. We did everything together. He was, it seemed, all I had for a family.

As the day drew nearer for him to be leaving Meriden, we would be together most of the time, talking about how we would see each other again one day, after we 'grew up'. We talked about how maybe his mother could take me home with her too. It all seemed so easy to us.

Finally the day came. Willy was dressed up in his best clothes and his kitbag was packed. I still had to feed the pigs, and so said goodbye to Willy, not fully realising how final saying "goodbye" really is.

I left him in the main hall of the house, where he waited for his mother to come and get him. I don't think anyone was absolutely sure what time exactly that she would come for him, though she was expected first thing in the morning. She would be coming on a bus.

Just like Willy and I had done so many times together, I went to the kitchen and got the steaming potato peelings and other stuff for the pigs. Then I mixed in the sweet-smelling pigfeed powder together with the hot swill, and headed off to the pigsty.

I walked down the path to the pigsty, deep in thought, already missing Willy. There was no one to chat to or fool around with. Already I felt his presence missing.

How well I remember those next few minutes in my young and impressionable life. As I recall, I was inside the pigsty, pouring the swill into the trough, the pigs as usual bustling around me, when I heard Willy and his mother. Willy was talking excitingly as they were walking down the narrow country lane past the pigsty, his voice echoing between the high hedgerows.

Hardly daring to speak for fear of him hearing the sadness in my voice, I called out, "Goodbye, Willy, bye."

Willy and his mother stopped talking and came over to the hedge and we talked for a moment. Then with good intentions, promising to write to each other and vowing to stay friends all of our lives, we said goodbye again, and Willy and his mother continued on down the lane.

While we were still within earshot, we both called back to each other.

SUFFER LITTLE CHILDREN

"Goodbye, Willy" I shouted, and he replied, "Goodbye, Reg, goodbye. Look after Belly for me. Goodbye, Reg, goodbye."

I called "Goodbye" back to him a couple of times more, and he called back each time, like kids would, all the time he was walking away until we couldn't hear each other any more. Then he was gone.

I never heard from Willy again, but I've always remembered him and have wondered many times if Willy would still remember me, and our early years together at Meriden.

These were some of the happy, yet sad, and certainly most memorable times of my childhood life. What was to happen during the next three years is a different story. If I'm glad of anything, I'm glad Willy didn't have to go through these next few years with me.

~°~°~ The China Plate ~°~°~

It wasn't long after Willy had left Meriden that I was told that I was to be moved again. Just like the other times when I was to be moved, once again my kitbag would have been packed and a chaperon would have been arranged to travel with me, or I would have been put on a train with a luggage label attached to me, noting who I was and my destination, much like any package that was being sent somewhere would be.

If I was travelling on my own, which was not often the case, I would be aware that there was no one, for the moment, watching me. For me, this was a responsible moment; I was actually in charge of myself. Such moments were rare and generally only occurred when I was in transit.

On this particular journey, after arriving in London something very unusual happened. A man met me. He was to be my chaperon, and so travelled with me on the Underground (subway) to Kings Cross Station, which is actually in just another suburb of London.

There was nothing strange or unusual about that, of course. However, what was strange was that this man gave me a present. I remember that he put his hand into the paper carrier bag he was carrying, and took out yet another paper bag. In the bag was a china dinner plate. Then he handed the china plate to me, and said something that puzzled me. I don't remember exactly the words that were said at the time, except that he would have said something like "Here. Have this. It's a plate,

SUFFER LITTLE CHILDREN

and it's for you to keep".

I remember looking up at him, and may have said, "A plate, for me" and, in wonderment, adding, "to keep?"

The plate was a rather large white china dinner plate with a floral pattern on it. To this day I can't imagine why the man, a total stranger to me, would have given a small boy of about nine years old a dinner plate. But a china plate it was, and he gave it to me.

I'm sure that I liked the plate, and to some extent would have cherished it. It was china, and it simply looked nice to me. But above all, it was mine and only mine. I kept and treasured the plate for quite a long time, perhaps a couple of months, though it might have only been a month – I don't really remember how long.

I wouldn't have used the plate to eat off, as we only used white porcelain-covered metal plates in most, if not all, of the orphanages I had ever been in up to this point in my life.

What happened to the plate eventually, I don't know that either. It probably got broken or stolen. But I remember it well, because I had owned something, even if it had only been a china plate.

The 'plate' incident happened on that particular trip from the lovely little village of Meriden and the gentle life of a family-run orphanage, to my new orphanage, and to what I was to find out would be the harshest and the most demoralising orphanage I was to be in. It was called Bayfordbury.

7

BAYFORDBURY – Part 1

~o~o~ Mr Scougall ~o~o~

I was met at the Hertford North railway station by the headmaster of Bayfordbury, Mr Scougall. He drove me in his little Ford car, provided by Dr Barnardo's Homes, to Bayfordbury, which was to be my new orphanage.

Mr Scougall was, as well I remember, an intimidating man to me, a very small boy of no more than about nine years old. He was well over six feet tall, big, and heavy. He must have weighed in excess of eighteen stone (two hundred and fifty-two pounds) and looked very overweight, one might even say fat.

Mr Scougall, at about fifty-five years old, looked fierce and rather frightening to me at first glance. Perhaps it was because he had a face that looked like that of a bulldog and jowls to match, or maybe it was because of his thick, dark untidy hair, overgrown bulging eyebrows, and a typical ruddy English complexion. Whatever it was, he immediately brought dread to my soul, and I remember well that, like the other boys I was to meet and live with at Bayfordbury, I was afraid and feared him from the first moment I ever saw him.

Mr Scougall bringing me back with him to Bayfordbury was much like a heartless farmer going to market and bringing home a new calf, lamb, piglet or such to be raised with the other creatures on his farm, and I was a lamb, seemingly for the slaughter. This may sound a little dramatic but as one will understand as one reads on, this is much like it was.

There would have been little or no conversation, but if asked a question, I would answer, "Yes, Sir" or "No, Sir". I would not, as we were always being told, speak unless spoken to.

SUFFER LITTLE CHILDREN
~o~o~ Bayfordbury, The Mansion ~o~o~

The town of Hertford was at the time a rather small, bustling town located about ten miles north-east of the outer suburbs of London, in the beautiful county of Hertfordshire.

We drove to the other side of Hertford on the main road to St Albans, a road I was to come to know like the back of my hand because we 'dicky boys' (as we Dr Barnardo boys often called ourselves) would walk the two or even three miles into the town of Hertford, very often.

Upon arriving at Bayfordbury we came to the main gates into the Bayfordbury estate. Beside the gates there was a gatehouse – many of the old British mansions had gatehouses – which one of the orphanage masters and his family lived in.

Mr Scougall hooted on his car horn and a man scurried out and opened the gates.

After passing through the huge wrought-iron gates, we then travelled about a half a mile up the driveway, and there it was: a very large white mansion, Bayfordbury.

We stopped at the big, wide-fronted steps, which led up to the main entrance of the Bayfordbury mansion. A total of six huge round white stone columns gave the steps an overwhelming feeling of grandeur, which made me feel very small.

At one end of the mansion, built into one of the stone gables was a big three-foot diameter clock with Roman numerals, and at the other end of this rather long mansion was an impressive weather vane, also about three feet in diameter.

The entire three-storey building was constructed of almost pure white stone, much like limestone, but, of course, a much harder stone. The windows were tall and wide, indicating that the rooms inside the mansion were big and spacious.

Unbeknown to me at that time, I had now entered the realm of Mr Scougall and misery – misery that was to last for the next two and a half years. This was to be by far the worst orphanage for young boys one could imagine – a terrible place where I and many other unfortunates were to have to live or, I might even say, survive in.

SUFFER LITTLE CHILDREN

*Bayfordbury
Front View of Mansion*

Rear View of Bayfordbury

SUFFER LITTLE CHILDREN

*Bayfordbury (Basement) Dining-Room
Much like it was in 1943 - 45
(PHOTO TAKEN IN 1989)*

*Bayfordbury Dormatory
This was my dormitory in the basement in 1943 – 45
At that time there wasn't any water in the basement.
(PHOTO TAKEN IN 1989)*

SUFFER LITTLE CHILDREN

I was told to take my kitbag to a dormitory in the basement of the building. It was a bleak-looking room with whitewashed walls, the floors being cold grey flagstone. The windows, because they were in the basement, had iron bars on them for security reasons. Because the windows were partially below ground, they faced directly at the wall of a stone-walled courtyard, which was entirely below ground level. There were about fifteen beds in my dormitory.

Bayfordbury was a huge domicile, the front facade of the building being as much as two hundred and fifty feet long. As well as the two main floors, there was an extensive attic area, and a full lower level one might call a basement.

The headmaster and his staff lived in a large part of the upper, more luxurious part of the mansion. We, the boys, lived, for the most part, in the basement level.

To better describe the basement, I should explain that when the huge old domicile of Bayfordbury was built during the Georgian period, the entire area around the mansion had been excavated to a depth of about twelve feet, in such a way as to form what might have been called a 'dry' moat, but what was actually called the courtyard, resulting in the so-called basement level being mostly above ground.

The courtyard area was completely paved with flagstones, in the same way as was the rest of the inside basement level that we lived in.

Looking out of our dormitory window we would, as I have mentioned, be looking straight at a stone wall about eight to ten feet away. This same situation applied to our, the boys', dining room, ablutions and the entire basement area.

In Britain no one called areas below ground level, basements. Such areas are only called cellars. Generally speaking, no one ever lived in a cellar, except for perhaps servants. In a smaller domicile, cellars were mostly built to store coal or coke and the likes.

Our dining room in the basement had a cemented vaulted ceiling. The walls were stone and the floor, like the courtyard and the rest of the basement, was flagstone paving. The walls and ceiling were painted with whitewash, which always looked dirty and generally grimy. From the ceiling there were several naked light bulbs hanging on simple electrical wires. These types of lights were common throughout our entire living

SUFFER LITTLE CHILDREN

quarters in the basement.

I can't believe Lady Clinton Baker – the owner of Bayfordbury – had anything to do with where we boys lived in her home, and I really don't believe that she had stipulated that 'the orphans' must be made to live in the bowels of her mansion. But, with the exception of one or possibly two dormitories, where the older boys slept, that was where I, and certainly most of us younger boys, lived much of the time.

The ablutions, which included the toilets, bathtubs and showers, were all at the other end of the basement from where the dormitories and the dining room were. All of the toilets, baths and washbasins were in one huge room. There were no cubicles. The walls throughout were again, basically whitewashed. This all-inclusive room was called 'the ablutions'.

The showers in the ablutions, which had probably been temporarily installed just for us boys, consisted of two rows of inch-and-a-quarter iron pipes suspended horizontally about seven feet above the floor, with about ten simple T fittings, and spaced about four feet apart. These sloping, horizontal water pipes allowed the water to come out of the holes, primarily by gravity.

As one can easily imagine, the system didn't work too well. When the showers were in operation there would be plenty of water coming out of the first few holes where the supply came in, and hardly any coming out of the last few holes. Even then, the water that did reach the end of the pipe where the last boys were would be uncomfortably cold.

We would scramble to get the first few holes, but mostly the big kids would get them while we little kids would shiver, trying to shower in cool or even cold water.

While we lived in this otherwise beautiful Bayfordbury mansion, the only room we would be allowed in upstairs during the day was the playroom, and we only went into this room when we all had to assemble, or sometimes if it was raining. Our 'occasional' playroom was probably a ballroom when Lord and Lady Clinton Baker were in residence there.

There was a piano in the playroom, and sometimes on Sunday mornings before church some, even five or six of us little kids but not the older ones, would stand around the piano and sing hymns and songs while Mr Scougall thumped away on the piano.

SUFFER LITTLE CHILDREN

I remember several of the hymns and songs Mr Scougall played and which we sang, like *'All through the Night'* and *'As I Was Going to Strawberry Fair'*.

One of the songs that we sang and which I thought I knew the words of was the Scottish song:

> *The camels are coming, Hurrah! Hurrah!*
> *The camels are coming Hurrah! Hurrah!*

I found out many years later that it wasn't 'the camels' at all that were coming; it was the 'Campbells'!

~o~o~ Institutions – Borstals, ~o~o~ Dr Barnardo's Homes

I feel because there is some mention of Borstals in my book, that I should briefly enlighten the reader about borstals. Borstals originated in England in the nineteenth century, the name being taken from Borstal prison near Rochester, Kent. Borstals were built throughout Britain to reform delinquent boys of sixteen to twenty-one years old.

Borstals – now called Youth Custody Centres – were primarily for boys convicted of crimes. Such boys were considered to be too young for prison life and the influences of the hardened criminals. If their crimes were serious enough, like house breaking, stealing, arson and the likes, then they would in all probability be sent to a borstal for a number of years.

Those who committed the more serious crimes like assault or murder, and repeat offenders, would be sentenced and have to serve their sentences in adult prisons, though under what conditions, I have no knowledge.

Borstals were located all over the British Isles, in most large towns and cities. Understandably, nobody would want a borstal to be located near them. Everyone, including us kids, all knew what borstals were, and there was always some concern amongst the local community if such a school was located near it.

It was rumoured, and I say rumoured because I don't know that any of us knew for sure, that Mr Scougall had been the headmaster or

SUFFER LITTLE CHILDREN

warden of a borstal before coming to work for Dr Barnardo's Homes. If the rumour was correct, then one could better understand why Mr Scougall was such a severe, unforgiving person, determined to rule by the rod during his administration of us pre-adolescent and adolescent boys.

The 'outsiders', as we Dr Barnardo boys referred to those people who lived outside the orphanage system, commonly regarded us Barnardo kids as being boys just a little better, if indeed better at all, than borstal boys.

It seemed that the outsiders did not know, or did not want to understand, that the Dr Barnardo's Homes boys were not like borstal boys, and that we were not in the orphanage as the result of any criminal activity, petty or otherwise.

In actual fact, the reason, though there were actually many exceptions, that children were in an orphanage was because they had lost their parents and were alone in the world with no adult prepared to look after them. They were never there because they had committed crimes.

Regardless, we were considered and treated as wayward kids, and orphanages were considered comparable to borstal. If the children in outsiders' homes did anything wrong, their parents would frequently say to them, "You ought to be in borstal," or threaten them with "I'll send you to Dr Barnardo's Homes if you don't behave," almost all in the same breath.

Us Dr Barnardo kids were linked together, without thought, to the boys incarcerated at a borstal and in the minds of some there was hardly the slightest, if any, distinction.

~o~o~

As I grew older, I began to understand more and more how, in those days, society regarded orphans in general terms. It seems as though we were thought to be antisocial, bent on mischief and crime, and nothing more than beggars and street urchins. Many people would, no doubt, conclude that most of us would end up in prisons, and that in all likelihood we would amount to nothing, or achieve little during the course of our lives.

SUFFER LITTLE CHILDREN

And so, like most, if not all of us Dr Barnardo kids, I too was ashamed of being a Dr Barnardo's Homes boy. Parents of outsider children would tell their kids not to play with or to have anything to do with us, afraid that we would be a bad influence on them and lead them 'astray'.

They would say that we were poor, which of course we were. Unfortunately we had nothing but the clothes we were standing in, and even those, particularly in the church orphanages, were donated by somebody. However, such donations were very likely not given by the people who said we were poor or who made derogatory remarks about us. They, the outsiders who despised us, would, in keeping with their attitude towards us, be too mean to give or share anything, or even to be simply kind and tolerant of us.

Those same outsiders, who had little or no understanding or compassion for orphans or otherwise Dr Barnardo kids, would say we were dirty. But as it was we weren't: we were made to shower or bath almost every day. They would tell their children that they could catch antisocial problems like fleas, ringworm, and other shameful problems from us, and therefore should stay away from us.

The outsider parents might even say that their children could get other health problems from us such as chickenpox, measles, mumps and the likes – which they could, just as they could from any other children. But they made it sound like it would be more likely that they could catch these health problems from us, which made us feel much like the lepers would have felt years ago, in the now ancient biblical times.

We may well have been, and in all probability were, cleaner and healthier than many of the outsiders' kids. We were examined for cleanliness every day, and our hair was inspected for lice and fleas every week, and I don't recall many, if any, of us ever having fleas.

We had to brush our teeth twice a day, and we were forced to take horrible-tasting laxatives every week. I would think that, inside and out, our bodies were disgustingly healthy and clean for young boys, although maybe somewhat undernourished.

I must agree, though, with the outsiders when they said we looked scruffy and untidy. There would, needless to say, be some truth to this. The simple fact was that we did look scruffy. Many of our clothes, particularly those in the private orphanages, were 'hand-me-downs'.

SUFFER LITTLE CHILDREN

Most of those, though we didn't really care, had holes in them and were just worn out.

Understandably there wasn't anyone with sufficient interest, like a mother or even a father, who would make sure that all of our buttons were done up, and that our underpants were properly supported and didn't hang down below our short-trouser legs.

We were all too aware that we survived and lived on charity and public donations, because we were constantly being reminded of this fact by unthinking adults, through their insensitive children. As a result of their constant reminders, insults and taunts we were, to say the very least, ashamed of our predicament and ourselves, simply for being what we were: orphans or 'children in care'.

~o~o~

Needless to say, our situation was not of our choice or within our control. But that was our life, and live it we would. We had no one to complain to or sympathise with our fated way of life.

But the reader should not be over-sympathetic. We, in our own little world, not knowing any other way of life first hand, didn't feel sorry for ourselves, and were, for the most part, quite happy. I had good friends amongst the boys in Bayfordbury, most of whom were like brothers to me, and a few of these I would know for the next fifty to sixty years at least.

~o~o~ Dicky Boys ~o~o~

I must admit that we were, as the result of the outsiders' attitudes towards us, quite hostile to many of the outsider kids. Being brought up as we were, with no one to help defend us from bigger boys, bullies and the likes, we became very independent and self-reliant, and so, rather aggressive.

Within the orphanage system, most arguments would result in physical fighting. Boys didn't avoid or stop talking to each other because of disputes; we simply raised our fists and fought. When such fights ended, more often than not in a standoff, the incident that had resulted in the fight would be forgotten and the boys might even become fast friends.

SUFFER LITTLE CHILDREN

The masters, whether intentionally or not, would not stop us boys from fighting. It just wasn't the way. It seemed as though we were expected to find our place within our own unique society, or structure of the orphanage. Very few boys would be, as it was so often put, 'cry babies'.

A nickname we boys in Dr Barnardo's quite often referred to ourselves as was 'Dicky Boys'. The term or name was quite unique to Dr Barnardo boys, and was used throughout the whole of Britain.

Putting the term in context, we might say, when we referred to ourselves collectively, "Is that a Dicky Boy over there?" meaning "Is that a Dr Barnardo boy?"

If there were hostilities between an outsider boy and one of our Dicky Boys, we always went to the defence of our own. We were, after all, brothers in a way, bonded by circumstances. But even then we would never fight two of us against one; this would be part of our unspoken code and two against one was thought to be cowardly. Three against three or the likes was a different matter, but rarely did such confrontations actually occur.

If a bigger outsider boy took advantage and fought one of our smaller boys, one of our bigger or 'better' fighters, would commonly step up to challenge the bigger outsider boy, and so help the smaller boy. There was a true loyalty which unconsciously existed between us Dr Barnardo kids, and the outsiders knew it.

~o~o~

So here I was, to spend the next few years not only known by outsiders as a typical 'bad' Barnardo boy, but a 'scruffy' Bayfordbury boy as well – something which we were also known as.

~o~o~ Lady Clinton Baker ~o~o~

Many lords and ladies, wealthy landowners, and owners of large homes and estates loaned their properties to institutions like Dr Barnardo's Homes for extensive periods of time during the war.

Just as Winston Churchill had asked, almost everyone did his or her part during those stressful times. Such was the generosity of

SUFFER LITTLE CHILDREN

Lady Clinton Baker in 1942, shortly before I came to live at Bayfordbury.

Lady Clinton Baker had, generously no doubt, loaned her Bayfordbury estate to Dr Barnardo's Homes for the duration of the war. She had lost her husband, Lord Clinton Baker, several years before the war.

The Bayfordbury estate covered about 2,000 acres and consisted of woods, fields, a rather large spinney, and a small lake. There were two half-mile entrance driveways into the estate.

At each entrance to the estate there were gatekeepers' houses. Across the entrance roads into the estate were steel railings and big ten feet high wrought-iron gates, which were kept closed and were opened only for authorised vehicles. Beside each of the main gates were small gates for pedestrians, which us kids used at such times that we were allowed to go out into the town or elsewhere.

Lady Clinton Baker was a mystery to us. Her family's name was everywhere – in Bayford Church, Hertingfordbury Church, throughout the Bayfordbury estate on several trees dedicated to members of the Clinton Baker family, and on the First World War memorial at Bayford Church. The reader will become familiar with Bayford and Hertingfordbury as my story progresses.

I well remember the first occasion that Lady Clinton Baker visited us, because it was the first of the few times we were ever to see her. We had all received the day off from school because this grand lady was coming to visit us, and for this reason if for no other, that would have made us like Lady Clinton Baker.

On this, the first occasion, we were all made to shower, comb our hair, and put on our best clothes. Mr Scougall warned us that we would be severely punished unless we behaved and acted like deserving Dr Barnardo boys.

It was raining and windy on the day Lady Clinton Baker arrived, so we all assembled in the playroom. The occasion would be much like it might have been if the King himself were coming to visit us.

Lady Clinton Baker looked like a nice, rather 'posh' but otherwise ordinary-looking lady, except that she wore a big fur coat and a large fancy hat. She had a young girl with her about my age, who, like her mother, wore a thick fur coat and a hat.

Many of us kids, without any of the masters seeing us, were of

SUFFER LITTLE CHILDREN

course, sniggering. It was at about that time in our cheeky young lives when we used to say, if we saw a woman with a fur coat on, "Fur coat, no drawers." But we didn't know what we were talking about really, or what it could mean.

That day we had a special dinner of 'bangers and mash', which was a big treat for us kids. It's more than likely that a 'big show' would be put on for the likes of Lady Clinton Baker; she would be one of those patrons of Dr Barnardo's Homes who gave money to support us.

As I have mentioned, we rarely saw Lady Clinton Baker, but when we did they were always very special days.

~o~ John 'Baggy' Baggaridge and Fred Dyos ~o~

Bayfordbury itself had been opened by Dr Barnardo's Homes just a few weeks before I had arrived there in early 1943. There were about fifty to sixty boys in the home, and I didn't know a single soul.

As one could imagine, it's very confusing for a small boy to be moving into what seemed like a large institutional environment, where the majority of the other boys are quite a bit older and bigger. I was about nine, while the eldest was almost sixteen years old and so much bigger than me.

Until a short while ago, I had been living with a family in the tiny village of Wilnecote, and then in a very small orphanage in Meriden, where none of the other boys were more than a year older than their younger peers.

Whereas Meriden was a family-run little orphanage, with individual attention given to each boy, depending on the child's needs, Bayfordbury was a large and disciplined orphanage administered, I was to find out, by a man with an iron fist, and whose staff had no time or interest in the welfare of any individual boy, except to perhaps punish them.

~o~o~

Fortunately I was to make friends quickly at Bayfordbury, and soon learned to relax amongst my peers, who, in turn, were sharing the same fortunes or misfortunes as myself.

SUFFER LITTLE CHILDREN

Shortly after I arrived at Bayfordbury, I met up with Fred Dyos. Fred was quite a bit bigger, and much heavier than me.

A short while later, maybe a month or so, John Baggaridge arrived. John had been living at a Dr Barnardo's Homes Sea School, and for reasons unknown to him, as was often the case, he had been transferred to Bayfordbury.

'Baggy', a nickname he was to become known by, and I were about the same height, and although Baggy was slightly heavier than me, we were both rather small boys.

We three: Fred, Baggy and myself, sat at a table positioned at the very back of the dining room, together with a couple of other boys, who I can hardly remember. There were at least twelve heavy, ten-foot long wooden tables in the dining room, with wooden benches each side. Much the same as they were at Woodford Bridge, the tables and benches were all scrubbed white.

The ceiling of the dining room was vaulted, and appeared to be constructed of corbelled brick, then rendered with cement plaster, and whitewashed. The floors were of flagstone slabs, and the walls were also whitewashed. Except for the whitewashing, it's unlikely that anything had been done to improve the basement since the mansion had been built late in the eighteenth century. There was no other colour in the dining room, and no pictures or other decoration, thus giving the room a gloomy, forlorn atmosphere, much like one could imagine a workhouse dining room would look.

The tables and benches were spaced evenly down each side of the room, with a six-foot wide aisle down the middle between them.

Running laterally to the tables, at the front end of the dining room, where the entrance door was located, were two tables placed end to end and arranged so that the food for the meals could be set up and served to us as we filed by. As well, there were benches just on the server's side. These were for the smaller boys to stand on while serving food to the other boys.

I really came to know Baggy as the result of an argument at our dining room table. Whatever it was that caused the argument, couldn't have been very significant as I don't remember what the argument was about, but nevertheless it led to a fist fight.

SUFFER LITTLE CHILDREN

As with any boys in an orphanage, eight to fifteen-year-olds, or any age for that matter, our arguments would often continue until one would challenge the other to a "Do ya wanna fight?"

The honourable response (most of us had lots of pride) would commonly be "Yeah! Do you?"

So without any more discussion we agreed that we would, after the meal and when Grace had been said, meet outside on the grass in front of the mansion, in full view of the staff, if any were watching. Even so, and if they were watching, the staff would rarely ever get involved to stop a fight.

It was Mr Scougall's policy that us boys, young and old, had to "learn to stand on your own two feet", and so we would be left to sort out our own disputes or problems in one way or another, including fighting.

Baggy and I, with lots of the kids shouting "fight, fight", fought toe to toe for about what seemed like half an hour, but which was really about five or, at the very most, ten minutes. After punching each other and being somewhat breathless, we would be standing, with our fists up pugilistic style, staring at each other, only half-heartedly wanting to continue.

My peers thought of me as being a 'good fighter' and I had fully expected to beat Baggy, but I was wrong. Baggy was also a good fighter, and I knew the best I could hope for was a draw or a standoff.

After a short while in these standoff situations, one of us would commonly say to the other, "Had enough?" or "Give up?", hoping like heck the other would say yes! The other, too proud to give up, would reply, "No. Do you?", and so it would go on until they would get fed up with the posturing, and ultimately leave.

I remember well how our fight ended. Everyone except Fred left our fight and only the three of us were left to talk to each other. As I recall, both Baggy and I had had enough, and we both conceded that neither of us had won. It had been a good fight, as fighting went at that time in our lives.

Besides being a little bruised, and maybe one of us receiving a bloody nose, neither of us had been hurt but, most important, both of our prides were still intact.

Fred had stayed to the end, listening to our posturing, and then encouraged us to shake hands. He didn't take sides one way or the other. After a few minutes of talking all was forgotten.

SUFFER LITTLE CHILDREN

From that day on, and for the rest of our childhood and youthful years, Baggy and I became great friends, and shared a great deal of respect for each other, knowing neither could beat the other in a fight.

In later years, when we were in a much bigger orphanage and about sixteen years old, we were both selected to be in the school's boxing team and were quite proficient at the sport. We never had to box against each other as Baggy was to become heavier than me, and so we were in different boxing weight classifications.

Even to this day, more than sixty-three years later, though I don't see or hear from Fred any more, I am still in touch with Baggy by letter and often by telephone, and see him and his wife Lois from time to time, when we visit England from Canada.

~°~°~ The Gamekeeper ~°~°~

Down behind the Bayfordbury mansion, about a quarter of a mile away, in a deep valley surrounded by trees, was Lady Clinton Baker's gamekeeper's cottage. Even during the war the gamekeeper still lived there.

He lived alone except for his two dogs. He also had a few cages in which he kept ferrets, which he would use for 'rabbiting'.

We didn't go too near his area of the woods often, as we regarded him as being like one of the Bayfordbury staff, even though he wasn't employed by Dr Barnardo's Homes. Even worse, we also knew that the gamekeeper had a gun, and being influenced by our young imaginations and what he might do with the gun, we didn't go near him or his cottage, though we would spy on him from a safe distance away.

Baggy, Fred, and I would see the gamekeeper in the woods sometimes, but would try not to let him see us. He never waved when he did see us. Nor did he act friendly, so we assumed he wasn't a nice chap and simply avoided him.

The estate was abundant with small game such as pheasants, partridge, rabbits, hares and such, which the gamekeeper was bound to protect. In those days it was expected that he would shoot hawks, owls, badgers and foxes, and weasels, stoats and other predatory animals that would hunt the game birds and rabbits.

In the not-too-distant future, we were to get to know the gamekeeper

SUFFER LITTLE CHILDREN

a little, and found that he wasn't really as frightening a chap as we had thought him to be.

A local farmer would pasture sheep on the front lawns of the mansion, which in turn kept the grass short. In the spring we would see the ewes lambing, right there on our front lawns. Lambing was quite a common occurrence, as were the rams challenging each other during their butting duels in the spring.

Cows were kept in other fields on the property, and with them there would often be a bull. There would always be signs stating 'Beware of the Bull', but we seldom heeded the signs and were from time to time chased by the bulls, though I don't recall any of the boys being injured at all.

Quite a large area adjoining the mansion was out of bounds to us kids. To be caught in any of the 'out-of-bounds' areas was automatically a caning offence.

~o~o~ The Bucket ~o~o~

The foot and head frames attached to our beds were made of cast-iron piping, which was painted black – typical of most, if not all such institutions at the time, it seemed. The beds were narrow, with cotton or wool-filled mattresses. For us they were quite adequate. After all, we had never known anything much better, except perhaps at my now almost forgotten foster parents' home.

There were about fifteen to twenty boys in the dormitory I was in, which seemed to be about the normal number of boys in a dormitory at Bayfordbury. We all wore white nightshirts with blue vertical stripes to bed, most of which were either too long or too short for us, much like 'one size fits all'. There were strict rules about us not wearing our heavy cotton underpants or socks in bed.

During the war, daylight-saving time was set back two hours, which meant that when we went to bed at 8.30 p.m. it would still be light outside and would stay light until 11.00 p.m. in midsummer.

Each night the hinged wooden shutters, which folded into special wall pockets each side of the windows during the day, had to be closed. This was a war condition requirement. If any light could be seen at

SUFFER LITTLE CHILDREN

night through anyone's windows or doors in Britain, there were fines that could be issued to the careless offender.

After our dormitory shutters were closed for the night and after it was dark outside, the dormitory would be as dark as the blackest ink. There was no such thing as a night-light in those days.

The beds were generally laid out around the perimeter of the dormitory, with the headrails against the walls. The remainder of the beds were then randomly spaced throughout the centre of the dormitory.

Many of us boys, and there were many, would frequently sleepwalk, including myself. When we did we would often stub our toes or bump into someone else's bed, or even walk straight into a wall. Being totally disoriented after waking up from a deep sleep and unable to see anything, we would wake up absolutely confused.

Because it was so dark, we wouldn't be able to find anything or any reference point that would indicate to us where we were in the dormitory, and so we couldn't find our way back to our beds. What we often had to do was wake another boy up in order to find out who he was, and so use him as a point of reference in order that we could find our way back to our own beds. This was all quite normal, and happened to many of us quite often.

The nearest toilet was in the 'ablutions', located at the other end of the mansion basement. This was too far for us young boys to go during the night, so we were provided with a white, three or four-gallon porcelain pail. The pail, or 'the bucket', as we called it, was conveniently located right in the middle of the floor in each of the dormitories. If a boy had to go for a pee or even a 'number two' in the middle of the night, they would all have to use the same bucket. There was nothing else.

Quite frequently, when any of the boys woke up and had to use the bucket during the night, if the boy was wide awake and thought about it, it wasn't so difficult to find the bucket, but he would have to walk carefully. However, if the boy jumped out of bed half awake, or had been asleep and woke up whilst sleepwalking, that was a different matter, because he wouldn't know where he was or where exactly the dreaded bucket was located, amongst the maze of beds.

To make things even worse, the bucket, after it had been used several times during the night, would begin to smell. So the boys nearest

SUFFER LITTLE CHILDREN

the bucket would move it away from their beds, and so almost none of us would know exactly where the darn bucket was from night to night.

It was quite common for us boys, being half asleep when we got out of bed to use the bucket, to often miss the bucket completely and pee on the floor. On some nights too many boys would have had to use it, and it became full and actually overflowed.

But as bad as that was, it wasn't the most unpleasant thing that could happen.

By far the worst thing we could do, if we were sleepwalking or otherwise out of bed, and totally disorientated, was to trip over the bucket and knock it over.

The white porcelain bucket, with its wire type handle, would roll and rattle around on the wooden floor, spilling its contents everywhere.

The unfortunate boy who had tripped over the bucket would quite possibly have hit his shinbone, causing him to shout when he tripped. Then, to make things even worse, he would quite commonly fall over the heavy bucket and, if the bucket was half full or more, into the sea of pee.

When this happened, in the quiet of the night, most all of the boys would wake up and, knowing who had tripped and probably fallen, would giggle, forgetting that if they themselves got out of bed some time in the night, they too might well slip over in the mess.

Believe it or not, disgusting as it was, knocking the bucket over had its good, as well as its bad points, depending on what time of the night it was knocked over.

If the bucket was knocked over shortly after we had gone to sleep, then there wouldn't be much pee in the bucket, if any at all. However, whatever pee there had been in the bucket at that point would be spilled on the floor and would remain there for rest of the night, ready to be stepped in by any boy needing to use the bucket during the rest of the night.

The later it was at night that the bucket got knocked over, say in the early hours of the morning, the worse it would be, as of course there would be more pee and whatever else there was in the bucket, to spill on the floor, and therefore more to clean up.

After the boy who quite possibly may have slipped over into the pee got back to his bed, he would have to take off his wet nightshirt, and get into bed to dry off and get warm again.

SUFFER LITTLE CHILDREN

The final thing the boy would think of and have on his mind before he got back to sleep was that when he woke up in the morning, he would be the one to clean up the mess, before quite possibly being caned later.

~°~°~ 'Spinning Up' ~°~°~

In the winter, going to bed at eight thirty in the evening wasn't too bad but in midsummer, it still being light outside until about eleven o'clock, it was very hard for us boys, and we simply wouldn't be able to go to sleep.

Through the small cracks in the shuttered windows we could see daylight and also hear the lambs bleating for their mothers, just outside our windows.

The birds would still be singing their evening songs long after we were in bed. So naturally, there would still be the feeling of daytime. Knowing it was still daylight would keep our young minds active, and we would stay awake until the sun went down and it became dark outside.

Talking after 'lights out' was not allowed and we could be caned for this too. But for the most part, none of the masters came to check on us regularly. If we talked, and we did quite often, we did so very quietly.

Most evenings, after the lights were turned off, somebody would 'spin up'. Spinning up was what we called telling stories. We would make up stories of adventures and gruesome murders, and try to scare each other.

I was pretty good at telling stories and was often called upon to do so. Others would keep 'diggy eye'. Diggy eye is the term for one or several of us being delegated to listen or keep watch for masters and the likes when we knew we were doing something wrong.

If, when a boy was spinning up, the person keeping diggy eye heard a master coming, he would whisper, "Diggs." Immediately we would stop talking and pretend to be asleep, until the master or matron had left. Then we would continue with our talking or spinning up. Rarely did we get caught, but occasionally we did, and then we would be almost automatically caned.

My friend Flappers had only one story he would tell. The first time he told his story he got lots of grumbling. He would start his story, with his voice sounding like a sort of trembling, scary whisper:

SUFFER LITTLE CHILDREN

"One dark and stormy night, three men sat on a bridge. One man said to the other, 'Tell us a story'."

Then Flappers would pause for a moment, and then continue,

"And so the story began."

Flappers would then pause again, and then continue in the same scary voice,

"One dark and stormy night, three men sat on a bridge, and one man said to the other, 'Tell us a story'."

Then he would pause again, and in a creepy voice continue again,

"And so the story began."

Then, continuing in the same scary voice, he would say it all again.

"One dark and stormy night, three men sat on a bridge..."

And so he would continue until we caught on. After Flappers had repeated himself a few times, saying exactly the same thing, we grumbled and laughed. When he volunteered to 'spin up' again, we all would boo him and tell him to "Shut up".

~o~o~ Brutal Caning ~o~o~

Most punishments at Bayfordbury would be by caning, or being sent to bed without any dinner (supper) after coming home from the outsiders' school, or sometimes even both. The punishment of being sent to bed early could last for a few days or even a week, depending on what kind of mood Mr Scougall was in at the time he was punishing us.

Many times a master would merely hit us with his hands, knocking us off our feet, or even punch us. We grew to fear many of the more sadistic masters, who had no hesitation in practising their violent acts on us kids.

SUFFER LITTLE CHILDREN

For us, there was no one to appeal to or help us, and Mr Scougall and his staff knew it only too well. Kids would go to school with black eyes, swollen and bloodied lips and other obvious bruises, but no one would seriously enquire as to how we got them.

The masters simply got away with the way they treated us defenceless kids, without any thought of punitive action being taken against them.

I believe now that the outsiders, including the teachers, thought that we received our bruises as the result of us fighting each other. Many times their assumptions were probably correct, but more often than not our bruises were caused by the masters.

Caning was always administered by Mr Scougall, as though it was his personal privilege to do so. He would joke about 'getting his exercise' and come out with the old saying we heard so many times, "This is going to hurt me more than it will hurt you." This would be followed by a careless chuckle, like it was all just a joke to him. Needless to say, it was no joke to us.

If Mr Scougall was away from Bayfordbury for any reason, then the privilege of caning us was taken over by Mr Nash, him being yet another of the fearful characters who, so to speak, 'looked after us'.

When we were to be punished we would have to wait outside Mr Scougall's office for him to shout and tell us to enter. Often there would be as many as eight boys waiting to go into his office for punishment.

These would be very tense moments, and we would fidget in anticipation of what was to again be the inevitable caning. We wouldn't talk to each other, mostly because we were frightened and fearful for what was coming, and how many strokes of the cane we would receive. The number of cuts – we commonly called strokes of the cane 'cuts' – of the cane we received, would be dependant purely on Mr Scougall's mood at the time.

To know we had done something wrong, had been caught, and were waiting for the cane, was a terribly worrying feeling, very hard to explain – a feeling of dread, perhaps.

When our names were called and we entered Mr Scougall's office, Mr Scougall, as I recall, would always it seemed, to be standing there with his back to us as we entered, casually looking out of the window,

SUFFER LITTLE CHILDREN

tapping his thick stick in the palm of his hand menacingly. It was all so routine.

There would be no explanation or discussion. He would simply demand us to bend over and touch our toes. Then he would cane us on our backsides, so much so that we would have black-and-blue welts deep into our buttocks, to the point that they would sometimes even bleed.

Each stroke of his flailing cane would make us involuntarily cry out in pain. It wasn't just a schoolboy punishment like one may believe – it was absolute brutality and we simply had to suffer it.

I really believe that he actually enjoyed himself beating us, watching us in such pain, much like the perverted bully he was.

He would render as many as six to eight severe strokes, and sometimes even more strokes of his thick bamboo cane on us, depending on how well the individual boy was holding up.

To hear "I will beat you until you are black and blue" had a resounding meaning to us and, with or without a good memory, most of us boys couldn't help but remember those beatings.

While we were waiting outside Mr Scougall's office, waiting for our turn to be caned, it was frightening to hear each of the other boys shouting in pain while they were being caned. Naturally we would all shout and scream when we were being caned.

Often after a caning we would pull our trousers down and show the other kids our wounds. They would quite normally sympathise with the injured person and at the same time laugh to lighten the moment, just like I would if it were them on the receiving end. This probably helped to get us through those miserable years of Scougall.

~o~o~

Every Sunday morning after breakfast we would gather in the playroom and have to produce the toothbrush and comb we had been provided with. If a boy had lost either of these items, then this too, would be a reason for us to be caned, after which the toothbrush or comb would be replaced.

How we kept losing these things I will never know, but so many of us did. Perhaps we lost combs because we often had holes in our pockets,

SUFFER LITTLE CHILDREN

if in fact we had pockets at all. Often our pockets would be sewn up, rather than the staff going to the trouble of repairing the holes.

I was to be a regular recipient of the cane, as were so many others, particularly my closest friends, it seems. The cane would be administered for such things as talking during prayers or when Grace was being said in the dining room, or for being out of bounds.

There were so many more reasons for which we could be caned, including talking after lights out at bedtime, torn clothes, not being able to find our wash towels, or being late for meals. So many times the reason could be us inadvertently or unintentionally looking insolent at a master or a so-called 'nurse'. In fact, there were so many reasons I couldn't possibly mention them all.

There would, of course, be deserving reasons for us to be caned. Those, I believe I could understand and accept. But the others and the extreme severity of the caning, I just can't understand, even today.

The memories of Bayfordbury and the punishments we endured are still a vivid memory to me, though unlike some, I have not, to my knowledge, had any lasting psychological problems as the result of those terrible times.

~o~o~ A Reason for Caning? ~o~o~

On one particular occasion, which resulted in my being caned, and which sticks out in my memory, was the time when we were on a crocodile walk, going to Hertingfordbury Church. The crocodile was rather straggling and for whatever reason, we were not walking in the disciplined manner we were used to.

The road to Hertingfordbury Church is a quiet country lane with hedges on each side. Unthinking, I ran through a small gap in the hedge and out at another gap about twenty feet further along the hedge, and then rejoined the walk. Mr Nash saw me. He was very angry, and told me to report to the office to see Mr Scougall when we got back to Bayfordbury.

I know I would have been 'stewing' all through the church service, in anticipation of what was to come later when we got back to Bayfordbury, even though I could not understand exactly what I had done that was

SUFFER LITTLE CHILDREN

so wrong, or why Mr Nash was so angry.

After the service, and when we arrived back at Bayfordbury, it would have been about twelve thirty, which was dinnertime. I, having to report to the office, would have to miss dinner. Mr Scougall, who, in all probability, would not have made himself available (perhaps having his dinner) made me wait until the time was convenient to him, with no regard to the fact that I was missing my dinner. All this time I was standing outside his office, hungry and waiting to be caned. Not a fun time, to be sure.

The fear of the caning, and the missing of my dinner, was all secondary to my not understanding exactly what it was that I had done to deserve the cane, and there was no possible way I could appeal against my imminent punishment.

~o~o~

Such trivial offences and the severe consequences of the offence were the normal daily existence at Bayfordbury. The punishments and the ordeal of waiting to receive them must surely have affected the mental and emotional characters of some of us children.

It seems to me now, when remembering those days, that no thought was ever given by anyone as to the emotional toll such anxieties caused us boys. Without doubt, I feel such emotional abuse was just as detrimental to our characters and well-being as the unreasonable physical caning we received.

8

BAYFORDBURY – PART 2

~∘~∘~ Bayford School ~∘~∘~

Not long, perhaps a week or so, after arriving at Bayfordbury, I was told to join a crocodile march to go to Bayford School with the other eight and a half and nine-year-old boys.

I believe Fred Dyos was already going to Bayford School at the time that I arrived at Bayfordbury, but Baggy wasn't to arrive at Bayfordbury and so go to Bayford School until a few weeks or so later.

The walk from Bayfordbury to Bayford took us past a small two-acre lake, across a large field, through the woods (about half a mile) and then through another large field. Our journey to school and back, took us close to an hour each way, and entailed our climbing over two or three stiles, and opening and closing a couple of large, heavy wooden field gates, which took two of us boys to manage.

Coming out of the last field and through a big wooden gate into Bayfordbury Lane, we would be on the outskirts of the tiny village of Bayford. The narrow country lane, lined with dog roses and hawthorn bushes, and hazel nut trees that overhung a little babbling brook on one side of the lane, sounded alive with the chirping of chaffinches, sparrows, wrens and many other birds.

Continuing on to school, we would pass the quaint little village church of St Mary's with its adjoining graveyard. Walking along a further narrow country lane for about a quarter of a mile would bring us to the centre of the village of Bayford, and Bayford School. All in all, the walk was a little over a mile, or a mile and a half each way.

Bayford School was a two-roomed school house. Mrs Dunning was the school's headmistress and one of two teachers who taught there. She was a nice, rather portly lady, who lived in the house next to the school.

Us younger of the Bayfordbury boys, ten to fifteen of us, made up by far the largest number of children attending Bayford School. The

SUFFER LITTLE CHILDREN

ages of the children at this small village school ranged from about six to nine, or possibly ten.

In Mrs Dunning's garden there were perhaps three apple trees. The trees produced beautiful yellow apples. The apples, we were told, were called 'Transparent', and she would give us some from time to time as prizes for good work. I remember winning many of these apples for learning and reciting several poems and passages from books, including the first paragraph from *Black Beauty*, which begins:

> *"The first place that I can most well remember was a large pleasant meadow, with a pond of clear water in it. Some trees overshadowed the pond and rushes, and water lilies grew at the deep end..." etc, etc.*

It was at Bayford School where I also learned and memorised Edgar Allen Poe's poem, *'Eldorado'*. I was taught to say the poem with a rhythm, as though nonchalantly riding a horse along a desolate trail. It went:

Gaily bedight, a gallant knight,
   in sunshine and in shadow,
Journeyed long, singing a song,
   in search of Eldorado.

When we came to the next part, we were to recite the poem slowly, indicating, with expression, that the knight was growing weary of his journey.

> *But as his strength, failed him at length,*
>   *he met a pilgrim shadow,*
> *"Shadow," said he, "where can it be,*
>   *this land, called Eldorado."*

Then, when the 'pilgrim shadow' spoke, we were to recite in a ghostly, trembling voice:

SUFFER LITTLE CHILDREN

"Over the mountains of the moon,
  Down the valley of the shadows,
Ride, boldly ride," the shade replied,
  "If you seek for Eldorado"

For my having learned and reciting the poem with the expression she wanted, I won one of her big, beautiful 'Transparent' apples.

I also won an apple for learning and singing a song that went:

Agatha Green was about seventeen,
  And Agatha's craze was to fly.
She shouted one day, when her uncle did say,
  "Come for a cruise in the sky."

The song went on about Agatha and her uncle gliding high in the sky, above the billowy white clouds. It all sounded lovely until something went wrong and the glider crashed, and Agatha Green and her uncle were both killed.

Why Mrs Dunning would teach us such a song, I don't know. We all thought it was very sad. Still, I didn't mind too much because, like I said, I won an apple for my performance of it.

Almost amazingly though, I learned all of this at Bayford School, at the age of nine.

Baggy and Fred weren't as good as me at reciting and winning apples, so after school we would go into Mrs Dunning's garden and 'scrump' a few each. She would complain to the class that some of us kids were stealing her apples and that if she caught them they would be in trouble. Little did she know it was her star pupil and his friends, swiping her apples as well as winning them.

I remember too, her teaching us the parables from the New Testament of the Bible. The parables sounded like fairy tales and so we would listen to them intently, hearing how Jesus brought the dead to life and made the blind man see. Unlike much of the Bible, these stories we could understand.

SUFFER LITTLE CHILDREN
~o~o~ The Rabbit with Red Wings ~o~o~

Once, at the school's Christmas party, which was held in the Bayford village hall, Mrs Dunning put on a concert for the parents of the children who attended her village school. We, the kids, sang, danced and recited what we had learned during the year.

She also had us put on a play. I played the lead part in a play, and was the rabbit in the play called *The Rabbit with Red Wings*. I remember too that a little girl my age, Elaine Alger, played my mother, and for something or other that I did wrong she had to put me over her knee and spank me. It's all so funny to think back on now. I have sometimes wondered if Elaine Alger remembers the little orphan boy from Bayfordbury who was her 'rabbit' son that she had to spank in the school play.

~o~o~ The Outhouse Toilet ~o~o~

The toilets, or lavatories, as they were called in England, at Bayford School were located at the end of the playground. They were not flushing toilets as we know them today, but were lavatories or outhouses that had to be emptied by a man with a horse and cart every day, or perhaps every second day.

The man would come and lift out the huge container buckets from both the boys' and girls' toilets, and hook them onto a yoke he rested on his shoulders, much like how a Dutch milkmaid carries milk.

Then he would walk through the playground with these two large buckets swinging backwards and forwards, until he got to his horse and cart.

After placing the full buckets on his cart, he would then replace the buckets in the boys' and girls' toilets with empty ones, and then drive his horse and cart away with the full ones. We all knew what he was doing, and kept well out of his way for fear of being splashed.

I remember one of the village outsider boys once saying that the 'bucket man' takes the buckets to Bayfordbury for the orphans' tea. As I remember, Fred didn't think it was very funny and it started a fight.

SUFFER LITTLE CHILDREN
~o~o~ Here's to Bayford School ~o~o~

Every day during the war all children, the outsiders as well as the Bayfordbury boys, each received a half-pint of milk every morning at playtime. The milk came in a small glass bottle with a cardboard cap on top. Cream would form on the top inch or so of the bottle. We would savour this part of the milk slowly, just sticking our tongues in it carefully until the cream was all gone.

Us orphans would get our milk free, as would other outsider kids whose families couldn't afford to buy it. The other children would bring their 'milk money' and pay for their milk. If there was a bottle of milk left over after everyone else had received theirs, or if a child was absent from school that day, the spare bottle would be sold to any kid who could pay for it. I think it cost about a ha'penny.

Once in a while Mrs Dunning would pay for the extra bottle and give it to one of us Bayfordbury boys. She really was a lovely, caring lady, though I'm not sure if we appreciated her fully at the time.

I, like many children, didn't really like milk, but we were nevertheless required to have it, and were made to sit at our desks and drink it before we were allowed outside to play.

On one particular occasion I had done something or other wrong in the class, and Mrs Dunning had made me stay in the classroom and miss going outside to play. As was usual, she went to her house just next door to have a cup of tea.

I was now left alone in the classroom to read a book or 'write lines', or even do nothing – I don't really remember – but it would have been something rather tedious or boring.

I must have had lots of time on my hands on this particular occasion to waste, so I stood on a chair and made silly drawings of little 'stick' people with silly faces all over the rather large blackboard. To top it off, I scribbled Mrs Dunning's name underneath it all.

Just as she did every day, Mrs Dunning came back from her house and into the playground, and rang her school bell. The kids then filed back into the classroom, with Mrs Dunning following them. Just as soon as the other kids saw the chalkboard they giggled, or laughed, which made me realise that perhaps I had done something else wrong,

SUFFER LITTLE CHILDREN

and that, again, I could be in for some more trouble.

Mrs Dunning was mildly annoyed with me and said she was going to send a note back to Bayfordbury to tell Mr Scougall I had been cheeky, which I knew I had. She often said she would tell Mr Scougall if we 'played up', but she never did.

Mrs Dunning then told me to go out to the lavatory and then come straight back to the classroom.

Well, the incident wasn't quite over yet and, unfortunately, I again exceeded myself with regard to my mischief.

Unfortunate as it was, I went outside and across the playground to the lavatory, just as Mrs Dunning had instructed me, and on the way back to the classroom I picked up a stone and threw it at the school house.

I remember saying, just as I threw the stone, "Here's to rotten old Bayford School."

As bad luck would have it, the stone went right through a glass windowpane and broke it. Of course, the window that broke had to be the one nearest to Mrs Dunning's desk, in the front of the class.

But that wasn't the only thing that happened. To add to the problem, the stone knocked over an extra bottle of milk that had been placed on the window sill. The bottle, full of milk, fell onto the flagstone floor beside her desk, and smashed.

Mrs Dunning was now very annoyed, and she gave me the cane on my hand. It would not have been a hard caning: she was too nice and much too gentle a person for that. She said she was going to tell Mr Scougall about what I had done, but, just as with the many other times she said she would, it's unlikely she ever did.

~o~o~

Mrs Dunning, without any doubt, would have known Mr Scougall for what he really was, and in a much different way than we would. I'm sure she wouldn't have approved of him or the way he was looking after us young children. The fear at the mere mention of his name, and the way we were treated at Bayfordbury, would have shown in our faces and in our demeanour.

Mrs Dunning was a lovely middle-aged lady with lots of understanding

SUFFER LITTLE CHILDREN

for us Bayfordbury boys. We kids must have taxed her patience terribly but, for the most part, she tolerated our naughtiness well, and gave us good and lasting memories which, for me, were to last a lifetime.

I knew too that Mrs Dunning, despite the naughty things I did, always liked me. She very often had an affectionate smile just for me, I believe, which I recognised and loved. Us kids, and most certainly myself, appreciated and loved affection from people like her. I really did like her. Sadly, most people in any authoritative position over us were not like Mrs Dunning.

Eventually, perhaps three years into the future, I would meet her husband and, coincidently, even be taught by him also.

~o~o~ Fred and the Fat Ball ~o~o~

At twelve o'clock – dinner time – we, except for a few of the village children, would all leave Bayford School and walk in an orderly manner to a big green hut or, as it was called, the village hall, which was about a quarter of a mile away, in the centre of the village.

The village hall was just one big hut. Inside there were three or four long tables with bench seats each side. Unlike at Bayfordbury, there were linoleum tablecloth coverings on the tables. We always sat in the same places each day to have our school dinner, which would be brought to us at the tables.

Our midday meal or school dinner was cooked for us by the village ladies and provided through a governmental school system programme. We looked forward to our outsiders' school dinners because, compared to the Bayfordbury meals, the Bayford village school meals were much, much nicer.

There were far less 'eyes' or black spots in the potatoes, or caterpillars in the cabbage. Nor would we have to eat stale bread. However, there would still be fat on the meat. In actual fact, in those days fat was thought to be good for growing children.

Even at Bayford School, the rules regarding wasting food were still the same. All of the kids still had to eat up every scrap of food on their plates, which included greens, crusts, fish and, worst of all, the fat on the meat. Due to the shortage of food throughout the entire British

SUFFER LITTLE CHILDREN

Isles, brought about by the war, it was expected that nothing would be wasted, particularly, it seemed, by us children.

~o~o~

Something that happened at one of our school dinners at Bayford was very funny, and I shall always remember those dinners for it.

John Baggaridge, Fred Dyos and I always sat together at one of the long tables with the other kids. Fred sat opposite me, and Baggy beside me.

Mrs Dunning or maybe a parent or two of the outsider children would walk up and down behind us kids to make sure we ate up every scrap of food on our plates. The saying 'waste not, want not' was one of many predominant sayings of those days, and it applied everywhere, including at Bayford.

On this particular day we were served beef stew. Everything was fine about the stew; it had carrots, potatoes, parsnips and – one of our favourites – dumplings. As well, I thought I had a particularly big dumpling on my plate until I noticed, to my horror, that it was just a big ball of greasy, slimy cream coloured fat. The fat ball was at least an inch and a half in diameter. It was the nastiest piece of greasy fat one could imagine. Due to the fact that we were not allowed to leave anything on our plates, even a huge lump of fat like the lump I had on my plate, I began to panic. It was too greasy to put in my pocket and I wouldn't dare drop it on the floor.

So, like the good generous friend I was, I said to Fred across the table, "Ay! Fred, Do ya want my dumpling?"

So, naturally Fred immediately said he did. Hardly being able to stop from laughing, I waited for the teacher or parent to pass by our table.

When the teacher finally passed by us and it was all clear, I stuck my fork into the big lump of greasy fat and said to Fred,

"OK, Fred, open your mouth!" and, leaning across the table, stuffed the huge lump of fat into his mouth. Normally Fred would have spat the fat ball straight back at me.

However, just then, as comical luck would have it, one of the ladies in charge happened to turn around, and came back to our place at the table.

The lady seemed to be looking straight at Fred. Fred, with his mouth full of this big lump of horrible fat, had to chew it up and swallow it.

SUFFER LITTLE CHILDREN

I can still see Fred's face and him gagging, trying to swallow that revolting lump of fat. Later Baggy and I rocked with laughter. It was a story that Baggy and I were to tell and laugh at for several years to come, even though good old Fred was no longer around.

Over the years it still makes me laugh, remembering Fred's cheeks stuffed full with this thick greasy lump of fat and him having to swallow it.

~o~o~ Gleaning ~o~o~

After the farmers had taken off their wheat and picked up their stoops of straw, Mrs Dunning would take us into the newly harvested cornfields to go 'gleaning'. We called all grain fields, including wheat, oats and barley, 'cornfields'.

For us to go gleaning meant that we would pick up any ears of wheat we could find, and put them into a bag. Later, Mrs Dunning taught us that we could take some of the ears and rub them between our hands and, by doing so, could separate the wheat from the chaff. Then we would eat the grains of wheat.

The wheat that we collected on those trips with Mrs Dunning, Mrs Dunning would feed to her chickens. Often when we were wandering in the fields on our own, we, too, would glean the wheat ears and eat the raw grain ourselves, just like Mrs Dunning had shown us.

We would also go on 'nature walks' with Mrs Dunning and she would point out and tell us about the various flowers we would find. She would also point out and tell us something about the various wild birds and any other wildlife we would come across during our walks.

Mrs Dunning was an interesting teacher who had lived most, if not all, of her life in the village of Bayford, and was most at ease in the country. She showed us many of the things we could eat that grew wild in the fields and woods – things like elderberries, hawthorn leaves (which we called bread and cheese), vinegar leaves and many other wild vegetation, which would not hurt us if we ate it, though needless to say we could get 'belly aches' from time to time.

She also pointed out the poisonous berries like deadly nightshade, and told us a general rule to remember, which I always did.

SUFFER LITTLE CHILDREN

If it's blue it's true,
But if it's red your dead!

The meaning was that if the berry was blue, like those on the elderberry bush, bluish blackberries, sloes and many more, then generally speaking we could eat them. But if the berries were red, like those of the deadly nightshade or the berries of the yew tree, then they were generally poisonous and should be left alone.

We also understood that this was only a simple guide, and didn't apply to all plants or berries. I don't recall any of us boys becoming sick as the result of 'foraged' food.

~o~o~

Mrs Dunning also taught us, both boys and girls, how to play 'rounders', a game similar to baseball but played with a tennis ball. We also played cricket and, of course, football. She helped teach us the rudiments of these sports and encouraged us to play them.

When we played rounders, the first thing we did was to pick sides. Because there were not really enough of us kids on each side to properly play the game, the team 'in' (meaning the ones batting) would, with the exception of the child actually batting, all be 'fielders'.

This meant that a fielder trying to get the 'batter' out, had to run after a hit ball, retrieve it, and throw the ball to a base in order to get the batter out, very much like in baseball.

On one occasion, an occasion that sticks out in my memory, a boy named Winter ran after a 'hit' ball, as was, of course, expected of him. All the rest of the kids on the fielder's team were cheering encouragement to Winter to throw the ball to a base and by doing so, get the batter out.

Winter, on the other hand was on the same team as the batter and so after picking up the ball he just stood there nonchalantly whistling, and wouldn't throw the ball to a base until his team mate had completed his 'rounder' and scored. The fielding side – girls as well as the boys – chased after Winter to catch him and, in fun, beat him. It was very funny at the time. Even Mrs Dunning laughed.

SUFFER LITTLE CHILDREN

This and many other occasions like it, were all part of those happy and unforgettable days at Bayford School.

~o~o~ Potato Picking ~o~o~

Just as most men, if they didn't volunteer, were drafted into either the Navy, the Air Force or one of the various army units, women, if they didn't have children to look after; and girls, after leaving school, were also required to do something to help the 'war effort'.

Many women joined the WAACs (Women's Army Auxiliary Corps) and the WRNS (Women's Royal Naval Service), which were units in the women's armed forces, while others were assigned to work in ammunition factories and such.

There were many, many ways women and girls served Great Britain during the war besides going into the armed forces.

Because there was a great need for farm labourers and men not being available, due to most of them being in the armed forces, the Women's Land Army was formed. The Land Girls, as they were called, either lived in or travelled to farms, to help farmers work the land. All of what the Land Girls did, I don't really know, except that they worked for the farmers, doing the milking, planting potatoes, seeding, haying, and helping with harvesting crops.

~o~o~

In late August or early September, under Mrs Dunning's supervision, all of us children from Bayford School would go 'potato picking' for the farmers in the immediate area. The farmer and the Land Girls, having planted the field with seed potatoes in the spring, needed to harvest them in the autumn.

This, again, was part of the war effort and we were not just expected, but were required, to assist the farmers with the harvesting

Fred, Baggy, and I would always try to be together in the fields. All of us boys and girls would be placed in one long row, which stretched the full width of the field.

To harvest the potatoes, one of the Land Girls driving a tractor with

SUFFER LITTLE CHILDREN

a single-furrow plough would come by us and turn over the now dying tops of the potato plants, exposing the mature potatoes. At this point we were required to pick up the potatoes and put them into the burlap sacks provided.

Potato picking, though perhaps a backbreaking job for adults, was not particularly hard work for us young kids. It took the Land Girl eight to ten minutes to drive the tractor the width of the field, turning over the soil and exposing the potatoes. During the time of her passing us, we would pick up the potatoes, put them into the sacks, and then wait for her to come by again, exposing more potatoes for us to pick up.

Being able to pick up the potatoes in our immediate area in about three minutes or so, left us with plenty of time on our hands. So we couldn't do that job either, without playing around.

Commonly we would go to the hedgerow and find a thin stick about two to three feet long. Then we would sharpen one end of the stick.

We would push our sticks into a potato and with a flick, toss the potato at other boys in the row. This in turn would prompt others to get sticks and fly potatoes back at us. It was great fun for us kids.

Often we would see Italian prisoners of war helping the farmers and the Land Girls in the fields. The Italians, like the Land Girls, were always nice to us, even though we had difficulty understanding the Italians.

~o~o~ Bayford Church ~o~o~

The vicar from the little church in Bayford, Reverend Brown, (I believe his name was Brown) would come to Bayford School and give us scripture lessons. It was at that time that I learned the Catechism.

St Mary's Anglican Church, which we passed twice a day going to and coming back from Bayford School, is a beautiful little village church. Its classical seventeenth century design with its prominent steeple dominated the village's quaint architecture. The beautiful stained glass windows, the protruding gargoyles, and ancient gravestones, helped to give a serene tranquillity to the village.

I, together with the rest of the children at Bayford School, were taught to sing the hymns relevant to all the different aspects of the holy

SUFFER LITTLE CHILDREN

year like Easter and Christmas, including the Harvest Festival, (which in Canada we call Thanksgiving). These were just some of the services we would celebrate in their respective seasons.

Bayford Church

The quaint little village of Bayford
Looking from the door of the church

SUFFER LITTLE CHILDREN

The sermons, which would last for what seemed like an hour, but which were really only a little more than half an hour, were very tedious for us young and fidgety children to listen to.

Often, when we thought no one was looking, we would turn around or talk to each other during the sermon. This too, would result in a caning from Mr Scougall, who, with several of his staff, would also attend morning prayer and evening song services with us.

We would alternate our church attendances each Sunday between Hertingfordbury Church and Bayford Church. The Hertingfordbury services were, as I recall, even more boring than those at Bayford Church.

~o~o~ Incendiary Bombs and Shrapnel ~o~o~

During our dinner breaks at Bayford School, which lasted about an hour and a half, we were allowed to wander around the village and walk in the nearby country lanes. There were almost no cars or motorised vehicles on the country roads in those days – only horses and carts, which were not much danger to us kids.

We would mostly wander in the fields, collect hazelnuts, chestnuts, and conkers, and also pick blackberries, in their seasons.

Officially, I believe, we were expected to stay in the school playground during our dinner period, but I think Mrs Dunning turned a 'blind eye' to us going out into the village and down the local country lanes.

We would also go to the Bayford railway station, stand on the little humpback bridge and watch the trains go under. The noisy trains would send up their smoke and steam and engulf us in the steam engine's acrid smoke, which in turn would make us hold our breath while soot and coal dust would get in our eyes.

Sometimes we would hear of a German or an RAF aeroplane that had been shot down. When we did, we would head across the fields to see it. Often we would find shrapnel in the fields or on the roads.

~o~o~

Shrapnel pieces are fragments of what was molten steel from ammunition, such as gun shells from anti-aircraft guns; and pieces of metal

SUFFER LITTLE CHILDREN

from damaged aircraft, which had become red-hot molten pieces of sharp and now very jagged cast-iron metal.

During an air raid, shrapnel flies around, indiscriminately killing and maiming anyone it may come in contact with. It was a very dangerous 'fall out' or by-product of air battles and bombs.

After shrapnel cools, it becomes a sculptured, beautiful yet ugly, twisted piece of heavy, sharp and jagged-edged cast iron. Children and grown-ups alike would collect shrapnel as souvenirs.

~o~o~

On one occasion Fred, Baggy, and I found a whole case of unexploded incendiary bombs. The bombs, we were told, would most likely have been dropped by a German aeroplane that had been damaged by anti-aircraft fire, or in a 'dog fight'.

It was known that if a German plane was badly damaged, it would usually unload its bombs by basically dropping them, or dumping them in the cases or the baskets that they were stored in, so that the pilot could maintain buoyancy. This action would also help to make the damaged plane as light as possible and consequently save fuel, which in turn would help the damaged plane get back to its base in France or Germany.

Incendiary bombs were designed to ignite upon impact with a hard object, and start fires. It was not an explosive type bomb, and didn't really do anything apart from simply penetrating structures and starting fires.

Why the incendiary bombs that we had found had not exploded when they hit the ground, we never knew, but they hadn't. Over the next couple of years we found many bombs – not only incendiary bombs, but also other explosive-type German bombs, which had not exploded. In absolute ignorance we would actually throw the bombs as far and as high as we could to make them explode, but they never did. We just called them 'duds'.

Sad as it was, many children were killed or severely injured by playing with unexploded bombs. We were constantly being warned not to play with them, but children typically like us, without parents to be concerned about them, didn't listen. All I can say is that we were very fortunate not to have been injured or killed.

SUFFER LITTLE CHILDREN

Well, on the particular occasion of our finding the case of incendiary bombs, it's quite possible that we too had a very close encounter. Anyway, we took the full case of bombs – about twenty-four of them – which would have been quite heavy for us to carry, back to Bayford School, and handed them out to any kid who wanted one.

What a panic, lots of the outsider kids went home carrying a presumably live incendiary bomb. The master or a senior boy, who came from Bayfordbury to supervise our walking home from school, took all the rest of the incendiary bombs away from Fred, Baggy and me and handed them 'in'.

When I think back on what we did with those bombs, it makes me smile. By handing out those bombs to the other outsider kids, we had inadvertently distributed bombs throughout the village. A tactic the Germans would never have thought of.

The Home Guard or the ARP came and collected the bombs and we were questioned as to where exactly we found them. Ironically, considering the unforgiving attitude at Bayfordbury, we didn't get into any particular trouble that I can recall.

I ponder, even now, how it could be that we could get such terrible beatings for such minor, mischievous things and yet, dramatically putting it, for 'bomb distributing' or 'bomb running', if that is what it could be called, we went completely unpunished.

As the result of our passing around the incendiary bombs the ARP came to Bayford School and Bayfordbury, and we were given extensive talks about things that were of imminent danger to us, such as incendiary bombs and the likes.

We were warned not to pick up anything we might find, like toys, sweets, or other such articles, because any of these could be 'booby trapped'. But it's difficult for a child to distinguish between what toys and the likes could be dangerous and what are not, when items of interest could simply be just left around for us to find.

We were told that it would have been the German sadists who would have developed the idea of booby traps directed at children.

Although I personally never did actually hear of any child being hurt as the result of such a booby trap, there were probably hundreds of children who were injured or even killed.

SUFFER LITTLE CHILDREN
~○~○~ Brick Fights ~○~○~

Young boys as a group, whether they were outsiders or orphans, are commonly hard to handle. As I believe the reader would gather, we were no exception. We would fight, wrestle and throw stones at objects, and no doubt, do damage to property.

We would also throw stones at each other and have what we would call a 'brick fight'. I would never suggest that we were, by any standards, 'angels' or even 'good kids', but we never really got into serious trouble. I'm quite sure too that the village grown-ups regarded us Bayfordbury boys as naughty children. But they tolerated us for what we were and never did treat us badly.

Needless to say, and as one may guess from reading this book, the people who taught at Bayford School, and the village people, as well as the parents of the outsider children who were involved with us, were totally different people to the Dr Barnardo's Homes staff at Bayfordbury.

At Bayford School we were looked after and taught by outsiders like Mrs Dunning, those who were the parents of the outsider children, and the villagers of Bayford. They were ordinary, everyday, caring people, whereas at the Bayfordbury orphanage we were looked after by a sadistic headmaster and his, for the most part, equally brutal staff.

~○~○~ Goodbye Mrs Dunning and Bayford School ~○~○~

After about a year or so of my being at Bayford School, I said my goodbyes to Mrs Dunning and the outsider kids in Bayford village, whom we had become good friends with, including perhaps, my secret love, Elaine Alger.

A short while earlier, Baggy, Fred, and I, together with the other boys who were changing schools, had been told that we would no longer be returning to Bayford School after the summer holidays, and that next term we would be going to the small town of Ware, to attend the 'Ware Senior and Central School'.

There was a certain amount of sadness about our leaving the comfort of Bayford School and the happy times we had had there. But at the same time, we were growing up and looking forward to our next, 'big boys' life.

9

BAYFORDBURY – Part 3

~o~o~ Daily Routine ~o~o~

Our becoming older boys and having to change our schools also meant that our daily routine at Bayfordbury was now to be changed quite extensively. The new routine would become the normal routine for Fred, Baggy and me, and last for the remainder of the time we were at Bayfordbury, which would be about a further year and a half.

It was basically a simple routine and, with some exceptions, much like it would be in any institution. During the school semesters we would, from Monday to Friday, be made to get up every morning at 6.00 a.m. and make our beds.

Regardless of whether anyone had knocked the bucket over during the night, somebody was required to empty it each morning and wash it out.

The rest of us, after getting up, would go to the ablutions and brush our teeth, wash, and slick our hair down. Then we would dress for school.

The dormitory I was in had no rugs or any sort of floor covering on the flagstones, which made them very cold to stand on in the mornings, particularly in the winter, or at any time for that matter, so we would stand on our clothes in order to keep our feet off the extremely cold stone floors.

Each day, two or three designated boys would sweep out the dormitory. The floors, being flagstone, had cement between the slabs of stone, resulting in them never looking particularly clean.

We would clean our boots with black boot polish and then shine them, trying not to get 'blackening' or boot polish on our long grey socks.

Every second or third day, at about a quarter to seven in the morning, we would line up outside the dining room and take our cod liver oil or other medicines such as a laxative, whether we needed it or not. All of these supplemental medicines were horrible tasting, but we routinely took them.

SUFFER LITTLE CHILDREN

Then we would file into the dining room for breakfast. We would all say the morning prayers, in a routine parrot form, and then the daily announcements were made by the duty master.

Often, when a boy had looked insolent or had 'answered back' to a master in such a way as to, unintentionally, offend the master, the boy would get a severe caning. Mr Scougall would often cane the boys who were to be caned before breakfast, in front of the other boys – the idea being that the caning would teach us all a lesson.

Then Grace would be said, thanking the almighty for the food "we are about to receive".

Breakfast would always be the same: porridge, either lumpy or very thin. Sometimes we would have 'bread and milk' which, if there was sugar on it, which wasn't very often, we thought was a pretty good breakfast.

We liked bread and milk, even though the bread was the leftover bread from several days earlier. Often there would be dead cockroaches or silverfish in it, which we would simply scoop out of our bowls with our spoons or fingers and, if the unsuspecting victim wasn't looking, put the insects on someone else's plate.

I know it sounds almost unbelievable when one reads my story today, but cockroaches and silverfish were quite common in our food at Bayfordbury. But that wasn't so unusual in most institutions.

After removing any insects we might find, we ate up whatever else was on our plates without thinking too much about it. It was far from the worse thing we suffered at Bayfordbury.

After breakfast, Grace would be said again, thanking the lord for the nice food we had received, including the various insects. Then selected boys would clear up the tin plates, cutlery and other pots and pans, take them to the 'wash house', and wash them up.

Other boys' jobs included washing the wooden tables and benches. If we were picked to sweep the dining room floor, we wasted no time but of course did it. These were all daily routine jobs that we had to complete before school.

After the dining room clean-up duties were done and inspected – something which had to be done before the school coach left – we lined up and were examined to check that our hair was combed and our boots

SUFFER LITTLE CHILDREN

were satisfactorily cleaned. We would probably remain reasonably tidy until we got off the coach, if that long.

The coach would leave Bayfordbury sharp at a quarter to eight in the morning, which, providing we were on it, left us plenty of time to get us to Ware Senior and Central School on time.

Occasionally we would be late for some reason and miss the coach. Missing the coach was a real problem, as we would now have to walk or run, and inevitably be late for the outsiders' school.

Being late for school would result in a punishment at the outsiders' school, but what would be much worse was that Mr Scougall would also be phoned, and told of the boy being absent or late. The boy would then be caned when he got back to Bayfordbury after school, and sent to bed without any tea.

At the end of the school day, about 3.30 p.m., we would all get on the coach again and return to Bayfordbury. If a boy was to miss the coach going back to Bayfordbury in the afternoon for any reason, like being 'kept in' as punishment for talking in class or for being late for school in the morning, or simply being too slow getting to the coach on time, he would have to walk the two to three miles home to Bayfordbury.

If, after walking home, the boy was too late for tea, then he would miss tea, and after being caned, would be sent to bed with nothing to eat at all.

The routine for teatime was much the same as for breakfast, except for the chores. Each evening after tea we would move all of the tables and benches to one end of the dining room, and sweep the flagstones spotless.

Before the cleaning was considered finished, the dining room would be inspected by the master on duty and, as the master would insist, "If so much as a crumb is found..." and so on. Then we would have to move all the tables and benches again and sweep the floor all over again.

After the dining room was found to be satisfactorily clean, we would then be allowed to go out and play or do whatever we wished until 7.30 p.m., at which time we had to go to our dormitories and get ready for bed.

On Saturdays, eight to ten boys would wash and scrub the flagstone floors in the dining room on our hands and knees, with stiff-bristled brushes and big blocks of carbolic soap, each of us having a bucket of water and a scrubbing brush and a cloth.

SUFFER LITTLE CHILDREN

There was a rotation system for showering, which meant that we showered on an age group system, every second or third day – the youngest on, say, Mondays; the next age group on Tuesdays; and the older boys on Wednesdays, and so on. Then we repeated the cycle. No one showered on Saturdays or Sundays.

By 8.00 p.m. most of us would be in bed. The shutters would be closed and the lights in the dormitories turned off at 8.30. Some of the older boys – boys who were about sixteen years old and who slept in a different dormitory to us – could stay up until 8.30 p.m., and then they too would have to be in bed and their lights turned out by 9.00.

That was our normal weekly routine, and it rarely varied during the school term.

~o~o~ Cheating for Survival ~o~o~

Every boy at Bayfordbury, as it would be in most orphanages, I would believe, had an identification number. I can still remember most of the school numbers that I had at all of the larger orphanages I was in, particularly from Bayfordbury on. My number at Bayfordbury was number 24.

At each orphanage we would be given any number that was available at the time we arrived there. Selected at random, the numbers we were assigned would, always, in all likelihood, be a different number than at the previous orphanage we were at. We were, as was expected, required to remember our numbers immediately, as our numbers were what we were usually known by.

The staff never used our Christian names. I would be identified as only '24, Longman'. It's quite possible that none of the masters or the other staff members or many of the other boys in the orphanage would know that my Christian name was Reginald. Only my peers and friends called me Reg.

Many, many boys had nicknames such as 'Baggy' and 'Flappers', the latter because he supposedly had big ears. There was also a boy we called 'Snotty' (his nose was always running) and of course there was 'Taffy' Evans, 'Jock' McLean and many other Jocks and Taffys. I personally never had a nickname that stuck.

The only attempt to label me with a nickname happened to be at

SUFFER LITTLE CHILDREN

Bayfordbury. For a while, in the early days of my being there, some of the boys started calling me 'Long Tongue', probably because I talked too much, and at another time they started to call me 'Professor', possibly because some of the boys thought that I pretended I knew everything. Fortunately, neither of these names were to last or stay with me very long.

I can, and always will, I suppose, remember my Bayfordbury number – 24 – for one particular reason. Why I remember it was OK then, but I am not particularly proud of the reason now. However, I would rationalise it as being a survival or a self preservation thing.

~o~o~

Every time after we had had our shower, we would run straight from under the shower to the changing room to get our towel, toothbrush and comb.

Then we would immediately run back to the master on duty, absolutely naked, and show him each of the items. We were required to do this so as to show the master that we hadn't lost any of them. Everyone's towel had their school number on it, marked in two-inch blue indelible ink.

The master would inspect all of us to see that we had washed behind our ears, backs of our knees, and feet. Then he would tick off our number so as to keep track that every boy had showered and had not lost any of his 'ablution kit'.

If we had lost or couldn't produce any item of our ablution kit, then Mr Scougall would cane us later.

The items lost would then be replaced by the orphanage. If a boy lost, say, his comb, he would try to replace it one way or another, either by stealing one from another unsuspecting boy or, if possible, getting another one by shoplifting it from Woolworths, though I don't remember ever shoplifting a towel.

As it was, one day after showering I ran back to the changing room and couldn't find my towel. Panicking, I presumed that some other boy must have lost theirs and taken mine. I had no idea really where it could have gone; it just wasn't anywhere around. It wouldn't seem to be easy to lose a towel but, nevertheless, I just couldn't find it.

SUFFER LITTLE CHILDREN

So, without hesitation, I looked around and then swiped another unsuspecting boy's towel in the changing room. I must have thought it all out pretty well, as I changed the number from 21, which was marked on the other boy's towel, to 24 – my number. Then I ran back to the master on duty and he ticked me off the list.

The boy whose towel I had swiped saw my/his towel and looked at the number. I had changed it with an indelible pencil. Such pencils were common at the time. One simply licked the end of the pencil, and it marked just as though it was an ink pen, and the ink wouldn't wash out.

The other boy could see my handiwork and the fact that I had changed his number from 21 to my number 24. So, of course, he went and told the master that I had swiped his towel and changed the number.

The master shouted out my name and told me to bring my towel to him. I showed him the number, which, provided one didn't look too closely, looked like 24. The master looked at it, but obviously not closely enough. Then he shouted at the boy and said, "That's clearly 24, Longman's towel." Then he clouted the other boy around the ear and told him to go and find his own towel.

The boy, needless to say, would have got the cane. This would have been one of those typical 'eat or eaten' situations which our peers would just laugh at. Quite possibly the other boy and I would have had a fight over this, which would have been typically the situation, but I don't really remember.

Although I was a very small boy, I was thought to be a good fighter. As a result of my fighting ability in a world where the fittest survived, these crafty and somewhat devious ways helped us in our personal preservation. Unfortunately, for those meek or timid boys there was absolutely no one to appeal to.

~o~o~ Ware School ~o~o~

The town of Ware was a very small town in those days, and is located about two to perhaps three miles the other side of Hertford. We were to see much of Ware over the next year or so.

Having to attend Ware Senior and Central School, our lives were to change again. No longer did we go to the little village of Bayford and

SUFFER LITTLE CHILDREN

the relative comfort of Mrs Dunning's two-roomed school house, or win apples and have our school dinners in the little village hall.

Now we were at a large outsiders' school that had lots of classrooms, indoor washrooms, and a huge gymnasium where we had our assemblies and, at dinnertime, our school dinners. Also there were lots of teachers, many of whom I never did get to know.

Going to school now, instead of there being about ten to fifteen of us walking across the fields and through the woods, we travelled in a coach through the town. All or certainly most of the other boys were older and bigger than Fred, Baggy, and me.

The coach would pass right through the middle of Hertford and then travel on the main road beside the railway track, and as we entered Ware we went over the 'New Canal' and then on to Ware Senior and Central School.

Crossing the main road into Ware, there was a railway crossing with huge white gates, which the stationmaster would operate manually when a train was coming.

It was a very busy train track going from London to the north of England, and part of the LNER (London North Eastern Railway). Our coach would often be stopped and we would have to wait for a train to go through.

Even though the railway crossing was located on the main road right in the centre of town, I never ever heard of any accidents resulting from that railway crossing.

Between the railway tracks and the road we travelled on, was the New Canal, which working barges travelled on. I was taught that the New Canal was built to bring water from the River Lee to the City of London shortly after the Great Plague and the Great Fire of London.

~o~o~ Mrs Blackwell ~o~o~

My teacher at Ware School was Mrs Blackwell. Mrs Blackwell was a large woman who wouldn't tolerate any nonsense. I remember well that when Mrs Blackwell got angry she would go very, very red from the base of her neck to the top of her forehead. She always seemed to wear a black dress.

SUFFER LITTLE CHILDREN

Mrs Blackwell was to be our teacher all the time we were at Ware Senior and Central School.

Baggy and Fred were both in the same class as me, and we all sat within talking distance, hence the frequent walking home after school as a result of our 'staying in' after the rest of the school went home. As the result of our having to stay in, we would miss catching the coach, which in turn would automatically mean our getting the cane when we got home to Bayfordbury.

It was Mrs Blackwell's task to teach us arithmetic, English, geography, and art in the broadest sense. Music, woodwork, gardening and gymnastics were taught to us by other teachers.

~o~o~

It didn't take much to get Mrs Blackwell angry; at least I certainly didn't find it hard. She clipped me around the ear many a time for one thing or another. I remember on one particular occasion when she clouted me around the ear, and although I suppose I deserved it, I have never forgotten it, probably because I was so cheeky in a way.

On the occasion that I refer to, during one of her art classes she took a tennis racquet from under her desk, and after waving the racquet around a few times she placed it on the blackboard chalk rail and told us to draw it.

Like the cheeky little sod that I was, I drew a square tennis racquet and showed Baggy and the other kids around me. We were giggling and generally fooling around just as Mrs Blackwell came up behind me. I hadn't noticed her quietly creeping up, seemingly studying my drawing.

When she noticed I had drawn a square tennis racquet she was livid. I can, even now, easily remember her colour instantly changing to the fiery lobster-red she was known for.

Without a single word, she gave me a really good clout across the back of my head, so hard that I hit my head on the desktop.

I shouted and made a fuss and pretended that I didn't know why she would have hit me. Looking me straight in the face, her eyes glaring, she told me that I was fooling around and that I would have to stay in after school and draw the tennis racquet again.

SUFFER LITTLE CHILDREN

Pretending that my feelings were hurt and regretting that I had fooled around, I told her that it was a tennis racquet just as she had asked us to draw, but that my racquet was in its square wooden restraining case.

I remember she looked embarrassed and even apologised to me, which I think made me feel pretty guilty. I can't think, when thinking back on the occasion, that I even knew a tennis racquet had a wooden restraining case at the time, though I suppose I did. Luckily though, I didn't have to stay in after school and miss the coach.

~o~o~

On another occasion Mrs Blackwell told us to draw anything we wanted to, so I drew an eagle's head. I must say, as did Mrs Blackwell, that my pencil drawing of the eagle's head was quite good. She told me to take my drawing home, and so I did, and sent it to my grandmother, who in turn kept it on top of her piano in a photo frame for many years to come. I will be writing more about my grandmother later.

~o~o~ Girls ~o~o~

The outsider kids brought sandwiches or a piece of cake to school to eat during our ten-thirty morning lunch break. Us Bayfordbury kids didn't have anything to eat at all for this break, so if we made friends with the outsider children (against their parents' wishes, of course) some of them, like a girl named June Chalkley, would often give us a little of their lunches.

June Chalkley sat immediately behind me, next to another girl. Me being so shy, June, with the exception of Elaine Alger, was quite possibly the only girl in the world that I would even have talked to in those early years. June, however, would pass me 'love letters' and tell me silly things like how much she loved me, and I suppose I wrote the same kind of things back to her.

In the classroom, I sat near a boy named Derrick Morgan. He was another Bayfordbury boy just like me except, unlike me, he was quite at ease with the girls and flirted with them constantly, even initiating the sending of 'love letters', or notes to several of the girls in the classroom. I never thought of Morgan as being a sissy, but that's what boys who liked girls would be called in our primitive society.

Once, June gave me an orange. I don't think I had ever seen, let alone eaten an orange up to this point in my life. Oranges weren't easy to come by during the war. Sometimes June would give me part of her lunch at lunchtime, while Baggy and Fred would jokingly beg me to give them some, which naturally I'm sure I did. We would share everything we had with each other, like best friends would.

I liked June. She was a pretty little girl, who had what I would call a sad or melancholy look. Perhaps she looked a little like Elaine Algar. Her hair was cut in the 'pageboy' style. She didn't smile much, but when she did, and if she smiled at me, I would be shy and involuntarily blush very noticeably.

As I mentioned, I'm sure I liked her very much, but at the same time I pretended that I didn't really want anything to do with her, or any girl for that matter, for two reasons.

First and foremost, I was very shy and I, like many other boys at the orphanage, had great difficulty talking to or even looking at girls. Us boys, being brought up in an exclusively boys' orphanage, didn't know anything whatsoever about girls. They simply weren't part of our lives.

All that we really knew about girls was that girls wore frocks, dresses and knickers (because we saw their knickers during gym lessons) and that boys wore short trousers. The word 'girl' was basically never mentioned and no one even tried to explain to us what girls were in relationship to boys. We were simply not informed about girls at all.

The second reason was that if any of us boys did have anything to do with girls, which very few did, the boy would be thought of as being a sissy by the other boys. Boys in an orphanage would have great difficulty keeping their heads up if they were labelled as being a sissy.

~o~o~ The Chinese Auction ~o~o~

Just prior to Christmas one year – about 1945 – Mrs Blackwell told us that we were going to have a 'Chinese auction' and that we should

SUFFER LITTLE CHILDREN

bring our pocket money to school on the given date, so that we could buy things at this auction.

I presume now that the outsider children's parents and families donated things to be auctioned and also provided money for their kids to buy things with.

I remember too, how I had saved my pocket money, which would have amounted to a ha'penny (half a penny) so that I, too, could buy something at the auction. I would have had no other money, absolutely nothing else, just a ha'penny.

Perhaps I should mention at this time, that in the 'old' English coinage system there were twelve pennies in a shilling, and twenty shillings to a pound. Hence, two hundred and forty pennies (pence) to a pound. A ha'penny was half a penny.

~o~o~

Every week we Bayfordbury kids would receive pocket money; how much depended on one's age. The oldest boys, who were fifteen years old, got as much as tuppence (two pennies) a week, but not more. I would have received about a ha'penny a week.

To give the reader an idea of how much a penny was worth at that time, I can tell you that the cost of a postage stamp to send a letter anywhere in Britain at the time, was tuppence ha'penny (two and a half pence).

Hypothetically, at the rate of pocket money that I received, it would have taken me five weeks to save enough money to send a letter to my grandmother, though in actual fact we never paid postage at all to send letters as Dr Barnardo's paid our postage.

If we did write letters, which we didn't very often, we would hand them to a master for them to be mailed. Before mailing, all of our letters were read by a master and were most probably censored.

I can't remember anyone ever saying anything about what we had written in our letters. I would presume now, all these years later, that anything that the masters wanted to delete, they just did. We, in turn, would never have known if they edited our letters or not. They, in all probability wouldn't mention anything about censoring our letters.

SUFFER LITTLE CHILDREN

However, we would mostly spend our pocket money on sweets such as chocolate bars, toffees, nougat or perhaps liquorice sticks or something like that. Even then though, without a sweet ration coupon, I'm not sure how we could be able to buy sweets at all.

We thought even a ha'penny was a lot of money at that point in time, though it couldn't really buy very much. However, a ha'penny was a ha'penny and was everything we had. Actually, it cost a penny to go to the public lavatory in those days, so we didn't use public toilets very often, if ever.

~o~o~

Back to Mrs Blackwell and her Chinese auction. On the day of Mrs Blackwell's auction, after we had settled down and were all sitting in our seats, Mrs Blackwell laid all the things she was going to auction on a table in the front of the class.

Everything on the table looked wonderful to me, and I was anticipating the prospect of being able to buy something and taking it back to the orphanage with me.

Then, as expected, she chose something from the table and put it on her desk in front of her.

The item she was going to auction was possibly a toy car, a toy cowboy revolver or something like that – certainly something which she thought would appeal to us children.

Then she started us bidding. I don't think we really understood the rules of a Chinese auction very well. Certainly, I can't believe I did.

Mrs Blackwell raised the item she had chosen, say a toy gun, above her head and said, "Who will give me a ha'penny for this?"

As I recall, my hand shot up. I was the first child to raise my hand, thereby bidding on whatever it was, though I can't remember now exactly what it was that I was bidding on because, as you will see, I didn't get it.

Being excited at the prospect of bidding, I think I thought that it was the boy who raised his hand first who got the item being auctioned. I was surprised to find out I was wrong.

Anyway, I remember raising my hand and bidding my only ha'penny for the item she was holding up above her head, and saying with great enthusiasm, "I will Miss, I will."

SUFFER LITTLE CHILDREN

Mrs Blackwell told me to bring my ha'penny up to her desk and put it in the bowl, which she had placed in the middle of her desk.

Just as she asked, I bounded up to the front of the class, put my ha'penny into the bowl, and was about to pick up my prize, when Mrs Blackwell said, "Does anyone else want to bid on this item?" adding, "Who will give a penny?"

Immediately another boy or girl raised the bid to a penny and, like me, came to the front of the class, and put his or her penny into the bowl. Then another child raised the bid to tuppence, (two pennies) and so on.

To my great disappointment I, being outbid, lost my only ha'penny, as did the other kids who bid less than the highest bidder. To top it off, at the end of the Chinese auction we didn't get our money back or anything at all to take home.

I spent the rest of the auction time watching the other kids bid and obtain things, while I, needless to say, didn't have any money left at all to bid with.

This, then, was what Mrs Blackwell called a Chinese auction. What the auction was in aid of, I have no idea. It was possibly, or, I might even say, that it was quite probably for Dr Barnardo's Homes.

Facetiously speaking, I might suggest that I gave my ha'penny to Dr Barnardo's Homes so that they could give it back to me for my pocket money the following week.

Regardless, I still remember the event as being a rotten swindle, even more so now, bearing in mind that that ha'penny, the ha'penny that I had dropped in Mrs Blackwell's pot, was my entire week's pocket money, and for it, I got nothing.

~o~o~ **Vegetarian** ~o~o~

At Ware Senior and Central School, we still received our morning half-pint of milk, just like we had received it at Bayford School. We drank it at our morning break before we went outside to play.

Many of us children didn't like milk but, just as it was at Bayford School, we were all required to drink it. It was all part of the children's supplementary war rationing programme.

SUFFER LITTLE CHILDREN

The outsiders' school dinners were, by Bayfordbury standards, very good, but still many of us would say we were vegetarians, in order not to have to eat the boiled and mostly greasy fat that was commonly part of a stew or other such meals.

Just as it was at Bayfordbury, Bayford School and almost every where else in Britain during the war, we all, as I have mentioned several times, had to eat everything put on our plates or we would, as we would be told, "have to sit there until you do". However, if we said we were vegetarians, instead of meat we would be given cheese.

Many of the outsider kids, like us, said they were vegetarians because they too didn't like the fatty meat so often served to us, but like us, many of them too didn't particularly like cheese either. Still, it was easier to put cheese in our pockets than greasy fat.

~o~o~ Reciting the Bible ~o~o~

It was in Mrs Dunning's class at Bayford School that I found to memorise the sometimes many paragraphs we were required to learn was quite a manageable task for me. Now in Ware School, Mrs Blackwell would often have me recite whatever we were told to learn 'off by heart' to the entire class. I wasn't particularly good at anything else at school in those days, but I could remember and recite verse and the likes quite well.

I now believe, these many years later, that Mrs Blackwell was perhaps somewhat religious, as we spent many hours having to learn paragraphs from the King James version of the Bible.

My favourite book in the King James version of the Bible was, and still is, St Matthew. Much of what is written in St Matthew Chapter 6, I was able to, with help I don't doubt, understand, unlike most of the rest of the Bible

Together with the rest of the class, including Baggy and Fred, I was required to learn off by heart many paragraphs from St Matthew Chapters 5 and 6, and to this day I can still remember quite a bit of it.

Later, I will tell the reader how I got into trouble with the chaplain in another orphanage, by quoting St Matthew Chapter 6, verses 19 to 21.

SUFFER LITTLE CHILDREN

The most accomplished of the scriptures that I learned was in the King James version of the Bible's New Testament's first book of Corinthians, Chapter 13.

1. *Though I speak with the tongues of men and of angels, and have not charity, I am become as sounding brass, or a tinkling cymbal.*
2. *And though I have the gift of prophecy, and understand all mysteries, and all knowledge; and though I have all faith, so that I could remove mountains, and have not charity, I am nothing.*
3. *And though I bestow all my goods to feed the poor, and though I give my body to be burned, and have not charity, it profiteth me nothing.*
4. *Charity suffereth long, and is kind; charity envieth not; charity vaunteth not itself, is not puffed up,*

The chapter continues on and is actually thirteen verses in total.

We were required to learn the entire thirteen verses off by heart and be able to recite them. I don't remember if all of us children managed to learn them all, but I did and got lots of praise from Mrs Blackwell, though, unlike Mrs Dunning, she didn't give me an apple!

~o~o~

In later years I was to learn, at my eldest son's wedding to be exact, that the reference to the word 'charity', which is used extensively in King James's version of Corinthians 13, was translated in the new or otherwise modern version of the Bible to mean 'love'. The translation baffles me and I still find it somewhat difficult to accept.

We were taught the word 'charity' to primarily mean a benevolent act, or a generous act towards the poor or needy, which to me is more fitting when taken in context with the teachings in Corinthians 13.

~o~o~

It was the softer side of Mrs Blackwell that brought our attention to Matthew, Chapter 19, verses 13 to 15.

SUFFER LITTLE CHILDREN

Which states:
13. Then there were brought unto him little children, that he should put his hands on them, and pray: and the disciples rebuked them.
14. But Jesus said, "SUFFER LITTLE CHILDREN, and forbid them not, to come unto me: for such is the kingdom of heaven."
15. And he laid his hands on them, and departed thence.

It seemed significant to me at the time, that out of the entire world, at least Jesus loved us, 'the little children', and I too, even though I was an almost unwanted orphan, was one of those little children.

~o~o~

Notwithstanding what I have just written, I can't say that I was ever really a true believer in Christianity.

With all the teachings of the church and, by the doctrine of my benefactor Dr Barnardo, our compulsory church attendance twice and sometimes three times each Sunday, and the long tedious sermons we were made to listen to at all of the Sunday services, I was simply bored to tears.

Such forced religion was somewhat counter-productive for us young boys, and I believe we turned a deaf ear to it all.

The constant prayers every morning, so much church on Sundays and the other special days in the Holy Year, together with all of the religious instruction we constantly received, was really too much for us.

The learning of sections of the Bible off by heart, together with the general religious influences we were constantly under, made us, I believe, unconsciously resent the need for so much religion – a subject we just couldn't understand.

During the course of my life to this point in Dr Barnardo's Homes, I must have been made to read or listen to someone else read the Bible, cover to cover, several times. The King James version is very hard for a child to comprehend and therefore, for the most part, becomes extremely tedious.

I know off by heart and can sing, even today, many of the hymns we sang in those days. As it is, I still listen to hymns almost every Sunday

SUFFER LITTLE CHILDREN

morning in our home, and enjoy them for the memories they bring to mind.

However, as a result of the religious 'brainwashing' thrust upon us throughout our entire upbringing in Dr Barnardo's Homes I, like many of my orphaned peers, am not a better Christian. Actually, I am by definition probably an agnostic. Certainly I question the logic of Christianity, as such.

I know I was given every opportunity to learn and understand the scriptures, but I simply couldn't believe that what we were taught regarding Christianity was really true.

I did, as did many of my peers I believe, presume that if we lived a life in keeping with the Ten Commandments, then we were living a righteous life. I rationalised too, and felt sure that God would understand, that if I couldn't, nor could I be made to believe in Jesus and the stories of the Bible, that He would understand this.

~o~o~ Mr Tustin, Our Music Teacher ~o~o~

We were taught music at Ware School by Mr Tustin. Mr Tustin was a Scotsman and known for having no nonsense in his class. He would carry a thin bamboo cane up his sleeve and if the need arose, he would let the cane slide down his sleeve into the palm of his hand, and hit the offender with it.

Mr Tustin was not by any stretch of the imagination a bad or sadistic person like the staff at Bayfordbury. In fact, we liked him, but nevertheless he was somewhat severe. His carrying a cane up his sleeve was his way of keeping our attention, in a funny sort of way.

Mr Tustin taught us many songs that I still know and play on my reed organ to this day. Songs, which include:

* *Ye Banks and Brae, oh Bonny Doone*, and:

* *Where the pools are bright and deep,*
  Where the grey trout lies asleep,
  Up the river and over the lea,
  That's the place for Bonnie and me.

SUFFER LITTLE CHILDREN

There was another song that Mr Tustin taught us in his singing classes, though I don't believe it could ever be sung in any civilised school today.

The whole school in full voice sang the song I refer to, which, again, we learned off by heart under Mr Tustin's tutoring.

The song, a very old sea shanty, would sound terrible in this day and age, but at that time its derogatory undertones had little meaning. The words of the song were:

> *I nebber see da' likes since I be born.*
> *When a big buck nigger wid 'is sea boots on, says,*
> *"Johnny come down from Shilough, poor ol' man.*
> *Don't wake her, don't shake her,*
> *Don't wake that girl with the blue dress on,*
> *Till Johnny come down from Shilough, poor ol' man."*

There were several more verses to the song and the word 'nigger' is mentioned several times throughout.

Unbelievable as it would be today, this song, an old British sea shanty, was sung by the entire school when any of the pupils attended their singing lessons in Mr Tustin's class.

In those days, I must say, the word nigger was not a terrible word and meant absolutely nothing to us children, even less so in a derogatory way. Nigger was purely a word which we called black people, much like a Scotsman was called Jock, an Irishman Paddy, a Welshman Taffy or an Englishman a Limey.

To the best of my knowledge, offence was never taken by anyone hearing anyone else using the word nigger. There weren't any coloured boys or girls at Ware Senior and Central School that I can remember. However, in another orphanage I was at some years later, there were coloured boys, which I will mention as my story progresses.

~o~o~

Gardening was another lesson taught at Ware School. Mr Lawrence was our gardening teacher. He taught us how to grow most of the common

SUFFER LITTLE CHILDREN

vegetables and how to plant celery and leeks in trenches in order to keep the desirable quality of those vegetables: long and white.

He also gave gardening lessons to adults in the evenings. Everyone was encouraged to grow their own vegetables during the war. Most towns and villages provided 'allotments' free of charge for anyone to grow their own vegetables. Again, it was all part of the war effort.

I remember one incident during a gardening class, when one of the boys in Mr Lawrence's class stuck a garden fork right through the middle of Baggy's hand while he was weeding or picking up small stones. The boy was digging, loosening the weeds in Baggy's area.

I think they basically treated Baggy's hand by putting iodine on it and a bandage for a couple of days. It wasn't a serious accident, and Baggy didn't suffer any long-term damage. But, to this day, Baggy still has the scar in the front and back of his hand where the fork had gone right through it.

~o~o~ Heading the Wooden Ball ~o~o~

Remembering a rotten trick I played on Fred Dyos still makes me laugh when I think of it, even today. It happened one day when we were at Ware School while playing at 'heading' a tennis ball. Baggy, Fred and a few others of us would often play football (soccer) with a tennis ball during our dinnertime break.

On this particular occasion though, we were just heading the tennis ball. The idea was simply to keep heading the tennis ball up in the air and not let it touch the ground. We would count how many times the ball would be headed, and would continually try to beat our last record.

Well, on this particular occasion one of us headed the ball and it went over a tall cast-iron picket fence. We could see through the picket fence, and saw that the ball had bounced through an open window and disappeared into one of the gardening department sheds.

Being the smallest, I was 'bunked-up', and over the fence in order to retrieve the tennis ball.

As I climbed through the shed window, one can imagine my surprise to find that there were about fifty to sixty balls, all about the same size

SUFFER LITTLE CHILDREN

as our tennis ball, spread all over the floor, making it a little hard to find which one was ours.

The strange thing was that all of the other balls, which looked so much like our dirty tennis ball, were made of wood. To top it off, the wood they were made of was a heavy hardwood, perhaps oak.

After a little searching, I found our tennis ball and put it in my pocket, and then, with my wicked mind at work, I picked up one of the wooden balls and climbed back out through the shed window.

After I had climbed out of the window and while I was still on the other side of the fence, I shouted to Fred that I had the ball, and would throw it out for him to head.

So, I threw the wooden ball as high as I could, over the fence towards Fred. Fred ran under it, headed it, and as is the object of the game, he tried to head it as high as he could.

Well, there was a loud plunk as the ball landed hard, right on Fred's head. I'm sure that Fred saw stars, because it was such a solid, heavy wooden ball. Everyone doubled up laughing, except Fred. Fred doubled up too, but he wasn't laughing.

Fortunately as a boy, even though I was very small, I was a really good runner.

Needless to say, Fred chased me around the school field to give me 'what for', but he didn't catch me. After he had cooled down he showed us his head. He had quite a large bump on the side, which lasted for a day or so. It was all quite funny.

~o~o~

Fred now lives in Australia but I'm quite sure that even to this day, he still remembers me as being that 'rotten little sod', though, like Baggy and myself, Fred would remember the occasion as being great fun and a time to remember.

~o~o~ Feeding Little Birdie ~o~o~

On another occasion, Baggy and I were wrestling while we were waiting for the coach to take us back to Bayfordbury after school one day.

SUFFER LITTLE CHILDREN

During our fun wrestling, Baggy had me bent over backwards.

He was straddling me and looking down into my face. I was looking up at him laughing, until he said, "Feeding little birdie" and then dribbled spit into my mouth.

I didn't like the idea of Baggy spitting in my mouth so, still bent over backwards, I managed to pick up a stone that was within my reach and I hit him right on his kneecap with it. I know it hurt him but I didn't care: at least I got away.

I am, to this day, still in touch with Baggy and he still remembers that 'feeding little birdie' incident and the well-deserved crack on the knee he got for spitting in my mouth.

~o~o~ 'Trashy' or 'Span it' ~o~o~

Even though we didn't have any worthwhile toys as such, we did have some things which we thought worth having, such as a piece of cheap jewellery chain (probably Bond Street jewellery, shoplifted from Woolworths), a large machine washer, a small brass bolt, an empty bullet shell or a piece of shrapnel. We might even have had a broken penknife, or perhaps some marbles.

With these treasures, we would play a game called 'trashy' or 'span it' with the other kids. We wouldn't risk losing a penknife or something we really valued, but most other things we might.

'Trashy' or otherwise 'span it', was played by one of us tossing one of our pieces of 'trash', as we called our treasures: perhaps a cigarette card, or a washer or something, about six to eight feet in front of us. The other boy would then, throw his 'trash' and try to get it on top, or close enough for him to be able to 'span it'.

To 'span it' and to win the 'trash', the last boy would spread his hand flat out on the ground, and if he could touch the two items with the tip of his thumb and his little finger, then, and only then, would both pieces of 'trash' become his.

If he could not span it or touch the two items with one hand spread out, then it would be the other boy's turn to simply move his trash just enough so that he could span them both.

Then it would be the winner's turn to toss an item first and the other

SUFFER LITTLE CHILDREN

boys turn, the one who had just lost his 'trash', to try and win back his 'trash' or whatever the other boy had tossed out in front of them.

We would spend many fun hours playing span it or trashy, and sometimes win lots of trash to treasure, until we lost it again to someone else.

10

BAYFORDBURY – Part 4

~o~o~ How Well We Remember ~o~o~

Life at Bayfordbury was very hard for us young children. Since leaving Bayfordbury well over sixty years ago, I have, in the past few years, met up with two of my old Bayfordbury friends – one of them, John Goodger, a very good friend who I will write about later; and the other, who I have already mentioned several times, my lifelong Bayfordbury friend John 'Baggy' Baggaridge.

These friends also remember well, the misery we suffered at the hands of Mr Scougall, Mr Nash and the majority of those who made up the rest of the staff at Bayfordbury. But in particular, we all remember in much detail those two almost sadistic men, Scougall and Nash, who were I believe, unwittingly, and I might even say irresponsibly, employed by Dr Barnardo's Homes to look after us children in our early, impressionable years.

We, as young boys, found our own way of life, and would avoid as best we could the Bayfordbury staff because of our fearful contempt of them.

~o~o~ Loyalty to Each Other ~o~o~

If there is one distinctive value that most orphans learn early in life, it would be loyalty to their friends. Their virtual abandonment by the rest of society forces a bond between those unfortunates living in conditions like Bayfordbury – a loyalty similar in many ways to that which exists between devoted army buddies in battle.

The most evident factor in this regard is that the kids all stick together in many cases, closer even than natural-born brothers and sisters.

We may and did fight each other on many, many occasions over countless differences of opinion and to also, I would suppose, establish our position amongst ourselves in our unique society, much like

SUFFER LITTLE CHILDREN

animals do relative to dominance in their respective species. But when confronted by outsider kids we would, with few exceptions, stand together as one, which more often than not proved to be to our advantage, and something which we would invariably benefit by.

I'm sure the outsider kids would say, "Don't tangle with those 'banana' kids. [That's what we were called sometimes.] They're a tough bunch," or words to that effect.

When one thinks about it, boys don't, in normal situations, have to fight so aggressively with self-abandonment, or have the need to fight as much as we did among ourselves.

Fighting in orphanages amongst ourselves was just one indication of our social aggressiveness. On the other hand, however, if one of our Bayfordbury boys got into a physical confrontation with a bigger outsider boy and the odds were unfair, one of our bigger Bayfordbury boys, we could guarantee, would step in to defend his smaller or younger peer.

Pound for pound, we were a tougher bunch than the outsiders, if not in physical strength, then in resolve and tenacity.

We were a tough bunch, no doubt hardened by our need to independently defend ourselves. The fact was that growing up in orphanages, we lived, unknowingly, under the old philosophies or sayings such as, 'survival of the fittest' and 'The bigger they are, the harder they fall'.

These sayings are not new clichés: they were around when I was a child and probably long before. But they fit the lifestyle of orphans in an orphanage environment, and we all learned to live by them.

~o~o~ Fighting ~o~o~

In all of the orphanages, it was always necessary to learn to defend oneself. If another boy challenged you to a fight, or you challenged someone else, then only you could see it through. Sometimes you walked away a winner, or you simply took a beating and learned to better handle the situation that led to the fight the next time.

Very often, a fight would basically end in a 'standoff', with both boys prepared to recognise and respect the other. Boys would seldom fight each other a second time for the need to see who could better the other.

SUFFER LITTLE CHILDREN

Quite often a fight would actually serve to bond a friendship – a friendship in some instances that could last a lifetime.

Of course, I, at one time or another, took my share of being beaten in fights, just like any other boy, whether from outsider kids or my orphanage peers. We were always cautious and aware that we could meet our match at any time and anywhere. I certainly did on many occasions.

None of us boys would step in to stop a fight. We simply encircled a fight and watched.

However badly a boy was losing a fight, he would not kick or bite and certainly never use a weapon like a stick or a stone. We always fought in accordance to what we called and thought were the 'Queensbury Rules'. Knives or chains as weapons were not even considered in those days, even by the worst of characters.

There was an unwritten code amongst the boys in all of the orphanages that I was ever in. If a boy did not fight fairly, he would be branded a coward and would lose a great deal of respect.

If any boy were to pull another boy's hair or scratch, he would be thought of as being a sissy because, as we thought, only girls did these things when they were nasty or very angry. To be called a sissy was one of the most degrading insults a boy would have to bear.

Many times we would fall foul of and suffer beatings from bullies or a few of the bigger kids at Bayfordbury. The masters would rarely interfere; they merely turned a blind eye and even ignored bullying.

Any boy who would 'tell tales' about another, or report a punishable offence or dispute of any kind to a master would be walking a fine line and would most certainly be given a hiding and quite likely be shunned by many, if not most of the boys in the orphanage.

Such boys would lose the trust and respect of the other boys. To add to their disgrace, they would also be held in contempt and despised by their peers for a long time to come.

Those same boys would often be picked on and suffer at the hands of those they had 'snitched' on or betrayed. Eventually, they would learn the 'code', and learn to live by it like most of the kids did. New boys would learn the code of loyalty just as soon as they entered the lifestyle of living in orphanages.

Very quickly the majority of boys learned to stand on their own two

SUFFER LITTLE CHILDREN

feet, as the saying goes. If a boy was too intimidated by the other boys, or didn't have it in him to defend himself, he was labelled as being a 'softy' and left alone.

Now that I think back and remember those boys we called 'softies', I realise now, that for them to act like softies, that this could have been a form of self-preservation, much like one doesn't make eye contact with an adversary unless they are prepared to challenge them. Although really, I don't think any boys we thought of as being softies, would have actually planned it that way.

~°~°~ Bayfordbury Staff ~°~°~

We all, with few exceptions, disliked and feared the Bayfordbury staff. They had 'Godlike' powers over us. It was as though these grown-ups were on one side of the fence, and we, the orphans, were on the other, much like prisoners and their jailers.

Upon further reflection today, and remembering those men and women whom we called master, matron, or nurse, I would believe most of them at Bayfordbury were probably in their late thirties and early forties.

Bearing in mind the minimal qualifications they no doubt were required to have to look after us, it is no wonder we were being looked after by such often unthinking, belligerent and unqualified men and women.

The men we called masters would normally have been called to serve in the Armed Forces, if perhaps they hadn't had something wrong with them in a physical, or possibly even in a social or mental way – who knows?

Some would rationalise that we orphans had huge chips on our shoulders and so needed to be continually disciplined. Many thought, no doubt, that we blamed society as a whole for the fact that we were institutionalised.

This was not the case. We were simply orphans or, for one reason or another, unwanted children, and only rebelled primarily because of the harsh treatment we received from our custodians. The rebellious attitude, if we had any such attitude at all, was only present at Bayfordbury. Only at Bayfordbury were we treated with such aggression and by such belligerent staff.

SUFFER LITTLE CHILDREN
~°~°~ Punishment to the Extreme ~°~°~

One of the most fearsome punishments that I, and most of us kids at Bayfordbury observed, was the time when a boy of about fifteen years old ran away.

His name was Valance. Valance did a bunk one evening; for whatever reason, I don't think any of us kids knew, though there could have been many reasons.

When at any time any of us boys did a bunk they, being orphans and for the most part alone in the world, would not have had any kind of sensible plan or a predetermined place to run to.

Unfortunate as it was, Valance ran away to a familiar place – one of the few places he did know – which was about two or three or, at the very most, four miles away.

Such was his pathetic yet innocent plan, he ran away to Ware Senior and Central School, the only familiar place he knew that he could run to – a place, I'm sure, where he couldn't help but know he would get caught at. Yet in reality it was like running away from one prison to another for all the sense it made and for what good it would do him.

Without a plan or any sympathetic person to run to, he quite possibly only ran away from Bayfordbury looking for attention, yet subconsciously wanting to be caught, like many of us did, no doubt.

Arriving at Ware School some time during the late evening, he hid and slept in one of the dustbins that were standing just outside of one of the school's side entrances. In the morning a school caretaker or worker found him and, as would be expected, took him to his boss, Mr Evans the headmaster. Mr Evans dutifully called Mr Scougall, and Valance was returned to Bayfordbury by the police.

We knew at breakfast time that Valance had done a bunk. Even before we had left on the coach to go to Ware School, a rumour had already been circulated that Valance had been caught and was being returned to Bayfordbury. This was all quite normal and we didn't think much more about it at the time.

We knew that Valance would be caned. Lots of boys ran away from Bayfordbury and they would all be returned and caned; it was to be expected and quite normal.

SUFFER LITTLE CHILDREN

However, as it turned out, nothing that happened that day was normal. Later in the afternoon, when our coach drew up in front of the steps at Bayfordbury's main entrance, we could see Mr Scougall, Mrs Scougall, Mr Nash, Matron and another master all standing at the top of the steps, Mr Scougall in particular looking very stern. The stone steps leading up to the main entrance into Bayfordbury were about thirty to perhaps forty feet wide, flanked by six eighteen-inch to two-feet diameter white stone columns.

There were about ten steps leading up to the main entrance podium. In the centre of the podium a big armchair had been placed, and standing off to one side was Valance, looking obviously nervous and scared. The whole scene was much like one would imagine at a medieval public hanging.

We disembarked from the coach and lined up, as was the usual procedure, in front of the huge front entrance steps. There was an unusual feeling of suspense as the coach drove away. We were all very quiet and no doubt nervous because of the unprecedented event that seemed to be unfolding.

Needless to say, we were all quite tense, anxiously waiting for what was about to happen to Valance. We could easily anticipate that Valance was going to be caned: that would be normal. But what was to happen on that day was not in any way, even at Bayfordbury, normal. We had often seen each other punished. Mr Scougall, it seemed, loved to punish us in front of each other. But this procedure and the atmosphere of the moment was quite different.

Mr Scougall, this hulk of a man, stepped forward and angrily pulled Valance up beside him by his shirt. Then he went on to tell us what we already knew: that Valance had run away. Then he said something to the effect that he was going to make an example of him and that if any of us ran away in the future, we could expect to receive what Valance was going to get.

I'm sure that we all thought that Valance was going to get a good caning, perhaps more severe than usual. But to our horror, and something which we had never seen before, one of the masters held Valance and at the same time he and Mr Nash, pulled Valance's braces off his shoulders and pulled his short trousers down and completely off, exposing his white bare buttocks.

SUFFER LITTLE CHILDREN

Then Mr Nash and the other master bent Valance over the big armchair and held him down, while Mr Scougall, swinging wildly, beat Valance's bare bottom with his stout cane.

After about six or seven strokes, Mr Scougall stopped beating the screaming Valance while Matron, in the pretext, it seemed, of being concerned, looked briefly to see Valance was all right. Then the hulking Mr Scougall beat Valance several more times.

We could all see, from where we were standing some twenty feet or so away, the welts swell and turn blue on Valance's bare buttocks with each stroke of the heavy cane. Needless for me to say, it was extremely stressful, even fearful for us nine or ten-year-old boys, though nothing like it was for Valance.

Valance literally screamed with pain, but was held down and unable to move until the caning was finished.

For us to have to witness this punishment is hard to explain. It was like our little world had gone mad. None of the boys spoke, no doubt because we were too frightened to even move or blink an eyelid.

We were often punished with the cane, and very severely, but never on our naked buttocks. His was the worst punishment that I had ever observed, or was ever to observe again. The memory of what happened that day will follow me to my grave.

For Valance the brutality and the pain, to say nothing of the humiliation he suffered that day at the hands of those sadistic masters at Bayfordbury, would be unforgivable, and would, no doubt, stay with Valance for the rest of his life.

I remember also Valance being helped to walk, by one of the masters who had held him while he was being caned. He was then taken away through the main entrance doors to the mansion, while we were simply told to carry on as usual.

Valance was put into isolation and had no visitors for several days. In actual fact none of us saw him for at least five or six days after his ordeal. He recovered all right, as far as we would know, but how such a humiliating beating would affect him in the future, I would never know.

Running away was really little more than an impetuous, mischievous, and an unthinking act by us boys. One would just leave the routine of institutional life and keep going. Eventually, when the boy

SUFFER LITTLE CHILDREN

became hungry and cold enough, he would usually panic, and often come back to the orphanage of his own accord.

There were no objectives, or anywhere to run to. Invariably the boy would eventually approach the first policeman he saw and 'give himself up'.

Often the police, without anyone else's help, would easily spot us and bring us back. We were always dressed the same. In our grey or blue short trousers held up by braces; grey shirts and grey socks, we all looked the same, like scruffy little urchins dressed in reasonably good clothes.

I don't recollect any boy doing a bunk and staying away for more than a day or two at a time. They always were returned or came back to the orphanage within a couple of days, one way or another.

This was not the last time boys ran away from the orphanages I was in, but, as I have mentioned, I don't recall any boy running away from Bayfordbury again. A fearful lesson had been taught us by Mr Scougall sure enough, but at what expense to the emotions of us young vulnerable boys and in particular, to Valance?

Some time in the future another master tried to punish me in a similar manner to the way Valance was punished, but without success. I will explain more about this further on in my story.

~°~°~ Out of Bounds ~°~°~

The 'out of bounds' areas around the Bayfordbury mansion were mostly fenced in with ornate walls and decorative wrought-iron railings. However, it was quite easy for us to climb over the walls and fences and to get into the out of bounds areas.

In many of these out of bounds areas, Lord and Lady Clinton Baker had, over the years and during their extensive travels throughout the world, brought back many exotic trees and shrubs, and planted them in what they had called their 'Tropical Gardens'.

Included in the exotic plants they had planted were overgrown areas of bamboo, beautiful fig trees, and other somewhat strange looking tropical and semi-tropical plants and trees like palms and the likes.

The bamboo shoots grew in great patches, almost like weeds. We

SUFFER LITTLE CHILDREN

would cut the slender shoots and use them for the arrows we would make for our bows. We would make 'feather' flights from heavy paper. These, we learned, kept the arrows straight in flight. Some of the arrows we would sharpen the end to a point and bind with wire to give weight to the front end. The bows we would make from yew trees, which we believed Robin Hood's bow was made from.

~o~o~

We became good archers of sorts, and would practise with our bows and arrows for hours on end. For the most part, being King Richard's men, we would shoot the arrows at those imaginary Prince John's men, or maybe home-made targets. It would have been too dangerous for us to actually shoot the arrows at each other.

Our crude King Arthur swords or Arabian cutlasses, which had curved cardboard hand shields, we also made ourselves. Our fun included being the Sherwood Forrest characters. Naturally we all wanted to be Robin Hood.

Fred, being bigger than Baggy and I, was always Big John. We would commonly argue about who had to be Maid Marian but we had to have her in our games so that we could rescue her. I believe I might well have reluctantly been Maid Marian from time to time, just as we all would have, except for perhaps Fred.

Sometimes we would be Indians, looking for imaginary cowboys, who were shaped like tree trunks, to aim our arrows at.

We also made spears with the bigger bamboo shoots and would bind sharp stones on the ends to give weight. We became fairly accurate at throwing these too.

As best my memory serves me, I don't recall anyone ever getting hurt from an arrow or a spear during our aggressive games, though we often got our fingers and knuckles banged or bruised during our over-enthusiastic sword fights.

I, like many other boys, became quite good with a catapult. After a lot of practice many of us kids could hit targets from quite a distance. Ammunition was easy to get: we simply picked stones up from our gravel driveways. From time to time we would also have brick fights.

SUFFER LITTLE CHILDREN

One group of 'friends' or maybe they weren't friends, would take on another group, and we would fire stones from catapults, or throw larger stones, at each other.

Of course, once in a while one of us would get hit as the result of this sort of fun, but again, I don't recall anyone getting more seriously hurt than a big bump on the head or a small cut on the scalp.

~o~o~ Foraging ~o~o~

Like many of the boys at Bayfordbury, Fred, Baggy and I would go on foraging expeditions across the fields to find edible wild berries, nuts and such to eat. Some of the more common things for us to find in their respective seasons were sweet chestnuts, hazelnuts, blackberries, and many types of vegetation. As kids we were always hungry, and there was no 'mum', or anyone else, who would give us anything to eat between our regular meals, which, as such, were often insufficient anyway.

The types of leaves, nuts and berries we could eat, we first learned from Mrs Dunning, and then from other older boys at Bayfordbury who had lived in other orphanages. These boys would bring with them their knowledge of foraging and ways of life, and combine their knowledge of such things with that of their peers.

With these combined experiences, we forged a kind of primitive way to satisfy our constant need to eat, or perhaps I should call it 'snack'. In so many little but nevertheless important ways, it was all an unforgettable way of learning which helped to give us, for good or bad, our own unique form of independence.

We never forgot what Mrs Dunning had first told us of many of the wild leaves and fruits we could look for, and her wise old saying:

If it's blue, it's true
(like elderberry and sloe) and
If it's red, you're dead
(like deadly nightshade and yew berries).

Some of the odd types of leaves which we foraged for were the young hawthorn leaves (we called them bread and cheese); the seeds of a

SUFFER LITTLE CHILDREN

type of thistle; leaves we called 'vinegar leaves'; and nasturtium leaves, which we called 'mustard leaves' because they tasted like mustard. There were many other wild plant leaves and berries we ate – too numerous to mention.

We would also pull up huge swedes, which farmers grew for cattle feed, from the farmers' fields. Then we would just clean them off on the grass or on our clothes, take off the outer dirty, tough skin with our teeth, and eat the swedes raw.

Such practices were commonplace with us kids at the time, and may even have been with the outsider kids, but we did it simply because we were always hungry. We would also, after discarding all of the leaves, eat the pith inside cabbage stalks.

We would, needless to say, often go 'scrumping' (stealing apples). Not just orphans went scrumping; almost all kids seemed to. I would think that we orphans were probably more brazen in our raiding of the orchards. We would climb over fences around people's gardens, even knowing that there were dogs in the their yards or orchards.

Usually we would go scrumping for apples, pears, plums and gooseberries. Quite often angry farmers or people waiting for us to show up would chase us, and many times we would get caught.

If a farmer, or anyone for that matter, did catch us, they would frequently clout us around the ear and threaten to call the orphanage. But generally speaking, no one did.

Scrumping wasn't a serious offence in those days, though if adults were caught scrumping they would quite probably be prosecuted for stealing, though I have never heard of anyone ever being charged for scrumping. Children were simply called rascals, and reprimanded on the spot.

~o~o~ Hertingfordbury Choirboy ~o~o~

As a boy, I know that I was not, by any stretch of the imagination, considered 'angelic' by anyone who knew me or had charge of me. But, without flattering myself, I must say I was rather a nice-looking little boy and could easily have been mistaken for being a quiet, well-behaved and somewhat intelligent boy.

SUFFER LITTLE CHILDREN

Whether the way I looked was the reason or not, I really don't know, but I suspect it was. Regardless, one day I was instructed by Mr Scougall to join the St Mary's Church choir in Hertingfordbury. I never was, and nor did I consider myself, a particularly good singer.

There were perhaps three boys, three girls, and maybe four men in the choir altogether. Two of the three boys were from Bayfordbury. I was one of them, and a boy named Williams was the other.

Hertingfordbury is a small village located three miles from Bayfordbury, in the opposite direction to Bayford.

Sometimes we went to Bayford Church on Sunday morning and Hertingfordbury Church in the afternoon, and reversed the order the following Sunday.

Williams – we mostly addressed each other by our surnames, though I can only recall other boys calling me Reg – and I would go for choir practice on Thursday evenings, and then sing in the choir on Sundays. We were paid a ha'penny for choir practice and a penny each time we sang during a Sunday service: a total of three ha'pennies a week. We were allowed to keep a ha'penny each and the orphanage kept the rest.

It's rather ironic that I used to donate a penny a week to the orphanage and live in the orphanage too. It was like I was paying a penny a week for my keep, which at Bayfordbury was really too much.

~o~o~ Williams, 'Kayaking' ~o~o~

One Sunday morning, when the rest of the Bayfordbury boys went to Bayford Church, Williams and I, as was usual, walked to Hertingfordbury Church, which, as I have mentioned, was about three miles away.

While dawdling along the same beautiful little country road – the one that I had received a caning for just because I ran between two openings in a hedge – we had to cross over a little humpback bridge.

On this particular Sunday, dressed in our Sunday clothes, Williams and I happened to look over the little humpback bridge that crosses over a tributary river which flowed into the River Lee.

On the bank of the small river just below us, we saw a small kayak turned upside down.

The river, with its crystal-clear water dotted with large and small

SUFFER LITTLE CHILDREN

rocks was, at this point, just a lazy slow-moving river about twelve to fifteen feet wide, and perhaps two and a half to three feet deep.

As would seem quite normal to us young boys at that point in time, Williams went down to the riverbank, turned the kayak over, and found there was a paddle in it. So, he slipped the kayak into the water and got in. In doing so he had to climb inside the small fabric opening which enclosed the top of the kayak. The opening in the fabric cover may have been a little on the large size for Williams, but otherwise was OK, it seemed.

He then pushed himself off the bank and started paddling into the middle of the river. All the time I was still leaning over the stone bridge, watching him.

While I was laughing, and at the same time watching him turning and trying to control the kayak, Williams was struggling, but nevertheless seemed to be doing pretty good and was moving well. I continued to watch him as he made his way slowly under the bridge. Then I ran to the other side of the narrow bridge, expecting to see Williams come out the other side.

As I watched, the kayak came out from under the little bridge as was expected, but Williams wasn't in it. I called out, "Williams, Williams" to him a couple of times, but there was no answer or any sign of him.

Reflecting today, I can't understand why I wouldn't have been more concerned, but at that time in my young life I just wasn't. Without, as I say, much concern for Williams, I watched the kayak drift down the river and go around a bend and out of sight.

Still there was no sign of Williams. I, unbelievable as it may seem, called out a couple of times for Williams and then I just carried on down the country lane on my way to Hertingfordbury Church, not wanting to be late for the service.

I remember clearly how Williams came into the vestry. We were changing into our black-and-white robes as he entered. He was almost soaking wet. Fortunately there were no adults in the vestry – only us boys and girls. Had there been any adults they would have sent him home and then, of course, he would have been caned.

Williams took all his clothes off except for his underwear, and put them on the radiator to dry. Then he put on his robes. As is usual, it

SUFFER LITTLE CHILDREN

was quite cold in the church but Williams didn't say a word. He knew he would have been in serious trouble if any one of the adults, and particularly the vicar, had noticed.

Williams told me later that he had apparently tipped the kayak over under the bridge and fallen out and was standing up to his waist in the water when I was calling him. He said he answered me, but that I obviously didn't hear him. So, he climbed out of the river, took his clothes off, and rang them out as best he could. Then after getting back into his wet clothes he ran all the way to church.

~∘~∘~ Hertingfordbury Village ~∘~∘~

Many times after choir practice or evening song, in the foggy autumn evenings, we, Williams and I, would see the lamplighter come and light the gaslight at the church gate.

The lamplighter, with a ladder over his shoulder, would ride his bicycle to the lamppost. Then he would put the ladder against the 'hangman's bar', pull on a chain to release the gas, and at the same time light the mantel with a lighted, long candle-waxed wick.

The light from the gaslight must have been a very subdued light, or I can't think that it would have been allowed during those war years.

The girls, who were a little older than us, and some of the older village boys, would after the boys climbed up the lamppost to get a light for their cigarettes, stand under the lamplight and smoke.

On the choir practice nights, the village's outsider kids would often go to the fish and chip shop and get themselves some fish and chips. Williams and I would cadge some from them.

Those were some of the nice memories I have of a little English village's way of life – a stark difference to the harsh life we endured in our other world, just three miles away, at Bayfordbury.

~∘~∘~ Bayfordbury Food ~∘~∘~

The food at Bayfordbury, except for perhaps the potatoes at Woodford Bridge, must have been the worst food I would ever have eaten, certainly to that point in my life. To this day, I can't recall ever having food which

SUFFER LITTLE CHILDREN

could remotely be considered as being anywhere near as bad as that at Bayfordbury.

Cockroaches and silverfish lived in abundance throughout the basement areas we lived in, and were seemingly unchecked. Mice and rats were commonplace, we ourselves partly adding to the problem. It wasn't unusual to see these vermin scurrying around our dormitories or almost anywhere in the basement where we lived, and even more so, where the kitchen and dining room were located.

We weren't really concerned about the mice or rats, they didn't frighten us or were we reviled by them, nor were we aware of the diseases that such vermin carried.

Part of the mice and rat problem was, no doubt, caused by ourselves. Some of the kids would keep 'tame' rats or mice as pets. They would have to save portions of their meals and smuggle the food out of the dining room in their pockets to feed them. Most of these pets, black, white and even tri-coloured rats and mice, were commonly kept beside the boys' beds, until they eventually died or got away.

Such as they were, the pet mice and rats would in turn breed with the wild rats or mice. It was commonplace to see grey, white, black, or mixed coloured types of these vermin scurrying across the floors, and to hear them squeaking at night.

Most of the problem with the food we ate wasn't so much to do with rats and mice though. It was primarily because we kids were made to prepare most of the food we ate ourselves, without any supervision by the staff. The rest of the problem would have been cleanliness of the kitchen, the abundance of cockroaches and silverfish, and simply careless cooking.

We all, eight to fifteen-year-olds, with few exceptions, would have to clean and cut up the cabbages, wash the potatoes, clean the carrots and so on. In fact, we had to prepare almost everything we ate.

Such work as vegetable preparation and washing dishes was tedious to us irresponsible boys. We younger boys followed the example of the older boys, who in turn would want to get the work done as quickly as possible, without regard for the end results.

The actual preparation of the vegetables was always the same. The potatoes were washed in one of the bathtubs that we bathed in, in the

SUFFER LITTLE CHILDREN

evenings. To wash the potatoes all we did was to merely put the bath plug in the tub, empty a sack of potatoes straight into the tub, and turn the water on.

Then, with a stiff-bristled yard broom, we would swish the potatoes up and down in the tub several times, then just pull the plug out of the tub and drain the water out.

Without any further inspection by anyone, all that we did after that was to simply slide the potatoes up the sloped end of the bathtub and into huge steel pots, which they were then boiled in.

The potatoes were never peeled or the eyes taken out. They were not, to my knowledge, ever inspected or examined by any staff member, or even by the boys cleaning them themselves, including me when it was my turn to prepare the vegetables.

The potato washing procedure was routinely carried out day after day by different boys, including Baggy, Fred and myself, us being just as irresponsible as anyone nine, ten or even fifteen year olds would be.

Cabbages, maybe ten for a meal, would then be put into the same tub, the outer leaves taken off, and the cabbages washed. Following our inadequate cleaning, the cabbages would then each be cut into six or eight pieces. Just like the potatoes, they would then be slid up the end of the bath into the cooking pots, without further inspection given them either.

The same cleaning preparation was given to all such vegetables like carrots, parsnips and turnips. All would have been irresponsibly prepared similarly.

~o~o~

One of the worst vegetables, the one that I and many of us boys disliked most, was marrow. These we crudely peeled and removed the seeds, and then the marrow was chopped into chunks and boiled. It was much like eating thick water. Still, we got lots of marrows to eat, and they were horrible. But it was wartime and, like everything else we were served, we had to eat it.

At weekends and holidays we had our dinners in the orphanage. The rest of the week we had dinner at the outsiders' school, where the

SUFFER LITTLE CHILDREN

food was properly prepared and cooked much better by far, than at Bayfordbury.

~o~o~ Food Servings ~o~o~

The method of serving the meals at Bayfordbury was routine, though most unfair as far as the younger boys were concerned.

After Grace had been said at each meal, the master in charge would call out an age group, starting with the oldest boys, aged fifteen. Then, according to the procedure, all of the fifteen-year-old boys, though there weren't many of them, would go up to the serving tables to be served 'buffet style'.

Then the fourteen-year-olds would do the same, followed by the thirteen-year-olds and so on, until it was our turn. Following the ten-year-olds, my age group – the nine-year-olds – would then go up to the serving tables to receive their servings of whatever was left in the pots. There were very few eight-year-old boys at Bayfordbury.

When it was our turn to file up and receive our helpings of the meal there were, understandably, absolutely no choices as to what we would eat, except two – eat what you were given or go without.

The unfairness of the entire procedure was very evident. The fifteen-year-olds were, generally speaking, the tough guys, so of course they would intimidate the younger boys serving the meal. By doing so, they would receive the best of everything being served each day. The master who was supervising the meal just didn't seem to care what went on.

My group felt the disadvantage of the system most. There were only a few kids younger than we were during those early days when first I arrived at Bayfordbury.

Most often, when it was our turn to go up to get our dinner there would be only the poorest quality of the food left. What we were expected to eat was not much better than the food that Willy and I used to feed to Belly and Pinky at Meriden.

But what I have described so far wasn't the worst of it. We all – the older boys and us little kids – would receive two potatoes each. After all of the boys older than us had gone up to get their meal, and the servers had picked through the potatoes for them, it would be our turn.

SUFFER LITTLE CHILDREN

Most of the other older boys would be sitting down scoffing (eating) their meals and supposedly enjoying them, while we were still waiting to be served, feeling very hungry, much like we were starving.

Eventually, when our age group was called out by the master, Fred, Baggy and I, together with the rest of our age group, would finally be allowed to go up to the serving tables to be served our dinners.

Unfortunately for us younger boys, being literally at the bottom of the 'food chain' we could only get what was left over in the cooking pots, which would consist of big, pure lumps of fat, bones with no meat, half-rotten carrots or parsnips, crusts of bread and, worst by far, two miserable potatoes.

The cabbage and most vegetables, including the residual grey water, would be served with a ladle or a big serving spoon, and scooped onto our plates from the bottom of the huge steel cooking pots. The water, we would drain off our plates by simply tipping it onto the floor when the master wasn't looking.

Many times after being served our dinner, we would get back to our tables and then find that one of the potatoes was completely rotten and unable to be eaten, and that the other supposed potato would often be nothing more than a stone, about the same size as a potato, and so looked exactly like a potato.

To make things worse, just as soon as we left the serving table to return to our tables to sort through the food on our plates, the fifteen-year-olds were going up to the serving tables again for 'extras'. So we wouldn't even get the chance to go up and get our stones or rotten potatoes exchanged for another potato, if there even was one.

We would find lots of caterpillars and other insects in our cabbage, and sometimes we might have only a cabbage stalk. Often the carrots would be so wormy or rotten that we couldn't give them away.

Then there was the meat. Us younger kids would get all the fat and bones, with very little meat at all. It should be remembered that with the bones, stones, slugs and snails and the often absolutely rotten vegetables, all of which was primarily our meal, meant that with some meals we had very little or almost nothing to eat at all.

It might easily have been said that we brought some of the misery on ourselves and therefore how could we complain. After all, we had

SUFFER LITTLE CHILDREN

prepared the food ourselves and thus 'reaped what we sowed'.

Of course, this is all true, but we must also bear in mind that many of us were only nine and ten-year-old, unsupervised kids. There is no doubt that we were irresponsible, as were all the boys at Bayfordbury, even the older ones. But then again, someone was being paid and charged with the responsibility of looking after us.

~o~o~ Sunday Teatime ~o~o~

At about 4.00 p.m., prior to our walking to church for evening song, we would have Sunday tea. Teatime is a meal, not just a drink – and it was always the same.

Sunday teatime never varied from week to week, and primarily consisted of two slices of bread and two patties of margarine for the older boys. For the younger boys it was the same, except we received one slice of bread plus one patty of margarine. We also all received two sardines and a bunch of watercress each.

Fortunately, the best part of the Sunday tea was that we also received a rock cake and a teaspoon of marmalade.

The one particularly miserable thing which made our Sunday teatime so memorable was the watercress.

It seemed like the supplier of the watercress, probably a local farmer, had an agreement to supply Bayfordbury with perhaps two bushels of watercress each Sunday.

There was nothing wrong with the actual watercress, except the way it was served to us. The farmer or whoever supplied the watercress, would, it seems, merely fork the watercress out of the river into bushel baskets. Then he would bring the bushel baskets of watercress to Bayfordbury, and that would be the extent of his contract. But, like all of the other food served to us, it plainly was not inspected at all.

After going up for our tea, in our age groups just as I have explained we did for our dinners, we would receive our slice of bread and coin of margarine and two sardines, and watercress, rock cake and marmalade, all on one porcelain covered steel plate.

Generally the watercress, which was beautifully green and fresh, always had lots of live active water insects and other creatures in it, but

SUFFER LITTLE CHILDREN

what was most common of all, and what we liked least, were the water snails clinging to it.

Without serious complaint though, we would take the little creatures out of our watercress and let them wander around the table, then eat the rest of the watercress.

The water snails were not as revolting as they may seem; they were simply alive and unappetising. We still ate the watercress and were not too concerned about the snails, except that we didn't want to accidentally put one of these horrible little creatures into our mouths and unintentionally chew them. Crunching down on the odd snail would result in us spitting the mess back out onto our plates, making the other kids laugh.

On one particularly unforgettable occasion, after returning to my table with my tea, I actually found that I had a stickleback (a type of minnow) in my watercress.

Obviously it confirmed that the watercress hadn't been inspected at all, or otherwise surely someone would have found the two-inch long minnow in it.

Understandably it would have been considerably more work, and cost more, for anyone to remove all of the water snails. There were just too many of them, some of them being very, very small. But a stickleback – that's hardly difficult to see!

~o~o~ Bread Slicing ~o~o~

A chore, which one of the fourteen or fifteen-year-old boys would have had to carry out, was the slicing of the many loaves of bread for each meal. The bread slicing was done on a mechanical bread-slicing machine.

The bread slicer was not an electric-powered machine – such machines had not been invented then. It was strictly a hand-operated machine, which meant that a boy would, with one hand, turn a flywheel located on one side of the bread slicer and, with his other hand, slide a large loaf of bread up to the slicing blade.

The revolving blade would then slice the bread to the thickness it was set for (about three quarters of an inch or more), letting the slice of cut bread fall into a large wicker laundry basket. The basket was about four feet square and about two feet deep.

SUFFER LITTLE CHILDREN

On one occasion that I well remember, the boy slicing the bread cut one of his fingers on the bread machine blade. The cut was not too serious, I would suppose, but enough to make his finger bleed a bit.

So, on most of the slices of bread following him cutting himself, he made a red cross with his bloody finger, right through the middle of each slice of bread, corner to corner. Expecting that he could get into trouble if the duty master saw it, he put the bloodied bread down to the bottom of the laundry hamper.

And so, as the boys came up to the serving table in their respective age groups to get their meal, they took their allowance of two slices of bread each as they passed the bread hamper.

When it was our age group's turn to go up for our meal, the bread which had been down the bottom of the hamper was now the only bread left for us, the younger boys, to have.

So now, besides our having to shake off the silverfish and cockroaches which seemed to be always present at the bottom of the bread hamper, Fred, Baggy, and I had to take one slice of bread each, and our bread was the bread at the bottom of the hamper, the slices that had the blood on them.

Then, after getting back to our tables, we had to scrape and pick the blood off our bread before we could eat it. It was tough being the youngest boys living at Bayfordbury, for many such reasons.

Naturally, the staff ate very well. We couldn't see exactly what they had to eat, but we could smell their food while it was cooking, the aroma wafting down through the corridors and, if we were outside, through the open windows. We could only imagine what it would be like to have bacon, fried onions, mushrooms, roast potatoes and even toast.

The cook prepared the staff's food separate to ours, and so everything would have been much better prepared than the food we ate. Also the staff would have the advantage of having access to all our ration books, and would have taken the best of the food for themselves. We would only have had the bare necessities from our food rationing allocation.

SUFFER LITTLE CHILDREN
~o~o~ Bed Wetting ~o~o~

I did, from time to time, until the age of about ten or eleven, wet my bed – another thing which made my life very unpleasant at Bayfordbury.

Wetting the bed was, we were made to believe, a deliberate and thoughtless act and also a disgusting thing to do, and so we were made to feel very ashamed of ourselves. Every morning after wetting the bed we would be so afraid of the consequences to follow.

We couldn't help wetting the bed and panicked when we found out that we had 'had an accident'. Most times we wouldn't even know we had wet the bed until after we woke up in the morning, at which time we knew that we would be caned by Mr Scougall.

Such punishment was thought, by Mr Scougall and his staff at Bayfordbury, to be the best way to cure bed wetting.

Any doctor today, with any understanding of children, would advise a parent or any adult in charge of the child, that wetting the bed is not a wilful act and that, with understanding and psychological help, the problem can in most instances be treated and cured, though even then it's far from easy.

In our case, we simply had to suffer the punishments and, unknowingly, have to wait and outgrow the problem.

If at Bayfordbury a boy had so-called 'deliberately' wet his bed two days in a row, he would be especially punished by being disgraced as well as being caned.

Such boys were required to stand outside the dining room while Grace and prayers were being said. Then the 'wet beds', as they were called, were made to file into the dining room, one after the other, with the wetted sheets draped over their heads and faces, and then routinely be caned in front of the other boys.

Some of the boys, perhaps six or seven, wet their beds almost every night and so the physical abuse to their bodies and emotions, and the disgrace and humiliation they suffered, was a daily occurrence.

After the unfortunate habitual 'bed wetters' had been disgraced and punished, then the rest of the 'one time' or occasional bed wetters would file into the dining room to receive their caning.

Even without the ceremonious draping of the wet sheets over our

SUFFER LITTLE CHILDREN

heads, the caning, in front of the other boys, was nevertheless an emotional, degrading and humiliating experience for us young boys.

~o~o~ A Beating from Mr Nash ~o~o~

On one particularly morning I woke up to find out that I had wet my bed. When realisation had set in, there was that usual dreaded sinking feeling, because I knew I would be caned and shamed, along with any of the other boys who had wet their beds during the night.

I recall that on this particularly unforgettable morning, I had just been down to the laundry tubs to wash out my sheets, which was the usual procedure for any boy who only occasionally wet his bed, and, not realising it was breakfast time, I was walking down the long, dimly lit corridor towards the dining room, singing a hymn.

I remember the occasion well. The hymn I was singing was *'There Is a Green Hill Far Away'*. Not realising that prayers were being said in the dining room at the time, I was singing the hymn at the top of my voice. The hymn is about Jesus, having been crucified. Little did I know, but I was about to be almost crucified myself, so to speak.

The stone walled corridors, combined with the hard flagstone floors and ceilings, made my rather immature high-pitched voice echo loudly throughout the basement corridor.

Later, Baggy and Fred told me they could hear me getting closer and closer, and my singing getting louder and louder. Like most of the other boys, they too were giggling, knowing that I was going to walk right into the dining room singing. As well, they could easily guess what would happen next.

Not knowing that prayers were being said and also being unaware of what awaited me, I casually strolled into the hushed dining room, still singing at the top of my voice and as loud as I could:

> *There is a green hill far away,*
>   *Without a city wall,*
> *Where our dear Lord was crucified,*
>   *He died to save us all.*

SUFFER LITTLE CHILDREN

Mr Nash, whom we feared almost as much as Mr Scougall, was a tall, rather thin man, and very agile. He had a thin chiselled face and dark, maybe even black, hair.

Together with his dark, well-shaved 'bluebeard' jaw, dark eyebrows and black heavy horn-rimmed glasses, he always looked ominous to the extreme. He had on a grey pinstriped suit. My memory of Mr Nash, the way he looked and how he treated me that morning is still most vivid in my memory, and it still makes me quite angry when I occasionally remember what happened to me that day.

As I entered the dining room I suddenly became aware that there was a hushed and eerie tension in the room, like something disastrous was about to happen. My first dread was realised when I came into the dining room and saw that Mr Nash was on duty.

He was standing just inside the door and sideways to me as I entered the dining room, staring straight ahead, breathing heavily. He was obviously tense and very angry. In utter fear, I stopped singing immediately.

Instantly I realised what the hushed atmosphere in the dining room was about. I remember well the fear I felt, knowing I was in for a beating. What I didn't know was to what extent.

Mr Nash, even though he had been saying the morning prayers, was smoking a cigarette and inhaling deeply. He had stopped saying whatever prayer he had been saying, and was patting his thigh, obviously very angry, and impatiently waiting to hit me.

Looking straight ahead, Mr Nash continued puffing heavily on his cigarette. He didn't even glance at me. Then in a quiet, kind of venomous voice said, "Come here, Longman."

Nervously I shuffled about a foot closer to him. I was still about eight feet away. Still looking straight ahead, he repeated himself. "Come here, Longman."

Almost every boy in the room could see me.

The room seemed even quieter now. There wasn't the slightest sound. It was so quiet one could have heard a cockroach tiptoeing across the floor.

I shuffled a little closer, waiting for the explosion of his fist. Instead, Mr Nash put his arm out and with a bony finger, pointed to a spot on the floor much closer to him.

SUFFER LITTLE CHILDREN

"Come right here," he ordered, in the harsh tone of authority that he was known for.

Every boy in the dining room knew what was going to happen. I too, of course. I would have been very alert at this point, my mental reflexes primed, waiting for him to strike. It was as though he was the predator and I the prey. I was very tense as I waited, motionless, hoping to avoid his fist.

Slowly, driven by fear and not daring to disobey him, I stepped closer to where he had instructed me to stand.

Just as I reached the spot that he had indicated with his finger, it happened. He moved so fast I didn't see his fist coming as he knocked me right through the doorway and into the corridor.

I, temporarily stunned by the blow, fell over backwards into the corridor wall. But he still hadn't finished with me. He seemed to spring outside the door and then he hit me several more times with his fists, in an extreme fit of anger.

At this point, the other boys in the dining room couldn't see me or Mr Nash in the corridor because we were actually outside the dining room, but they could hear what was going on. Baggy and Fred said that they thought I could have ended up in hospital that day.

They also said that they had never heard Mr Nash so angry, even though they, like many of the boys, had seen him angry many, many times. Many of them too had suffered his wrath for no good reason, but this was an extreme situation.

After beating me, and still in such a rage, he shouted at me, "Get out of my sight!" and that I would not get any breakfast, adding, "I'll deal with you later", as though he hadn't done anything to me so far.

I remember also that I went outside in front of the mansion, and climbed onto one of the big white round stones that lined the driveway and continued crying, like any nine-year-old child would.

Then to add to my misery I heard a window being lifted open on the second floor. To my absolute dread, I heard Mr Scougall's voice.

To almost any compassionate eye, seeing this little boy sitting crossed legged on top of this perfectly round, ornamental white stone, nose bleeding, bruised and crying, leads me to see a vision of a heartbroken, sad little elf, hopelessly lost in the world.

SUFFER LITTLE CHILDREN

But not so Mr Scougall. Mr Scougall called from his window and said, "What are you doing out there, Longman? Aren't you supposed to be in the dining room having your breakfast?"

"Yes, Sir," I replied, trying hard to stop crying.

"Then why aren't you?" Mr Scougall enquired.

I told him that I had misbehaved at breakfast. To my relief, he merely grunted something and closed his window.

Unbeknown to us boys, Mr Scougall had, just a day or so earlier, suffered a heart attack and was recuperating in his staff quarters.

I heard nothing more about the singing incident from Mr Nash or Mr Scougall. I can only believe that Mr Nash felt ashamed of himself or that he simply felt that I had been punished enough, which I certainly had. I will remember that beating for the rest of my life.

The entire episode was, to me, a little like the David and Goliath contest, I being David and Nash, Goliath. The difference was, Nash had the slingshot as well as the size.

~o~o~

But that wasn't to be the only brutal beating Mr Nash gave me. I will tell you more about that later in my story.

The day was, many years later, when I actually knew where Mr Nash was and I was sixteen years old and, to some degree, an accomplished amateur boxer, that I fantasised about finding Mr Nash and going to see him to make him account for that and the other beatings he had given me. He was the ultimate bully and quite likely, like most bullies are, a coward at heart.

However, several years later, when I was about to leave Dr Barnardo's Homes to go out into the world on my own, I was to learn from another boy that Mr Nash had been promoted and was now the headmaster of another Dr Barnardo's home, in Bognor Regis, Sussex.

Fortunately I was able to put the idea of going to see Mr Nash out of my mind, but I shall always remember him, as I am quite sure many of us who knew him always will.

SUFFER LITTLE CHILDREN

> *"I climbed onto one of the big white round stones that lined the driveway and continued crying."*
>
> A beating from Mr Nash

Although many years later, this was nevertheless the very stone which I, as a small boy of nine years, climbed up on and cried, after being beaten by Mr Nash while at Bayfordbury

11

BAYFORDBURY – PART 5

~○~○~ Albert 'Flappers' Foot ~○~○~

Another special childhood friend that I haven't mentioned very much so far was 'Flapper' Foot. Mr Scougall first labelled Albert Foot 'Flappers', shortly after Flappers arrived at Bayfordbury. In his sardonic, humorous way, Mr Scougall said that Foot had big ears, and as of that day, he always called him Flappers every time he spoke to him.

From then on Albert Foot was only known by most of the boys and the staff, as either Foot or Flappers. Flappers kept that nickname for all the time I was to know him, which was until I finally left the custody of Dr Barnardo's Homes in 1950.

In many ways, and I say this in an affectionate way, Flappers was, though I hate to admit it, as adults would put it, "a bad influence" on me. The epitome of trouble that he was, I liked Flappers a lot. He was, during the years that I knew him, the closest resemblance to that of Charles Dickens's 'Artful Dodger', if ever there was one. He was always in trouble and many, many times I was right there with him.

None of the things he did wrong were terribly wrong, but they were bad enough for him to get caned often. Of all of my friends, he was caned more often than any of us and often deserved it (says the kettle, calling the frying pan black!).

Flappers was this 'character' until the last day I was to know him, which was when we were both about sixteen and a half years old, and I was to leave Dr Barnardo's Homes and we went our different ways.

Flapper Foot was a well-built, rather heavy-set boy and a couple of inches taller than me. He had olive coloured skin and although all of us boys, including Flappers, had our hair cut extremely short at the back and sides, he had a thick mop of hair as black as the blackest crow. My hair, too, was also just as black at the time.

It didn't even occur to us to talk about it, as it simply didn't matter enough, but now, whilst reflecting, I suspect, because of Flappers' olive

SUFFER LITTLE CHILDREN

coloured skin, that he was from a bloodline originating in somewhere like Spain or South America of perhaps a couple of generations earlier.

When I wasn't 'knocking around' with Fred and Baggy, I would be with Flappers. We would go scrumping together and dodge into the pictures to see films that we could never afford to pay to see, as we had almost no money.

We would bring punishments on ourselves by playing in the out-of-bounds areas, deliberately hiding from the ever-watchful eyes of the Bayfordbury staff. Being out of bounds was also, like so many, many other misdemeanours, a caning offence.

I know that people reading this childhood upbringing of mine and what I have written may well say I was a 'rotten little sod', and that much of the punishment and the canings I received were deserved. To some extent I would have to agree with them, though, with some allowances, I would give a measure of doubt to this appraisal of myself and think of myself as simply being a mischievous young boy at this early age. Like Flappers and many other boys, I was not deserving of the violence we were constantly exposed to at Bayfordbury.

~o~o~ The Sport of Shoplifting ~o~o~

On Saturday afternoons we were usually allowed out of the orphanage to go into Hertford or anywhere else we may wish to go, just so long as we were back again by four thirty for tea.

It was required that before we went out of the Bayfordbury grounds, we changed into our best clothes. Our best clothes consisted of a grey flannel jacket and short grey trousers, grey long sleeved shirts, and a Barnardo's tie.

I'm quite sure that if we had kept ourselves tidy, we would have looked like very well brought up children. But unfortunately, in the absence of proper concern or interest in us as individuals, we plainly looked like a bunch of scruffy little urchins.

The steel studs on the soles of our boots, together with the steel caps on both the heels and toes, made our boots 'clip clap' loudly on the pavement when we walked.

We would walk the little more than two miles into Hertford easily.

SUFFER LITTLE CHILDREN

Sometimes, quite often actually, we would even dodge on the double-decker buses.

I still remember the number of the bus which passed by Bayfordbury, going between Hertford and St Albans; it was 341. Why I should remember this bus number, I have no idea, but like many such details, I just do.

Dodging on the bus was never a sure thing. We would just get on and wait for the conductor to come to us for our fare. Needless to say, we wouldn't have the money. If the conductor was a man he would shout at us or simply tell us to get off the bus, but by this time we would have travelled about a quarter of the way to town or more, which was better than walking all the way.

Sometimes, if it was a lady bus conductor, she would often just smile and tell us to get off the bus if a bus inspector got on.

Flappers and I, as well as lots of other Bayfordbury boys, would go into Hertford with the definite intent of going shoplifting.

I'm quite proud, and yet at the same time ashamed, to say that both Flappers and I were very good at shoplifting. We were almost, it seemed, habitual shoplifters, though we did it mostly for fun, as did many of us orphans.

Today, in writing about our being shoplifters, I'm not condoning the act, of course. But while telling you the story of my childhood as an orphan, I'm merely telling the reader that this is what I was, and that this was what we did. For us, shoplifting was simply nothing more than great fun, somewhat challenging, and exciting. We didn't sell anything we stole; we just traded the stuff with the other kids for the things they had shoplifted.

It should be known that there was no criminal intent in our actions of shoplifting, and that we were not knowingly criminally minded. We did not break into houses or business properties, and we didn't roam around in gangs or accost people, or start fights with our outsider peers.

We did not, and I refer to most, if not all, of the Bayfordbury boys, deliberately cause trouble in any way that would interest the local police.

We would never, and I mean never, swear. In fact, with the exception of words like 'bloody', 'hell', 'damn' or 'sod', which even these we would never say, we didn't even know the more common four-letter swear-words of today, let alone the meaning of some of them.

SUFFER LITTLE CHILDREN

We weren't cheeky to adults, and nor did we ever or, should I say, rarely, play 'hooky' from school. In most ways, apart from the shoplifting, we were, with few exceptions, generally honest, law-abiding young boys.

I would also add that we were far from saintly boys. But being institutionalised, we were in a situation where such activities as shoplifting and fighting, possibly resulting from rebellious feelings, were almost inbred in us.

I don't recall any of us boys, and I mean any having to be sent to a borstal for any criminal offence whatsoever.

Generally speaking, shoplifters, even adults when I was a child, were not necessarily prosecuted like they would be today. We knew, of course, that what we were doing was wrong, and although I may be sounding like we weren't scared, we would actually be scared stiff whilst shoplifting, because we knew that we would be severely punished by Mr Scougall if we were caught stealing, even though shoplifting wasn't really called stealing, it seems, in those days.

One could be aware that only a century or so before us, a person, or even a child, under the hammer of an unforgiving judge like the infamous Judge Jeffries could be hanged for stealing just a loaf of bread. This, at the time, was not an unusual punishment for such acts.

But, as with so many oddities in our lives at the time, I would suppose that even though the punishments were very severe, the shoplifting all somehow seemed worthwhile.

As one could easily imagine, to the townspeople we would be a terrible nuisance and an obvious source of anguish to them. They, from time to time, would catch one of us boys and give him a good clout around the ear, but that was about all they did.

Grown-ups in those days would hit a child spontaneously, without concern for being prosecuted. But generally speaking they did not, with the exception of the Bayfordbury staff, beat children unreasonably.

I could in some way try to justify our shoplifting by pointing out that because we had no money, or any likelihood of getting any from anywhere, we couldn't actually acquire anything at all unless we shoplifted it.

For us to simply buy a tuppenny comb or a toothbrush, if we had lost ours, would require us to save our pocket money for perhaps three, or

SUFFER LITTLE CHILDREN

even four weeks. Of course, we wouldn't have time to save to buy any of our lost items, as the inspections to determine if we still had them occurred weekly. Alternatively, to shoplift a 'lost item' or be prepared to receive a severe beating, was hardly something we would give much consideration to.

So, if it occurs to the reader to sit in judgement of us, bear in mind our lifestyle and the impoverished environment we lived in. Such as it was, I urge the reader of my frank and honest story to read it for what it is, and not to be morally judgmental.

I must admit it and say, that I feel no bravado in what I write. Mine is not a story requiring sympathy and certainly not condolence. I can only say that this is how it was and how I must tell it.

~o~o~ Flappers, Our Leader ~o~o~

On the subject of shoplifting however, Flappers was without a doubt our leader and, like Dickens's 'Artful Dodger', he would show the 'new' boys how it was done.

There wasn't really any trick to it. Flappers mostly gave us encouragement. All we really did was to wait until no one was looking and then slip whatever article took our fancy into our pockets, or inside our cotton shirts. Flappers was, now that I think about it, simply giving us the nerve to actually shoplift.

Woolworths was our main target. It was, and still is, at the time of my writing, located on the main street in Hertford. It's not a huge department store as one would find today, but it was big enough so that the shop assistant girls who worked there couldn't watch us all the time.

Woolworths didn't sell expensive articles. In fact, they were commonly known for only selling cheaply made things at low prices.

We would steal the silliest of things like 'Bond Street' jewellery (their own brand name of very cheap jewellery), darts, scent, batteries, torches (flashlights), also smoking pipes, cigarettes, toys, and lipstick. We even stole HP sauce, Marmite, pepper and just about anything that took our fancy. These are just some of the things that I remember.

None of us boys smoked or even tried to, as far as I know. Naturally, we didn't wear jewellery – nor would we dare to – so we wouldn't have

SUFFER LITTLE CHILDREN

had any need for it. We didn't play the proper game of darts; we just threw the darts up into trees and thoughtlessly left them there.

Generally speaking, we didn't dare take much of anything that we had shoplifted back to Bayfordbury – only items that we believed wouldn't attract attention. If we had anything worthwhile in our possession, then the masters would guess that such items had been stolen and easily catch on to us. Needless to say, that if we had been reported by a shopkeeper for shoplifting or found out by any of the staff at Bayfordbury, we would certainly have been justifiably severely caned.

With the exception of some of the items like the batteries and torches, and also the HP sauce, Marmite and pepper, I can't think of what we did exactly, with all of the silly contraband we swiped. As it was, we would hide the Marmite, HP sauce, pepper and the likes, inside our shirts or in our pockets, and take these 'luxury' items into the dining room at mealtimes with us. Then we would share them with the other kids and spread them on our stale or sometimes even mouldy bread.

We sprinkled the pepper on our stale bread with nothing else, not even margarine on it. Pepper was quite tasty on our porridge too, especially when there was no sugar or jam to put on that bland-tasting stuff. Baggy and Fred, who really didn't do much shoplifting, thought it was great. When we ran out of things, we merely went back to Woolworths again and got more.

From time to time boys would get caught shoplifting by the Woolworths staff. They would simply give the boy a good telling-off, or perhaps, if the staff member was a man he might even clip the boys around the ear and chase them out of the shop. (In Britain we called all stores shops.)

But chasing us out of the shop didn't help Woolworths much. We weren't really afraid of outsider girls, and would come back the following Saturday and just avoid any of the Woolworths staff who knew us.

Occasionally, one or two of the boys would get caught by the Bayfordbury staff by foolishly bringing the 'stuff' back to Bayfordbury.

The offence of shoplifting was not considered much different than from any of the other things we did wrong, and the punishment would have been no different either. It was always caning.

SUFFER LITTLE CHILDREN

I must say though, that I don't recall many of the boys being caught and punished at Bayfordbury for shoplifting.

~o~o~

As I have mentioned, we didn't really want most of the things we stole; we weren't stealing with criminal intent or for profitable gain. It was just something we did, and mostly for devilment.

I can't tell you why we would steal the cheap jewellery or scent, though I can remember that Flappers and I had a tin box with a lid – probably a biscuit tin – which we would have found at the Bayford dump.

The box was about twelve inches by twelve inches and about eight inches deep. As I recall, we took the tin box into the out-of-bounds area and dug a hole under a tree in the Tropical Gardens, and buried the tin box with some of our 'loot' in it.

I can't remember us actually ever going back to get the box or even getting the stuff out of it. It's quite possible, even quite likely, that the biscuit tin, with the Bond Street 'gold' jewellery still in it, is still wherever we hid it, that is if the tin box, or the 'gold' even, hasn't rotted away (like Bond Street jewellery just might) or some other 'thieving kid' didn't find the box and take it.

We did, however, use the torch batteries and bulbs. We would make home-made torches (flashlights) and play with them after lights out in the dormitories. By cutting out paper shapes of spiders or people, we could have shadowy puppet-type plays on the ceiling.

It was also great fun to play chasing outside in the dark with the torches before going to bed in the early spring or late autumn, particularly if the torch had a good spot beam. I'm sure we didn't give much thought to the 'blackout' rules.

As I have mentioned, Flappers and I never did get caught shoplifting while we were at Bayfordbury. We did however, eventually get caught, but not until after Bayfordbury was closed and we had all moved to Eastbourne in Sussex.

~o~o~

SUFFER LITTLE CHILDREN

To this day, some sixty or more years later, while revisiting Hertford with my wife Donna, I was emotionally moved to find that the same Woolworths is still there, in the same place and on the same street – Castle Street – in Hertford, and the shop is absolutely unchanged.

The only thing that was missing for me was that wicked sod Flappers and his rotten apprentice-in-crime, though I suppose I have to admit, one of us was there.

~°~°~ Special Outings ~°~°~

On special occasions, maybe once or twice a year, the Odeon cinema in Hertford would invite us Bayfordbury boys to come to the pictures. This was a tremendous treat for us, more so than they could possibly imagine.

There were those who, knowing our situation or social deprivation, donated time and provided much enjoyment for us Dr Barnardo kids.

The pictures that I remember we were invited to go and see were *National Velvet*, starring Elizabeth Taylor, who we all fell in love with. We also were taken to see *Lassie Come Home*, *My Friend Flicka*, and my favourite, *The North West Mounted Police*, starring Gary Cooper as Johnny.

The *North West Mounted Police* story was about Louis Riel in British Columbia.

The only other times we went to the pictures were when we dodged in. We would simply follow two adults or a group of older people into the cinema, as though we were with them.

Flappers would grab my arm, and pull me along with the people who had paid and who were going into the cinema. I feel quite sure that often the people we were 'tagging along' with, knew what we were doing, and just didn't care. The usherettes were mostly young girls and I suppose, too nice to question what was going on.

Once, in perhaps 1944, shortly before Christmas day an organisation invited us Bayfordbury boys to come to a Christmas party at the Corn Exchange. The Corn Exchange, which was situated in the centre of town, was a major administration building in Hertford.

Besides being used for other functions, the Corn Exchange was also used as the courthouse when the quarterly county assizes were held

SUFFER LITTLE CHILDREN

in Hertford. In several years to come, I was to have to attend the court there in connection with a murder trial, which one of our Barnardo boys committed. I will write more about this serious event in due course.

However, on the occasion of us attending the Christmas party at the Corn Exchange, we played a game where all of us boys, including the outsider children, had to run around the floor to music.

When the music stopped, we had to drop to the floor. The last three to sit on the floor were out and had to go and sit down.

This went on until there was just one boy or girl left. The winner would receive a prize. I remember how proud I was to be the 'last boy' left and for me to win and actually take home a puzzle. Even a puzzle was a treasure in those days for us kids.

~°~°~ My First Christmas ~°~°~

Bayfordbury was the first place that I remember, orphanage or otherwise, that I ever had had any Christmas at all. Until then, strange as it may seem, I don't think I had even heard of Christmas, or if so, it had no significance to me.

I now would have been nine years old and soon I would be ten on the 28th of December, though I didn't really know when my birthday was at the time, as I had never been told, it seems.

Actually, I had never been wished a 'happy birthday', received a birthday card or a birthday present. Nor had I ever even seen a birthday cake. Later, in about 1947, I was to learn that my birthday was on the 28th of December and that I was born in 1933. However, by then I would have been fourteen years old.

Perhaps when I was fostered in Tamworth I may have been there between Christmases and therefore didn't actually spend a Christmas or a birthday with my foster family.

Regardless, and remarkable as it is, I had, to this point in my life and to the best of my knowledge, never received any presents, or was even aware of any Christmases at all until, of all places, Bayfordbury.

Quite possibly it had something to do with the war – I really don't know – but past Christmases had come and gone without, to my knowledge, my ever realising or being told that it was Christmas.

SUFFER LITTLE CHILDREN

As it was, a month or two before Christmas in about 1943, not long after I had arrived at Bayfordbury, I remember that we were told we could go into a big room on the main floor opposite the playroom, and see the Christmas tree.

It was a huge tree, which must have been about eight to even nine feet tall, with huge branches. There were beautiful silver balls and other shiny glass trimmings on the tree, including lots of real wax candles, all of which were unlit. The tree was also draped with strands of tinsel.

On Christmas Eve we were again invited to come to the room and to stand around the tree to sing Christmas carols, which we had been taught by Mrs Dunning at Bayford School.

This time, the Christmas tree was even more decorated than the first time we had seen it. Now the candles on the tree were alight, the twinkling little flames casting flickering shadows on the walls and ceiling.

High on top of the tree was a pretty fairy in a sparkling white dress, holding a silver wand. It really seemed like a strange but wonderful Christmas, and such an exciting time to us kids.

Of course, the candles were spaced such that there was minimal chance, if any, of the tree catching fire. It all looked so nice and magical to us kids. Our excitement peaked and imaginations ran wild in anticipation as to what we would receive for a Christmas present from Father Christmas.

Tied to many of its sturdy branches were gifts, many of which were wrapped in coloured wrapping paper, all of which further intrigued us. Other presents were in plain view, like popguns, toy rifles, cap guns, colourful wooden swords, big cars, lorries and aeroplanes, lead soldiers, and lots of other exciting toys.

We had been told that all of us were to receive one present each. We had never known such a time. There were no names on any of the presents and so we didn't know who was going to get what.

That night we all went to bed knowing the next day was Christmas Day. Unknown to us, during the night someone – a master, no doubt – came into our dormitory and quietly placed a sock, full with good things, on the foot of each of our beds. It was done so quietly no one woke up until one of the boys, who had probably gone to the bucket, found his sock at the end of his bed and woke the rest of us up.

SUFFER LITTLE CHILDREN

Then the lights went on and we all were awake. It would have been pretty early in the morning still when we were pulling whatever was in our socks out including walnuts, sweets, and even pomegranates.

Almost everything would have seemed quite exotic to us, we had never seen pomegranates before.

I don't remember all of the things that were in our socks, but there may have been perhaps a small wooden toy, colouring pencils, thin paper books and other types of things like that. Most of the stuff would have been too insignificant to remember, though it wouldn't have been insignificant to us at the time. Nevertheless, it was all very exciting.

Boys were going into the other dormitories to see what the other boys had got in their stockings. There would have been lots of swapping of things, the bigger boys getting the best of the deals.

Over the course of Christmas time it seemed like the rules at Bayfordbury were relaxed a little. We could speak at the breakfast table and even walk around the dining room. Unlikely as it was, I don't think we even said Grace or prayers, and certainly no one was caned that day, even the 'wet beds'.

Generally, it seemed we could do anything we wanted to. We may not even have had to wash or brush our teeth, as no one would be there checking on us.

Just before going to church for the Christmas Day service us younger boys had to stand around the piano in the playroom and sing Christmas carols while Mr Scougall, like the reformed Mr Scrooge, played the piano.

Then off we went to Hertingfordbury Church in our usual crocodile march. When we returned to Bayfordbury we had our Christmas dinner.

What we had for dinner, I don't really remember; though it wouldn't have been chicken or I would certainly remember. However, I do remember that for 'sweet' (dessert), we had Christmas pudding. Inside the pudding, there were silver thre'penny pieces, which a few of the lucky ones got.

Later, we had our Christmas tea, which included jelly, blancmange, bread, butter, and jam. As well, there was a piece of Christmas cake for each of us.

SUFFER LITTLE CHILDREN
~o~o~ My Christmas 'Fish' ~o~o~

After tea, we all went to the room on the second floor again where the Christmas tree was. The candles were all alight again and flickering brightly, again casting their magical shadows throughout the huge oak-panelled room with its twelve-foot high ceiling.

After singing Christmas carols and spending a few minutes once again looking at the wonderful presents under and on the tree, the big moment that we had all been waiting for came.

The many days of waiting and anticipation, leading up to Christmas and the expectation of our receiving a Christmas present from Father Christmas (Santa Claus), who I don't think we even doubted existed, had really come.

Together with all of us eager boys standing near and around the tree, were Father Christmas, Mrs Scougall, and their grown-up son, all smiling and helping us enjoy the moment.

Mr Scougall's son, who like his father, was very tall, climbed up a step ladder and lifted a present off the tree and handed it to Mrs Scougall, who in turn handed it to Father Christmas. Father Christmas then called out a boy's name and number.

Then the boy would eagerly come forward and Mr Scougall, ironically now, 'dear old Father Christmas', would hand to the boy whatever present he had in his hand.

As there were most probably no actual names on the presents, I would believe that the names were simply read from a list with all of our names on it, and the boys received randomly whatever was taken off the tree.

I remember watching one of the boys receiving the popgun, which I really wanted most; another the tin lorry; and yet another, the wooden sword and so on.

Eventually, Father Christmas called out my name. Like any of the other boys, I bounded forward in great anticipation of receiving my surprise, a present just like I had dreamed of, and my first ever Christmas present.

Now it was my turn. I was going to get a real Christmas present. 'Dear old Santa Claus' had called out my name, 'Number 24, Longman'. It would have been hard to contain my excitement.

SUFFER LITTLE CHILDREN

Father Christmas smiled through his big woolly white beard and moustache and handed me the small long thin present, which was about twelve inches long. I didn't mind that it wasn't a big present; it could still be something really good, like even a penknife or a torch, even though it did feel a little on the soft side and wasn't very heavy.

Undaunted at the size and weight of the present, I was nevertheless very excited at the prospect of receiving something I had dreamed of.

Like the rest of the boys after receiving their presents, I took it into the playroom. With Baggy and Fred watching, I tore off the paper wrapping and became instantly, and profoundly disillusioned, and extremely disappointed.

What I had received for my first and only Christmas present from 'dear old Father Christmas' or otherwise rotten old Scougall, turned out to be a stuffed, shiny green, plastic-like fabric fish.

The fish was about eight inches long. It had white shirt buttons for eyes and red stitches for a mouth. It couldn't swim, it didn't wind up, nor could it do anything at all. It didn't even squeak and I couldn't eat it. It was just a silly 'dolly' fish.

To this point in my life, I don't think I had ever been so disappointed as I was at that moment. Even to this day I don't think I was ever so let down.

In all probability, some little girl in a school somewhere in Hertford had made the stuffed fish in her sewing class at school and donated it to the orphanage for, as the teacher or parent would have told her, 'a poor little orphan'.

I remember that I had tears in my eyes. It was the only present for Christmas that I was going to get. Of course, many other kids would have been very happy with their presents, and others just as disappointed as I was, but that was life.

There was much about that 'first Christmas' that was good and exciting and certainly most unforgettable. It was also, possibly and quite probably, the biggest let-down that I can remember, even to this day.

~o~o~

SUFFER LITTLE CHILDREN

We have to remember that it was wartime and that many children under other circumstances received absolutely nothing. But at that time in my life and at my age, I could only think that anything at all would have been better than a silly old green plastic fish. I remember Fred and Baggy laughing at my fish a few days later. Although I can't recall what present they each received from Father Christmas, I know it was better than my stuffed fabric fish.

It took quite a few years for me to be able to laugh at my story about the first Christmas in an orphanage that I could remember. What I did with the fish, I don't really know. Perhaps I released it into a pond somewhere, as no one else would have wanted it. But how well I remember that silly plastic fish.

~o~o~ 'Blacky' the Rook ~o~o~

Every day, early in the morning before school, summer and winter, two boys were made to get out of bed and go down to a cottage near the gatehouse to pick up the daily papers for the staff. This job was given to two different boys to do for a week or two at a time.

On one particular day, when it was Fred's and my turn to get the newspapers, a particular and memorable thing happened.

As it was, it was a cool and misty morning with lots of dew still on the ground. While we were walking through the field on the way to the cottage we heard a commotion coming from a short distance away.

The sound we could hear was a distressed squawking noise coming from inside a big old hollow oak tree. The tree was in the middle of the field next to the hedge we were walking beside, no more than about a hundred yards away.

Because it was a Saturday, we didn't need to rush to get back to Bayfordbury to catch the coach and so typically, like boys would, we decided to investigate the squawking.

We scrambled through the blackberry bushes in the hedge and ran over to the tree where the noise was coming from. Inside the hollow trunk of the big old tree, about six feet up, there was a huge black looking bird. It appeared to be caught on something.

Fred told me to climb up inside the tree and grab the bird. Fred was

SUFFER LITTLE CHILDREN

quite a bit bigger than me and quite possibly could have got stuck inside the tree, and although the bird looked pretty fierce, I agreed to do it. Fred 'bunked' me up, and I climbed up inside the tree. With Fred calling out encouragement, I grabbed the tail of the bird.

With this huge bird viciously trying to peck me, I gradually, bit by bit, pulled it gently down the inside of the trunk of the tree, until finally Fred was able to be of assistance and hold its wings together.

One way or another, the bird's wing had got slightly damaged, either when it got stuck or by me trying to free it – I really don't know. Nevertheless, it wasn't seriously hurt.

As it turned out, the bird was a big old rook. With the exception of a possibly sprained wing and a couple of broken feathers, it was in reasonably good shape.

Fred wrapped the big rook in his pullover and we brought it back to Bayfordbury and into the woodshed, where we put it temporarily into a wooden box that we found.

The woodshed was part of the main building, the area actually being called 'The Woodshed'. There was a second floor in the woodshed, with wooden stairs leading up to it. No one ever used the woodshed so, after crudely framing in the underside of the stairs and finding some chicken wire, we closed it in, forming a rather large enclosure.

We made a wire door out of some other old pieces of wood and the remaining chicken wire, and then we put 'Blacky', which is what Fred named the rook, in the cage.

For a short while Blacky looked rather sad and forlorn, but a little while later he started hopping around the cage and after squawking for a while, settled down.

We had put a crude splint on his wing, which in all probability may not have been very damaged in the first place. Regardless, its wing healed OK.

Fred and Baggy, as well as myself, would save something from our meals and there were always scraps of mouldy bread to be had. We would also save pieces of meat or fat, taking care none of the masters would see us, and wrap the scraps in paper and put them in our pockets to feed to Blacky later.

In the beginning Blacky wouldn't eat anything, so we would hold him and force the bread and meat scraps into its mouth. Then we would

SUFFER LITTLE CHILDREN

dribble spit down his throat. Eventually, Blacky ate everything we gave him.

At first Blacky was very nervous of us when we had put him in his cage, and would try to peck us with its huge beak, so of course we would approach it very cautiously. After Blacky had been with us for just a few days to perhaps a week, he was fine and acted quite friendly towards us.

It didn't take long before we could go into Blacky's cage and he would sit on our arms and squawk loudly. He didn't seem to mind being with us at all.

Then, after about six weeks or so on a particular Sunday, we went to church as usual. When, upon returning from church, Fred went to see Blacky in the woodshed, he found the door to Blacky's cage wide open and Blacky gone.

I wasn't with Fred when Fred discovered Blacky had gone. Fred came and told Baggy and me the bad news, and so we went looking for the bird. As luck would have it, there, on top of the woodshed's slated roof, we saw Blacky standing on its ridge.

Without hesitation Fred climbed up onto the slate roof, which was about twelve to fourteen feet above the ground, and tried to catch Blacky.

Slate roofs are often dangerous to walk on as the slates easily become loose and slide down the roof. That's exactly what happened on this occasion. Fred stepped on one of the loose slates and slid off the roof, falling to the ground below. Fortunately the ground was wet and muddy and Fred only broke his arm.

We took Fred to the nurse, who then sent him to the hospital in Hertford to have his broken arm set. With Fred having his arm broken and being in hospital, Baggy and I were feeling quite 'down', because as well as Fred being hurt, Blacky had escaped and, we believed, flown away and gone for ever.

Later in the evening, hoping, but certainly not expecting to see Blacky there, I went to the woodshed and looked in Blacky's cage and there, to my absolute surprise, was Blacky. I couldn't believe my eyes. He was in his cage, standing on his perch, squawking loudly, expecting to be fed.

I gave Blacky some of the bread and scraps we had kept in reserve, and closed his cage door. That was all there was to it; he was tame.

Because we didn't know anything about rooks, crows or jackdaws

SUFFER LITTLE CHILDREN

prior to our acquiring Blacky, we didn't know that such birds are easily tamed and become very friendly pets.

After Fred came home from the hospital later in the day, I told Fred the good news and from that day on we didn't put Blacky in his cage at all, but Blacky always went back there to roost at night.

We had Blacky for what seemed to be quite a long time. All the other boys knew Blacky and coaxed him to the point where he would land on just about anyone's arm. He would perch in the huge cedar trees in the front of the Bayfordbury mansion, where, it seemed, he waited for us to come home from school.

One day, after several months had passed, we came home from Ware school and Blacky wasn't there to greet us. We looked for him, but we never saw Blacky again. What happened to him, we never really knew.

We liked to believe that perhaps Blacky had reverted to the wild again and purely flew away. We never entertained the thought that a fox or the like could have killed him. We simply accepted his 'going home to the wild' as a happy ending.

~o~o~ Making Butter ~o~o~

It was at Bayfordbury that I learned how to make butter and, unknowingly at the time, buttermilk.

We never received our butter ration in the orphanages even though, like everyone else in Britain, we were entitled to it.

The staff would have our rations of butter while we ate margarine, which, though it was also rationed, was, of course, not the same thing, not that we really knew the difference.

So, for a short period of time, much like a fad, many of the boys would save their milk at breakfast or teatime. We would even 'cadge' (beg) milk from other boys and fill a 'Corona' bottle (a pint-size pop bottle) to about two thirds full.

We would then add to the milk a small amount of salt, which was easy to come by, and then put the stopper on the end. Corona bottles came with their own stopper attached to the bottle with a wire clasp.

After that, it was just a matter of constantly shaking the bottle of milk which, needless to say, was quite tiring. When we were eventually

SUFFER LITTLE CHILDREN

tired out and couldn't shake it any more, we would roll the bottle on the grass. We would do this too for several hours altogether.

Eventually a small lump of butter would form and then get bigger, much like a snowball collects more snow when it's rolled on the ground, though the process is much slower.

After about two days of intermittently rolling the bottle when we had time, the lump of butter would grow to about a third of the size of the inside of the bottle. The rest of the milk and salt would become buttermilk.

The only problem was how to get the butter out of the narrow-necked bottle.

It would have been very difficult to break the neck off the bottle without getting fragments of glass in the butter, plus we wouldn't be able to use the bottle again, so that wouldn't be a good idea.

So one of the boys came up with the ingenious but simple idea of how to get the butter out of the narrow-necked bottle.

The idea was: one would basically tie a button onto a piece of string or strong cotton thread, and then drop it down inside the narrow neck of the bottle, wiggling it around until it sunk below the butter. Then we simply pulled up the button, and with it came blobs of butter. The butter wouldn't come out in one piece, of course; it came out in dribs and drabs, blob by blob. We ate the butter straight out of the bottle, or even on bread we had saved purposely from the dining room.

We drank the salty, watery milk remains, though at that time we had never heard of buttermilk and I wasn't to hear it called that for several years or so in the future and after I had moved to Canada to live.

~o~o~ Doodlebugs ~o~o~

In 1944 the war was still raging in Europe and throughout many parts of the world. German planes were still coming over to bomb London and industrial targets in the other major towns and cities throughout Britain. However, because the battlefronts were mostly concentrated in Europe, air raids didn't occur so often, and certainly they were not so intense.

But by now, the Germans had invented a new and even more frightening weapon. The V-1 rockets, which we called 'doodlebugs' or 'buzz

SUFFER LITTLE CHILDREN

bombs', were the concern of mostly Londoners and those living in the southern counties of England. The V-2 rockets were to come a little later and were even more terrifying.

The doodlebug engines had an unmistakeable droning sound of their own, and quite unlike the sound of a German or any other aeroplane. Almost everyone could distinguish the sound between a German, and a British or American aeroplane.

However, the sound of a doodlebug was different again. It had a throbbing sound, which was very distinguishable from any other flying machine.

While one could actually hear the engine of a doodlebug there was no need to be overly afraid. However, when the engines stopped, that was the time to have to worry.

After a doodlebug's engine stopped, the huge flying bomb as it was, dropped like a stone and exploded on impact, covering quite an extensive area, damaging or destroying anything within a quarter of a mile. Besides being a formidable and dangerous weapon, it was also psychologically effective.

From the time the engine of a doodlebug stopped, and until it reached the ground and exploded, there wouldn't be time to run to the air raid shelters.

We were taught, as the result of special drills, to drop immediately to the ground and to lie down flat, face down, and wait for the imminent explosion. We were also told that if the bomb was close enough, we must not raise our heads until the debris had settled. For the most part the doodlebugs were destined for London and generally missed small towns like Ware.

On one memorable occasion, on a particularly hot sunny day while we were at Ware School, a doodlebug must have malfunctioned in some way, because while we were out of our classrooms and in the playground having our morning break, we heard its now familiar sound.

As it was, we heard the doodlebug overhead, but before we fully realised it the flying bomb exploded high up, right over Ware school.

We didn't have time to drop to the ground. The explosion was deafening. Some of the debris fell on the road near the playground but no one, to my knowledge, was hurt.

SUFFER LITTLE CHILDREN

It was said afterwards that perhaps the doodlebug had overheated or had had an electrical problem in some way. In either event, it was a very close call.

On another occasion, a doodlebug landed in the woods near Bayfordbury – the same woods we used to pass through on the way to Bayford School. The woods would not have been more than a quarter of a mile from the Bayfordbury mansion.

The blast from the doodlebug blew out most of the windows on one side of the mansion, and many trees were blown down. The glassless window openings were boarded up for several weeks after that.

Most of the mansion, in fact the entire mansion, was shrouded in darkness, day and night for several days, until the electricity was restored again.

Again, no one was hurt in either of these explosions, but drills were intensified. I, having grown up unaware of the dangers of war, was now a little older and so, of course, worried somewhat more at the prospect of a doodlebug actually hitting the orphanage or Ware School.

Actually I don't believe the Germans would have intended to waste their doodlebug bombs like the two we encountered, on schools and orphanages. The doodlebugs that had come close to landing on us, like most of them that had been sent over from France, were for the most part intended for London.

I believe those doodlebugs, like many others, had just gone off course, or overshot their mark. Hertford and Ware are located about ten to fifteen miles from the outskirts of the London suburbs.

~o~o~

There were two cinemas in Hertford: the Gaumont and the Castle. On another occasion, a doodlebug or perhaps a V-2 rocket, which did do damage and cost lives, was the one that landed on the Castle cinema, located right in the centre of Hertford and just a stone's throw from our favourite 'shopping' place, Woolworths. The cinema was severely damaged and so it was closed until after the war. Sadly, during one of our visits to Hertford in 1994, we found that the Castle cinema had since been demolished, and now there is no evidence that the cinema was ever there.

SUFFER LITTLE CHILDREN
~o~o~ John Thomas and the Mouse ~o~o~

Stealing from one another was not a common, or a wise practice, for at least two reasons. The first reason was that there was nothing other boys had that another boy wanted enough to risk getting caught stealing it. The only things a so-inclined boy may have risked stealing were perhaps sweets and other such treats, sent to some more fortunate boys by parents or other family members.

The second reason, which in fact would have been of more concern, would be that if a boy was caught stealing from another boy and the other boys found out, the offender would be shamed or beaten up by his peers and severely caned by Mr Scougall if he, too, found out.

We had a theory amongst us boys, which was really quite simple. If one had something worth stealing, then give it to the boy who one might expect to steal it, and let him look after the item for you. Then he just couldn't steal it.

~o~o~

One morning at breakfast, Mr Scougall detected an argument between two boys and asked the reason. Reluctantly I'm sure, one of the boys, Brian Pain, responded to Mr Scougall's questions and accused a boy named John Thomas of stealing one of his mice.

Yes, that was his name: John Thomas. Some time or several years in the future, we were to call a certain appendage to our bodies affectionately by the name of 'John Thomas', but I won't bother to mention anything further about that in this particular story.

As I started to say, John Thomas was accused of stealing one of Pain's mice, and while doing so, accidentally killing two more.

Apparently, Brian Pain kept white mice in the top drawer of his bedside table. Several boys had pet mice and most of them also kept their mice and rats in their bedside table drawers. This was quite a common and an acceptable thing to do. In fact, Bayfordbury seemed to approve of the practice.

Of course, the boys let the mice breed and they did, just as mice do. Some of the boys would trade their mice or give them away as favours

SUFFER LITTLE CHILDREN

or for one reason or another. It was simply a small-time 'pet trade' business. No one seemed to care that these mice would often get away and join the wild mouse population.

Anyway, someone had apparently slid open the top drawer of Pain's bedside table and taken one of his mice. When whoever it was closed the drawer, two other mice were looking over the front edge of the drawer, looking to see what was going on, or even planning to escape.

When the drawer was closed, perhaps rather quickly because perhaps someone was coming, their heads got caught in the top edge of the drawer and they were both killed.

Brian Pain believed Thomas was the one who took his mouse and also caused the death of the other two. Unfortunately for Thomas, they were arguing about the whole thing, when Mr Scougall heard them.

Mr Scougall called Thomas up to the back of the dining room, right beside where Fred, Baggy, and I were sitting, to question him and ultimately punish him.

Mr Scougall, his monstrous frame towering over Thomas, said to him in his typically booming voice, "You stole Pain's mouse, Thomas, didn't you?"

"No, Sir," answered Thomas defensively.

"And when you closed the drawer, you killed two others, didn't you, Thomas?" persisted Mr Scougall.

Thomas was obviously frightened. He knew he was going to be caned and there was nothing he could do. His situation was hopeless; he wasn't going to be able to convince Mr Scougall otherwise. Mr Scougall had already judged Thomas and found him guilty.

"I didn't, Sir, I didn't. CROSS MY HEART, I DIDN'T," Thomas insisted, desperately pleading his innocence.

Mr Scougall then with a smile said, "CROSS YOUR ARSE, YOU DID!" and then instructed another boy to go and get his cane.

Thomas had pleaded his innocence to no avail, and was caned severely. All caning was severe; there was no rational or reasonable way of us being caned by Mr Scougall. We were caned much like one would beat a carpet to clean the dust and grit out.

Whether Thomas actually did steal Pain's mouse, I never knew, but it didn't matter – Mr Scougall was convinced that he did, and that was

SUFFER LITTLE CHILDREN

that. He was the law of the orphanage and there was absolutely no reasoning with him and or any possible appeal.

But what had made this incident so unforgettable was the fact that Mr Scougall had said a swear-word. Swearing was a capital offence for us and no boy would dare to swear. For several days later, lots of boys recalled Mr Scougall's swearing, with a degree of amazement.

~º~º~ Mr Scougall's Humour ~º~º~

Mr Scougall had a sardonic sense of humour. He would commonly tell jokes and ridicule boys who were to be caned or punished in front of the rest of us. We would laugh at his jokes, afraid to let him see us not laughing. But mostly the jokes he told were to amuse himself or his staff, and we wouldn't understand them. But we would laugh anyway.

Once in a while he would tell us a joke or two, a couple of which I can still remember and even now still find a little humorous.

One of the jokes, which he told during an assembly in the playroom one day when we were having to show our toothbrushes, combs etc, was about the old man who was sleepwalking.

He said:

> "An old man was sleepwalking, with his arms outstretched in front of him and spread slightly apart in the classic sleepwalking fashion. As he walked, he came upon a door, which was open about halfway. The old man's arms were such that the open edge of the door went between his outstretched arms and as he walked forward, the edge of the door bumped him on the nose. 'Ouch,' exclaimed the old man, waking up, 'That's the first time I've realised that my nose is longer than my arms'."

Mr Scougall was an unpredictable man. We could never know how he would be each day, or even hour by hour.

Every Saturday morning after breakfast we would all assemble in the playroom, and he would address us.

SUFFER LITTLE CHILDREN

Sometimes he was jolly and joking, and at other times he would bring boys forward and, in a furious rage, punish them in front of the rest of us, which naturally made us all very nervous most of the time we were anywhere near him.

Unpredictable as he was, it was at these times that he told us jokes. Another joke he told was about a mouse – a joke that we all genuinely laughed at, and which we repeated to each other and to the outsiders at Ware School.

The joke was about a little mouse that had just escaped from being caught by a big fat cat in this big old house. In running away from the fat cat, the little mouse came across a glass of beer sitting on a table in another room. The mouse was so thirsty from running that it swallowed the entire glass of beer down in one gulp.

The next moment the mouse was bending its little arms and flexing its little muscles and shouting in a drunken stupor, "Now bring out that darn cat; I'll eat him alive!"

But joking with us kids was not the normal way we would remember Mr Scougall. They were just lighter moments during a rather fearful time in my childhood.

~o~o~ Organised Unfair Sharing ~o~o~

Our sweet ration was shared out in a rather unfair manner. Most sweets were either toffees or hard-boiled sweets. The method of distributing them, which occurred on Saturday mornings during our assembly, was that Mr Scougall would call out the older boys first in their age groups, just as was the normal method at mealtimes.

The older and therefore naturally bigger boys would file up to a table in front of Mr Scougall, then one by one they would reach into a large open bowl or basin and grab a handful of sweets.

As would be expected, big boys would have big hands and small boys would, of course, have small hands. Each of us was required to put our hands, with fingers down, into the bowl and grab whatever amount of sweets we could in one grab. We were not allowed to turn our hands over. Any that we dropped back into the bowl, we didn't get. This was our share of the sweets and that would be all we would get.

SUFFER LITTLE CHILDREN

Most times the bigger boys would get eight to ten sweets in one grab, depending on the size of the sweets, whereas Baggy, Flappers and I, and all the little kids like us, would get only four or five sweets.

Fred would fare a little better than us and get perhaps six or even seven sweets. We would always compare how many each of us got and commonly grumble.

Sometimes during their respective harvesting seasons, boys would be selected to go into the 'out-of-bounds' areas, though chestnuts grew almost everywhere, and collect the ripened chestnuts, which had fallen to the ground.

Then they would be shared out in the same unfair 'dip and grab' method, the bigger boys getting a bigger share, just like how our sweet ration was shared.

Without anyone's permission we would often go to these out-of-bounds chestnut trees and collect our own chestnuts, but we made sure we didn't get caught.

~o~o~ Conkers ~o~o~

We would play a game simply called 'conkers', which entailed breaking each other's conkers. We were not unique in playing this game. It was played by schoolboys throughout Britain in those days and quite possibly still is.

Conkers, otherwise known as horse chestnuts, grow profusely in Britain. They grow on common land and are easy to obtain.

To play the game, first we would make a hole through the middle of a horse chestnut with a nail or a meat skewer. After tying a knot in one end of a piece of string or perhaps a shoelace, we would then thread the string through the hole in the conker. That was it; we were ready to challenge our peers to a game of conkers.

The challenged boy would then hold up, or 'dangle' his conker, while the other boy tried to smash and break the other boy's conker, by swinging his and hitting his opponent's conker with it.

If we broke the other boy's conker, our conker became a 'oner' or a 'twoer', depending on how many competitors' conkers it broke. If, for instance you were playing against a conker which was already a sixer,

SUFFER LITTLE CHILDREN

and your conker was already a threer and you won, yours would then become a tenner.

I remember too, boys would hit each other's knuckles, which, if it happened a couple of times, could well result in a fight.

12

BAYFORDBURY – Part 6

~o~o~ Chilblains and Chaps ~o~o~

In the windy, chilly autumn, when the cool and damp mornings made us shiver and want to hug the hot radiators in the otherwise cold basement corridors of Bayfordbury, we were still made to go outside to play.

Generally speaking there was nowhere in this huge mansion that we lived in and called home that we were allowed to go to during the daytime, summer or winter, unless it was either raining or on special occasions.

On those cold and miserable days, if no one like the masters or matron were looking, we would huddle around the hot radiators, putting our hands on them to get them warm.

Chilblains were a common problem amongst us boys, particularly at Bayfordbury, it seems. We were constantly being told not to put our hands on the radiators. This practice, together with the wind and dampness was, we were told, the major cause of chilblains.

Chilblains would make our fingers swell, and eventually the skin on our knuckles would crack and bleed.

If we were seen with our hands in our short-trouser pockets we would also get into trouble, and if we were told too often, our pockets would be sewn up. We wore nothing on our heads and had no scarves or gloves.

On top of this, when we showered and dried ourselves with the bare thread towels that were provided us, the towels would not dry us, and so we would develop 'chaps'.

We were told, which I believe we knew, that the chaps were the result of us not drying ourselves properly after showering, which was probably true. But because the bigger boys, who showered before us, would swipe our towels and dry themselves on them while we were still showering, the towels would already be wet through by the time we came to dry ourselves.

SUFFER LITTLE CHILDREN

Combined with the fact that we wore only short trousers, summer and winter, we became very exposed to getting severe chaps. The cold winds during the late autumn and throughout the winter months would play havoc on our legs.

Our short-trouser legs stopped about two inches above our knees. This is where the chaps occurred, with the short-trouser legs constantly rubbing against our bare legs.

The skin on our legs would become red and raw as the result of the chaps, making us walk with our legs apart in a futile effort to stop the shorts from touching our now painfully chapped legs.

A big tin of 'chap ointment' was provided for us to put on our chaps and chilblains. This ointment worked really well and very quickly the chaps and chilblains healed.

Unfortunately, as soon as the chilblains and the chaps healed, we forgot about them and again continued to warm our cold hands and feet on the radiators.

Because we didn't or couldn't dry ourselves, again, for the same reasons as before, the cycle repeated itself and the chilblains and chaps would return time and time again throughout the autumn, winter and early spring. The problem was a constant cycle, and we didn't have the will to keep our hands off the radiators, and so help prevent the chilblains from coming back.

~o~o~

It would have been during those winter months of chaps and chilblains that Baggy, Fred, Flappers and I would have been about ten going on eleven years old. When thinking back to those days, it seems that this was the same time that we were beginning to realise that we could make our hair look nice.

So, by combing our hair using the carbolic soap we washed and showered with, and water, we could slick our hair down and make big waves in it. Slicked down hair or wavy hair was the fashion for men and boys at the time.

The outsider boys would put nice-smelling Brylcream in their hair, and it would stay slicked down or hold a wave for most of the day,

SUFFER LITTLE CHILDREN

whereas ours, by using just soap and water would only stay nice until it dried, and then it would dry hard and set solid, like it was a mould.

Not being able to buy Brylcream and if we didn't shoplift it, we would sometimes substitute the Brylcream with the chap ointment and smear that on our hair. The white chap ointment even looked like Brylcream, and despite the fact that it smelled like we had just come from the sick bay, it worked well and kept our hair tidy too.

I can hardly believe it as I write, but you must believe me that if there wasn't any chap ointment, we sometimes even put our rations of margarine or even pork dripping in our hair. As it didn't look any different than if we used Brylcream, it was great for us. We were quite oblivious of the fact that it probably smelt terrible, thus solidifying our persona of being 'scruffy little urchins'.

I don't recall any of our teachers or masters telling us about our hair looking any different than the outsider boys, or that it smelt objectionable at all, and I doubt that our outsider peers dared, because that too, may have started a fight.

We were continually being told not to use the chap ointment on our hair by the Bayfordbury masters, basically because the ointment would run out and become in short supply. I would suppose now that the chap ointment could have been rather expensive as well.

~o~o~ Beating (for Hunters) ~o~o~

In the late autumn when typically the weather is cool, damp and often rainy, most of us, including the younger and older boys, would be told we were required to go 'beating'.

Beating is a countryside activity where lords and ladies, estate owners and the very rich would hire local villagers for the day to beat the bushes and flush out game such as rabbits and hares, pheasants, partridge and the likes, for them to shoot.

By our living on the Bayfordbury estate we were a convenient source of child labour for just this job.

If the 'beating' was to take place away from Bayfordbury, we would be driven by coach or in cars to the selected location. But most often the beating or hunting 'meet' would take place on the Bayfordbury estate or

SUFFER LITTLE CHILDREN

on an adjacent property, where we would have to walk to.

At about five thirty in the morning on a predetermined Saturday we would get up, have our breakfast and assemble outside in the brisk early morning air, rain or shine, and wait for our instructions.

Beating, it seemed, always coincided with the time of the year when our chaps and chilblains were seriously hurting us. Walking in the wet undergrowth amongst the thorny blackberry canes and stinging nettles, and scrambling through hawthorn hedges, was not much fun either.

To add to our misery, the rabbits and pheasants often hid in the stinging nettles and amongst the bramble bushes, where we were instructed that we should make an extra effort to flush out the game.

Rubbing against stinging nettles or scratching our chapped legs on the hawthorn bushes was painful, and could, of course, make 'beating' quite miserable.

If any of us boys were not careful, we could easily get soaking wet stumbling into the water-filled ditches, something which could only add to our already miserable time on certain occasions.

What with cuts and stings on top of the constant pain caused by our chaps and chilblains, and also being cold, and soaked to the skin when it rained, we found that 'beating' wasn't all fun.

I well remember that I would get chilled to the bone walking through the dripping woods, particularly so if I was the one instructed to stand at the edge of the woods, where the bramble bushes grew, or in the corner of an open field, with no protection from the wind and rain.

Sometimes it would rain and be windy all day, with no let-up. Having no raincoats or weather protection of any kind, we would often get soaked to the skin.

Lady Clinton Baker's gamekeeper would be in charge of the beaters and organise the day of beating for the 'small game' hunting. He, too, wore thick corduroy breaches, much like the gentry we were beating for.

Like a gamekeeper would, he wore a traditional floppy country-type hat with a big pheasant feather in it.

It would be the gamekeeper's decision, depending on the availability of game, if, and on what part of the estate, the hunt would take place.

Following the gamekeeper, who no doubt would have studied the game situation, we would always, it seemed, walk to the furthest

SUFFER LITTLE CHILDREN

boundary of the Bayfordbury estate, through the wet grass, to a field or the woods as had been predetermined by him, and that would be where the beating would start. We would probably cover approximately three to four hundred acres in a single meet.

The arrangements or plan was simple. One or two boys would be sent to the corners of the wood or field. Once in position, they would be required to just stand there and keep tapping or banging a corner fence post or a tree with a stick, and generally making a noise. These 'corner boys', were instructed to keep shouting and constantly make as much noise as possible. This would help stop the game from 'doubling back' or running off to the side.

As for the rest of us boys, beating required that we went to the outer edge of the woods and spread out in a long single line, about fifteen to twenty feet apart, and then walk forward, banging the bushes and tapping the trees and, just like the other boys, making as much noise as we could.

As was the intent, the beaters would flush any game such as rabbits, hares, pheasants, partridge, woodcocks and even pigeons out of their natural hiding places, and head them in the direction of the 'shooters'. As many as eight to ten or even more shooters or otherwise gentry with shotguns would be waiting to shoot the game as it came within range.

The shooters were made up of local landowners, lords and ladies, and the 'upper class gentlemen' from London.

They would come to Bayfordbury in their big luxurious cars: Rolls Royces, Bentleys and the likes, which would make Mr Scougall's little Austin look pretty small. From time to time they would simply meet us Bayfordbury boys at a predetermined estate or hunting place.

Each of the gentry would be dressed in hunting breeches, tweed jackets, and heavy hunting cloaks. They would also have riding boots and sporty-looking hats, and carry hunting sticks (portable seats). Most, if not all of them, would bring their own servants or 'gun bearers' for the day.

The 'shooters' would be organised by the gamekeeper and positioned about twenty feet apart in such a way that as the 'flushed game' came past them they would shoot it, and their trained dogs would instantly fetch the 'bagged' game. For safety's sake, they were not supposed to fire in front of themselves, in our direction.

SUFFER LITTLE CHILDREN

Their gun bearers or servants, would carry their employer's accessories, load and reload the shotguns, and also direct the dogs.

Some of the servants or gun bearers would handle two guns: one for birds, and the other for the bigger game such as rabbits and hares. We would see the gentry drinking from their brandy flasks. For them it was as much a party day as a hunting day.

Whether it was because of the brandy or simple carelessness, we wouldn't have known, but some of the gentry were not as careful of where they fired their shotguns as may be expected, especially after a few drinks.

On one occasion that I remember, a boy actually did get shot. A rabbit or hare ran out in front of one of the shooters, who in turn must have swung around and fired, hitting one of the boys in the leg.

Hearing that a boy had been shot, we all went over to where the boy was, expecting him to be dead. When we were kids we believed that everything or anybody who got shot would automatically die. That's how it was with us 'cowboys and Indians', and in the pictures we saw.

Actually, the boy only had a couple of pellets, or 'shot', in his leg, so he was sent back to Bayfordbury for attention. We didn't hear any more about it, so I suppose he was all right afterwards. The lord or whoever accidentally shot the boy may well have given him sixpence, and that was the end of it – Bayfordbury probably took half, so the boy would wind up with only thre'pence, if he was lucky.

We would stop beating at about noon to have lunch. The orphanage would pack sandwiches for us boys, which were fine. We got what we expected: bread and jam or even bread and 'dripping'. Dripping is the fat that comes out of a beef or pork roast and left in the bottom of the roasting pan.

Almost everyone ate dripping in those days and just about everybody liked it. I don't know where our dripping actually came from, though I would expect that it was donated to us by the local restaurants or the likes. A big container of water was provided for us to drink, with about ten tin cups between the thirty to forty of us.

The gentry's servants, on the other hand, would set up portable tables with white tablecloths, wine glasses, salt and pepper shakers and sauces etc. Their food was arranged buffet-style for themselves. To us it looked like a 'posh' banquet.

SUFFER LITTLE CHILDREN

Although we were kept well away from them, we could see what they were having to eat. They had delicacies like chicken or pheasant legs, pork pies, and other types of savoury pies and pasties. They too would have sandwiches, although theirs were somewhat better than ours: they had no crusts on the bread and were cut into delicate little triangles. They would also have fruit such as apples and pears and oranges.

The slices of bread our sandwiches were made with were commonly called 'doorsteps' – very thick slices of bread, about three quarters to an inch thick. The primary reason for giving us such thick bread was to cut down on the amount of margarine or dripping etc needed to make a sandwich. Also, doorsteps would fill us growing boys up more quickly.

When the gentry had finished with their meal, their gun bearers or servants had their fill. After that, they would invite us to finish off their leftovers.

It disturbs me now to remember how the gentry and their servants seemed amused by our enthusiastic rush to get their scraps. I don't think they could remotely believe the difference between the poor quality of the food we ate and the food that they brought to the hunting event.

~o~o~

Later in the afternoon the gentry would have tea, 'Camp' coffee, or other hot drinks, but we wouldn't have anything until tea time. Usually we wouldn't get back home to Bayfordbury until some time after six in the evening, around the time it was getting dark.

If it rained the gun bearers would hold umbrellas over their respective employers, which would have made it all a little more bearable for the 'shooters', while we boys continued walking and beating, all the time constantly being soaked to the skin.

Depending upon how much game there was, the beating would go on until dusk – rain or shine. We would be quite tired towards the end of the day. After all, we had been walking, shouting and beating the bushes and trees all through the day, from about six or six thirty in the morning.

For the gentry and their servants etc it wasn't so bad – they had had refreshments during the afternoon. But we boys, having had nothing

SUFFER LITTLE CHILDREN

to eat since midday, would be absolutely ravenous. Such activity for us young boys, including stomping through the woods and fields, and knowing the adults were eating and drinking, certainly made us envious to say the least.

It was something of a relief when the gamekeeper eventually declared the day over.

The lords and the other dignitaries would then divide up the game between them. They would choose the pheasants or partridge they wanted, while their gun bearers would tie the bird's legs together as a 'brace'. Rabbits and hares were also tied together similar to the birds, and taken to their respective owners' cars.

I would believe that those hunting would have had to pay or donate money to Dr Barnardo's Homes for our services. This, together with the fee paid to Lady Clinton Baker, would make it quite an expensive day out for them.

It was, notwithstanding the discomfort we may have suffered during the day, a good day for us though, as we received perhaps sixpence a day from Dr Barnardo's for our services. The money was kept for us by Mr Scougall and given to us as pocket money, which we would take to the Hertford Spring Fair. The spring fair was always held in May, on 'May Day'.

Sometimes we would go beating for as much as five, or even six times during the course of the autumn beating season and, if we were lucky, earn as much as three shillings, which was quite a lot of money for us Dr Barnardo kids in those days.

Beating, nevertheless, would get quite tiring, and was never as much fun after the third or fourth time in the season as it was the first or second time. However, we had no choice, and simply went beating whenever we were told to.

~o~o~ Summer Living at Bayfordbury ~o~o~

During our summer holidays from Ware School there was a different routine at Bayfordbury that I should mention. Mr Scougall would tell us all to clean our boots and put them under our beds. We never wore running shoes, or 'plimsolls', as they were called. Such shoes were thought to be bad for a growing child's feet.

SUFFER LITTLE CHILDREN

All through the summer months, from when the outsiders' schools closed and until we returned to school again in early September, we wouldn't wear our boots, except for church and special occasions. The object was to save money on our boot repairs.

It was also a rule that we would only wear our shirts when we were told we could, which again was for going to church and other special occasions. Our summer shorts were made of light cotton, which had a single strip of elastic in the top to hold them up. They were all navy blue.

Because there weren't any buttons on our cotton shorts for the braces to hold the underpants up, we didn't wear underpants either.

With austerity as a prime objective, and also because of the war rationing on all clothes, including boots (we never ever wore shoes), we ran around all through the summer more than half naked.

And so, during the entire summer, we would get up in the mornings, wash, brush our teeth and then come to breakfast without boots, socks or shirts and dressed only in our navy blue cotton shorts.

Occasionally the elastic in our shorts would break, or stretch to the point that it wouldn't hold our cotton shorts up, so then we would have to tie string around our waists.

~o~o~ Outdoor Dining ~o~o~

It was Bayfordbury's policy that during the two summer months of July and August, while we were on our summer holidays, we didn't eat in the dining room at all, even in the mornings, if at all possible.

In fact, we only ate inside if it was raining, but that would have meant bringing all the tables and benches in, which would have been quite a lot of work even though there were lots of hands to do it.

So for the most part we would suffer any small amount of drizzle and, generally speaking, always eat outside during the summer. I can't really remember when we ever ate in the dining room during the summer holidays, though we probably did from time to time.

Eating outside had its good points and bad points. While we were eating outside the cleaning up wasn't so bad. We only had to pick up some of the bits and pieces of food from off the grass – a task which was much simpler than having to sweep or wash the dining room floor.

SUFFER LITTLE CHILDREN

We could, when none of the masters were looking, throw pieces of fat and other food that we wanted to get rid of far enough away from the tables not to be noticed. Badgers, hedgehogs and other animals would clear up any scraps during the nights, if they weren't eaten up first by the birds.

Once a week, all the tables and benches would be picked up and moved about thirty feet. That way we would have a new dining room floor every week.

But there were several real 'down sides' to this outside, or 'summer picnicking'. Sometimes dining outside was quite uncomfortable. Eating outside in the often constant drizzling rain, sitting on wet benches and trying to keep our bread from being soaked wasn't the fun it might seem to be.

With the sun blazing down during midsummer, flies, wasps, hornets and other insects would become a constant nuisance. The insects, competing for our food, regularly landed on it, and from time to time stung us.

Being outside from dawn to dusk, many of us would become quite sunburned. The sunburn would invariably turn into huge sun blisters, covering our shoulders and backs. We would break the blisters ourselves, resulting in lots of water-type fluid draining out.

If we went to the nurse, which most often we didn't, she would prick the big blisters and put calamine lotion on the rest, which, to some extent, provided some relief from the itching.

With or without the calamine lotion, our skin would peel and we would look much like snakes when they're shedding their skin. After we had finished peeling, we wouldn't blister again that summer.

Big, commercial-sized jam jars, half filled with water, with a little jam around the rim and down the inside of the jars, were put in the centre of each of the tables. It didn't take long for the jars to be infested with wasps and the occasional hornet.

The hornets were the insects we were most concerned about. We were told by the older boys that a sting from a hornet could kill a horse, so we didn't take the threat of hornets lightly.

Ants, spiders, and flies were basically a nuisance, but wasps and hornets were of more concern.

On one occasion, one of the boys was eating his bread and jam, when

SUFFER LITTLE CHILDREN

a wasp landed on his jam just as he was putting it into his mouth. The wasp stung him inside his mouth, and he had to be rushed to the hospital in Hertford. The boy came home later and though his mouth was quite swollen, he was otherwise OK.

~o~o~ Raiding Wasp and Hornet's Nests ~o~o~

Raiding wasp or hornet's nests was always a challenge. We would dare each other to push a stick into their nest if the nest was inside a tree; or if it was outside of the tree and attached to a branch, we would dare each other to climb the tree and go out onto the branch to knock it down. Climbing a tree to get at a hornet's nest was particularly risky, as it wasn't so easy to get away if they attacked. A wasp's nest was a different matter, but we were still very cautious.

Many times those stinging insects would actually chase us, and we would run away laughing. We often got stung and it really hurt, but we gave each other no sympathy and would invariably laugh at each other for getting stung, and still continued raiding the nests.

~o~o~ Swimming in the River Lee ~o~o~

On particularly hot days, a master or sometimes a senior fifteen or sixteen-year-old boy would take us to the River Lee to go swimming.

We would walk barefoot in a 'crocodile march', keeping over to the side of the road, out of the way of traffic travelling on the rather narrow road from Hertford to St Albans.

The black soft asphalt on the road was often very hot on our bare feet, and if we stepped on a stone or anything hard or sharp, it hurt the soles, sometimes making them bleed.

As we walked, we would scuff the tops of our big toes and they too would often bleed. But we would bear the discomfort and I can't remember that we minded the walk too much. Certainly we didn't complain, because we were going swimming.

The scuffing of our unprotected toes, now that I recall, showed clearly on the tops of our boots when we were wearing them. The tops of our boots always showed lots of wear, caused, no doubt, by our not picking

SUFFER LITTLE CHILDREN

our feet up when we walked.

The road which ran beside the River Lee was full of twists and turns, and even though it was the main road between Hertford and St Albans it was also, like most roads in England at the time, quite narrow.

Our walk to the part of the river that we swam in was about two to three miles from Bayfordbury, but we eagerly walked it without concern or complaint, in anticipation of going swimming. Swimming, or merely going to the river, was a big treat for us.

The cars, coaches and the No. 341 double-decker buses would slow down as they passed us, and the passengers would wave and smile at us as they passed and we would wave back enthusiastically.

By the time we got to the place to swim we would be thirsty, and with the sun beating down on our heads and bare backs, we couldn't wait to get into the river.

The River Lee was a clean, fast-moving river for the most part, dotted with big stones, but it mostly had a smooth, sandy bottom.

At a bend in the river – the spot where we were always taken to to go swimming – there were long wavy weeds drifting in a rather slow, lazy current. There were also plenty of minnows and sticklebacks and other small fish in the river, which we would chase and try, unsuccessfully, to catch.

After we arrived at the place where we could go bathing, we would take off our shorts, which were all we had on, and swim completely naked in the river.

The buses and cars would, it seemed, slow down to watch us bathing. Instinctively we would lie down in the river to hide ourselves, though we weren't really overly bashful about being seen. There had never been any privacy in our lives and we didn't react too much to curious passers-by.

The river wasn't under any circumstances dangerous, and wasn't really deep enough for us to be able to actually swim in, but that didn't stop us from being able to completely submerge ourselves.

I remember the water being so clear that we would drink it from our cupped hands any time we liked, with absolutely no concern. After all, this was the same river that our watercress, which we were served for our Sunday tea, came out of.

SUFFER LITTLE CHILDREN

After we had swam long enough, or when whoever was in charge of us decided, we would put our shorts back on and then walk back to Bayfordbury again. We didn't have towels to dry ourselves with.

Following such a walk to go swimming, and there were many such trips, we would naturally be very hungry and ready for our tea.

But often, even during these memorable and happy times, there was still a blanket of misery hanging over some of us from time to time. Sometimes we were, as the result of some minor thing we had done wrong earlier, required to go to bed without any tea.

Having to go to bed without our tea would, of course, be particularly upsetting, seeing that we would be so hungry after swimming and having walked all the way to the swimming spot and back.

Other boys, or friends of those boys who had been punished and sent to bed and who would miss their tea, would save them something from their own tea, or whatever they could scrounge from other boys, and bring it to the dormitory when they came to bed later.

It's hard to realise now, but I still remember well how good those crusts and scraps of bread tasted on such occasions when I was made to miss my tea, particularly after going swimming earlier.

Only those boys sent to bed early without any tea were allowed to go to their dormitories before bedtime. If a boy was caught in a dormitory without permission, he would be automatically sent to bed as a punishment. However, there were boys who, out of love or fondness for their pets, still risked going to their dormitories to feed or see their mice and rats.

~o~ Bayfordbury and Dr Barnardo Songs ~o~

If we were going somewhere on the coach, like Ware School, or when we were walking in a crocodile march to go swimming or somewhere like that, we would often sing songs. Many of them were all about Dr Barnardo's Homes and so only sung by us Dr Barnardo kids.

We would, led by any one of us boys who just wanted to sing, spontaneously sing the songs about our way of life in Barnardo's. One such song went as follows:

SUFFER LITTLE CHILDREN

There is a mouldy shack on Bayford hill,
  Where we get 'goshy' grub, that makes us ill.
Eggs and bacon we don't see,
  We get sawdust in our tea,
And we are gradually, fading away.

The reference to Bayford was not really referring to the village of Bayford exactly. It was simply that 'Bayfordbury' would not fit the song. Bayfordbury was actually in the parish of Bayford.

Another one of those songs that we sang, which sounds a little like it was sung in defiance of our keepers, was really a song acknowledging the fellowship of our own unique society. These songs were accepted by Dr Barnardo's Homes and the staff as being harmless, and were never, to my knowledge, suppressed. There were more verses to this song but this is all I can still remember:

Come to Barnardo's, make no delay,
  Just round the corner, you'll find the way,
Sitting on the doorstep, eating mouldy cheese,
  Come to Barnardo's Homes.

Almost without exception new boys, just as soon as they arrived at Bayfordbury, would learn these songs, including others, and be able to sing them in just a short while after arriving. There were several such songs. None of them had any 'rude' inferences. This would not have been allowed.

Many of the songs, which were perhaps no more than just a chorus of a song, and there were many, were the same in other Dr Barnardo's homes, though some were unique to the particular orphanage we lived in.

~o~o~ American Soldiers ~o~o~

Not too far from us there was an American army base. The base must have been fairly close to Bayfordbury, though we didn't really see much of the Americans.

SUFFER LITTLE CHILDREN

However, as an organised unit they would from time to time come through the Bayfordbury estate on maneuvers or on training exercises. They would travel through Bayfordbury in convoys of trucks, Jeeps, Bren gun carriers, and huge tanks.

Passing through the rather small field gates must have taken quite a bit of care, as I don't recall any damage being done to the property by the convoys or their manoeuvres.

Often the soldiers would stop and have their coffee or tea breaks and meals on our grounds. The Americans were very friendly towards us, and would encourage us to say, "Got any gum, chum?" which they would give us willingly, it seemed. They were all called 'Yank', like "Hello, Mr Yank."

Unfortunately kids in those days, and particularly us boys, were not allowed to chew gum, and would be punished even for that.

The American soldiers would sometimes ask us to sing our orphanage songs, and for singing them they would give us the occasional chocolate bar or other things to eat, including gum to chew. They would sit on the grass and tell us stories while smoking their huge cigars. They seemed to have plenty of time for us.

~o~o~ Bird Nesting ~o~o~

In those Bayfordbury days, amid the miseries we suffered at the hands of the staff there were, of course, good times.

Boys being boys, one of the enjoyable things we did was going bird nesting. The intent was not to hurt birds or to destroy their nests, but to collect their eggs.

We would try to find one egg of each type of bird and 'blow it'. We understood that birds couldn't count past three, so if there were four eggs, which more often than not there were, we would take one.

To 'blow' an egg entailed making a pinhole in each end of the egg and to blow the insides out, leaving an empty egg shell.

If the egg was 'addled', it meant that the chick had started to form inside the egg, or that the egg had gone bad.

In such instances the insides could not be blown through the pinholes, and so the egg was no good for collecting, and discarded.

SUFFER LITTLE CHILDREN

We would look for various types of bird's nests along the hedgerows, in the spinneys, beside the riverbanks and under bridges. We also looked in the fields and meadows for nests hidden in the long grass, such as those of skylarks, which were very hard to find.

Amongst the worst places to find nests were in the hawthorn bushes and in the formidable gorse bushes. These were always a challenge and left us with cuts and scratches on our bare legs and arms.

Blackbirds, thrushes, chaffinches, various tits, and several other types of bird's nests were quite common and easy to find. Other birds, such as owls, hawks, kingfishers and skylarks and the like were not so easy.

It was quite easy to find a swan's nest in the rivers. However, finding their nests was the easy part. The hard part was actually getting the egg. The swans were vigorous defenders of their nests, and considered quite dangerous if they could get close enough to us.

After we each had one egg of a particular type of bird, we would not bother to raid any of those nests again. From time to time, someone would want to swap an egg from a type of bird they didn't have, so then we would go searching specifically for a particular nest.

Swapping eggs between us was a serious business. Some kids would be fortunate enough to discover a hard-to-find nest, with eggs in it. These eggs would be good bargaining collateral for anyone, and therefore it would take quite a bit of negotiating to get to swap an egg for them.

I can well remember the most rare bird's nest Flappers and I were ever to find. On this particular occasion, while Flappers and I were out looking for bird's nests, we found a kingfisher's nest under a small humpback bridge.

It was very hard to get to the nest as it was in the middle and on the underside of the small bridge, and to fall would land us in the river. Still, we managed to get to the nest and in this instance took one egg each. We kept one of those eggs for a long time and eventually sold it, along with our entire collection, to a boy at Ware School for a shilling.

SUFFER LITTLE CHILDREN
~o~o~ The Owl's Nest ~o~o~

Another occasion, which remains in my memory, was the time Flappers and I found an owl's nest high up in an old oak tree.

The nest, we believed, was in a deep hollow in the trunk of the tree, about twenty to twenty-five feet above the ground. It was decided that I would climb the tree to check out and see if there was indeed a nest in the hole. It was fairly hard to climb but we were very young and had no fear of heights, and nor did we contemplate ever falling.

Even though I was climbing up this rather high tree, at this point we couldn't be sure that there was even a nest in the hollow, let alone eggs. But that was the challenge: checking out every possibility.

It turned out that there was a nest and there were eggs in it. To my delight, they were owl's eggs. There were five or more eggs in the nest and the owl was nowhere to be seen thank goodness, for that could have been yet another problem.

Because the nest was so high up in the tree, I had to hold on carefully, using both hands while climbing down the tree, and so I had to put two of the rather large eggs into my mouth. We often put eggs in our mouths if we had to climb down a tree.

It would be difficult to forget this escapade. While climbing down the tree with these two eggs filling my mouth, something caused me to jerk or slip a little. The jolt made me clamp down on one of the eggs. Naturally the egg broke and, to my disgust, it was rotten or addled.

The taste was terrible. In trying to get the egg out of my mouth, the other egg broke and it too was just as rotten. I remember Flappers just standing at the bottom of the tree, laughing. I know that I felt pretty sick after eventually climbing down the tree.

~o~o~

We would keep our blown eggs in a flat box. The box would be about two inches deep. Then we would line the box all around and on the bottom with cotton wool. The eggs would look very impressive, all neatly arranged in sizes and colour. We would care for them as though they were the crown jewels.

SUFFER LITTLE CHILDREN

To remember those days in the Bayfordbury countryside is a fond memory. Saturdays and Sundays were the best times, providing we didn't have work duties to do first. Unfortunately, after we got home from school, and if we went bird nesting in the evenings after tea in the springtime, we only had an hour or so before bedtime.

It's been more than sixty years now, but I still remember well those good, though not really carefree times, when Flappers and I were about ten years old and we would go bird nesting.

Many times over the years, I have wondered if my good old friend Flappers ever gave thought to those often happy times. Or would he only remember the miserable times at Bayfordbury and the man who bullied us, and who first ever called him Flappers?

~o~o~ Bicycle Wheel Hoops ~o~o~

The kind of fun that we would make for ourselves included going to the Bayford village dump and bringing parts of old bicycles back to the home and then putting them together, piece by piece, until we had a crude frame with wheels, handlebars and a seat.

We couldn't find a chain for the bike and so we would just 'freewheel' down the hilly roads within the Bayfordbury estate, and walk back up again and repeat our rides. The rims on the wheels wouldn't have tires on them, as we could never find inner tubes that weren't perished or any good.

Like anything else we did like this, we would have to take care not to get caught, either at the dump or while riding the bikes down the hills because, like many things we did, these again would be caning offences. But we did them, it seems, regardless of the consequences.

Another form of fun would be to use tireless bicycle wheels for hoops, to run with. After removing the spokes from the wheels we would get a curved piece of stick, which we would then hold one end in our hand and place the other end in the rim, where the tire and inner tube would otherwise go, and then run with it.

Three or four or more of us boys would run effortlessly together for miles beside the hoops, down the country lanes around Bayfordbury and in the little country lane that leads to and around Bayford.

SUFFER LITTLE CHILDREN

On one occasion that I remember, Baggy, Fred and I were running along one of these narrow country lanes, which was just wide enough for a single car to travel on, when a car came around a bend in the lane.

Fred could hardly stop and just managed to get out of the way in time to avoid being knocked down.

His hoop, which Fred had lost control of, fell over right in front of the oncoming car. The driver of the car, as he was approaching us, leaned out of his car window and shouted at us to keep off the road. While he was busy shouting at us, he unintentionally ran over the steel hoop and got a flat tire.

The man must have been someone of some importance, because he seemed 'well to do' and had a car. During the war petrol was rationed but even then, not just anyone was permitted to have a car, or could get petrol coupons.

I remember that we meekly stood there and took a good telling-off. Then we watched and even helped the man a little, to change his wheel. After the tire was changed he gave us a shilling between us. Sharing the shilling, we would have received four pence each. A shilling was a lot of money for us at the time.

~o~o~ Crude Field Hockey ~o~o~

We would cut branches out of the woods and make crude 'field hockey' sticks. The sticks would be about three feet long and have a big knob or a gnarled joint at the end. With a tennis ball being the only other piece of equipment needed, and two sides of about eight to ten boys on each team, the game was on.

We would play on our football pitch and basically all chase the tennis ball together, trying to hit the ball between the football goal posts, to score.

There was no order to the game, no rules, no referee or anyone in charge. We simply made up the teams and off we went, charging after the tennis ball. There was no safety equipment, no passing or teamwork. It was just good fun and we played it for hours.

Many kids would get hit with the sticks on their hands, head, legs and shins, or just about anywhere. There was no finesse about this

SUFFER LITTLE CHILDREN

game; we simply enjoyed it.

Unfortunately boys would accidentally hit other boys with their sticks and so, naturally, fights would break out. But they were just momentary spats and, again, no one that I can remember ever got seriously hurt.

Vaulting was another thing we would do. We would cut a small tree or a large sapling down and make a stout pole about six to seven feet long and then, like a pole vault jumper, vault over low hedges, fences and streams.

It seemed like we could sail over these barriers as though we had wings.

~o~o~

In those days we made our own fun. We had no money to go to the pictures, no family which we could go and visit, no girls to distract the older boys and, sadly, no dogs to play with. If there wasn't anything planned by the orphanage, we invariably made up things for ourselves to do.

Such things, just as I have described, wouldn't have cost us anything and would, I'm quite sure, have been just as much fun.

This would have been one of the 'up sides' of being in an orphanage: there were always other boys to participate spontaneously in the various unorganised team activities and related fun.

~o~o~ Picking Wild Mushrooms ~o~o~

Almost daily, before we went to school in the late summer and autumn, we would, when it was our turn, be made to get up just after dawn and were sent out into the cow pastures to collect wild mushrooms. This was not really a bad chore, and I must admit I enjoyed the rather easy challenge of finding mushrooms.

We would, in the early morning light, wander through the cow pastures, listening to the crows and rooks, and looking for and collecting the fresh mushrooms, which we would find in the 'fairy rings'.

We all knew the correct type of mushroom to pick. A general rule was that if its underside was a pearl-coloured pink and it looked and

SUFFER LITTLE CHILDREN

smelled like a mushroom, it probably was. But if there was any doubt, we simply had to try and peel it.

If one takes the membrane at the outer edge of the mushroom and can peel it off quite easily, then it is, in all probability, a good edible mushroom as long as it also has the other characteristics mentioned earlier. Even when we were out picking mushrooms, we still had to judge the time right. It was very important that after we got back from picking mushrooms, we washed, had breakfast, and still caught the coach in time for school.

I don't know if any one of the staff ever did get sick as the result of a poisonous mushroom. If so, we never ever heard that any of them did.

The mushrooms were never served to us boys. The most we could get out of finding and picking them was to smell them cooking, complementing the bacon, eggs and fried bread, which was the breakfast the staff would eat.

In the springtime we would be told to walk along the riverbanks and collect moorhen eggs. These too, we would hand over, almost automatically, to Mr and Mrs Scougall for them to have for their tea.

~o~o~ Exploited ~o~o~

As I think back and recollect those days, even today, as I write, it's only too easy for me to see how we children were so blatantly exploited.

Those demands of us young boys, our being made to collect mushrooms, pheasant and moorhen eggs for those selfish caregivers at Bayfordbury, reaped no rewards for us kids.

Together with all the hardships, this was our life and we didn't really think too much about it at the time. Life went on, and still most of us didn't really realise that we were being treated so differently from outsider kids.

We simply had no comparisons which we could make, except they, the outsiders, had mums and dads, whereas we had masters and matrons to care for us. The outsider kids called their caregivers Mum and Dad, Uncle and Aunty, whereas we called ours Sir and Matron.

Of course, I had been fostered for a short while, but that was so long ago that by now it was almost forgotten, and rarely came to mind.

SUFFER LITTLE CHILDREN

Abuse, in the context of children, was not a word anyone used or recognised at that time, and most certainly not in orphanages. We just didn't seem to know that there was a better way of life or that there were any laws, if in fact there were such laws in those days, to protect us.

It never crossed our minds, and nor could we rationalise, that somewhere, anywhere, there was love and understanding for children like us, and so, understandably, we didn't really miss it.

There was absolutely no one that we were aware of who would sympathetically listen to us, or to whom we could tell any of our fears or grievances to. The only authority outside of Bayfordbury and Mr Scougall's domain that we knew anything at all about was the police, and we wouldn't dare approach or speak to them, for fear of reprisal.

We couldn't speak about Bayfordbury or the abuse we received there with our 'outsider' teachers, as this, too, would be just too risky.

We knew that speaking to any other outside authority would, without doubt, result in us receiving almost unspeakable punishment. Also we couldn't comprehend that anyone would believe us, even if we did have the nerve to tell them.

13

BAYFORDBURY – Part 7

~∘~∘~ Holiday with Gran and Granddad ~∘~∘~

One day, in early July 1944, a week or so before Ware School was to let us out for our summer holidays, Mr Scougall pointed to me in his usual authoritarian way while we were in the dining room one morning, and told me to go to his office after breakfast.

Needless to say, I thought I had done something wrong or otherwise had been reported for something that I had done and was not aware of, which, I would have thought, would result in my being caned. He never had, generally speaking, anything kind to say to us boys, so what else could I think?

Fortunately, Mr Scougall had summoned me to tell me that my grandmother had been in touch with Dr Barnardo's Homes, and that she wanted me to go and spend three weeks of my summer holidays with her.

I had heard of other boys who had gone on holiday with their mothers, or perhaps their fathers who were on leave from the Army. They might even spend their summer or Easter holidays with other members of their families from time to time.

But for me to be going somewhere to live outside of the orphanage, even though it was only for three weeks, was unbelievably exciting. I could hardly believe it was happening to me.

I didn't know my grandmother. I had no idea what she looked like or what she would be like even, or if she would like me. I had received a letter or two from her over the years, but I couldn't put a face or personality to the letters.

I understood what a relationship with a grandmother was, as I had had a grandmother of sorts when I lived with my foster family in Tamworth. But this was my very own grandmother, the realisation of which was somewhat hard for me to really comprehend.

SUFFER LITTLE CHILDREN

As soon as Mr Scougall had told me I was going, I lived for the day I would be leaving Bayfordbury and seeing my grandma. I don't think I gave much thought to my grandfather or anyone else. Mr Scougall had said, "Your grandmother has asked..." and that was the person that I associated my good fortune with.

Every day I talked to Fred, Baggy, and Flappers about my going to my grandmother's house, and I absolutely dwelt on the subject to the point that they must have been tired of hearing about it.

For the next week or so, I simply just waited and waited for the time to come when I would actually be on my way to Taunton to see my grandmother. For me, this was much like a fairy tale might be to an outsider child.

I know I will never be able to explain my excitement. I was actually going to a real home, a home like my old foster home, where there would be a bedroom and a private lavatory for just the people in the house. There would also be a kitchen and other small rooms, all of which added up to a place called a home, a real home.

Poor old Fred and Baggy weren't going anywhere. Fred had a father somewhere, as did Baggy, but they never heard from them at all, even at Christmas or at any other time. In some ways, having a father or a mother and never hearing from them ever, was perhaps even worse than being an orphan, who has no mother or father, and as such, never expects to hear from them.

I would have been ten going on eleven years old at about the time I was to go 'home' to see my grandmother.

I packed my now familiar kitbag myself, probably under the supervision of Matron, who would make sure I had all my clothes, including my nightshirt, toothbrush, comb etc. She would also have given me my ration book to take with me.

Mr Scougall, who was unusually very nice to me on the day of my leaving, took me to Hertford North railway station in his car. I then travelled the short distance on the train to Kings Cross railway station on my own.

A lady chaperoned me across London on the 'tube' to Paddington railway station. She would have recognised me as being "the boy with the Dr Barnardo's Homes kitbag".

SUFFER LITTLE CHILDREN

After we arrived at Paddington Station at a predetermined location, we found my grandmother there waiting to meet us. My chaperon had a few words with my grandmother, gave her my ration book, and then she left.

I recall my looking at this old lady, my grandmother, trying to remember her, but I couldn't remember her at all. The last time I had set eyes on her was when I was about three or four years old and had been living with my father, stepmother, and sister Barbara in Taunton.

My grandmother held my hand tightly until we boarded the train to Taunton; she didn't seem to want to let it go. At the same time, she seemed to be studying me, though I didn't know why at the time.

Today, on reflection, it seems reasonable to believe that my grandmother had been looking at me to see if she could see in me a likeness of her own deceased son Bert, who had been killed five years earlier, at just thirty-four years old.

Unknown to me, her meeting me could have been a happy, yet at the same time quite a sad time for her.

It wasn't long before I was to learn that I was a mirror image of my father. In later years I was to see photographs of him, and could almost believe that they were photographs of myself.

It was an emotional time for me too. It felt like I was in a fantasy world. It's very hard to explain, but here I was, holding the hand of my own grandmother, the only person that I could remember that I had ever actually met who I could call my family since I had said goodbye to my sister Barbara several years earlier in the now foggy, hazy years of my infancy.

I can remember that I adored my grandmother immediately, and couldn't take my eyes off her. I thought over and over again in my child's mind, this is my grandmother and she is my family, my real family, and I had to try hard to believe the reality of it all.

Mr Scougall and the harsh life at Bayfordbury, in just the few hours since I had left, was already beginning to be forgotten and life was becoming wonderful. Unlike in my life at Bayfordbury, it seemed as though I had no cares or worries in the world.

My gran and I sat opposite each other in a third-class carriage. We talked, and she told me that my sister Barbara was also coming to stay with us, and that we would meet her tomorrow at the railway station.

Even though I could hardly remember Barbara, I was again excited

SUFFER LITTLE CHILDREN

at the prospect of seeing my own sister.

Gran also told me that she was still trying to arrange for our older sister Carol, who lived in Nottingham, to come to Taunton to see Barbara and myself.

The idea of seeing Carol was not quite so exciting, as I didn't remember ever having seen her at all. I was aware that I had a sister Carol, but only vaguely. Sad as it may seem, I couldn't remember having lived in the same house with Carol, though in my infancy I had of course.

Sitting in the train watching my grandmother, I can remember well that she had a little wart on her chin and that a long black hair grew out of it, and it fascinated me. Although she looked pretty old to me, she was really quite lively and had an elfish, yet kindly looking face.

She was probably about sixty-five years old at the time. I immediately felt a loving kinship about her, and after just a few days she never looked old to me again.

~o~o~

After we arrived at the Taunton railway station my grandmother took my kitbag, and then we walked home to her house. On the way, an old man walking and pushing a bicycle up a hill stopped to talk to us. He turned out to be my grandfather.

He didn't say much, if anything, to me at all. He just exchanged a few words with my grandmother and then he continued on his way. We continued on our walk to my gran's – Gran is what I called her – house.

My grandparents lived at 99 Winchester Street. It was a terraced house with a small garden and a very low garden wall in the front of the house. At the back of the house, enclosing the back garden, was a fairly tall garden wall with a wooden gate.

We went in the front door of the house and into the parlour.

The house was much like I had imagined it would be, and a little like the house in Wilnecote. The rooms were very small but warm, in the friendly sense of the word. These cosy rooms, which, compared to the huge cold rooms in the Bayfordbury mansion, where I would have to say was my normal home, and where I usually lived, made my grandparent's house the 'real' home I had always imagined.

SUFFER LITTLE CHILDREN

My grandmother had a little terrier dog, which was very excited when we came into the house. I can't recall the dog's name, but I do remember later taking it for walks on a lead in the fields near 'our' house.

I remember too, hearing at least two clocks ticking in the house. I had never heard a clock chime before. One of the clocks chimed on each quarter, as well as striking the hour.

I can still remember those clocks; they remind me so much of my grandparents.

This then, was my grandparents' house, which in later years I grew to know very well and even love. It was not a grand house, nor was the furniture of particularly high quality, but nevertheless it was, to me, not just a house, but also a proper home.

My grandfather, who I called Granddad, came home later for his afternoon tea. He still didn't speak very much to me, but simply acknowledged me and asked me a few questions and then carried on with his normal routine.

He never failed to listen to the news on the big cabinet radio in the parlour, to hear how the war was going. He didn't speak to anyone when the radio was on and no one would speak to him. He seemed to always be staring at something straight ahead and concentrating, quite possibly remembering how it was with him in the First World War, when he, with his eldest son, my Uncle Reg, were serving in the Army.

My grandfather would get cross with me, or anyone else, if they made a noise while the news was on. No one was allowed to even make a sound, or my grandfather would grumble and tell whoever it was to "Go into the other room."

My grandparents had had four sons serving in the armed services during the Second World War, until my father had been killed – three in the Army and the other in the Navy.

~°~°~ Meeting My Sisters ~°~°~

The following day after my arriving in Taunton, my grandmother and I walked to the Taunton railway station and waited for the train from the north to bring my sister Barbara home to my grandmother's.

SUFFER LITTLE CHILDREN

Barbara was coming from an orphanage in Ripon, in Yorkshire. I hadn't seen Barbara since we parted at Barkingside so many, many years earlier, when I was just five years old.

My grandmother bought two 'penny' platform tickets for us, and as the train came rumbling into the station we looked at all the young girls, searching for which one was Barbara. I don't remember Dr Barnardo's Homes girls having to have navy blue kitbags like the boys did.

My grandmother was the first to recognise Barbara, by I suppose, the blue jumper dress she wore. She had probably been told how she would be dressed and what luggage she would be carrying.

I doubt that my grandmother would have known Barbara, or Barbara her, without help from Dr Barnardo's as they hadn't seen each other for several years – possibly since 1938, when we had left Taunton to go to live in the Millbank Barracks in London.

Barbara, being two years older than me, was about twelve years old now. She was, as I recall, perhaps a little on the plump side but nevertheless quite attractive. She had almost red hair. The other girls at the orphanage in Ripon called her 'Carrots'.

When she saw me she was all smiles. She hugged me and at the same time had tears in her eyes. All through the years, following our being admitted into Dr Barnardo's Homes, she said she had constantly thought about me, her little brother.

Barbara was as pleased as I was to be coming 'home' to Gran's house and, even if it was only for a short while, to be away from the institutional way of life we were forced to endure.

We walked home to Gran's house and no doubt were excited to be together. Gran was a very relaxed and yet lively person to be with, and very easy for children to like. She constantly smiled, and had a devilish, pixie-like way about her.

Barbara, Gran and I slept in Gran's big bed together. I can still remember how we sank into the wide, feather-filled mattress and covered ourselves with the down filled duvet. It was so luxurious when compared with my narrow iron bed, with its wafer-thin mattress and threadbare blankets that I had at the orphanage.

Barbara and I didn't talk much about our lives in Dr Barnardo's Homes. We just knew how the other felt about having no immediate

SUFFER LITTLE CHILDREN

*My sister Barbara and I
Photo taken during our first
holiday with Gran in 1943*

SUFFER LITTLE CHILDREN

family like a mother and father, or even seeing or hearing about each other.

Barbara knew that we had another sister more so than I did, but at that time in our lives we had no idea where she was. We only knew Carol hadn't been put into the orphanage with us. Neither of us had at any time ever heard anything about Carol, and no one in Dr Barnardo's ever spoke to either of us about her.

Barbara once told me that she had tried to write to me several times over the years we had been apart, but that she never heard back from me. Unfortunately, all I could tell her was that if she did write to me, her letters never reached me.

Once in a while (following this visit to my grandmother) Gran would write to me and from time to time would send me two shillings and sixpence (half a crown). The money was kept for me at Bayfordbury, to be given to me to spend on special occasions such as visiting my grandmother.

~°~°~ Meeting Aunty Molly and Cousin Jill ~°~°~

It was during the first few days of my being in Taunton that I met my Aunty Molly and my cousin Jill. Immediately I loved Aunty Molly. She was the most funny, gentle and adorable person I had ever met. Aunty Molly had sparkling blue eyes and the most beautiful smile, quite possibly inherited from my grandmother.

I knew almost immediately that if I could have chosen a mother she would have been, without the slightest doubt, my first choice.

There was mention from time to time of 'Sid' – Aunty Molly's husband and, of course, my uncle. Uncle Sid was a staff sergeant in the Army, fighting the Germans in Europe at the time I came 'home' to Taunton. I wasn't to meet him for another few years.

Aunty Molly's daughter, my cousin Jill, was also a favourite with me. Jill was a little more than a year younger than me. She had very dark hair and her mother's sparkling eyes, and also a girlish lilting laugh.

Jill had a demeanour about her which seemed, and I mean only 'seemed', haughty and somewhat aloof. She constantly taunted me in a devilish way and we often squabbled, like a brother and sister might.

SUFFER LITTLE CHILDREN

While I was on holiday in Taunton that year, Jill and I were almost inseparable, and became very good friends for, as it turned out, the rest of her life.

~○~○~ Blue Anchor ~○~○~

A few days after Barbara arrived at Gran's, our grandmother rented a caravan for a week, in a small coastal hamlet called Blue Anchor, which is located on the Bristol Channel not far from the town of Minehead.

Aunty Molly and Jill also came to Blue Anchor for a week's holiday at the same time. The caravan was very small – in fact, it was a one-room caravan which had a little cooker, and no toilet or sink. But, most important, it had beds enough for Barbara and I to sleep together, while Aunty Molly, Gran and Jill slept in a slightly bigger bed together at the other end of the caravan.

With five of us in the caravan together it was probably a little crowded, but no one seemed to mind.

All of the caravans in the field we camped in were small and, although they were on wheels, they had been stationary for many years, even from well before the war.

During the days, we would go to the beach, and when the tide was in we would go swimming in the sea.

Quite often we would also go to the areas where there were plenty of rocks and seaweed, and pick winkles – little edible sea snails which cling to rocks and seaweed.

After getting back to our caravan, my grandmother and Aunty Molly would boil up the winkles and we ate them. These were the first winkles I had ever tasted and although they were snails and didn't look very appetising, they were nevertheless quite delicious.

To eat them we simply removed the 'front door', and with a pin, pulled the little cooked snail out from inside its shell, and ate it. They really do look revolting, so much so that if one studied them, they probably wouldn't eat them at all.

~○~○~

SUFFER LITTLE CHILDREN

The seashore at Blue Anchor is quite stony at the top of the beach, but then after about twenty feet it becomes nice and sandy. After about thirty to forty feet of sand, as one walks further out towards the sea the sand changes from nice clean sand to a thick, slimy, slippery mud. The mud gradually gets deeper and deeper as one walks out towards the sea, and it is naturally more difficult to walk in.

On one particular occasion that comes to mind, Jill and I slowly walked out into the mud to see how far we dared to go. Jill had a new pretty dress on, which besides costing plenty of money, needed clothes coupons in order to buy it.

She had tucked her dress into the top of her knickers, which was a common thing for young girls to do in those days, so that, of course, she wouldn't get her new dress wet or dirty.

Well, at first we were just walking and talking and daring each other to take one step further into the deeper mud, and then another step and so on.

Then one of us, 'the rotten little sod', playing too rough, pushed Jill over and into the thick, slimy wet mud. As she struggled to get up, with me helping her, she became absolutely covered in the mud. Her new dress looked like a floor cloth, ready to be discarded.

Jill cried, which made me feel bad, and I couldn't console her. Besides feeling bad, I was also quite worried and concerned as to what was going to happen to me when we got back to the caravan.

That was the only time ever that Aunty Molly looked a little disappointed in me, but still she wasn't terribly angry. Her disappointment didn't last long and soon she was laughing at the state Jill looked when she had seen her. In later years both Aunty Molly and Jill would still remember, and laugh at what happened that day.

~o~o~

Even though it was still wartime there seemed to be no threat from air raids at Blue Anchor, though directly across the Bristol Channel from Blue Anchor was the big Welsh city of Cardiff. We still had to observe the 'no lights at night' rule.

Cardiff was a big industrial city with a large naval port, so the

SUFFER LITTLE CHILDREN

Germans regularly bombed it. From Blue Anchor we could see the searchlights beaming across the sky all through the late evenings before we went to bed, but there were no air raids during the week we were in Blue Anchor, or at least we didn't see any.

My grandmother and Aunty Molly took us to Minehead, to the pictures, one rainy day. The picture playing was a film called *The Virginian*. I remember that Barbara, who would have been about twelve or perhaps even thirteen at the time, didn't understand the meaning of the title, but I remember her telling me that she thought it was going to be a 'rude' film. I had no idea what she was talking about.

Being absolutely carefree and free of the constant watchful eyes of the Bayfordbury staff, the time I spent at Blue Anchor with Gran, Aunty Molly, Jill and Barbara was a very happy time in my life, and I will always remember it.

~°~°~ Sister Carol ~°~°~

After the second week of Barbara and I being on holiday in Taunton, our grandma managed to arrange for Carol to come from Nottingham to Taunton for a week's holiday.

Together with Gran, Barbara and I met Carol at the Taunton Station, just like when Gran and I had met Barbara.

Carol was a very pretty girl with a slight build and auburn hair, much like Barbara's but not quite so red. She seemed particularly gentle and spoke very quietly. Also, much like myself, she was very shy. It would have been at least seven or eight years since all three of us had last been together and so, unfortunately, we didn't know each other very well at all. I would only have been about three, and Barbara five, when Carol had been sent away to live in Nottingham.

So, here I was with my two sisters, my grandmother, lovely Aunty Molly and dear Jill. Life was just wonderful.

The food that my grandmother gave us was like no other food I had ever tasted since perhaps I had left my foster home.

We went to the pictures a couple of times and I was on holiday in a real family home, 'my' family home. It was unbelievably marvellous.

In the third week of my holiday at Gran's, it was time for us to have

SUFFER LITTLE CHILDREN

to leave my grandmother's home and return to the places we had come from: Carol to Nottingham, Barbara to her orphanage in Ripon, and I to mine, the dreaded Bayfordbury.

Carol left Gran's first. Before she left she took me to a toyshop and bought me a bright, golden- coloured tin sword. It was the perfect toy for me. I believed that because it had a curved handguard, it was a pirate's cutlass. I fastened the cutlass around my waist with the cloth belt that it came with, and wore it everywhere I went during my last few days in Taunton.

It was very stressful saying goodbye to Carol, my eldest sister, and I tried hard not to cry. She, too, had tears in her eyes, not knowing when we would see each other again.

Unknown to us at the time, Carol's life in Nottingham was equally as bad as ours, or even worse. She had only been at Gran's a week, but now she would have had an insight into the happy family life she too longed for. At fifteen, she would have been even more aware of what she had missed and was still missing in terms of a family life, more so even than Barbara and me.

Carol, like us, would have longed to have had her own father and mother to love her, and a sister and brother for her to care for and grow up with, including a proper relationship with her gran and granddad. No doubt she would have given her soul for a chance to have had her own aunts, uncles and cousins to become familiar with, just like other families had.

But she, like us, had very little to go back 'home' for. Unlike Barbara and me though, for Carol it was possibly even worse because, in retrospect, it was as though Carol lived in an 'empty shell', without even the comfort of having other children around her who were in the same situation as she was in – an orphan – and was living on the unorganised or, perhaps, unpredictable charity of others.

We saw her off at the railway station and waved until the train was out of sight. Unlike the joyous feelings we had when Carol had arrived at the station, this time we left the station speechless, sad, and in tears.

Almost the next day, Barbara had to leave. The goodbyes were just as hard as when Carol had left. But we had known our holiday would come to an end.

SUFFER LITTLE CHILDREN

Barbara had not spoken much to me about her life in Dr Barnardo's Homes, although I think she did say that Ripon was not too bad and that she was treated well there. But still it was sad to say goodbye and naturally we cried, not knowing when we would see each other again.

~o~o~

I can't really remember very much about my grandfather at that time. He was always busy with other things, and was still going to work on a regular basis. In about seven years or so in the future, I was to come to know him quite well, and found him to be, well, perhaps a little grumpy but nevertheless a likable old man.

Next door to my grandparent's house was my grandfather's garage. At one time the garage was a thriving business, selling petrol, and my grandfather and his son Reg also repaired automobiles, horse carriages, carts and other such vehicles. I was to learn, many years later, that my granddad's garage was one of the first garages in Taunton. At one time my father, and uncles Reg, Jack and Harry, all worked with my grandfather in LONGMAN AND SONS garage.

~o~o~ Flowers for Aunty Molly ~o~o~

The next day, the day after Barbara had left Gran's house to return to Ripon, I decided to go to Aunty Molly's house to say goodbye to her and Jill, because I, too, was leaving Gran's to go back to Bayfordbury the following day, and may not get another chance.

On my way to Aunty Molly's, and as I was crossing a main road in Taunton, a big lorry stopped and the driver got out and came over to me.

I didn't know who the chap was, but he said he was Uncle Len, my aunt Rose's husband. I must have met him while I was in Taunton, but with so many new people now in my life, I couldn't remember him.

As it was, Uncle Len gave me two half-crown pieces and said one was for Barbara, and the other one was for me. He told me to say goodbye to Barbara for him. Then, after a few more words, he got back in his big lorry and drove off.

SUFFER LITTLE CHILDREN

I felt a little guilty at not having told Uncle Len that Barbara had already left Taunton and had gone back to her orphanage a day or so ago. But, like that same 'rotten little sod' that I was, and listening to my conscience – Flappers – I pocketed Barbara's half-crown without giving it a second thought.

After Uncle Len had driven away, I continued walking towards Aunty Molly's house and, as luck would have it, there, lying on the pavement, was a lovely bunch of flowers. Somebody had obviously dropped them. So I picked up the flowers and again continued on my way to Aunty Molly's house.

I gave the flowers to Aunty Molly like they were a going away present. Aunty Molly was touched by my thoughtfulness and as I was saying goodbye to her and Jill she gave me a big hug and held me for a while.

I remember particularly well Aunty Molly hugging me that day. No one else had ever shown such affection towards me before. Jill and I didn't say much; we were just too sorry to be saying goodbye.

Saying goodbye was, under most circumstances, very heart-wrenching for me, but particularly so when I said goodbye to Aunty Molly and Jill. I'm sure that on my way back to my gran's house I would have felt very sad and full of disappointment at having to leave them.

~o~o~

Then before it had fully registered, my holiday at my grandmother's house with my gran and granddad was over. Meeting my Aunty Molly and my cousin Jill and having Barbara and Carol with me, was all over. It was time to leave 99 Winchester Street.

Leaving 99 was very, very upsetting. Gran carried my kitbag and off we went to the Taunton railway station to catch the train back to Paddington. I remember that my gran didn't speak much. I think she was just as sorry at my going as I was, though, it seemed, she could never know just how sad and emotional it was for me. I'm sure I was deep in thought, realising where I was going and that I would eventually be back at Bayfordbury again.

With my sad face and obviously unhappy demeanour, and wearing

SUFFER LITTLE CHILDREN

a big oversized army officer's cap (though it could have been a bus conductor's cap) which my grandmother had found in a cupboard under the stairs and had given me, and with the colourful tin sword swinging around my waist, I could only have looked like a forlorn little carnival character, with a face like I was going to the gallows.

When we arrived at Paddington station we met my chaperon, who smiled at me. She had a few words with my grandmother and then said we should say goodbye to each other.

Again, I would have been very upset, and no doubt cried at having to leave my grandmother. She, too, was quite upset.

She hugged and then kissed me goodbye and with that, the chaperon and I left Gran standing on the platform at Paddington and went to the Underground or 'tube', as it was often called, to travel across London again, to Kings Cross railway station.

After arriving at Hertford North station, the man who I feared most in the whole world was there to meet me and drive me back to Bayfordbury. Mr Scougall, who had no time for any of us boys, didn't speak to me, except to say, perhaps, an unemotional "Well, Longman, did you have a good holiday?" or commenting on my hat and sword.

After getting out of Mr Scougall's car and pulling my kitbag behind me, several boys came up to me to look at my sword. They were fascinated with my cap and wanted to try it on. Very quickly I was back into the familiar way of living and surviving in Bayfordbury.

14

BAYFORDBURY – Part 8

~o~o~ Back to Bayfordbury ~o~o~

It didn't take long for me to get back into the Bayfordbury way of life. Although I sadly missed my gran and the life in Taunton, I was still very pleased and excited to see my friends at Bayfordbury again. They were, after all, almost a sort of family to me.

Naturally Fred, Baggy, and Flappers were just as pleased to see me as I was to see them. I had lots to tell them about the outsiders 'good life' and the things I had done.

At first it seemed to me that I had been away for a long, long time, but within just a couple of days my memories of Gran's house and Taunton would begin to fade, and I would be back to my more normal way of life at the orphanage.

They – my friends and the rest of the boys in the orphanage – had been having the same summer as I had experienced with them the previous year. So far this summer, as was now usual, they hadn't been wearing shoes, socks, shirts, or anything except for their cotton shorts.

Very quickly and without any thought at all, I found I was dressing the same as before, eating the same terrible food, and generally falling back into the normal, institutional way of life again, almost as though I had never even left it.

It was about mid-August when I had returned from Gran's, and so the usual summer rules were in effect at Bayfordbury.

Besides having to eat outside under the blazing sun or in chilly winds and drizzle, we still had to go to bed at eight o'clock during the warm summer evenings, even though it would be light outside. Often the sun would still be shining long after we had gone to bed.

Just as always, summer and winter, our wooden window shutters would be closed, the dormitory lights turned out, and the bucket placed somewhere in the middle of the dormitory floor, waiting to be knocked over some time during the dark night. Nothing had changed.

SUFFER LITTLE CHILDREN

I would lie in my hard, narrow bed, realising that now I had had a tiny taste of the outsiders' way of life. Also I remembered sadly that just a few days earlier at this time in the evening, I would have been outside in the fields walking with my gran and her dog or with my sisters, visiting Aunty Molly or fooling around with my cousin Jill. I might even have been swimming in the sea at Blue Anchor.

This was the way of life that the outsiders seemed to live all of the time. It somehow just didn't seem fair.

~o~o~

The rest of the summer, after I had returned to Bayfordbury from my grandmother's house, passed much like the previous summer.

Nothing had changed. We would still walk in our bare feet with just our shorts on to go swimming in the River Lee and with the traffic going by, the passengers on the buses waving to us. As well, we still scuffed our toes on the hot asphalt road, our shirtless backs blistering in the blazing sun, just like they did in previous years.

Even with these discomforts, we still enjoyed the swimming excursions; they were enjoyable breaks from the otherwise institutionalised way of life in an orphanage.

Late summer was the time to go scrumping for apples and gooseberries, and to start playing football and field hockey, just like we did every year. Then, with the summer holidays over, we would return to Ware School.

Later, as the summer faded and autumn arrived, we would go looking for chestnuts and hazelnuts and other fruits that ripened in their seasons.

Going back to the outsiders' school was fine with us, because it was a welcome change to the Bayfordbury routine. The boys and girls we knew and whom we were friendly with would tell us about their summers. Mrs Blackwell would make us write essays about how we spent our summer holidays. So, of course, I would have lots to write about after seeing my sisters and grandparents.

SUFFER LITTLE CHILDREN
~o~o~ Approaching D-Day ~o~o~

A few months before my grandmother had arranged for me to go to Taunton, the war had taken a new course and now the allied forces were positioning themselves to take the offensive towards the German fronts.

There was a new optimism in the British news and at Ware School. Mrs Blackwell would speak about the war during our school classes. She would put colourful maps of the world on her blackboard, and try to explain to us where the German lines were, and where the German positions were the strongest.

~o~o~

It was, as I recall from a young boy's perspective, one day in early June 1944 when we first heard the rumblings of huge convoys consisting of hundreds of army trucks full of soldiers. There were also many, many other army vehicles. The convoys passed by our Bayfordbury gates, making a tremendously loud thunderous noise on the small country road.

We had over recent years seen many big armoured convoys, but this was different. In this particular convoy, besides the troop-transporting vehicles there were also hundreds of tanks and armoured cars, Bren gun carriers, Jeeps, artillery guns and supply trucks.

Most of us boys, including, probably, all of the staff, went down to the main road to see the immense convoys of armoured vehicles – British and American.

As I recall, it was early in the morning on the day we first heard the rumbling of the heavy vehicles coming from the direction of Hertford. The convoy was so long it must have continued passing by our Bayfordbury gates all day and well into the late evening. At the time, we boys didn't understand what the huge movement of troops and armoured equipment was all about.

A few days or so later, several hundreds, if not thousands of aeroplanes, many of them towing big troop transport gliders, flew over Hertford and Bayfordbury. The aircraft covered the sky like a huge cloud, stretching as far as the eye could see in all directions.

SUFFER LITTLE CHILDREN

It was all very exciting and certainly a big attraction for us, much like a carnival would be. This was the beginning of the Allied Forces' liberation of Europe.

As it eventually turned out, this major movement of troops and equipment was the beginning of the end of the war with Germany.

~o~o~ VE Day ~o~o~

On the 8th of May, 1945 the war with Germany, which began in 1939, was over. Although we believed it was over, in fact it wasn't exactly over. Unbeknown to us boys, the British and their allies which formed the British Empire were first at war with Germany and Italy. The war with Japan, primarily involving America and which the British were still deeply involved in, was still ongoing and wouldn't be over until the 15th of August, 1945.

The Americans didn't enter the war against the Germans until after the 7th of December, 1941, more than two years after Britain and the Commonwealth had desperately been defending itself against the might of the German and Italian armies, and the formidable German air force.

The Americans had not entered the war, even though Britain, (with the aid of the Commonwealth countries), had had to desperately defend itself in what was called 'The Battle of Britain', and what was intended to be the Germans' imminent invasion of Britain.

When Japan attacked America, by bombing Pearl Harbor on the 7th of December, 1941, Britain and the Commonwealth, with hardly a day's deliberation and without any hesitation, sided with America against the Japanese. And so, the British Empire was now allies with America in virtually resolving two wars.

VE (Victory in Europe) day really meant that it was only the war with Germany that was over. The war with Japan still wasn't yet over, and wouldn't be for another few months to come.

Still, the Germans had been the main enemy of Britain and the Commonwealth and so, as far as we were concerned, the war for us was over. We didn't understand really, that the British Empire was still fighting alongside the Americans against the formidable Japanese.

On VE Day there were big celebrations everywhere. We collected

SUFFER LITTLE CHILDREN

dead branches from the woods on the Bayfordbury estate and built a huge bonfire for the VE celebrations.

Ware School was closed for a few days and so, of course, we all stayed home. There was an atmosphere of total relaxation everywhere.

On the day of the celebrations we had sports like sack races and egg and spoon races. We had a special meal with nicer food, including cake.

~o~o~ One of the Happiest Days of My Life ~o~o~

After a few days of being back to school, something happened that made a certain day one of the saddest days for some people, and yet at the same time one of the happiest for others, including me.

The saddest, I would presume, were for those like Mrs Scougall and her son, whilst the most jubilant boys in the entire world on this particular day must have been the boys in Bayfordbury.

When this wonderfully big event happened, it was to us Bayfordbury boys, at this point in our lives, the biggest and most joyful event ever to happen. It was happier even than Christmas, and also a bigger event than my going home to Gran's house.

It all happened, as far as we were aware, quite unexpectedly, almost right out of the blue, so to speak.

This, one of the most memorable days of my life – the 10th of September, 1945, to be exact: a day I shall always remember – started much like any other day.

We had gone to Ware School in the morning, in our usual jostling manner on the coach, joking with some, or fighting with others.

Even on the way back to Bayfordbury, everything again was just as normal. The boys having to go to bed without any tea were probably feeling 'down in the dumps', whilst others were planning to go looking for chestnuts or perhaps hazelnuts after tea.

However, upon arriving back at Bayfordbury from Ware School, we couldn't help but notice that something was quite different.

The coach stopped, as it normally did, at the bottom of the huge entrance steps to the mansion.

Elevated above us on the big stone podium was Mrs Scougall, sprawled out in the big armchair – the one they had savagely thrashed Valance on –

SUFFER LITTLE CHILDREN

sobbing uncontrollably, with her son trying to console her. Mr Nash and his wife, and most, if not all, of the staff, were standing dutifully beside them with their heads tilted forward.

Except for the 'doom and gloom' look on the podium (perhaps we had lost the war after all) the stage looked set much like it was on the day when Valance had been so brutally caned, except no one on the podium had looked particularly sad on that day.

At this point none of us could have guessed what was going to happen. I'm sure some of us might have thought that some other poor soul was in for a thrashing.

But really there was a difference. One prominent person was missing, which we all immediately noticed. The missing person was none other than Mr Scougall.

We had hoped that maybe he wasn't well, and would be away for a few days or even weeks. We may even have mused that perhaps he had done a bunk.

We filed out of the coach and as usual lined up, three deep, waiting for an announcement. What came next served to be one of the happiest statements I was ever to hear in my entire life.

Mr Nash stepped forward, and with his head slightly bowed, told us what he thought was the saddest news possible. Unknown to those on the podium, the announcement he made was so uplifting for most of us, much like a great weight had been lifted in our young lives. It turned out that what Mr Nash so sadly told us was to change our way of life at Bayfordbury completely.

Mr Nash didn't tell us Mr Scougall was sick, or that he would be away for a while. That would have been good news enough. Instead, after a brief dramatic silence, he told us that Mr Scougall had had another heart attack and had died during the day.

I remember how Fred, Baggy and I, and probably Flappers, glanced sideways at each other, trying to suppress our wicked smiles, while at the same time trying to look sorry. Most of the boys undoubtedly felt the same as we did. They all had – certainly most of them at one time or another – been sadistically beaten by this now deceased brute of a man.

SUFFER LITTLE CHILDREN

We naturally pretended to be sorry for the death of this man, yet we couldn't show our real feelings. Mr Scougall was dead; he was actually well and truly dead. He could never beat us again.

We were so overwhelmed with happiness it was hard to contain ourselves, yet at the risk to our lives, we dared not show it. Mr Nash was still here, and in our wildest dreams we didn't expect that he would die as well. With the two of them gone, well, that would be even better than our having won the war.

Then there was even more good news. (It makes me laugh still just to write about it.) We were told the funeral would be on Thursday next. Therefore, we would have to take the day off from school.

Just how much good news could one receive in one day without cheering out loud? It all felt like we should be shouting "Hip, Hip, Hurrah" several times over.

Strangely enough, and this is absolutely a fact, only one boy showed any sorrow or remorse at all, that boy, strange as it may seem, was John Thomas, the boy who 'crossed his heart' and swore he hadn't stolen Pain's mouse, but was caned for it anyway.

I'm sure all the rest of the boys felt as my friends and I did. We felt nothing but almost overwhelming happiness and an extreme feeling of relief.

We were then dismissed, leaving Mrs Scougall sobbing on the podium, with her son trying to comfort her and at the same time leading her back into the mansion, with the staff solemnly following. The rest of us boys, with our heads bent in a posture of sadness, walked away from the main entrance steps, our hearts and souls undoubtedly uplifted.

~o~o~ 'Good Riddance to Bad Rubbish' ~o~o~
(As the Saying Goes)

We went to school as usual the next day and everyone, including the outsider kids and the teachers, had all heard the 'sad' news. We pretended to be sad too, but found it hard to hide our happy change of fortune.

Generally speaking, no one really blamed us boys for not caring about Mr Scougall dying. Many of the outsiders, if not most of them at

SUFFER LITTLE CHILDREN

one time or another, had heard of the tyranny we faced at Bayfordbury. There had always been some sympathy for us in that regard, though many of them probably thought that he was still the best person to be in control of "those Bayfordbury boys".

~o~o~

On the Thursday, the day of Mr Scougall's funeral, we dressed in our Sunday clothes and walked to Hertingfordbury. After we arrived we were made to line up each side of the gravel pathway leading to the main entrance to the church.

All of the mourners and any interested villagers had to walk down the path, between us rows of 'mourning' Bayfordbury boys, to enter the church. Ironically, we served as the sort of 'guard of honour' for the man who we feared and despised more than anyone else in our lives.

Williams and I didn't have to sing in the choir, because there was no choir for Mr Scougall's funeral.

The mourners would probably have thought that we all loved and respected our now deceased headmaster.

In all probability it looked that way, and one could, if one didn't know better, think it was all quite sad. Yet, in actual fact it was really quite the opposite, of course.

The entire event of Mr Scougall's passing was to us more like Christmas Day; we were all so happy.

Then the coffin was carried down the path between us boys and into the church. The service was conducted, with nice words being said about our almost hated bully of a headmaster – words which we would no doubt have quietly sniggered at.

After the service, the coffin was carried out to the back of the church to its burial plot.

I remember seeing Mrs Dunning briefly at Mr Scougall's funeral. She saw me and gave me her lovely smile. I wanted to go and speak to her, as I hadn't seen her for at least a year, but the opportunity wasn't there.

That was, apart from one other occasion a few years later, to be the last time that I was to see Mrs Dunning – a person I shall always remember and admire for her gentleness towards us unfortunate victims of society.

SUFFER LITTLE CHILDREN

James Somerville Scougall
died Sept. 10th 1945
IN A LIFETIME OF SERVICE TO
YOUTH HE REMAINED YOUNG

SUFFER LITTLE CHILDREN

~o~o~

Some sixty years later I, for the first time since leaving Bayfordbury, revisited the beautiful village of Hertingfordbury and Hertingfordbury Church with my wife Donna. While at the church we found, after much searching due to it being overgrown with weeds, Mr Scougall's gravestone.

I found it so ironical to see written on his headstone an inscription that made me smile. The inscription reads:

IN A LIFETIME OF SERVICE TO YOUTH,
HE REMAINED YOUNG.

I think it would have been more appropriate if it had read:

IN A LIFETIME OF BEATING THE YOUTH IN HIS CHARGE,
HE REMAINED FIT AND STRONG, UNTIL IT KILLED HIM.

All we could think about during and after the funeral service was that now, at last, it was all over. For some reason, I believe we knew that Mr Nash would become the new acting headmaster, something which we also believed would be pretty bad for us, but we didn't fear him quite like we feared Mr Scougall. In any event, now there wasn't Mr Scougall and Mr Nash; there was just Mr Nash.

~o~o~ Enter Mr Castle ~o~o~

After just a couple of weeks following the demise of Mr Scougall, life for us Bayfordbury boys was to change yet again, and much for the better.

Dr Barnardo's Homes sent a new headmaster to Bayfordbury. His name was Mr Castle. He came with his wife and two daughters. Both of his daughters were about nine or ten years old, which was pretty close to my age, and for the next few years they grew up with us though, being girls, they didn't really associate with us very much.

Mr Castle had just retired from the position of being the chief of police in the Sudan. He was a big man, about the same build as Mr Scougall, but under no circumstances could he be considered fat. He was about fifty to

SUFFER LITTLE CHILDREN

perhaps fifty-five years old, and though he was firm in his dealings with us, we were to find out that he was a fair and understanding man.

He reformed the harsh disciplinary methods previously administered at Bayfordbury. There would be no more caning, though he did from time to time 'dish out' corporal punishment.

Instead of a thick cane, Mr Castle used a huge plimsoll (running shoe), which we called 'the slipper'. It too hurt, but it was a different kind of pain. It stung and although it really hurt, it didn't make the cheeks of our backsides bleed, like with the vicious canings that Mr Scougall had administered did.

Mr Castle didn't often punish us with the slipper. The slipper was only used as the last resort, and only when we repeatedly did the same serious offences. Quite often Mr Castle would simply speak to us about our mistakes or mischief, and most often that was enough.

I believe too, that Mr Castle would meet with the Hertford community leaders from time to time, because we were invited to join a football league, and participate in other activities in the town.

Bayfordbury had a reasonably good football team and although I played football, like all of us boys did, I don't remember myself as being a particularly good player. The Bayfordbury Hornets, as our team was called, always gave a good account of themselves.

Life at Bayfordbury under Mr Castle's administration became quite different. The fear of caning and of the staff hitting us with their fists was gone. Even though Mr Nash was still around, I don't think he dared abuse the boys like he used to. Mr Castle would not have tolerated any abuse, or have permitted bullying by the staff.

~o~o~ Closing Bayfordbury ~o~o~

One morning in the winter of 1946, when I would have been just about twelve years old, Mr Castle told us to assemble in the playroom, and with Mrs Castle and their two daughters present, he informed us that our days at Bayfordbury were coming to an end.

Mr Castle had only been at Bayfordbury for a short time when he broke the news and told us that the entire orphanage was about to move, and that Bayfordbury was going to be closed completely.

SUFFER LITTLE CHILDREN

This was a welcome, but also a profound change to our lives, which would again affect us boys and our way of life. As it turned out, it was for the most part better, though not entirely so.

He told us that in about a week's time we would all be leaving Bayfordbury for the last time, and go to live in Eastbourne, in Sussex.

We had no idea where Eastbourne was, though we did know it was beside the sea somewhere. As it is, it's on the south coast, about sixty to seventy miles from where we were living in Bayfordbury.

That day we went to school and told everyone that we were leaving Ware Senior and Central School, and moving. It was very exciting and, generally speaking, we were glad to be leaving.

Many of us associated Ware School with Bayfordbury, and wanted to be rid of most of the memories we had of the time we had spent there.

But even so, Ware School held some nice memories for us: the snowball fights, with us Bayfordbury boys against the rest; Mrs Blackwell's 'Chinese auction'; Mr Tustin's little 'up his sleeve stick'; Mr Lawrence's gardening lessons; and many other such memories, all of which would stay with me for the rest of my life.

But, there were also plenty of reasons why we wanted to leave Ware School, chiefly because we were so often reported by the Ware School teachers or Mr Evans, the headmaster, to Mr Scougall for things we may or may not have done. Many times, if something was missing, like a football or a cricket bat, or if a boy had been seen in an outsider's garden or shoplifting, and the outsiders didn't know exactly who it was, they would commonly blame us Bayfordbury boys.

If there was a report of such an incident, and if Mr Scougall didn't know who the culprit was, he would first of all ask the boy responsible to come forward, which he never did, and if there was no particular one individual to punish, then Mr Scougall would punish all of those boys who attended Ware School.

Such punishments would include the entire orphanage going to bed immediately after we arrived back at Bayfordbury. We would not have any tea, the dormitory window shutters would be closed, and no lights would be allowed to be turned on.

During such punishments, to make things even worse, the no-talking in the dormitory after lights out would be rigorously enforced, and there

SUFFER LITTLE CHILDREN

would be strict monitoring by the masters. If boys were caught talking, they would either be caned or sent to bed after school every day for a week.

These communal type of punishments we would, it seems, mostly associate with Ware School, as many of the accusations regarding mischief often came from there. So naturally, besides being pleased to be leaving Bayfordbury we were, to some extent, also pleased to be leaving Ware School.

~°~°~ On the Move ~°~°~

On the day before our move to Eastbourne we were told to pack whatever we had in boxes or bags, and have them ready to be put on a coach first thing in the morning. We went to school and said goodbye to everyone, including Mrs Blackwell, who was particularly nice to us and wished us well.

I also said goodbye to June Chalkley, but there was no particular sadness; we only liked each other from a distance.

Then we took our last coach ride from Ware School, and passed the Odeon cinema, where we had seen *The North West Mounted Police* and *National Velvet* and a few other unforgettable pictures.

We passed through the centre of Hertford, with its prominent monumental statue of a stag situated right in the middle of town. We also passed the ruins of the Castle cinema, which had been hit by a doodlebug and, for the very last time, we drove up the long driveway and past the gatehouse, to the Bayfordbury mansion.

The next day we all got up early, had our breakfast and ran around, taking one last look at our favourite places. Many of us, no doubt, couldn't help but remember the good, as well as the bad things that had happened to us at Bayfordbury.

I fleetingly remembered our big old rook Blacky and playing field hockey, cricket and football on the front field. Of course, I couldn't help but remember my unforgettable fight with Baggy on the front lawn – an incident which, as it turned out, was the beginning of what was to be a lifelong friendship.

It was somewhat nice to remember going beating for game on those cool, damp autumn mornings. And how could I forget that terrible

SUFFER LITTLE CHILDREN

beating Valance received on his bare backside, for simply doing a bunk?

I could now perhaps put behind me the memories of Mr Scougall opening his window and questioning me after Mr Nash had physically beaten me for coming into the dining room singing.

In a rather sad moment too, I happily remembered the good times with Mrs Dunning at Bayford School, and the Bayford School dinners. I also remembered Elaine Alger, with me being the 'rabbit with red wings'.

It was nice, too, remembering winning the apples, which came from Mrs Dunning's apple tree, and even the occasion when I broke her classroom window, and the bottle of milk episode, and her not reporting my naughtiness to Mr Scougall.

All of this was to be in the past now, including the other good times associated with Bayfordbury. But mostly we were glad to be leaving the bad times, the memories of Mr Scougall and the unfair and vicious beatings we had received from that abusive man.

As we boarded the coaches that were to take us to Eastbourne on that cool early morning in March 1946, I'm sure we were very excited. We would, I'm quite sure, have been laughing and fooling around, like young adolescent boys would.

Not many of us boys would have been sorry to be leaving Bayfordbury behind, along with the mostly bad times we had suffered there.

For the next several hours we travelled to Eastbourne on the coaches, happily anticipating a better life.

As we journeyed, we sang our old Dr Barnardo songs, and in particular and quite possibly for the last time, the Bayfordbury song we all knew so well:

There is a mouldy shack on Bayford hill,
  Where we get 'goshy' grub that makes us ill.
Eggs and bacon we don't see, we get sawdust in our tea,
  And we are gradually, fading away.

15

CHURCHILL HOUSE – Part 1

~°~°~ Moving to Eastbourne ~°~°~

I was a little over twelve years old in March of 1946 when we arrived at Churchill House, in Old Town, Eastbourne, Sussex.

Now, what had seemed like a long war was at last over. I had, to this point in my life and for as long as I could remember, been living in wartime conditions. Life, it seemed, was turning for what were to be better family conditions in Britain, but not necessarily for me yet.

The wartime defences of England's shores were already in the process of being dismantled and cleared away by the time we arrived at Eastbourne. The huge concrete anti-vehicle invasion blockades, which were the deterrent for German tanks and other vehicles such as mobile guns and troop transporters had there been an invasion of England by the Germans, were still quite visible, but many of them had already been removed.

The endless miles of curled, rusty barbed wire with seaweed, rags, and other unsightly debris clinging to it, were also undergoing the huge process of being removed from the beaches at the time we arrived in Eastbourne.

However, the signs and remnants of war were still evident just about everywhere. There were many posters warning of the dangers of unexploded bombs, artillery shells, and land or sea mines which could float or be washed ashore and up onto the beaches.

As well, there were graphic pictures of other types of floating booby traps, which could also drift ashore on the incoming tides. Combined with these signs and indicators of war, there were still bunkers or gun turrets, which had been used by the Home Guard, yet to be demolished or dismantled.

SUFFER LITTLE CHILDREN
~o~o~ Churchill House ~o~o~

Churchill House was not a huge or a particularly old mansion like Bayfordbury, but nevertheless it was still a very large domicile, with three floors filled with long corridors, steep stairs, and many very large and small rooms. The entire estate, which consisted of about five acres, was located in the heart of Old Town.

Old Town is an original part of Eastbourne. Many years ago the wealthy lived on the sea front, which was the prime area of Eastbourne in those days, while the tradesmen and other working people lived inland, in which later, and to this day, is called 'Old Town'.

Later still, it became fashionable for the wealthy to live in Old Town as well as on the 'front' and so, in the later part of the nineteenth century, the prestigious Churchill House was built there.

~o~o~

We arrived at Churchill House, in two or three coaches, at about twelve thirty – dinnertime. Because of the move, sandwiches were provided for us.

After assembling in the playroom we were told the fundamental things we needed to know about Eastbourne, including any changes in our daily routine. We were then shown to our respective dormitories.

After having lived at Bayfordbury for the past three and a half years, the rooms to be used as dormitories in Churchill House seemed quite small, almost cosy even. Whereas the dormitories at Bayfordbury had about thirty boys in them, here we had just six boys in each dormitory, three each side of the room.

There were perhaps seven or eight dormitories on two floors. Each dormitory was identified alphabetically, A to maybe H. We still had the same black cast-iron pipe 'head and bottom' ends on our beds, which had probably been brought to Eastbourne from Bayfordbury.

I was in dormitory B. Flappers was in dormitory F. I can remember he was in dormitory F because of something that was to happen in the near future that would certainly help to make me remember.

SUFFER LITTLE CHILDREN

Churchill House, Eastbourne, Sussex

I can't remember which dormitory Baggy and Fred were in, though I know they weren't in the same dormitory as Flappers or me. However, as we would spend quite a bit of time in each other's dorms, actually sleeping in the same dormitory didn't seem to matter much.

The dormitories were nicely painted and the wood floors were polished and shiny. The 'ablutions', which we now called lavatories, were much nicer than at Bayfordbury, and we even had bathtubs to bath in, instead of crude showers.

Fortunately, there were no requirements for us to have to close the window shutters any more, now that the war was over – although I'm not sure that there were architecturally built-in shutters for the windows at Churchill House. Thank goodness, the rooms would never be in total darkness at night again.

We didn't need to have a bucket in the centre of the dormitory floor at nights as the lavatories were just down the corridor on each floor. The cleaning of the lavatories was one of many 'general duties' which all of the boys were required to do from time to time on a regular basis.

SUFFER LITTLE CHILDREN

Inspections of our bodies for cleanliness, and checking to see if we still had our combs, toothbrushes, towels etc was all in the past. As a matter of fact I don't recall us losing such toiletry items after we moved to Eastbourne, and if we did, I'm quite sure that Mr Castle didn't punish us for having such deficiencies.

There were two playrooms. One of them was located in a nicer part of the mansion, while the other was located in a remote area of the home and which, as I recall, we called the gymnasium. We would play indoor hockey with a soft rubber puck, and rolled up newspapers bound tightly with string, which we used for hockey sticks.

The food at Churchill House, even though it was still rationed, was much better too. Everything, including the preparation of the vegetables and the bread slicing, was done by the employed staff. There was even a proper lady cook.

~о~о~ Bedewell School ~о~о~

A few days after we arrived at Churchill House we had to be enrolled in our new outsiders' schools. Because there were so many of us, we were divided into two groups. One group went to Bedewell School and the other to Bourne School. Both of these senior schools were the same in every respect except that they were in two separate areas of Eastbourne, about a half a mile or so apart.

Eastbourne was a fairly big town even in those days, but not so big that we couldn't walk from one end of town to the other in perhaps an hour. The schools were about fifteen minutes apart if we ran all the way.

It was decided that Fred, Flappers and I were to go to Bedewell School, but poor ole Baggy had to go to Bourne School. It didn't make too much difference really, as we would often meet at dinnertime to swim in the sea or otherwise 'muck around' along the sea front.

I had two teachers that I remember reasonably well at Bedewell School, besides several more who I can't remember very well. One was a youngish chap called Mr Grey. The other was a lady, who also wasn't very old. Her name was Miss Gardener. She was my 'home' class teacher. I liked Miss Gardener. Besides being rather pretty she was always pleasant, and encouraged us to learn.

SUFFER LITTLE CHILDREN

Unfortunately, my 'scatterbrain' attitude towards school, until the time we came to Eastbourne and Bedewell School, was, I know, not very good. What with my having been moved so much, from orphanage to orphanage and school to school, I would excuse myself and say that because of all the moving, that it was no wonder I would have found it hard to settle down in school to learn.

I have, to this day, just one school report card from my childhood. This report is for my first term at Bedewell School, and it's signed by Miss Gardener. If I couldn't justify why it was so bad, I would be ashamed of it. The report shows that I came twenty-fourth in our class of twenty-eight. I don't have, nor have I ever seen, any other of my school report cards, that I can recollect.

~o~o~

In later years, when I had children of my own, I would encourage them to do well at school. I would tell, or even emphasise to them, to first of all "learn how to learn", and that without a good education life could be difficult. I never did show them my 'only' school report card, as I would have been a poor example for them to follow.

~o~o~

Eventually I did settle down at Bedewell School and thanks to Miss Gardener, although I didn't excel in any of the academic subjects, I did eventually catch up with my schooling, generally speaking.

It was at Bedewell School that I was first to get into a boxing ring. Our gym teacher showed us the rudiments of the sport and told us to pair off and, in our turn, get into the ring. We were required to put on oversized boxing gloves and the teacher merely told us, in effect, to 'go to it'.

The heavy oversized sparring gloves helped stop any of us from hurting each other. Because the gloves were so big and heavy, we boys simply couldn't punch each other as quickly as we might have been able to if the gloves had been lighter, tighter, and therefore harder.

Even though I was very small I was, even at Bedewell School, thought to be a good fighter amongst my peers. But fighting in the 'ring'

SUFFER LITTLE CHILDREN

for sport is quite different from scrapping amongst ourselves. Boxing, though we were not to learn much about the sport at that time, has far more finesse to it than just putting on boxing gloves and getting into a boxing ring.

I can distinctly remember the first time I ever got into a boxing ring, and how nervous I was. I remember too that I held both gloves up in front of my face, in a defensive manner, and then punched or counter-punched with both of my gloves at the same time, much like a piston.

The gym teacher told me the proper way to defend myself and how to lead with my left hand only, but I took no notice of him and continued the two-handed punching strategy, which seemed to work OK for me. I know now that I must have looked rather foolish during my boxing debut, but I really didn't care at the time. I was to, just a few years in the future at yet another orphanage, learn how to box properly. I will write about this later.

~o~o~ Mr Castle in the Sudan ~o~o~

Mr Castle would tell us stories about his life as chief of police in the Sudan. Besides being a big man he was, with his bent nose and huge hands, a tough-looking man.

Although he was such a big man, and looked a little like a retired heavyweight boxer or wrestler might, he seldom ever got angry. He never, ever hit any of us boys with his hands.

As the police chief, Mr Castle had had some tough times in the Sudan. The British police stationed out there, we were led to believe, were a rough bunch, much like the English equivalent of the French Foreign Legion.

One of his stories was that while he was serving in the Sudan the British picture, *The Four Feathers* was made in his district. He told us how there was a scene in the picture in which a massacre of British troops supposedly took place, and after the massacre, vultures came to feast on the corpses.

The way he told his stories was very graphic and he made them sound so true, which he always said they were, and I had no good reason to doubt him.

SUFFER LITTLE CHILDREN

He went on to tell us that to get the vultures to circle overhead for the filming of *The Four Feathers*, two horses were killed to attract them. Mr Castle told us how the filming crew spread old army uniforms and weapons around the dead horses, and that the vultures circled for hours before they landed to feast.

I remember Mr Castle as being a very tolerant man. He and his family would from time to time accompany us on walks on the South Downs. It was often during these walks that he would tell us of his adventures in the Sudan.

He did punish us, of course. Just like at Bayfordbury, we would have to bend over a big armchair. Then he would give us a few good wallops on our rear ends with his huge plimsoll (sneaker) slipper. Have no doubt, the slipper certainly hurt and so, as with the cane, we would naturally try to avoid having to receive 'capital punishment'.

Fortunately, the slipper wasn't used to punish us very often, but when it was, the standard punishment for doing something considered very wrong was perhaps four whacks. An extreme punishment might be six whacks. Although he didn't beat us with a stick, we were nevertheless still very concerned about getting the slipper.

We all liked Mr Castle and his family. Mrs Castle was always very friendly, but had little to do with the actual looking after us. Besides caring for us, the Castles were also raising their two daughters, who, generally speaking, were kept apart from us.

~o~o~ Miss (Nurse) Rand ~o~o~

Miss Rand, who we called Nurse Rand, was just a young woman, small and petite, between twenty and twenty-four years old, I would believe.

She was in charge of the sick bay. If we had any minor or otherwise treatable ailments, like a boil which had to be dressed, or bumps, cuts and scrapes, or even chickenpox or mumps, then we would go to see her, and she would attend to us.

Nurse Rand was an unfortunate widow, and a victim of the war. It was said that her young husband had been a fighter pilot and was killed during the critical Battle of Britain, about three or four years before we had come to live at Churchill House.

SUFFER LITTLE CHILDREN

I think of Nurse Rand as being a rather quiet person in a sad way. She was, we thought, a very pretty lady who never had even the slightest cross word for anyone.

In considering her situation, I believe now that Miss Rand had come to work for Dr Barnardo's Homes to help take her mind off her enormous loss. Looking after us kids helped her, like with so many other young women at that time who had lost loved ones, to get over her otherwise empty life.

Nurse Rand had a bicycle, which was a ladies' bike, of course. Often I would go and ask her if I could borrow it. It was a new bicycle and had a modern three-speed gear change on it. Fortunately for me, the saddle height never needed adjusting, because Nurse Rand wasn't much, if any, taller than me.

One way or another, Fred had built himself a reasonably good bike. It had brakes that worked, two good wheels with tires that didn't constantly go flat, and a chain that didn't break very often, which, if it did, needed new links for replacements. Actually his bike operated pretty well considering that he made it completely from scratch, without spending much, if any money.

Only one other boy, whose name I can't recall, had a bicycle, which his mother had bought him.

Fred with his bike, I with Miss Rand's bike, and Baggy, if Baggy could borrow the other boy's bike, would go racing around Eastbourne. The bikes would, it seemed, fly like the wind.

The streets and roads in Eastbourne are quite hilly and so we could get up quite a speed going down the hills, though along the actual sea front it was quite flat. There weren't many cars on the roads in those days, so it wasn't particularly dangerous for bicycles.

However, on one particular occasion, when just Fred and I were out on bikes and racing around the main streets in the town, a policeman signalled for us to stop.

Without proper regard for the policeman, and not really caring, we didn't stop. I would suppose we simply didn't give a darn, and carried on without a care in the world. After all, he wasn't one of our masters.

Many of the police in those days also rode bicycles, and so the young policeman, on his 'roadster' bike, gave chase. We rode as fast as we

SUFFER LITTLE CHILDREN

could, down several streets, until the policeman eventually caught us.

He took our names and found out that we were Dr Barnardo boys from 'Old Town'.

For our own sake, I now believe, we were reported to Mr Castle, who gave us a severe talking-to, and told us we weren't to ride our bicycles in town any more.

But after a while we (perhaps he forgot his instructions) continued to ride around the town, but there were no more incidents with the police.

~o~o~ Sea Scouts ~o~o~

It was Mr Castle who, much like he did in Hertford, was able to influence the local townspeople to embrace and invite us into their community. I don't believe Mr Scougall ever made this kind of effort on our behalf.

Mr Castle's efforts to integrate us into the community paid off, because shortly after we arrived in Eastbourne we were encouraged to join the Boy Scouts and other clubs. I remember that I joined the table tennis team in Churchill House and that we played in a table tennis league, playing against grown-ups' teams in the town, and we did quite well.

Fred, Baggy and Flappers, and a few of the other boys and I, joined the Sea Scouts. With little effort, we learned the Scout's Promise and Laws. I can't say that I can still remember all of the laws, though I can still remember a few. However, I have no problem remembering the Promise.

I promise to do my best, to do my duty to God and the King,
To help other people at all times, and obey the Scouts' Law.

We also had to learn and to pass our 'Tenderfoot'. In several different ways we also helped to put on fund raising entertainment, the money going towards Britain's war debt to America.

~o~o~

On one very memorable occasion our sea scout troop was entered into a regatta (race) against other clubs and sea scouts in the area. Our troop had two boats entered. One boat had all our 'big' or older

SUFFER LITTLE CHILDREN

(fourteen-year-old) sea scouts in it. The boat I was in was our second entry.

Our scout troop didn't own a boat, so we didn't practise at all.

The idea was to row in a rhythmic and coordinated manner as fast as we could, and so, of course, win the race. As it was, we rowed our hearts out.

There were about six of us boys on each side of the big old wooden, twenty-five foot long rowboat, and each of us had one long, very heavy, oar each.

The coxswain, an older sea scout, was shouting "In out, in out, in out" almost frantically as we raced along the shore in front of the promenade, There were lots of holiday makers watching us, some shouting encouragement to their favourite team.

Eastbourne was, even then, a fairly popular holiday town. Many Londoners come down to Eastbourne for weekends, and even spent their summer holidays there, particularly now that the war was over.

Our scout troop's best boat – the boat with the older scouts in it – came in first, to cheers and clapping of the spectators. The other boat – the boat that I was in – didn't do so well, and actually came in last out of about twelve boats.

Unfortunately, the oars were far too big for me and I just couldn't hold onto them. The part of the oar I had to hold in order to row was so thick that with my hands being so small, I found it hard to hold onto the oar. To top it off, the rest of the rowers' oars kept knocking into each other. To make things even worse, I dropped my oar, so we had to turn our boat around and go back for it.

As I have mentioned, our boat came last. Nobody seemed to care much; at least no one said anything to me, except Baggy and Flappers, who constantly taunted me and fooled around. Fred, fortunately for him, was in our other boat that actually came third in the race. He would have a different story to tell about that regatta.

The people who had cheered on our senior boat were now laughing and shouting to us in our boat, all in fun, of course. I don't think I would have been laughing at the time, even though I wouldn't have cared that we came in last. I would have been thinking that I was only too pleased to have the blinking race over with.

SUFFER LITTLE CHILDREN
~o~o~ The Scouts International Jamboree ~o~o~

A very happy and unforgettable event that took place when I was in the Sea Scouts was the International Jamboree held at Eastbourne.

International jamborees are always very big events in the scouting world. Scout troops from all over the world attend, including troops from Australia, America, Switzerland, Africa, New Zealand, Canada, and many European and other countries in the world.

The campsite was established near the woods, high up on the South Downs, overlooking the sea. Contrary to how it sounds, the Downs are actually rather high rolling hills that stretch for many miles along the south coast of England. Our troop was one of several troops that helped collect firewood and bring it to the many piles of wood for the visiting scouts to take back to their campsites.

There were about three thousand scouts in attendance at the Eastbourne Jamboree, which was to last three days.

During the first couple of days we learned how to chop wood safely, follow trails, and how to peel potatoes and prepare vegetables properly – something we hadn't had a chance to learn at Bayfordbury.

It's almost traditional that at scout camps like this jamboree, where boys sit around their own troop's campfire at night, the scoutmaster or another talented scout leader, tells scary stories.

However, what I remember most about that jamboree was that on the last night, we all assembled in a huge clearing, grouped according to our respective countries, and with our country's flags in full view. Each country sang what was perhaps one of their traditional scout songs.

The song that we sang, and which I learned at that very memorable jamboree, was a song I was to remember and teach to my wife and four sons when we would go camping many years in the future.

The song, said to be a famous scout song, has rather strange words, and was, I was to find out later, apparently written by Lord Baden-Powell – founder and Chief Scout of the World. The song goes as follows:

SUFFER LITTLE CHILDREN

Ging Gang Gooley

Ging gang gooley, gooley, gooley, gooley, watcha ging gang goo, ging gang goo.
Ging gang gooley, gooley, gooley, gooley, watcha ging gang goo, ging gang goo.

Chorus:
Heyla, heyla sheyla, heyla sheyla, heyla ho heyla, heyla sheyla, heyla sheyla, heyla ho
Golly wally, golly wally, golly walla, golly walla um-pa, um-pa, um-pa.

Repeat:
Ging gang gooley, gooley, gooley, gooley, watcha ging gang goo, ging gang goo.
Ging gang gooley, gooley, gooley, gooley, watcha ging gang goo, ging gang goo.

During the scouts' first International World Jamboree, Lord Baden Powell realised that scouts throughout the world spoke different languages. Because of that, he wrote this song, which no one understood the words or meaning of, and he called it simply 'a nonsense song'.

There were other songs we were taught at the jamboree, but this one, as was its intent, was the easiest to remember and I believe it was not only the silliest, but by far the most unforgettable.

A newspaper, the *Eastbourne Gazette*, took a photo of part of our troop with Lord Rowallen, and published it the next day. Lord Rowallen had become the Chief Scout of the world after Lord Baden-Powell retired.

Nurse Rand, because she saw my photo in the paper, went to the Eastbourne Gazette office and bought a copy of the photo, then gave it to me. I still have the photograph in our family photo collection, all these years later.

SUFFER LITTLE CHILDREN

Lord Rowallen (Chief Scout) at
the International Boy Scouts
Jamboree
Eastbourne – 1946

~o~o~ Scouts Paper Drive ~o~o~

Another memorable thing that Flappers and I did, which I'm not particularly proud of, was the time we found a purse with money in it, and kept it.

Although as I say, I'm not particularly proud of what we did, it nevertheless happened, and I feel bound to tell all.

Our scout leader asked if any of us would volunteer to go on a 'paper drive' one Saturday. Flappers and I, with only good intentions, said we would. So, as was quite normal, they gave us a two-wheeled handcart to collect the salvage paper in.

SUFFER LITTLE CHILDREN

The handcart was about four feet wide and four feet long and had about a four-foot long single tongue handle with which to steer it. It also had big wooden wheels, which were about three feet in diameter.

We were required to knock on people's doors and ask them if they had any old books or newspapers for our paper drive.

Most of the people on our predetermined route would have been informed that the scouts would be coming, and to have their salvage paper or books on their front doorsteps for us to just come and put the salvage on our cart.

At the house I am about to mention (for us, the lucky one, the house at the end of the rainbow, depending on one's point of view) the rotten thing happened.

I remember well that, as with the other houses on the street, we knocked on the door, but unlike most of the others, no one answered. So, we knocked again and still there was no answer.

Just then, just as we were about to leave, one of us happened to look on the step we were actually standing on, and there, on the step (at the end of the rainbow), was a little brown purse.

We picked up the purse, glanced inside, and saw that there was what appeared to be some change in it. Flappers – the 'Artful Dodger's' – eyes and mine met, and our minds were immediately made up. One of the codes we lived by, which at that time in our lives seemed to be OK, was 'Finders, keepers; losers, weepers'. This was a code we believed to be fair, and most certainly so on that day.

We had already knocked on the door and no one had answered, so Flappers put the little purse in his pocket and we carried on down the street.

After we had gone a little way down the street and away from the house where we had found the purse, we looked in the purse again. To our delight there was much more money in it than we had first thought. As it turned out, there was a one-pound note and a ten-shilling note, and also some silver and coppers in it.

It really was quite a lot of money. Grown-ups in those days only earned about three to four pounds a week.

We were quite pleased with our find, and without any concern or conscience that perhaps we were being dishonest, we shared out the

SUFFER LITTLE CHILDREN

money and headed straight for the sweet shop. We also shared the money with Fred and Baggy, who, like us, bought various things to eat and drink, and just got rid of the money.

Although I have mentioned that we had had no concerns as to who had lost the purse, that's not quite true. I know I wondered then, and have often wondered since, if the purse could have belonged to a retired pensioner or some other unfortunate person who couldn't afford to lose it. Even then, at the time when in our orphanage society, the 'dog eat dog' rule applied, I did for a short while feel a little guilty.

On the other hand, the purse could have belonged to someone who could well have afforded to lose it, and so, without taxing my conscience any further, I chose to believe the latter.

To put it all in perspective, we had found more than thirty shillings, which for us, was an enormous amount of money. At that time, going to the pictures and sitting in the cheap seats cost about sixpence, a bottle of ginger beer or 'pop' cost about tuppence a bottle, and a bus ride across the entire town of Eastbourne cost about thre'pence.

~o~o~ Scouts Garden Fete ~o~o~

Our scout troop would raise money in several different ways for many charities, even for Dr Barnardo's Homes, I would think.

On one particular occasion, the scoutmaster made arrangements with Mr Castle, and with Mr Castle's consent, the scouts held a 'garden fete' in the field that was part of the Churchill House estate.

The field was almost square in shape and about three acres in size. In one corner of the field several stalls were set up, perhaps fifteen to twenty altogether.

There were all types of events that took place at the stalls including popguns, which could be used to shoot a light toy or something off a shelf. There were darts to aim at playing cards mounted on a large sheet of cardboard or plywood, and small hoops to toss over prizes, and so on.

The stalls, or otherwise 'pitches', were situated all in one corner of the field, forming a rather large circle.

Flappers and I had a pitch to run, called a 'coconut shy' or, as was its proper name, an 'Aunt Sally'. The idea was for a customer to pay

SUFFER LITTLE CHILDREN

tuppence for three wooden balls, and to throw the balls at the coconuts. But as coconuts would have been difficult to come by so shortly after the war, we used turnips.

The turnips – about six – were balanced on top of posts. If anyone could throw one of their wooden balls and knock a turnip off, then the person would win a prize.

Flappers and I did a pretty brisk business. Typically, Flappers, I expect, suggested we siphon off our share of the 'take' before we handed the money in.

Behind us, at the side of the field, there were lots of bushes. So, we placed a tin in the hedge, making sure it couldn't be seen by anyone.

Then when no one was looking, we would take some of the money our stall made, and put it in the tin. By the end of the day we had made about one shilling and six pence each without raising any suspicion.

I'm not sure that we fully understood all of the Scouts' Laws properly. Of course we were honest little boy scouts, so who would suspect we would do anything to the contrary?

As it was, lots of the boys were dipping into their take, and no one was caught, as far as I know.

~o~o~ Paid a Penny ~o~o~

Each school day we were given a penny for a bus ride to school. Dr Barnardo's Homes wouldn't pay us to ride home from school, only to school. So, we had to walk back to the orphanage each day.

Quite often we would run to school in the mornings in order to keep our pennies. We never seemed to save many of our pennies though, and so I have to presume we spent them on silly, unaccountable items.

Vicarage Road, the road where Churchill House was on, was located next to the golf links. Often, on the way home from Bedewell School, we would take a short cut through the golf links in order to get back to the orphanage quickly.

On the particular day that I am going to mention, Fred and I were cutting across the golf links, hurrying, because both of us had to go to the 'gents' (toilet). We knew there was a 'public convenience' (another name they used to call the public toilets in those days, and still do

SUFFER LITTLE CHILDREN

actually) on the golf links. So, because of the urgency, Fred and I headed straight for it.

We were both busting to go to the gents so we ran the last fifty yards or so, our hands in our pockets, searching for our pennies.

It never cost anything to use a urinal, but it always cost a penny to use the WC, and this time we both urgently needed to use the WC.

There were just two WC cubicles in the gents. Being just ahead of Fred I ran straight to nearest one, just as Fred ran to the second door. I remember that we were both panicking and laughing as we ran into the gents because the situation was so urgent.

Rushing to get into the WC, I dropped my penny into the slot provided, so that I could open the door. How shocked and surprised I was at what I saw next.

As the penny dropped, I noticed a big note, a really big note on the door that read quite clearly, 'Out of Order'. But it was too late. I had already put my one and only penny in the slot, and it was gone.

The way the toilets flushed at that time was simply by a gravity system. After use, one just pulled down on a chain, which was attached to a lever on a three-gallon tank of water located above the WC, about seven feet above the floor and attached to the wall over the toilet. Water then rushed down a pipe and flushed the toilet.

Unable to stop myself, I rushed into the stall, looked around, and couldn't see anything at all wrong. The toilet bowl wasn't broken or even cracked, there was water in the actual toilet, and the overhead tank looked fine.

With a sigh of relief, I undid all my buttons, slipped my braces off my shoulders, and did my business. Relieved, I pulled up my short trousers, did up my buttons, put my braces back over my shoulders, and then it happened.

Still talking to Fred and telling him how there was nothing wrong in this stall and that perhaps someone was just fooling around writing silly notes and sticking them on the stall, I pulled the chain.

The water rushed down the vertical pipe from the tank to the toilet, in the normal way that it should, to flush the toilet.

The problem was that there was a very small, unnoticeable hole in the pipe, and it was located about chest high on me. The pressure of

SUFFER LITTLE CHILDREN

water coming down the pipe was such that the water shot straight out of the hole, and straight at me.

I remember frantically shouting and trying to get out of the way of the stream of water, but the door was bolted of course, and I was unable to get out. Fred stood on his toilet and looked over the partition to see what was going on.

I came out of the stall, soaking wet. Needless to say, Fred laughed and I never, as they say, heard the last of it. If the entire event had been a planned practical joke, it couldn't have worked better or have been funnier.

The whole outsiders' school and Churchill House heard about it. Even Nurse Rand laughed at me.

16

CHURCHILL HOUSE – Part 2

-~º~º~ Fatigues ~º~º~

Living at Churchill House, with Mr Castle as our headmaster and being near the sea, was such a difference for us boys as compared with the recent lives we had been living at Bayfordbury with the now deceased Mr Scougall.

We had loved the Bayfordbury countryside and its surroundings, and also the actual town of Hertford, and to some extent we missed it. But that was all. Here, close to the South Downs, the sea, and the beautiful town of Eastbourne, was more than compensation for what we had left behind.

But still it was not all fun. We were, of course, still somewhat underprivileged kids with, in many ways, rebellious characters. Although Mr Castle's guidance relaxed our fear of our keepers, there was still Mr Nash we had to be wary of.

If Mr Nash was on duty, we kept out of his way as best we could, though he would be in constant contact with us as we did our chores, which were called fatigues. The kind of fatigues we did included, among others:

- Weeding the flower gardens, and there were lots of them.
- Sweeping up the leaves, as well as the garden paths, with 'witches brooms'. These brooms were made from something like swamp willow twigs, and lashed together onto a pole handle.
- Raking the dead grass in the field, which was about three acres, in the spring and through the summer after a local farmer had come and cut the long and rough grass.
- Polishing the many pine floors throughout Churchill House.
- Cleaning and polishing the brass door knobs and push-plates on the doors to almost every room in the mansion.
- Cleaning windows inside the house.
- Dusting throughout the home.

SUFFER LITTLE CHILDREN

There were many, many other fatigues that had to be done regularly, but which are too numerous to mention, though most of them are similar to those I have mentioned.

Some of the fatigues would take hours to do and to easily distracted young boys, they seemed arduous and somewhat unnecessary.

Young boys, being what they are, didn't want to waste time doing fatigues and really only did the very least they could, simply to get the fatigue passed or accepted by the master on duty. If the fatigue wasn't done to the satisfaction of the master, then the work would merely have to be done all over again. Eventually we learned, for the most part, to be smart and do our fatigues right the first time.

I realise only now, as I write, that someone had to do these jobs and so, needless to say, it would be reasonable that we did them.

~○~○~ Poor Ole Flappers ~○~○~

On one particular occasion, when Baggy, Fred, Flappers and I were doing fatigues raking the field with about thirty other boys, we still found a way to get into trouble.

It was a relaxing type of fatigue; no one was making us work hard or overly watching us. The master who was in charge of us, Mr Brock, had left us to go for a cup of tea or something or other, like grown-ups did. And, as the saying goes, 'When the cat's away the mice will play'. Just like it would with most boys, the saying suited us perfectly.

While Mr Brock was gone, we eleven or twelve-year-old boys were playing 'cowboys and Indians'. Other boys were playing at other things instead of raking, or simply sitting on the grass, keeping digs.

In our playing cowboys and Indians, we started off by hiding behind the many piles of dried grass we had raked up. The piles, about two-feet-six high, were scattered around the field.

Gradually the game extended into the next field, which had lots of blackberry bushes and other types of dense bushes in it, that were ideal for hiding in.

However, this field – the field next to ours – belonged to another estate. We knew that the property was most certainly 'out of bounds' and that we shouldn't be playing in it. Quite probably the owner had

SUFFER LITTLE CHILDREN

appealed to Mr Castle to keep us off his land, and Mr Castle would have undoubtedly made every effort to keep peace between us Dr Barnardo boys and our neighbours.

Well, while several of us were out of bounds, Mr Brock came back and noticed we were missing, or perhaps he even caught a glimpse of one of us. The boy keeping diggy-eye of course, didn't see him coming.

None of us boys disliked Mr Brock. As it was, we actually liked him. In fact, we thought Mr Brock was a little bit soft on us, and because of that, we might well take advantage of him.

Although we wouldn't think about it too much, I believe we were aware and understood that the staff, including Mr Brock, still had a job to do and that a certain amount of discipline had to be upheld.

Anyway, Mr Brock saw Fred, Baggy and me and told us to come out of the neighbour's field and over to him, in our field. He hadn't see Flappers.

Then he told us to go up to the house and report to the office. Without glancing back at us, he left and headed up to the house to meet us there.

As we were leaving to go up to the house, and as usual, grumbling and feeling a bit sorry for ourselves, I saw Flappers. He was still in the other field between some bushes, walking towards us.

He had been too far away to hear us get caught and had probably thought that the game was over. He might even have been picking blackberries all the time Mr Brock was reprimanding us.

I shouted over to him, "Hey! Flappers. We got caught out of bounds and have to report to the office," and followed up with, "Mr Brock saw you too, and said you have to report as well."

Of course Mr Brock hadn't seen Flappers at all. I don't know why I told Flappers he had to report; it just came out, like another saying: 'misery loves company'.

Well, as it was, Baggy, Fred and I filed into Mr Castle's office. Mr Brock was there, explaining the fact that we were out of bounds and that he had told us to report to the office.

Mr Castle told us that there had been several complaints about us boys trespassing on our neighbour's property, and that we were going to get the slipper, in order to set an example to the other boys.

SUFFER LITTLE CHILDREN

We weren't surprised to hear our punishment. Being out of bounds always had been a corporal punishment and although the slipper hurt and we would avoid it if at all possible, here we were, and we were prepared to take our punishment.

Baggy was first to get about three whacks with the slipper; then Fred. Just as I stepped towards the 'flogging chair' there was a knock on the door.

Mr Castle stopped, stood up straight, and called out, "Come in."

Then the door opened slowly and Flappers stepped inside the office. Mr Castle asked him what he wanted. Flappers, looking at Mr Brock said, "I was told to report to the office, Sir."

Before Mr Brock could answer, Mr Castle asked, "What for?"

"For being out of bounds, Sir," replied Flappers.

Mr Castle said to Mr Brock, "Did you see Foot out of bounds? You didn't mention him."

Mr Brock smiled and said, "Actually I didn't, Sir. I only saw Longman, Dyos and Baggaridge, but if he was, I think he should be here also."

Flappers was glaring at me, when Mr Castle asked him, "Were you out of bounds then, Foot?"

Flappers, realising he would get into far more trouble if he were caught lying, had to tell Mr Castle he had been with us and replied, "Yes, Sir!"

The rest of us putting our hands over our mouths and, trying hard not to laugh, felt like a bunch of 'rotten little sods'.

I remember that Mr Castle, also seeing the funny side, smiled and said, "Then you had better stay, hadn't you, Foot?"

So, Flappers got three good whacks with the slipper, just like we did.

Flappers was a tough kid. We could have had a fist fight over the incident, but we simply had a good laugh at the whole event. I know Flappers would have remembered this story for many years to come.

~○~○~ Love Lane ~○~○~

Just like we did at Bayfordbury one of us, or perhaps we all helped to make a very crude bike, I can't really remember exactly who made it, though it was probably Fred.

SUFFER LITTLE CHILDREN

As it was, the bike consisted only of a frame, two wheels, a seat, and handlebars. It had no chain, pedals or breaks. It didn't even have tires on the steel rims, and it certainly didn't have a bell.

Fred was a little taller than the rest of us, and so for him the bike was just about OK for his height, but for Baggy, Flappers, and me, the bike frame was a little too tall for us and therefore the seat far too high, resulting in us having to help each other up onto the seat. Then we would push each other down the sloping 'Love Lane' until we got up enough speed for whoever was on the bike to 'stay up' and freewheel.

Love Lane, which was not much wider than a footpath – about three to four feet wide – and had tall trees and bushes that overhung it on each side. It was a fairly straight lane that sloped downhill for about two hundred yards or so. The surface of the lane was covered with a thick layer of coal cinders.

Coal cinders, called 'coke', are the ashes left over after coal has been incinerated in either a furnace or in anyone's home fireplace. Cinders are particularly brittle and very sharp to the touch. The lane was located just outside the back gate of the Churchill House estate.

The idea was simple. After being pushed, and getting up enough speed, the bicycle would careen, freewheeling down the hill completely out of control, until it eventually ran out of 'hill' after two hundred yards or so, after which the footpath 'bottomed out' and started an upward climb.

On one memorable occasion, when it was my turn for the bike ride, Baggy and Flappers, or Fred, ran beside me, pushing me as fast as they could. Then, because they couldn't run as fast as I was travelling, they left me to continue hurtling down the lane on my own, all of which was quite normal.

After they had left me I travelled on, absolutely out of control, at what seemed like breakneck speed, down the lane.

Quite a long way down the lane there were two people walking a medium-sized dog. The dog wasn't on a lead, which was quite normal at that time.

As I approached them, I was shouting to the people in order to draw their attention to me as there was no bell on the bike. The man and woman both moved tight to the side of the lane, waiting for me to go

SUFFER LITTLE CHILDREN

hurtling past, at the same time calling out something to the dog, thus drawing its attention to me.

Perhaps they were shouting urgently for the dog to "Sit, sit!"

Now that I think about it, maybe that's exactly what they did shout, because the dog did just that, it merely sat down right in the middle of the lane.

With only steel rims, it's very difficult not to slide on loose cinders under such circumstances if one tries to swerve. Unfortunately, with no control whatsoever, I could do nothing but try to keep the bike upright.

The obedient or otherwise petrified dog, sitting upright on its haunches, watched me come straight towards it and didn't move an inch. I, being unable to do anything about it, ran right over the dopey dog.

The front wheel of the bike simply slid off the dog's hindquarters. The bike, of course, went sideways and tipped over, with me flying over the handlebars and sprawling flat out, face down in the cinders.

The man and woman ran over, very concerned about me, and asked me if I was all right. I had cuts and scrapes on my hands, arms, knees and legs, and even a grazed nose. I was, it seemed, bleeding everywhere, otherwise I was all right. I'm sure I believed I was going to get into trouble, because I thought I was the one at fault, which without a doubt I was, and at that point would just have scampered away.

Fortunately for me the lady took out her handkerchief and cleaned me up as best she could, and told me how sorry they were. The dog was completely forgotten, but nevertheless was all right. The main concern for them was that I wasn't hurt.

Then to top it off and to my delight, the man put his hand in his pocket and gave me sixpence. I was very happy getting the sixpence, it was much better than getting the slipper from Mr Castle if I had been reported for riding the bike in Love Lane, something which wouldn't have been allowed in the first place.

~o~o~ Cheeky Beggars ~o~o~

Something rather hard to believe was our way of 'going to the pictures', which we would often do on a Saturday.

We were allowed to go into town on Saturday and Sunday afternoons,

SUFFER LITTLE CHILDREN

and even in the evenings in the summer, I believe, to do anything we liked, such as going to the pictures if we had saved any money, which would have been most unlikely. Sometimes we would just wander around the shops, doing a little shopping (or, should I say, shoplifting) or we might just go down to the beach, and in the summer, go swimming in the sea.

We still, even though we were now about twelve years old, didn't have any money to spend. Our pocket money may have increased, but it still would not have been more than tuppence a week, which we would spend on bread rolls or perhaps pop.

Generally speaking, we didn't have any money saved up, except for a penny or two from time to time. To go to the pictures cost about sixpence.

However, if we decided to go to the pictures, it would start with one of us typically saying to the other, "Shall we go to the pictures today?"

The other would reply, something to the effect of, "OK. Which one shall we go and see?"

The response could be, "Let's go and see *Tarzan and the Leopard Woman*. It's on at the Tivoli."

After deciding which film we wanted to see, we would head off down into Eastbourne and stand at the entrance into the cinema.

If the picture was an 'A' (adult) or 'H' (horror) picture, which it seemed many of them were, then children weren't allowed into the cinema without an adult.

The unbelievable thing we would do, which today I can hardly believe, but which we did many, many times, was to split up and approach people.

One of us would commonly approach a man and his lady friend (they would have probably been on a date) and ask them, "Would you take me in please, Sir?"

We would put our hand out with maybe a penny or even a halfpenny in it. The man, showing his date that he was the generous type, would most often say, "Oh that's all right; I'll pay for you."

Not wanting us to sit with them in the pictures, because perhaps they were courting, the chap would pay for the cheapest seat, at the children's rate, for us. So, for them the price wasn't too bad and they probably felt good as well.

SUFFER LITTLE CHILDREN

Each of us would have to find their own 'adults' to pay for us, though I must say, to be completely honest, that I only remember just Flappers and myself doing this 'cheeky beggars' act. I don't remember Baggy or Fred ever being as brazen as Flappers, and without Flappers' influence I probably wouldn't have had the nerve to ask to be 'taken in' either.

We would, if we had been sitting with them, always say thank you to the people who took us in and paid for us. Then, in the intermission, we would look around and then go and sit with each other. We never thought of ourselves as being beggars, though thinking back, of course we were.

In those days one could go into the pictures at any time during the showing of the picture. If the picture was halfway through, or even just ten minutes from the end, a person would quite often see the end of a picture long before they saw the beginning of the film.

If the film was a suspense or a mystery story, you would know 'who did it' before the crime was even committed.

One could also stay in the pictures and see the picture several times, or until the cinema closed at the end of the day, except in our case we would have to be back to the orphanage by tea time.

We did, I remember, knock on people's houses from time to time and ask if we could do 'odd jobs' to try and earn enough money to go to the pictures, but most people didn't give us anything to do, so we fell back on our "Please, Sir, would you take me in?"

~°~°~ Dodging in ~°~°~

One time when I went to the pictures, I managed to go in completely under my own resources as a result of my cheeky nature.

If on a Saturday or Sunday afternoon, we decided not to dodge into the pictures, but to basically just saunter around the town or go swimming in the sea, we may, quite spontaneously, decide to play chasing around the centre of Eastbourne.

Often there would be as many as eight of us boys, four on each side, running around the town, half of us looking for the other half. As each boy got caught, then the game was over for him or he would help chase down the other boys.

SUFFER LITTLE CHILDREN

The ones being chased would hide in shops, dodge down alleyways, hide behind cars or simply go anywhere – there were no rules. We wouldn't stop running or hiding until we were caught. Sometimes the game would go on for most of the afternoon.

On one particular and certainly memorable occasion, there were only Baggy, Flappers, and me playing the game, and they were chasing me. Both Baggy and Flappers were good runners, but so was I.

We would split up when we were looking for the so-called 'quarry', so the advantage was usually with the ones chasing.

Having run away from one of our pursuers, we would then have to hide, or if the other boy saw us, then we would then have to run from the other 'fresh' runner.

On the occasion I am referring to, I was running from either Baggy or Flappers, and was aware that he was catching up with me and that soon I would be caught. At the same time, I noticed I was running past the main entrance of a cinema. Without any hesitation whatsoever I ran straight up the steps, directly into the cinema lobby.

Because I had run so far into the cinema so as not to be seen by either of the other boys, I continued on without stopping, straight through the doors and passed right by where the usherettes usually stood collecting the paid entrance tickets, and into the actual cinema. Then, exhausted, I merely sat down in a seat.

The usherette must have just taken people to their seats somewhere, and didn't see me come in. To top it off and as luck would have it, I found I was sitting in the back of the cinema, which is where the more expensive seats were.

But a scruffy little urchin like me being in the most expensive seats was a bit risky, so I moved down to the front rows, which were considerably cheaper and where I would be less conspicuous.

Unlike today, the closer the seats were to the front of the cinema, the cheaper they were. Normally, when we dodged in, we would always sit in the first three rows so that we didn't draw attention to ourselves. Sometimes though, when the cinema started to fill up, we would go out to the lavatory and then come back out and go and sit down in a seat several rows back in the better seats next to adults, as though we were with them, and then the usherettes wouldn't notice us.

SUFFER LITTLE CHILDREN

Actually, it's only at this moment as I write, that I realise we were making a mistake sitting in the cheapest seats anyway, because that is exactly where they – the managers or usherettes – would come looking for us, the 'dodgers in'.

On the other hand, our sitting in the more expensive seats, and us still looking like the scruffy little urchins that we were, we could never have got away with dodging in and sitting in the more expensive seats without attracting attention to ourselves.

Regardless, on this particular occasion, when the usherette came back to the entrance doors at the back of the cinema where I was sitting, she came up to me. I thought she had caught me, but all she did, without looking at my ticket, was to tell me to go back to my seat up the front. I didn't care; at least I had lost Baggy and Flappers and was comfortably sitting in the pictures.

I can even remember the picture I saw on that occasion. It was a comedy picture called *The Ghost of St Michael's*, starring Will Hay.

Both Flappers and Baggy said that they had looked everywhere for me that afternoon. There was also talk about us trying to do what I did, together some time, but I can't remember that we ever did: it would have been simply too brazen. It probably wouldn't have worked a second time anyway, and certainly not with two or three of us at the same time.

~°~°~ Staff Qualifications ~°~°~

So many unforgettable things happened in the early days while I was at Churchill House. So many, in fact, that it would be difficult to write about all of them.

Such happier times for us boys were most certainly due to Mr Castle's leniency towards us. His clear understanding and perception of those unfortunate and yet unique young boys in his charge served us well and, no doubt, helped shape our careless characters.

Punishments under his direction, though we didn't realise it at the time, were well thought out and fair, and as such, we accepted them without hating our masters.

Receiving corporal punishment (slipper) was for the most part only administered for serious offences and to maintain discipline, such as

SUFFER LITTLE CHILDREN

being rude or excessively cheeky, stealing, constant fighting and being out of bounds.

Our being out of bounds could seriously affect our relationships with our neighbours. That was one of Mr Castle's prime concerns.

The slipper was administered quite severely but, most importantly, fairly. I believe that generally, none of us boys ever considered that we were badly treated by Mr Castle.

But as I have mentioned, there was always the intimidating Mr Nash lurking in the background.

However, even he had to watch himself while Mr Castle was around looking after our interests. Mr Castle was a much bigger man than Mr Nash, and being the bigger man commonly meant that Mr Castle would not have taken any nonsense or bullying from Mr Nash.

There were about five or six other masters altogether as well as Matron, who were very involved in looking after us. Theirs were the routine, day-to-day positions of being on duty, perhaps two of them at all times. Nurse Rand, too, was always around and often filled routine duties.

As I have mentioned, many of the cleaning duties were assigned to us boys on a daily or weekly schedule. We would sweep and polish our dormitory floors, dust, and polish brass doorknobs and other brass in the mansion.

We even learned to darn the holes in our wool socks and sew on buttons, under the direction of Nurse Rand. I believe it was Nurse Rand who taught us how to knit wool scarves and even dishcloths.

There were several workers on the staff who did the bulk of the cleaning duties, and a couple of cooks, most of whom we had little contact with and, therefore, knew little about them.

Being a master other than the headmaster in an orphanage must have been a somewhat uninspiring, or a rather boring job, without much challenge. After all, most of their time was spent merely patrolling and supervising whatever and wherever our activities were going on.

Such masters were not educators. They weren't qualified to teach us anything, except perhaps they taught us the rudiments of how to play football and cricket. They didn't do anything relative to the maintenance of the property, like painting, cutting the grass or anything physical.

SUFFER LITTLE CHILDREN

One duty the masters were required to do was that of night-watchman. This entailed patrolling the entire estate and the mansion during the night.

The duties of the night-watchman involved ensuring there was no smoke or fire anywhere in the mansion, or burst water pipes or gas leaks. They would also ensure that there were no trespassers or even burglars on the premises.

I'm sure we felt that if there was a threat to us by burglars or trespassers, Mr Castle would have 'eaten them alive'. Anyway, who in their right mind would want to break into an orphanage, to steal what? Tin plates and tin mugs and the likes? If there was anything worth stealing, Flappers and I would probably have found it and sold it. That's not really true; we weren't thieves. We were, if I dare say so, only shoplifters.

~°~°~ Fox in the Henhouse ~°~°~

One day, we were made aware that a fox had, during the night, killed one of the chickens Mrs Castle kept for her family's eggs, and that Mr Castle was going to shoot the fox.

Mr Castle had borrowed a double-barrelled, twelve-gauge shotgun from a neighbouring mansion, the owners of which also wanted the fox disposed of.

A gun to us was a big deal. Nobody normally had a gun. Only gamekeepers and the rich people who went hunting, like those lords or gentry whom we went 'beating' for at Bayfordbury, had guns.

Somehow this was different. Now Mr Castle had a gun. To us he was going to be our 'Jesse James' and hunt down the sly fox.

That night he and another master set themselves up on the ground floor of the mansion, facing the back garden, where the chicken house was. With the shotgun resting on the windowsill, they spent the night keeping watch through an open window.

I expect that Mrs Castle would bring them tea and crumpets, and that they made a party of it all, which lasted until the early hours of the morning or until they all fell asleep.

We were aware that for the first couple of nights Mr Castle stayed up most of the time, keeping a constant vigil, the shotgun always at

SUFFER LITTLE CHILDREN

the ready. But the fox never showed up and so he eventually gave up, believing the fox wouldn't come back again.

About a week later another chicken went missing. There were lots of feathers scattered all over the back garden, which clearly indicated that the fox was back. So now the other masters also took up the watch.

I believe they enjoyed this rather exciting experience. In most instances, being on the night watch duty would have been a tedious and even a miserable job. But, as one could imagine, this was a different experience.

Then – perhaps it was on the second or third night – one of the masters fired both barrels of the shotgun at something, and all heck broke loose.

The noise from firing both barrels of a twelve-gauge shotgun through a window from inside the mansion in the middle of the night was extremely loud.

We had never heard a bang, or rather two bangs, quite as loud for a long time. It wasn't like hearing the guns or bombs during the peak of the war. They were very loud but the noise of the shotgun echoing down the long corridors seemed so much louder.

Lights went on everywhere. Most of the boys in the dormitories woke up, and several were running into each other's dormitories. The place was like Bedlam. The neighbours, too, must have been woken up by the noise.

Several masters, including Mr Castle, were in the gardens with torches, looking for an injured or dead fox. None was found.

It was rumoured that Mr Brock thought he had seen a fox and had fired at it. But we really thought differently. We thought that he had fired it just because he had the urge to fire the gun, which until then, no one had heard go off.

After that night there were no more chickens taken. A few days to a week later, a fox was caught in a snare on the neighbour's farm. That was the last we heard of the fox.

SUFFER LITTLE CHILDREN
~o~o~ Angora the Rabbit ~o~o~

Mr Castle permitted us to keep small pets like rabbits, guinea pigs, mice and rats, just like Mr Scougall allowed us to at Bayfordbury. We couldn't, of course, keep dogs or cats: they would simply be too much for boys to keep in orphanages.

To us, the domesticated rat was not thought of as being a dreaded rodent or vermin, as it would be in its wild state. Instead, it was an intelligent and really quite an affectionate animal, which the boys who had them found out by their own experiences. I may well have kept a mouse as a pet for a short time, but I don't remember that I ever owned a rat.

The boys would train the mice and rats to do simple little things such as running up their coat sleeves, inside their shirts, and down their short-trouser legs. They would also let them out of their cages to run around on the dormitory floors. What they did with their rats and mice wasn't much more than what I have described, but it all seemed rather clever at that point in time.

I recall that Flappers at one time had a big Angora rabbit. The Angora, I understand, is one of the largest breeds of rabbits commonly kept as a pet. It is known for its very thick soft fur as well as for its size.

Flappers loved his rabbit and looked after it well. He would often take an apple off of a 'barrow boy's' cart (without paying for it) and then run, with me hot on his heels; with the barrow boy, who was not really a boy at all, but more often a rough-and-tumble type of chap, shouting threats after us.

At the same time as Flappers had the Angora rabbit, I owned a guinea pig. We would put the two animals on the grass together, but they simply ignored each other. Although they both ate the same kind of food, they wouldn't share a carrot or cabbage leaf or anything together. They didn't even run around together. We should have learned something from that, but we didn't. Well actually, we did learn something, but when we did, it was a little too late.

One day, someone acquired a tame ferret from somewhere and asked if he could put it in my guinea pig's cage. I said I thought that it would be OK, if Flappers would let me put my guinea pig in his cage with his Angora rabbit.

SUFFER LITTLE CHILDREN

It was evening when we put these two – the rabbit and the guinea pig – together. The next morning, when we came down to feed them, we found a terrible sight.

The big Angora rabbit had been fighting with my guinea pig during the night, and my poor little pet was dead. The rabbit had actually torn my guinea pig's ear completely off, and there was blood everywhere.

The blame fell on Flappers. Flappers always accepted that I could beat him in a fight, and so he conceded that it was all his fault that his rabbit had killed my guinea pig, which, of course, it wasn't really.

But with us kids being what we were, someone had to be responsible for everything, even someone's grumpy old rabbit. The end result to our argument was that I would now have half a 'share' in Flappers' rabbit.

How naive I was in those days now that I think about it. All that 'sharing' really meant was that now I could help feed the rabbit, and to sometimes be the one to 'swipe' the apple from the barrow boy's cart, just because I had a share in that blinking rabbit. Also sharing meant I had to help clean out its cage every two or three days.

On reflection, as I write this story all these years later, it could be that my friend Flappers, the 'Artful Dodger', was a heck of a lot smarter than I gave him credit for.

As Mr Scrooge said when reminiscing about Bob Cratchet,

"I would like to have a word with my friend Flappers about now."

~o~o~ The Handcuffs ~o~o~

Up till this time of our lives, none of my closest group of friends had ever been caught shoplifting, or should I say, got into serious trouble for shoplifting. From time to time a lady shop assistant would see us put something or other in our pockets or inside our shirts, and make us put it back. They would give us a little talking-to; or, once in a while, a man might grab hold of one of us and give us a 'clip around the ear', but that was about all.

Even at Bayfordbury, when we would go out shoplifting almost every day for a period in our lives, no one got caught. But this was to change.

We still used to go shoplifting even after coming to Eastbourne, and still the stuff we stole was of little, if any, use to us. But we thought

SUFFER LITTLE CHILDREN

it was good fun and in our little world we would think it was all very exciting and that we were 'living on the edge', so to speak.

I can't emphasise enough that for us wantons, shoplifting was just a periodic fad, like periods in the year when we played conkers, trashy, marbles, or went scavenging through the village or town dumps. We did all these types of activities for short periods of time, and then we moved on to other things.

I'm sure we didn't give any thought as to what effect our shoplifting had on the shop owners. For us it was all simply fun, though not without risks.

We knew that we must not be caught by anyone, particularly the shopkeeper, who in turn might report us to the police. This would result in the orphanage finding out and, needless to say, we knew that we would be severely punished. Regardless, we took some real chances on our shoplifting expeditions.

One of the most brazen acts I believe I ever did, was the time when we were out shoplifting, and we were in a toyshop.

It was a fairly big toyshop, bearing in mind that most shops weren't very big back then. All around the walls of the toyshop there were long wooden horizontal shelves. The shelves, which were spaced about ten to twelve inches apart, filled the entire walls from floor to ceiling. The ceiling was about eight feet high, which to us kids seemed pretty high.

On each shelf there were toys of every description: big and small tin cars, dolls, puzzles and games, large yachts, boats, cap guns and model aeroplanes. There were wind-up toys, electric trains, snakes and ladders games, and just about everything one could think of for children to play with, young and old.

Of all the toys in the shop that got my attention most, and which I suppose I thought I must have in spite of the risk, was a pair of shiny handcuffs.

Unfortunately, the handcuffs were hanging from a hook on the front edge of one of the top shelves, the shelf being at least seven feet above the floor.

The shiny silver handcuffs, together with a little key attached to them by a piece of string, looked absolutely real. They must have really attracted me, considering what I did next.

SUFFER LITTLE CHILDREN

I told Flappers what I intended to do and so he kept 'diggs'.

There were of, course, lots of other people in the shop, so it was just a matter of watching to see that the shopkeeper and the couple of shop girls were preoccupied with other customers, and that no one else was looking in my direction.

Even now, I can't believe how brazen I was. Seeing that the 'coast was clear', so to speak, I nimbly climbed up the shelves, which, as I have mentioned, were about twelve to fourteen inches apart. Then I gently lifted the handcuffs off the hook they were hanging on, and climbed down again, carefully seeing that I didn't knock anything else off the shelves.

I can still remember how high above everyone in the shop I was when I was taking the handcuffs off the hook. I had been in full view of everyone in the shop, just as though I was on a stage. Had I been noticed, I would have looked literally like a real 'cheeky monkey'.

Had the shopkeeper or anyone noticed or had questioned me, I certainly would have had some tricky explaining to do. As it was, Flappers would have been quite proud of me: I was, after that feat, almost as big a 'crook' as he was.

~o~o~ Chocolates in the Window ~o~o~

There were also some surprises that we didn't expect while in the act of shoplifting. In fact, one such surprise actually made us feel cheated ourselves, which wasn't really fair, dare I say, considering the risk we took.

On the particular occasion I refer to, Flappers and I were passing a sweet shop and there, in the shop window, just inside the entrance door, was a lovely looking medium-size box of chocolates.

The box was open and tilted slightly forward, displaying the delicious-looking dark chocolates. So, without much hesitation, we decided that with a little cunning, we would take one of the chocolates each. Sweets, including chocolates and anything made from sugar, were still rationed even though the war was over, and could not easily be obtained, except with sweet coupons and money. Having neither of these essentials, getting to eat chocolates out of a box of chocolates was not very likely.

SUFFER LITTLE CHILDREN

Determined to get one of the chocolates each, we casually entered the small sweet shop, pretending to be looking around. There were a couple of people in the shop buying sweets or something or other, and by doing so, they were distracting the shopkeeper.

Inside the shop, covering the window, was a light curtain, and the chocolates were just on the other side of the curtain.

Flappers nodded or otherwise indicated to me that the coast was clear and, as planned, I should swipe a couple of the chocolates.

So, I opened the curtain just a little so that I could see what I was doing, then reaching my hand inside, tried to take out a chocolate.

But the chocolate that I had a hold of seemed to be stuck, or was just a very tight fit in the box. It simply wouldn't come out of the box easily.

So I pulled a little harder, and then even harder until, still holding onto the chocolate, I found I had the entire box of chocolates in my hand.

I must have knocked something else over behind the curtain because there was the noise of something falling.

The shopkeeper heard the noise, looked over at us, and shouted something like, "Hey, what are you cheeky little sods doing?"

He was, at the same time trying to get from around his counter so that he could actually grab hold of us.

The shopkeeper didn't need to say any more. With the whole box of chocolates in my hand, Flappers and I ran out of the sweet shop and down the busy street as fast as we could go, with the shopkeeper in hot pursuit. This was all happening on one of the main streets in Eastbourne.

But, as I have mentioned, we were both good runners, and when we got a safe distance away we stopped and looked inside of the box of what we thought were delicious chocolates, anticipating a nice treat.

Then came the surprise. The reason the chocolates were so hard to get out of the box when I was reaching for them behind the curtain was because they weren't chocolates at all: they were just artificial display chocolates made out of wood, and painted an appetising chocolate colour.

To keep the wooden 'chocolates' in place, they had been glued to the inside of the box. Actually they were quite dusty and may well have been in the sweet shop window for years, perhaps even since before the war.

SUFFER LITTLE CHILDREN
~o~o~ The Day of Reckoning ~o~o~

Having become quite efficient as 'rotten little shoplifters' over the past couple of years, both at Bayfordbury and now at Eastbourne, our time for shoplifting and not getting caught was running out. Without warning and quite suddenly, it all ended quite dramatically and, as the saying goes, we were taught a lesson which I never forgot.

One evening, at about half past seven, after we had got our nightshirts on and were getting ready for bed, a boy came to my dormitory and said that Mr Castle wanted to see me in dorm F.

I knew, of course, that this was Flappers' dormitory, and naturally couldn't help but ponder as to what Flappers had done which warranted Mr Castle to summon me there.

Naturally quite worried, I went upstairs to Flappers' dormitory, and as I entered his dorm I could see immediately why Mr Castle had sent for me.

Laid out all over Flappers' bed was lots of the stuff we had shoplifted recently, including a nice shiny penknife Flappers had swiped. We had, for whatever reason, relaxed on our practice of not bringing shoplifted stuff back to the orphanage, and there it was, much of it laid out neatly on Flappers' bed.

I can see myself even now, looking quite innocently surprised and pretending not to know what the stuff was or whom it belonged to. There was lots of stuff: darts, pens, bottles of sauce, toys, Bond Street jewellery, scent, lipstick, pencil sharpeners – almost anything sold in places like Woolworths that one could imagine.

As I came in Mr Castle said to me in a stern, but inquiring voice, "Have you ever seen any of these things before, Longman?"

I looked at the stuff on the bed thoughtfully and carefully, then replied without any hesitation, "What? This stuff, Sir? No, Sir, I ain't seen none of this before, ever."

He said again in perhaps a more stern, yet not angry voice, "I'm only going to ask you once more, Longman. Have you ever seen any of these things before?"

Feeling a little worried, I nevertheless replied in a cocky, confident manner, "No, Sir. Honest, cross me 'eart, I ain't seen none of it before. Honest I ain't."

SUFFER LITTLE CHILDREN

Flappers, who had been listening to his Judas friend deny his story, said in desperation, "Yeh! You 'ave. You 'ave, Reg. We found it on the beach, remember? We found it on the beach. It was in a bag, remember? Remember?" He sounded desperate.

Then Mr Castle said, waving his hand across the bed and over all the stuff laid out on it, "Is that true, Longman? Did you find any of this on the beach?"

I replied, not looking at Flappers, hoping to put myself in the clear, I suppose, "No, Sir! No, Sir!" shaking my head from side to side. "I've never seen this stuff before. Honest I ain't."

Flappers was panicking now,

"Yes you 'ave, Reg. Don't ya remember, we were on the beach and– "

Mr Castle cut Flappers off, and said to another boy, "Put all this in a pillowcase and bring it down to my quarters, right away."

He then told me to go back to my dormitory, and said that he would be talking to us later.

So I left Flappers in his dormitory and returned to mine, deeply concerned, no doubt, knowing Mr Castle had caught us 'red handed', so to speak.

I can't believe now that I would have slept a wink that night. I knew we were in real trouble. I was absolutely sure Mr Castle hadn't believed Flappers' story about finding the stuff on the beach. I felt too, that he hadn't believed a word of what I had said either in my denial of having seen or having anything to do with it. After all, Mr Castle had been a very senior policeman before he had come to Dr Barnardo's to work.

The next morning, before breakfast, Flappers told me that I should have said we found the stuff on the beach just like he had said, and then we would have got away with it. I told him he was daft, and that no one would believe the story about finding a bagful of stuff on the beach – certainly not Mr Castle.

After we were all in the dining room and ready for our breakfast, Mr Castle came in, and the whole orphanage knew something was up. Mr Castle never came into the dining room generally, and most certainly not at breakfast time, on a school day.

Then, after the morning prayers and just before Grace was said, Mr Castle told all of us that after breakfast we should all get ready for

SUFFER LITTLE CHILDREN

school as usual, and then assemble in the playroom at 7.30, he had something very important to discuss.

~o~o~

I should mention that just a few months before Mr Scougall had died there had been an amnesty, or forgiveness period given by Mr Scougall for boys who had done something or other wrong.

Such leniency or forgiveness was arbitrarily given by the Bayfordbury masters, depending on how they felt at the time we approached them.

If a boy, having done something wrong, approached a master and 'owned up' or said he was sorry for what he had done, then the master would or could arbitrarily tell the boy, 'not to do it, or whatever it was he had done wrong, again' and let him off with a caution. But, needless to say, this special amnesty period only lasted for a short time, and there was only one of these so called amnesty periods that I can remember.

Naively, I thought it might be a good idea to try this ploy again, only with Mr Castle.

Now that I think about it, perhaps the forgiveness, amnesty or leniency period came about as the result of Mr Scougall being told by some authority that he was treating us too harshly, and that he should soften his disciplinary ways towards us. I don't know, of course, if indeed this was the situation or not.

~o~o~

So, with forgiveness in mind, I suggested to Flappers that we should go and own up and tell Mr Castle the truth: that we had stolen all the stuff, and that we were very sorry. There would be nothing to lose and just maybe we might even 'get off' with a warning or at the worst, Mr Castle would take it easy on us.

After convincing Flappers that it would be the best and honest thing to do – not that we cared so much about the 'honest' bit – we went to make our appeal to Mr Castle.

I remember well standing outside Mr Castle's family quarters and nervously knocking on the door. Mrs Castle opened the door and saw

SUFFER LITTLE CHILDREN

us, heads bent, looking as humble and repentant as we could.

Although she could have easily guessed what we were there for, she still asked in her gentle way what we wanted. I told her we wanted to speak with Mr Castle.

She told us to come in, and we followed her inside their quarters and into the dining room. Sitting around their breakfast table were Mr Castle and his daughters.

The three of them looked up from the table and Mr Castle said, "Yes?" in a knowing yet inquiring voice.

I replied, in a nervous voice, "We've come to own up, Sir. We stole the stuff and we want to say sorry."

This was how we used to say it at Bayfordbury during the period I've mentioned.

Quietly Mr Castle answered me and said, "I was quite sure you did, Longman. Now go and wait in the playroom and I'll see you and Foot there in a few minutes."

We left Mr Castle's dining room and passed through the rest of his quarters to the playroom. We thought, It's all OK now; we've owned up, so he will just give us all a good talking-to, and let us off.

About half an hour later – one of the longest half-hours in my life – all of the other boys had assembled in the playroom, and Mr Castle came in. He stood there for a moment with his hands clasped behind his back, looking at the boys congregated before him.

Then my heart must have skipped a beat, because following Mr Castle were two other masters carrying a big armchair. On the seat of the armchair was 'the big white slipper'.

We all, the whole orphanage, stood at one end of the playroom, waiting for Mr Castle to speak. He looked very stern but, as always, not angry. There was nothing personal in his tone or what he said.

He simply told us that that there had been several complaints from the local shop owners regarding us boys shoplifting, and he was going to put a stop to it. He told us how he had defended us kids several times, arguing to the effect that it wasn't his boys who they had seen shoplifting.

When he said he was going to make an example of us and that all of us boys should heed his words and actions, I thought, 'Now we're for it'.

SUFFER LITTLE CHILDREN

I don't think I heard anything else he said, though I'm sure he said much more.

Then he told Flappers and myself to come up to the front beside the chair, and told us that he was going to severely punish us. I remember too that he said that he thought Flappers was the main culprit, and for that reason, he would make an example of him in particular.

I was first to be punished. So I bent over the chair, my hands on the arms of the chair: typical of how we would normally receive the slipper.

I received four solid whacks from Mr Castle's huge slipper, jumping back each time with a loud OW! Have no doubt, it really hurt. But Flappers wasn't so lucky. He received six or even seven good solid whacks and made as much fuss as I did. I know first hand that, that blinkin' slipper, really, really did hurt.

The slipper, as I say, really did hurt, but what was more important, it taught most of us the lesson intended, without the punishment being brutal or sadistic – there were no severe welts grooved into our buttocks, and nor did we bleed like we did from those callous beatings which we received at Bayfordbury from Mr Scougall.

I never did think our punishment was unfair and although Flappers and I felt somewhat disgraced, we weren't intentionally made to feel humiliated in front of our peers.

As of that day, I never went shoplifting again, and I don't recall any other boy doing so either, though I would have to suspect that perhaps they did but simply weren't caught.

Mr Castle, without anger or being personal, had punished us and taught us the lesson he had intended, and I never forgot it. I can't say that it made me an entirely honest boy – I know it didn't – but I never went shoplifting again.

17

CHURCHILL HOUSE – Part 3

~o~o~ Back to Taunton ~o~o~

In the summer of 1946 my grandmother again made arrangements with Dr Barnardo's Homes for me to go 'home' to Taunton to stay with her for my summer holidays.

Just like the last time I had travelled to my gran's, in what seemed like a long, long time ago now, I was again very excited.

I would only have been told I was going 'home' a week or so before I was to actually go, in order that the excitement would not affect my daily routine.

~o~o~

Although Baggy's father lived somewhere in Essex, his father never wrote to him, visited him or ever invited him to spend his summer holidays with him. Baggy hardly ever spoke of his father if at all in a positive way, or in any way much, as far as I can remember. The only relative Baggy ever spoke of was his sister, who lived in Horsham, Sussex. He spoke of her in a fond way. However, she was just a little older than him, and I suppose she just couldn't afford to come and see him.

Fred had two brothers in Dr Barnardo's Homes. Both of them were at Bayfordbury with us and were now at Churchill House. One of Fred's brothers, Leslie (who we called Dicky for some reason) was a couple or even three years older than us. Because he was older, we didn't have very much to do with him.

Fred's other brother, Billy, was two years younger than Fred. Although we didn't have much to do with Billy either, Fred was always aware of what Billy was up to, or what scrapes he might get into. None of the other boys would pick on Billy, Billy being much smaller, without being accountable to Fred.

In such an environment as the orphanages we lived in, boys only

SUFFER LITTLE CHILDREN

associated with other boys their own age. If a boy, even a brother, was two years, or most certainly three years older or younger than another boy, then the boys, or sometimes brothers, it seemed, hardly knew each other.

In the case of Dicky and Fred, I didn't know for a long, long time that Dicky was even Fred's brother, though I did know that Billy was Fred's younger brother.

In the not-too-distant future Baggy and I were to find out, in a rather sad way for us, that Fred, Dicky and Billy were to be together as brothers in a different way of life, for better or worse, for the rest of their lives, as I will explain later in my story.

Fred and his brothers had no mother alive that they were aware of, but they did still have a father, though they never heard from him.

Flappers didn't have any mother, father, sisters, or brothers. Although like Flappers, I too, didn't have a father or mother, but at least I did have two sisters and a half-sister.

Flappers, on the other hand, didn't have a soul in the world, including uncles, aunts, or even grandparents alive, or at least, if any of them were alive they didn't show any interest in him whatsoever, and he wasn't aware that they even existed.

It seemed that other than the impersonalised Dr Barnardo's Homes, no one in the entire world cared if Flappers was alive or dead, happy or unhappy. Sadly, he had absolutely no one, anywhere, that he knew of who cared for him.

So none of my 'best friends' could go anywhere for their summer holidays. No one wanted them. They could only stay at the orphanage.

But living at Churchill House was not so bad in some ways. After all, Eastbourne was, and still is, a lovely holiday town where people came from all over the British Isles to spend their summer holidays.

~o~o~

On the day I left to go home to Taunton Mr Castle, like Mr Scougall had done, drove me to the railway station. Mr Castle reminded me to be on my best behaviour, and in a sincere way wished me a happy holiday, and put me on the train to London. I did not feel the same

SUFFER LITTLE CHILDREN

happiness leaving Mr Castle or Churchill House as I had when I had left Mr Scougall and Bayfordbury.

But I was happy nevertheless just to be leaving the orphanage way of life and going to see Gran, Aunty Molly, and Jill again. Unbeknown to me at this point in time, I was going to meet my Uncle Sid (Aunty Molly's husband and Jill's father) for the first time.

Just as had been arranged previously, a chaperon met me at Waterloo Station and took me across London on the 'tube' to Paddington Station.

My grandmother was there to meet me just as before, but this time she knew me and I her. There was lots of hugging, and then we were off to Taunton.

I remember more about this visit because I was now a year or so older and more aware of my surroundings. As we arrived at the Taunton railway station, a booming voice came over the loud speakers, announcing destination routes, which sounded something like 'Those wishing to go to Derby or Nottingham, to all change and go to platform two. Those wishing to go to Washford, Blue Anchor, Dunster, and Minehead, to go to platform five.'

There were many changes to other destinations announced, advising which platforms one should go to. It was all very worldly, and now I was part of it all.

Much like we did before, my grandmother and I walked back to her house at 99 Winchester Street, and what a lovely sight it was. I was home again. I knew that although the food at Churchill House was much better than that at Bayfordbury, it just couldn't be as good as my grandmother's home cooking.

I would still have given my grandmother an envelope with my ration book in it, because even in 1946, and until at least 1951, some things were still rationed.

My sister Barbara came home to Gran's a couple of days later and the excitement of us all being together again was such a warm and 'homely' feeling. My grandfather was still the same, and still didn't have much to do with us, but we didn't really notice.

Our Uncle Harry and his family: Aunt Babs and my cousins Brian and June, came to visit from Croydon in London, and stayed for a short while and so, though the house had three bedrooms, we still had to use

SUFFER LITTLE CHILDREN

the front room as a bedroom.

Barbara and myself again slept with Gran in her bedroom. I remembered my grandmother's feathered bed and her eiderdown duvet. Once again, it felt so luxurious.

Needless to say, with about nine or ten people in the house it, for a short time, seemed rather crowded.

The first thing I wanted to do the next day after all of the excitement had died down was to go and see Aunty Molly and Jill so, remembering the way, I walked the mile or so to their house.

Aunty Molly and Jill were expecting me and made me feel like I was family, which of course I was. It must have been a Saturday because my Uncle Sid was home, and not at work in the Post Office.

This was the first time I met Uncle Sid. He had only recently been demobbed from the Army. After six long years away from home on active service as a staff sergeant in the Royal Signals, he had rejoined the British postal service and again worked in the main post office in Taunton.

Uncle Sid was a good-looking, fatherly figure and on all accounts was a very pleasant and tolerant person who, it seemed, never got cross.

I remember on one occasion, being the 'cheeky little sod' that I was, telling Uncle Sid while he was smoking his pipe, and me not understanding the addiction or the habit of smoking, that I thought he only smoked his pipe to 'show off'.

He didn't ever seem to get annoyed, and was always kind and understanding of me. Nor did he raise his voice or ever seem to get angry with Jill or Aunty Molly. I quickly grew to love him like I did Aunty Molly and Jill.

~o~o~

I don't remember my sister Barbara really taking to the Pitman family like I did. To me, the Pitmans were the family I would have chosen to belong to if I were given the chance to choose. In many years to come, just before she died, Aunty Molly told my wife Donna and I that she always wished she had adopted me after my father had died.

As it was, when my father had died in 1939, Aunty Molly and Uncle Sid had just lost their baby son Derek, who was only three years old.

SUFFER LITTLE CHILDREN

On top of that, Uncle Sid, because of the threat of imminent war, had just volunteered for active duty in the Army.

~°~°~ Blue Anchor ~°~°~

After a couple of days of my arriving in Taunton, and after Barbara had arrived, we all went on the train to Blue Anchor to spend a week to perhaps ten days in the caravan again.

My grandma, Barbara and I had one caravan, which again we shared with Aunty Molly and Jill; while Uncle Harry, Aunty Babs, and my cousins June and Brian were in another caravan. Uncle Sid didn't come with us as he would be working.

Because it was quite crowded in the tiny caravan, my cousin Brian and I slept in a small tent pitched just outside the caravan. Although it was a pretty small tent, it was still quite comfortable.

The railway tracks ran just beside my gran's caravan, in fact passing no more than about forty to fifty feet away, and the tent Brian and I were in was even closer to the tracks.

The tracks were in a fairly deep gully with steep banks either side. Our tent was pitched on top of the bank, looking down on the trains as they passed. At night the trains would come thundering past our caravan site, making the ground tremble. The last train, I believe, passed by us a little before midnight.

On one particular night, while we were fast asleep, a steam train came rumbling through and as it passed our tent it spilled out red hot coals from its fire – the fire that boils the water to make the steam to drive the train.

The coals that spilled out ignited the dry August grass which grew on the banks beside the train tracks – the same bank where our tent was pitched on top of.

Upon hearing the crackling of burning grass I woke up Brian and we rushed outside, me in my Barnardo's nightshirt and Brian in his pyjamas, to see what was going on.

Much of the bank was covered in small stones and so it was not particularly dangerous, but it could have been.

SUFFER LITTLE CHILDREN

It certainly bothered me. From that time on until we left Blue Anchor that year, I was always alert when a train came by, particularly at night.

~o~o~ **Making a Kite** ~o~o~

My Uncle Reg and his wife Aunty Hilda came down to Blue Anchor for a few days holiday while we were there. Uncle Reg was a jolly type of man. I'll always remember him with a smile on his face, and a hearty laugh. Aunty Hilda, on the other hand, was considerably more reserved, but nevertheless a little feisty and I believe, perhaps a little hard to get along with.

For whatever reason, Aunty Hilda wasn't the most popular person in the Longman family, but I liked her and always felt she liked me. She and Uncle Reg had no children of their own.

One day while we were at Blue Anchor, Brian and I made a kite. We used to make kites in the orphanage, so I showed Brian how we should go about it. We got some thin straight sticks from the woods, and with some newspapers, made a crude kite.

However, while we were making it, we realised that what we didn't have was anything to stick the seams of the newspapers together with, as is necessary in order to make the kite stay together. So Brian and I discussed our problem of having no glue or sticky tape, and came up with a plan contrived by that same 'rotten little sod': me.

The plan was simple. I went over to Uncle Reg and Aunty Hilda's caravan, which was on the other side of the woods, in a different field, and told Aunty Hilda that Gran had cut her finger quite badly, and that she had sent me to get a piece of first aid adhesive.

Aunty Hilda was very worried, and gave me the whole roll of the first-aid adhesive that she had brought with her on holiday, for me to rush back to Gran's with.

I must have made too much of the cut finger, because Aunty Hilda came over to Gran's caravan to see if she could help. As it was, she quickly found out that Gran hadn't cut her finger at all. Needless to say, Gran and Aunty Hilda were quite annoyed with me, and by the time Aunty Hilda caught up with Brian and myself, we had used most of her Elastoplast up in sticking our kite together.

SUFFER LITTLE CHILDREN

Although Brian didn't get into any trouble at all, Aunty Hilda was very upset with me, and didn't speak to me for the rest of the holiday. Later, in several years time, we were to become good friends again and I even went to live with her and Uncle Reg for a while.

After all that happened that day, and even though I had upset Gran and Aunty Hilda, I still can't remember ever seeing that darn kite fly.

~o~o~ VE Day Anniversary ~o~o~

The holidays in Blue Anchor were very memorable. I spent a lot of time with Jill and Aunty Molly. Jill and I, much like we had done the other time we were at Blue Anchor, would go foraging along the beach, looking in the small tidal pools for trapped fish, and also eels and crabs.

Jill would be very 'girlish' in her touching anything which was slimy or which could nip, like crabs, even though they were very small. Like boys would, I would pick the crabs up and chase her with them. They were such unforgettable times and to some extent I felt a little like her protector when there was just the two of us playing together, and I loved it.

By definition, Carol and Barbara were my sisters of course, and although I must say I loved the idea that they were my 'real' sisters and 'my family', we were, nevertheless, almost strangers. We were not very close, as siblings should be, because, due to circumstances we didn't really know each other. However, Jill and I, even though she was my cousin and the only girl that I had ever known, bonded very quickly. She was purely a friend and I felt a natural kinship towards her.

Jill was rather sedate, even as a young girl. She walked very gracefully, always with her head held high.

To some, in later years, when she was about sixteen or seventeen years old, she was thought to be haughty and somewhat aloof whereas, in fact, she was just a lovely, down to earth, fun loving girl.

At the time when we were in Blue Anchor I was about twelve going on thirteen years old, and Jill was slightly more than a year younger.

Together we would wander for what seemed like miles along the beach. Jill was a good swimmer, much like I was, and so we would go swimming almost every day. We would also collect seashells and

SUFFER LITTLE CHILDREN

colourful stones, which were in abundance on the stony portions of the beach.

One day the Greenslades, the owners of the caravan site, informed everyone that they were going to have a celebration day to celebrate the anniversary of the end of the war.

VE Day, more so than VJ Day, celebrations were now to be an annual event, which would be celebrated in most cities, towns, and villages throughout the British Isles.

The celebrations included field sports such as running races, egg and spoon races and high jumping. Jill and I went into the three-legged race together.

How well I remember us falling over and over each other and laughing, eventually finishing just about last, with Aunty Molly and Gran laughing as well. We didn't win anything together during the entire competition, but it was such a lovely, happy occasion.

Boys under fifteen were invited to enter for a hundred yards sprint. Being prompted by Aunty Molly, I came forward to enter the race. The organisers noticed I was much smaller than the rest of the boys who had entered and being perhaps the youngest boy in the race, they gave me about a twenty-foot handicap.

As I have mentioned several times now, I was a fairly good runner as a boy – even into my late thirties – and I don't mean just for my size. I really could run quite well.

We all got ready to run and they blew the starter's whistle. I ran as best I could and finished way ahead of anyone else. I remember Gran being so pleased, and Jill cheering. I really did win the race easily.

But that was only the first heat. In the second heat they cut my handicap to about ten feet. Again, I won pretty handily. So, in the next heat I was lined up the same as the rest, without a handicap.

I still won that heat, but in the final race between the winners of all of the previous heats, I came in about fourth. Still Gran and Uncle Harry and all of the rest of the Longman family were very impressed.

Aunty Molly and Jill often recalled that day many years later, particularly the first heat. They said my little legs were a blur, running like heck for a shilling prize, which in the end I didn't get.

SUFFER LITTLE CHILDREN
~o~o~ Carol – Torquay ~o~o~

After we came back from Blue Anchor, my grandmother told Barbara and me that our sister Carol was in Torquay and that she had asked if we could go there to see her.

Torquay is about a fifty-mile trip by train from Taunton, and so Gran bought Barbara and me a train ticket and we headed off to see Carol, who was about sixteen or maybe seventeen years old at the time.

When we arrived at the Torquay railway station, Carol and about five other girls her age were there to meet us.

Carol and her friends were there on an organised Girl Guides' holiday trip. They had travelled down together from Nottingham to Torquay, in Devon, and were to be there for a week. A few weeks earlier Carol had prearranged with Gran to let Barbara and me go to Torquay to see her.

Carol looked lovely. She had long auburn hair and a pretty face, and was still the soft-spoken person I knew her to be. The girls, I remember, made a fuss of me. Barbara too, enjoyed Carol's friends; they all seemed to get along well together.

I remember too that we all wanted to go swimming in the sea. As it was, I wanted to go swimming too, but I didn't have a swimming costume, so one of the girls lent me hers. I remember that I dived off one of the wooden wave breakers and swam as fast as I could. I remember too, the girls being impressed with my swimming, or at least they pretended to be. Later we had fish and chips for tea, they bought us ice creams to, which was a big treat for me.

One of the girls took a photo of us all, which I still have to this day. Then the day was over. It was upsetting saying goodbye to Carol and the other girls, but Barbara and I had to catch our train back to Taunton.

I wouldn't have known at the time, but I wasn't to see Carol again for at least five to six more years, when I was in my late teens and in the army, doing my compulsory National Service.

SUFFER LITTLE CHILDREN

Carol and Barbara (front left), myself and
Carol's Girl Guide friends
Torquay – 1947

SUFFER LITTLE CHILDREN
~o~o~ Sad Goodbyes Again ~o~o~

Just like the last time I was in Taunton, the three-week holiday that I had come to Gran's house for came to an end. Barbara again left the day before me to return to her orphanage, which I believe was still in Ripon, Yorkshire.

I went and said goodbye to Uncle Reg and Aunty Hilda. Then on the way to Aunty Molly, Uncle Sid and Jill's house to say goodbye to them; strange as it may seem, I saw Uncle Len again.

The last time I had seen Uncle Len was when he had stopped and given me two half-crowns – one for Barbara and one for myself – and because Barbara had already left to go back to her orphanage I couldn't give her her's and so, fortunately for me, I was able to keep both.

On this occasion, seeing Uncle Len, although it didn't seem like a coincidence at the time, it was, of course. Uncle Len, as he was driving by, saw me, and again stopped and jumped out of his lorry and came over to me to say goodbye. Strange as it was, it was almost in exactly the same place on the street as the last time we said goodbye.

I'm not sure, but I would suspect that he gave me a shilling or two. People did that sort of thing in those days quite often. Then he said something quite strange to me, which I still remember to this day. He told me that this was "really" goodbye.

I didn't know Uncle Len very well and so when he said that this was "really goodbye", I didn't quite understand him. Then he continued on to tell me that I would not, ever, be seeing him again. He told me that he was very sick due to a kidney problem. He also said that as the result of his bad kidneys he was going to die soon.

I can't say that I fully understood what Uncle Len meant, in fact I'm quite sure I didn't. But we said goodbye and I was never to see him again.

So it was that I said goodbye to Granddad and everyone else whom I had spent my summer holiday with and who had been kind to me, especially Aunty Molly, Uncle Sid and Jill.

Much like the last time, Gran travelled with me up to London. We met my chaperon, who in turn took me across London and then put me on the train to Eastbourne.

SUFFER LITTLE CHILDREN

A few hours later I arrived at Churchill House and into a way of life which was so much better than the last time, when I had returned to Dr Barnardo's Homes at Bayfordbury. But nevertheless it was still quite sad and somewhat emotionally disturbing leaving the free-and-easy life at Gran's house and returning to the disciplined way of life in an orphanage.

~o~o~

It must have been just a few months or so later after returning from Gran's, that Mr Castle summoned me to his study and told me that, indeed, my Uncle Len had died. My grandmother must have written to Mr Castle and told him the news. I remember that I was quite sad and cried at hearing of his dying, even though I hardly knew Uncle Len very well.

18

CHURCHILL HOUSE – Part 4

~°~°~ Traditional Begging ~°~°~

November the fifth in England is Guy Fawkes Day. This is the day that gives all British children a 'licence' to virtually go begging for money. Orphans and the likes, though we in Dr Barnardo's Homes were not beggars; we simply took advantage of such days.

Like other kids, we would make crude effigies of Guy Fawkes, an historical character who in 1605 tried to blow up the British parliament buildings, or the 'gasworks', as they are often referred to by the London taxi drivers.

We would then tie the 'Guy' onto two crossed poles and drag it along the streets.

Fred, Flappers, and I would, most days, meet up with Baggy from Bourne School and do things like this together. We would only have one Guy between us, and share all the 'takings'.

As we passed by anyone in the street, we would put out our hands and ask, "Penny for the Guy. Penny for the Guy, please." Very commonly they would put a coin into our tin can or old cap, and carry on their way. Once in a while, if they recognised the way we were dressed (Dr Barnardo boys), they might put thre'pence or even a sixpenny piece in our tin can, but this didn't happen very often.

We would also go up to people's houses, knock on their doors, and ask them, too, for a penny for the Guy. This really was a traditional children's pastime, but only on Guy Fawkes day. It was quite a socially acceptable thing to do. Often, when the pubs were open, we would hang around outside pub doors, asking for the traditional 'penny for the Guy'.

On a good day or evening we could, if we made sufficient effort, collect as much as two shillings on our way home from school.

Two shillings would be enough to buy four individual packets of fish and chips. The fish and chips, with plenty of salt and vinegar on, were wrapped in newspaper.

SUFFER LITTLE CHILDREN

I don't know where the fish and chip shops got their newspapers from that they wrapped the fish and chips in, but that was the common practice. The shops simply put a small piece of wax paper on top of a couple of sheets of newspaper then simply wrapped the fish and chips up in it, and no one thought any more about it.

We, like anyone else, would walk along the streets eating our fish and chips directly out of the newspaper they were wrapped in. Although, to buy fish and chips for ourselves, was a really, really big treat, so we couldn't afford to buy them it very often.

On the evening of November the fifth Mr Castle would allow us to stay out a little later, so that we could drag our Guy to the 'common' and put it, with all the Guys that other children had made, on top of the bonfire and burn it. Many of the outsider kids would have 'sparklers', but we just couldn't afford them.

Guy Fawkes 'begging' would go on for about a week or so before November the fifth, but the day after, it was all over until the following year.

~o~o~ Carol Singing ~o~o~

About a week to perhaps even ten days before Christmas Day, we would go Carol singing on our way home from school to the orphanage. The evenings, as I recall, would often be foggy and damp, so much so that the mist or steam from our breath would usher out of our mouths when we talked or even breathed, and particularly so when we sang.

The chilly dampness of the late afternoons, combined with the foggy glow of the gaslights, gave an atmosphere of a quiet gloom yet a merry feeling at Christmas time, which was further cheered up by the sound of us and other children singing traditional carols.

We would stand outside someone's house and sing a Carol or two, or until someone came out and gave us a few pennies. The moment they gave us money or sometimes a mince pie, we would stop singing almost instantly it seems, and then go to the next house and sing.

We would try and go to as many houses as we could, in order to be able to make as much money as possible. Most people would give us a penny or a thre'penny piece. Once in a while someone might even give

SUFFER LITTLE CHILDREN

us a sixpenny bit, but mostly we would get pennies. Regardless, we were quite happy with anything we got.

I recall that on one occasion, on my way to scouts in the evening, I went up to someone's front door by myself and was singing at the top of my voice, but nobody answered the door. So I knocked and knocked and sang and sang, until eventually a young woman came to the door and gave me sixpence, which was simply marvellous, like finding 'the jackpot'.

I remember still that I had thought that because the lady had given me sixpence, that I should carry on and sing some more carols, so I sang and sang until she came out again, but this time she told me to "Bugger off, you little sod." She also said, "Listen, my husband's asleep and if he wakes up he'll give you a bloody good hiding" – I thought she could at least have added 'Happy Christmas'.

She had seemed pretty angry. Still it was all OK with me, as she had given me sixpence, and that was a lot more than I would normally expect. To make things even better, I didn't have to share it with anyone.

Like the little sod I was, I might well have, just for a joke, told Flappers to "Go to that house; the lady there will give you sixpence," and hope that just maybe her husband would come to the door while Flappers was singing, and whilst I watched from a distance.

~o~o~ For Better or for Worse ~o~o~

Christmas was the season and the time of year that the owners or managers of theatres and cinemas would invite us Dr Barnardo boys and other 'poor' kids to come to their theatre, to see pantomimes and conjurors perform, or even go to the pictures free – without 'dodging-in'.

We would also be invited to the circus. Most of the theatre and circus performances were probably 'dress rehearsals', prior to them being open for the paying public. Often we would be invited to charity parties at church halls and places like that.

Now that I think back on those days I'm just now beginning to realise, even though I hadn't realised it then, that we orphans, unbeknown to us, must have been somewhat pitied by some, who showed much genuine kindness towards us. But we would have hated to have been pitied, so perhaps it's better that we hadn't known.

SUFFER LITTLE CHILDREN

Many businesses, big and small; and church groups and charitable organisations would pursue obtaining gifts and entertainment experiences for us Dr Barnardo kids, particularly at Christmas. This was another side to the outsiders that we didn't really know much about.

As would so often be the situation, the people or organisations who did their best for us would go almost unnoticed by us, whereas those who endeavoured to malign or hurt us, we would, of course, remember.

~o~o~

For the rest of the year we were still the scourge of the area we lived in. Nothing would change regarding us Dr Barnardo kids, in the eyes of some.

But now that I was a little older – twelve going on thirteen – it embarrassed me, as it did most of the other boys my age and older, to be thought of in this way.

However, we could do absolutely nothing about it, except to accept life the way it was, and to play our cards the way they had been dealt.

I recognise now, these many years later, that maybe we brought much of the bad feeling towards us on ourselves. But then again I could make the somewhat valid excuse that there was little guidance for us to be 'normal' boys in society.

However, the way we were treated at Churchill House was nothing like the way we had been treated at Bayfordbury. As I have mentioned several times, Mr Castle was a fair and compassionate man. On rare occasions he did sometimes speak to us on an individual basis, with care and understanding. But bearing in mind that there were as many as sixty or more boys at Churchill House, it would have been an overwhelming undertaking for one man to counsel all of them individually.

~o~o~

Irrespective of however the reader may perceive how I am writing my story, it must be known that we never at any time really felt sorry for ourselves. It simply never occurred to us to feel this way.

SUFFER LITTLE CHILDREN

This was our life, and we still survived in the old manner just as I have mentioned, 'take what you can; there may not be another day tomorrow'. We plainly knew no other way of life.

For the most part, my life as a child growing up in the care of Dr Barnardo's Homes, though not being an orthodox way of life for a child, it was nevertheless, apart from certain occasions, a happy and memorable time of my life.

Not having known or properly experienced an outsider's conventional upbringing, I don't know that I would have wanted to change it.

~o~o~ Poetic Justice ~o~o~

One day, a couple of months before Christmas in 1946, Flappers and I were walking home from school, joking and fooling around in our normal casual manner. On our way, we passed a boy on his front lawn. The boy, I believe, was just a little younger than us.

Our attention was drawn to the beautiful large tin car he was playing with. Most toys like this car were made of tin, and beautifully painted.

The car was silver, with fine red lines on it, and had something like cellophane glass for windows. It was about eighteen inches long and looked a bit like a Daimler or a Rolls Royce. I have no doubt that it was probably very well made, and rather expensive to buy.

Well, as it was, something happened or otherwise distracted the boy from playing with the car, and so he ran into his house, leaving the big beautiful tin car on the grass, only about thirty to forty feet away from us. I know that I've mentioned that I had learned my lesson regarding 'shoplifting' and that I didn't go shoplifting any more. That was quite true. However, I didn't say that Flappers and I were totally reformed or that we were now 'good honest boys'. That wouldn't be quite true.

Flappers, the thieving little sod, looked at me, his rotten understudy, and then almost instinctively he ran over to the centre of the lawn and grabbed the car.

Just as Flappers picked up the car, another boy, who we hadn't noticed, saw us and shouted, "Hey, that's Johnny's. That's Johnny's car."

I remember us laughing and running like heck down the road, Flappers struggling to carry the huge tin car. We didn't give a single

SUFFER LITTLE CHILDREN

thought or a darn for the unfortunate boy who had just lost his beautiful toy car. We took the short cut across the golf links and home to the orphanage, now proudly carrying our beautiful trophy. While we were running and laughing we were saying, "Hey, that's Johnny's car. That's Johnny's," mimicking the boy.

After we got back to Churchill House I said to Flappers, "If Mr Castle sees this, he will surely wonder how we came by it." So, I suggested that we take the car to him and say that we found it in the road.

We also knew, so we thought and always understood, that if no one claimed something that had been found, that the item found would be given back to the finder. In this instance, for our being such 'honest' boys, the car would be given to us because we were the ones who had 'found it' and handed it in.

I said I would be the one to take the car to Mr Castle, because I doubted he would believe Flappers.

Flappers agreed with the plan, and so I took the tin car and gave it to Mr Castle, telling him that Flappers and I had found the car lying in the middle of a deserted road. (I would expect that I would make a point of not saying that we found it on the beach.)

After giving the car to Mr Castle, Mr Castle complimented me for being so honest, but that was about all that was said. He didn't say we would get the car if no one claimed it.

Nevertheless, because we knew Mr Castle was such an honest man himself (ex-Chief of Police and all that) Flappers and I took it for granted that Mr Castle would give the car back to us in due course. After all, we had learned that 'honesty is the best policy'. Everyone knew that.

After a couple of weeks, we thought that perhaps Mr Castle had taken the car to the police station, to the 'Lost and Found', and that was the end of it.

We were soon to find out that, when taking everything into consideration, it was not always so wise to be quite so honest.

~o~o~

Christmas at Churchill House in 1946 was probably one of the happiest Christmases I had had in an orphanage. I was twelve and would

SUFFER LITTLE CHILDREN

be thirteen on the 28th of December. Unknown to me at the time, this would be my last Christmas at Churchill House, with the many friends I had made over the past several years.

The playroom was decorated with yards and yards of home-made paper chains and other trimmings we boys had made, and also conifer cones we had collected from the cedar trees on the estate.

About a week before Christmas Mr Castle had a huge Christmas tree brought into the playroom – a tree not unlike the one Mr Scougall had obtained for our Christmas at Bayfordbury.

The tree was decorated with shiny ornaments, glass globes, tinsel, and candles to be lighted on Christmas Eve, but there weren't any toys or other gifts on or under the tree. We were all sure there would be gifts of some kind, especially now that Mr Castle was in charge.

That night – Christmas Eve – there was, as would be expected, lots of excitement. Before going to bed we all assembled in the playroom and, with Mr and Mrs Castle and their daughters, we sang Christmas carols.

Nurse Rand, in her soft gentle voice, read us the story: *A Christmas Carol*, Scrooge, of course, reminding us of Mr Scougall before Scrooge was reformed.

Before lights out we were told to hang one of our socks on the rail at the end of our beds, much like we had done at Bayfordbury. All of the socks looked the same – grey, with half-inch bands of red around the tops.

The excitement, with sixty or more boys chattering in their dormitories, telling each other what they expected or hoped to get in our stockings, grew and grew, taking us a long time to settle down for the night.

Boys were running into each other's dormitories well after lights out, and as with other Christmases, even the ones at Bayfordbury, discipline was somewhat relaxed.

Eventually we did settle down and went to sleep until the first boy in one of the dormitories woke up. The boy, feeling down to the bottom of his bed and finding that his stocking was full, woke everyone else. The lights in each dormitory were turned on and, as of that moment, Christmas had arrived.

Because all of the socks looked alike, and probably one size fits all, all that had to be done was to replace all of the 'look alike' empty socks with socks that had previously been filled. – It's taken me all these years

SUFFER LITTLE CHILDREN

to figure that out.

Each of us had a variation of a little gift: perhaps a dinky toy, pencils, or maybe a yo-yo. As well, we each received fruits such as a pomegranate, apple, tangerine, or some other interesting thing to eat.

Each of us also received a huge, Jaffa orange, stuffed tightly into the toe of our sock.

Then on Christmas Day, immediately after breakfast, we came into the playroom and saw our marvellous Christmas tree again, all alight with flickering candles shining brightly in the otherwise unlit room. To our surprise and delight, there were lots of toys, games, toy guns and the likes, all piled under the tree.

The best present of all though was a large tin car, which was the big beautiful car that Flappers and I, after blatantly stealing it, had redeemed our consciences by honestly handing it in to Mr Castle just a few weeks earlier.

I thought, as did Flappers, that the car would be given to one of us, as it was the exact same car that I had handed in to Mr Castle after our 'finding it'.

Alas! The blinking car was given to another boy. Flappers and I both agreed jokingly that honesty didn't really pay after all.

Why Mr Castle hadn't given the car to me or perhaps Flappers, I will never know. Maybe he had forgotten who had found and handed in the car. Or maybe he did know and had even guessed how we had come by it. I have absolutely no idea.

But one thing we did learn was that we didn't gain anything by our honesty, or dishonesty, depending on which point of view one wishes to take.

~°~°~ Making up Plays ~°~°~

During the winter months we were told we could all participate in plays or skits, which we could be asked to be in.

One of the masters wrote a short skit and cast Williams – the boy who fell out of the kayak when we were on our way to Hertingfordbury Church – and me in it. The play was called *The Bigger Family*. I played a little old man in the skit, my name being: 'Much Bigger'.

SUFFER LITTLE CHILDREN

Making up Plays
The 'Bigger' Family
I'm the one in Black, Williams
in White

SUFFER LITTLE CHILDREN

Williams, who was hardly any taller than me, was the only other character in the play. His name was 'Little Bigger'. The idea was that we were supposed to be arguing as to who was the bigger of the two of us.

I would say that I was 'Much Bigger', and then Williams would say that he was a 'Little Bigger' and so on. It was all a play on words.

A photo was taken of us both dressed up as little old men. The two of us were *The Bigger Family*. I still have the picture in our family album.

There were several other plays in which different boys played parts. The night was a great success, and a prize for the best play was given. The prize was a 'chitty' – a sort of gift certificate – to the fish and chip shop for every one in the play.

As the result of the success of the 'Plays Night', it was then decided that we would have another night of plays, only this time the boys would write their own. Mrs Castle and Nurse Rand would judge the plays and, as became the standard prize, the winners would receive fish and chips for their dinner.

I made up a play called *The White Knight*. Flappers played the part of the villain: the 'Black Knight'. It all sounded very original at the time.

Because it was I who made up and wrote the play, I was naturally the good guy, or hero: the 'White Knight.' Also, there was a fair damsel, played by John Goodger. I'll be writing more about John later.

The Black Knight had a relatively small wooden hatchet for a weapon, while I, being the White Knight, had a long wooden sword. All props were crudely made by us boys in a hurry, just for the plays.

We dressed up: I in a white undershirt and white pants, using my pillowcase like a diaper, and Flappers as the Black Knight, wore his navy blue gym shorts and a dark shirt – that's how we thought knights dressed. We both had had indelible ink moustaches and crudely made black cardboard glasses. – Thinking back how silly we were, knights didn't wear glasses.

I cannot now even imagine what the 'fair damsel' Goodger wore. He (she?) must have simply looked terrible. Of course, she wouldn't have had boobs – at that time in our lives we didn't even know that girls had boobs. Even if we had known, we wouldn't have been allowed to bring attention to such rude things.

We didn't rehearse any of the play at all. Even though I 'wrote' the

SUFFER LITTLE CHILDREN

play there was hardly, if anything at all written down: we just discussed the plot and the principle of what was to happen, and then merely ad-libbed it all, just hoping to win fish and chips for our dinner.

The gist of my play was that the Black Knight would kidnap the fair damsel, and the White Knight had to save her and win her hand. How original! Could one have ever imagined such a story before?

During the scene to save the lovely damsel (Goodg) I, being the White Knight with a very long sword, was to knock the rather small hatchet out of the hands of the Black Knight (Flappers), and slay him. That was the story.

However, Flappers had a different idea as to how the story should go, and so, during our duel, he spontaneously snatched the sword right out of my hand.

I, trying to get my story back on track, picked up the wooden hatchet that Flappers had discarded, and with a dramatic chop I accidentally (or so I said) hit the Black Knight right on top of his head, accidentally making Flappers' head bleed.

Flappers and I argued about it later. I said that I knew it would hurt, but after all, he did snatch my sword out of my hand. It was all just fun and being the friends that we were, we laughed about it all later.

We didn't win the fish and chips that time, probably because Nurse Rand had to leave the 'performance' to put some iodine and an Elastoplast on Flappers' head.

We had these play nights perhaps four more times or until they became simply too silly, so much so that Mrs Castle and Nurse Rand wouldn't come to watch them.

However, on the third play night, when others, just like I did, were putting on their silly plays – everyone by now was making the plays up as they went along, without any planning at all – I sang a song.

The song has rather a melancholy or even a mournful tune, and though there are contradictions in the words, it still sounds sad.

My performance won the hearts of Mrs Castle and Nurse Rand, who, as was usual, were the judges.

The song I sang went like this:

SUFFER LITTLE CHILDREN

I am a poor little orphan boy, my mother she is dead,
My father is a drunken man and won't give me no bread.
I went into the pantry to get a crust of bread,
My father came and caught me, and sent me off to bed.
I sat upon the windowsill to hear the organs play,
and thought of my dear mother, who's dead and far away.

Oh, I want to be buried in the same old grave,
next to my dear old mother,
Six little angels by my side, two to guard, and two to pray,
And two to carry my soul away.

I must have come across looking and sounding like a sad and lonely little orphan, because I remember both Mrs Castle and Nurse Rand had tears in their eyes, which they tried to hide, but still had to dab their eyes with their handkerchiefs.

Although my performance wasn't a play, they still gave me a chitty to take to the fish and chip shop.

~o~o~

Life at Churchill House under the administrative care of Mr and Mrs Castle was a happy time, and a time of good memories. The staff in general, and in particular, Nurse Rand, were very good to us, and treated us as best they could, without favourites or any special attention given to individual boys. This would have been Mr Castle's policy.

We were never beaten by any of the staff, including Mr Nash, who still none of us liked, regardless. The days of the harsh canings were all but forgotten, which was good for our own personal morale.

But in the very near future, our lives were to be turned around yet again. Again, violence would return to our lives, and the rod would not be spared.

We would see once again the misery of being punished without mercy. Brutal beatings would become the normal way of life again, and our fear of our keepers would return.

SUFFER LITTLE CHILDREN
~o~o~ Sad Announcement ~o~o~

One day, after our tea, Mr Castle came into the dining room and told us that after Grace, when we leave the dining room, we should all assemble in the playroom. He had an important announcement to make.

Once again, we were not accustomed to Mr Castle telling us to assemble unless something of particular importance was to happen, or something like, as in the case of Flappers and me, shoplifting, or perhaps major staff changes.

Other masters on duty would often require us to assemble for various reasons, like announcing clean-up duties and other routine requirements such as haircuts etc.

This time it was different. Mr Castle, the headmaster, had told us to assemble. We knew something important was going to happen, or be announced.

In great anticipation and as instructed, we assembled in the playroom. Mr Castle looked deep in thought and was reading something in his hand. Mrs Castle and their two daughters were standing beside him, but they didn't look happy. In fact, they seemed to be rather unhappy.

As well as Mr Castle and his family most, if not all of the staff were present, including Mr Nash, Nurse Rand, Matron and several other masters, who were all standing behind Mr Castle, seemingly unaware of what was about to be announced.

After we had all assembled and quietened down, Mr Castle commenced speaking.

What he had to say made us all, without any noticeable exceptions, very concerned, wondering what the future had in store for us again and what changes we might expect in our lives.

The last time such a dramatic announcement occurred was when we were told that Bayfordbury was to be closed, and that we were moving to Eastbourne.

As it was, Mr Castle had assembled us in the playroom to inform us, with a certain sadness in his voice, that he and his family were leaving Churchill House, and that a new headmaster would be coming to take over as of tomorrow.

He went on to tell us that he had been asked to open a new Dr

SUFFER LITTLE CHILDREN

Barnardo's home, in Clacton-on-Sea. He told us too a little about Clacton: that instead of a mansion, the home would consist of several cottages (much like Woodford Bridge or Barkingside) and that some of our younger boys may be moved there.

Mr Castle went on to tell us that he would be staying at Churchill House for about a week or so in order to show the new headmaster the routine running of our institution. He continued to explain to us where Clacton-on-Sea was and that it was about eighty miles away.

After he had finished his announcement to us and the staff, Mrs Castle, with obvious sadness in her voice, said how she had loved living with us all and how much she would miss us. Their daughters also were visibly upset, as they too had been very happy living in Eastbourne, and at Churchill House.

Mr Castle again told us that the new headmaster would be arriving tomorrow, and that we were to assemble again after tea so that he could introduce him to us.

There was a hush in the room. With few exceptions, if any, all the boys liked both Mr and Mrs Castle. They had always treated us well, and Mr Castle had kept the brutes like Mr Nash at bay. Now, with him going, we didn't know what to expect.

~o~o~

The next day, after we arrived home from school and after we had finished our tea we, just as we had been told, again assembled in the playroom.

This time we knew what we were assembling for, and so, as could be expected, there was lots of chatter and speculation as to what the new headmaster would be like.

Unlike the day before, this time all of the staff were already in the playroom when we arrived. A few minutes later, and after we had settled down, Mr Castle came into the playroom accompanied by a short man with crutches, together with his wife, who looked perhaps a little stern.

Mr Castle introduced Mr Fowlermott as our new headmaster and told us that Mrs Fowlermott would be our new matron. He asked, as would be expected, that we show Mr and Mrs Fowlermott the same respect that we had always shown him and Mrs Castle.

SUFFER LITTLE CHILDREN

This was the normal introduction when a new master, or in this case a new headmaster, and his wife were introduced to us. Then we waited for Mr Fowlermott to speak.

Mr Fowlermott was a middle-aged man, his wife being about the same age. I would say now when thinking back that they were about fifty to fifty-five years old. He had a thin crop of dark hair, big dark glasses and was of a slight build, with a rather gaunt face. The fascinating thing about Mr Fowlermott was the fact that he only had one leg. The other leg, which he didn't use most of the time, was made of wood. He had one of his trouser legs folded up to his crotch. The wooden leg, when he wore it, must have been either a bit too long or too short, because his limp when he walked was to the extreme.

Looking very stern and much like her husband, Mrs Fowlermott, too, had thick dark rimmed glasses.

She was quite tall, perhaps even six inches taller than her husband, and very thin. Later my friends and I all agreed that she was definitely a little prettier than Dracula's wife, but not by much.

Standing there, she wasn't smiling and her demeanour indicated to us that we should "look out or you'll know what to expect".

Mr Fowlermott cited to us the same old intimidating phrases that many new masters used when they were to first meet us: the often used phrase, which we had heard so many times before.

"If you play ball with me, I'll play ball with you; but if you don't play ball..." etc etc etc.

With this threatening or otherwise intimidating introduction, we could tell right away that life wasn't going to be the same any more. Mr Fowlermott didn't look like a nice man, and his wife looked severe, or even mean.

We were quickly to discover that what we had thought of them at our initial introduction was just about right on. Mr Fowlermott, we were soon to find out, was a severe punisher with the cane. Our first impressions of his wife were also correct. She was a bad-tempered woman, and should not have been in the position she held.

After a few days Mr Castle and his family were gone. One day, a few years later, I was to see Mr and Mrs Castle again at Clacton-on-Sea. I will write about that happy time later.

SUFFER LITTLE CHILDREN
~o~o~ A Turn for the Worse ~o~o~

Several times in the weeks to come, boys were punished for what seemed like minor offences. One such offence – one that I was to suffer for – was simply for talking in the dining room.

The no-talking rule had been relaxed during Mr Castle's administration, but now, just talking in the dining room during meals was not allowed. The punishment for this offence was commonly four strokes of the cane, and, in the case of a constant repeater, possibly six strokes.

Mr Fowlermott always administered caning in the same way as Mr Scougall had, though not quite as brutally, primarily because Mr Fowlermott was not as big or as strong a man as Mr Scougall.

Mr Fowlermott, although he only had one leg, would swing his cane like he was going to knock a building down. Like Mr Scougall, instead of just chastising a boy for minor disciplinary infractions, he would resort to the same unreasonable caning. Such was the saying 'Spare the rod and spoil the child' and the Fowlermotts adhered to this.

To make life worse now that Mr Castle was gone, Mr Nash resumed his old ways of hitting us with his fists and knocking us about. Many boys suffered his violent moods, and were often left bruised and feeling, no doubt, depressed as the result of his bullying.

Mrs Fowlermott, who we addressed as Matron, was just as bad or perhaps even worse than we had suspected she might be and, as I remember her, she was a very surly person. No one would speak or step out of line if she was anywhere near us. Certainly we would avoid her if at all possible.

~o~o~ Mr Nash, My Childhood Nemesis ~o~o~

Over the years during my younger days, I, like so many other boys, suffered physical abuse from some of the masters in the orphanages. Many of the beatings were just part of our way of life, and common at the time.

No one came to the defence of us boys – not the outsider schoolteachers, police, or anyone of authority or any other person that I am aware of. Beatings were miserable, to be sure, and quite often carried out by any member of the male staff. But then there were the exceptionally

SUFFER LITTLE CHILDREN

brutal bullies. In my case, as was the situation in Bayfordbury and now in Churchill House, there was Mr Nash.

~o~o~

One day – another day that I can't help but remember – was the day that Mr Nash again beat me unreasonably, as though I were his equal in size and strength.

On this particular occasion, and for the second time, Mr Nash beat me so severely that, like the other time at Bayfordbury, I'll remember it for the rest of my life. He beat me with his fists, kicked me, pulled me around by my hair, and even deliberately banged my head against the wall.

It all happened as the result of my not turning my mattress one morning: a simple, deliberate, but unfortunate mistake that I had no excuse for. It was a standard procedure in most orphanages but, as with so many boys, if no one was looking we often didn't.

Every morning, after being called to get up and out of bed at six o'clock, we would go into the lavatory rooms on our respective floors. There we would brush our teeth with pink carbolic tooth powder, wash our hands and faces, and brush our hair.

Then we would come back to our dormitories, get dressed and make our beds.

Why exactly we turned our mattresses every day, we as young boys had no idea, but nevertheless we turned them, just because we were told to.

However, we sometimes didn't. This infraction of the rules usually went unnoticed. If a boy was found not to have carried out this simple chore, then he would usually be simply chastised, and made to strip his bed, turn his mattress, and then make his bed again. That was about all there was to it.

Not turning one's mattress was not thought to be a very serious offence. With the exception of Bayfordbury, it would not have been a caning offence.

As it was, on the morning I refer to, Mr Nash came into our dormitory and, because we had finished making our beds so quickly, asked me if

SUFFER LITTLE CHILDREN

I had turned my mattress. I told him I had, though like many, or even most of the boys, I actually hadn't.

Mr Nash stared at me and then put his hand down my bed between the top and bottom sheets, and felt to see if it was still warm. Because I hadn't turned my mattress it was naturally still warm and so he knew I hadn't turned it.

Knowing his temperament, I immediately knew I was in trouble. As it was, I was standing beside the bed, close to him. He looked at me through the corner of his eye and without any warning, swung his fisted hand at me, hitting me on the side of the head and knocking me right over the bed.

Then he ran around the other side of the bed after me, pulling me around by my hair like I was a rag doll. Then he hit me again and again, knocking me back over the bed with his hands and fists. After he had kicked me several times and had deliberately banged my head against the steel bed rail as well as the plastered wall, I became dizzy and dazed, to the point that I threw up, sick to my stomach.

With my nose bleeding from having hit it on the steel bed railing, Mr Nash stormed out of the dormitory, still in a fitful rage.

Needless to say, I was extremely traumatised and distraught. The other boys in our dormitory, and the dorm next to ours, were hushed and afraid to make any noise for fear of drawing attention to themselves. I was only too aware of their concern for themselves. I too, would feel as they did when I observed or was aware of other boys being so badly treated by the likes of Mr Nash.

The boys in my dorm in particular, were nervous and somewhat traumatised by having seen me being so severely beaten and so didn't speak, for fear of Mr Nash coming back into our dormitory.

After breakfast, I went to the sick bay to have cuts on my forehead attended to. Nurse Rand was visibly disturbed by the state I was in. My eyes were swollen and red. I had a swollen lip, my face was bruised, and my forehead was cut and had been bleeding.

I remember that I wrote to my grandmother and told her about the beating. As was the normal practice, I handed my letter in to the office for mailing. A member of Dr Barnardo's staff always read and mailed the letters for us.

SUFFER LITTLE CHILDREN

Whether my grandmother received my letter and wrote to Dr Barnardo's Homes' head office in Stepney or not, I don't really know – she never did mention it; or if because my letter had actually been read by one of the staff members, as would have been normal, and who in turn didn't forward it on to my grandmother, I will never know.

Either way, shortly after I had handed my letter into the office Mr Nash came to me and acted much nicer to me. I would like to think that he had been cautioned about hitting us kids the way he did, but with Mr Fowlermott now the headmaster, I have my doubts.

~o~o~

In today's climate Mr Nash would, I'm quite sure, have gone to prison for the way he so often brutally beat us kids.

When Mr Castle had been our headmaster and therefore Mr Nash's boss, Mr Nash would never have dared to treat any of us the way he did. Unknown to us then, but understanding humanity a little better now, I feel quite confident in saying that Mr Castle had been our shield and protector against the likes of Mr Nash.

I have over the past few years met a couple of my old friends from Bayfordbury and Churchill House, one being my lifelong friend Baggy, and the other, John 'Goodg' Goodger, who I will be writing about later.

Both of these old friends clearly remember Mr Nash in much the same way as I do, and have their own stories to tell about the vicious beatings they received from him.

Unbelievable as it was, a year or so after leaving Churchill House to go to Goldings, Goldings being a more senior orphanage for older Dr Barnardo's Homes boys, I met three other boys who had come from yet another Dr Barnardo's home, in a town called Bognor Regis, Sussex.

The boys, who were 'spares' or 'weeds', had just arrived at Goldings, where Baggy, Flappers and I had moved to, and they told Baggy, Flappers and myself that Mr Nash had been promoted to the position of headmaster, and had been moved to Bognor Regis.

Their stories regarding the violent and the despised Mr Nash were all quite consistent with ours.

SUFFER LITTLE CHILDREN
~o~o~ Plans to Move ~o~o~

From time to time there would be an announcement informing us that we were invited to put our names down on a sheet of paper posted on the notice board if we wished to go to another Dr Barnardo's home for special occupational training.

On one such occasion we were told that if we wanted to go to 'Russel Coats Training School', that we should put our names down.

Russel Coats Training School was one of two 'sea schools', which also were part of Dr Barnardo's Homes. The other sea school was Watts Naval Training School – a military naval school established to train Dr Barnardo boys for a future career in the Royal Navy. Many boys who attended Watts Naval became high-ranking officers in the Royal Navy.

Russel Coats Training School, on the other hand, was opened to train boys for opportunities in the merchant navy. Needless to say, Britain had a great need for merchant seaman, and many boys made a good career in this service.

Fred, Baggy, Flappers and I, including several other boys, all put our names down to go to Russel Coats. Fred and I thought we would like to be 'ship's carpenters'. I really don't remember why Baggy and Flappers wanted to go to Russel Coats to become merchant seaman, but I suppose they had their reasons.

Quite possibly it was partly to do with us all wanting to stay together. The idea of travelling the world on merchant ships for the rest of our lives appealed to many young boys, including me.

I'm sure, too, that we thought that with Mr Castle gone and Mr Fowlermott now in charge, we could be leaving Churchill House within a few days and that, too, would have appealed to us.

The next day I went to Bedewell School and told a male teacher, not Mrs Gardener, that I was leaving, and was going to another orphanage a long way away. I think I must have indicated that I could be "going tomorrow".

The teacher wished me well and gave me sixpence, which didn't totally surprise me. People in those days gave kids money when they were going on holiday, or leaving to go to somewhere like, for instance, another orphanage.

SUFFER LITTLE CHILDREN

The next day we were told which boys had been selected to go to Russel Coats, and that none of us – Fred, Baggy, Flappers or I – were amongst those selected. They didn't tell us why, just that we were not selected. In fact, out of about fifteen boys wanting to go, only about three or four were actually to go.

So, I went back to Bedewell School the following day as usual, and sat in my seat. The teacher who had given me sixpence a few days earlier looked a little surprised. I think that he believed he had been cheated out of sixpence, but he didn't say so. However, he did ask me what happened and why I hadn't gone away to another orphanage. I simply told him I that I hadn't been selected to go, but that I might be going next time.

Then, just a few days, or perhaps a week after applying to go to Russel Coats, we were asked if any of us wanted to go to live in Australia.

We had no idea where Australia was at the time; it could have been anywhere, even near Clacton-on-Sea, for all we knew. If it was near Clacton we would be able to see Mr Castle again. Certainly we would get away from Mr Fowlermott and Mr Nash, and that seemed to be our biggest motivation to move.

So again, Fred, Baggy, Flappers and I put our names down to go to Australia. No one explained anything to us about Australia or that it was such a long way away, not that that would have mattered one way or another to us.

Such a move for us would be simply a change. One place or orphanage was, for us, like any other. We had no permanent home or people to miss, only our friends in the orphanage. I don't think I gave any thought about leaving England, my sisters, Gran, Aunty Molly, Uncle Sid or Jill. It was just an adventure and that we would not be gone for ever.

At this time in our lives we had no future or ambition, or really any aims in life, and there was absolutely no one, anywhere, guiding us.

The next day, just as before, I went to the same teacher and told him I was going to Australia. I must have convinced him that I really was going this time. So, the teacher gave me another sixpence, and once again wished me good luck.

About a month or so, after we had put our names down to go to Australia, we were told to assemble in the playroom for an announcement.

SUFFER LITTLE CHILDREN

It was then when we were told who was going to Australia. We were, of course, excited. By now we knew that Australia was on the other side of the world. We had seen pictures of kangaroos, boomerangs and crocodiles. There seemed to be lots of people riding horses and rounding up sheep, and miles of open spaces. It all seemed very exciting. We all wanted to go.

The names were then read out. Baggy and I were to be very disappointed for more than one reason. It wasn't just that we were not selected to go; it was worse than that.

Baggy, Flappers and I were not on the list of boys to go but, to our great disappointment, Fred Dyos was.

~o~o~ Goodbye Fred ~o~o~

I can't think whether I was embarrassed or not when I went back to school the next day, after we knew who was going to Australia. Actually, I can't recall what I told the teacher. I don't think he even bothered to ask. He certainly didn't ask for his sixpence back.

There wasn't much said about my going to Australia, but I guess the teacher thought he wouldn't fall for that one again. I can only imagine now that he had quite a chuckle with the other teaching staff about this little sod saying goodbye every second day, and him giving me sixpence each time.

Many years later I was to find out that when my grandparents were contacted by Dr Barnardo's Homes they had objected to my going to Australia, and so my name was taken off the application list.

The same thing apparently happened to Baggy. I don't know why Flappers wasn't selected; there would have been no one to object to his leaving England. Several other boys apart from us were also disappointed.

Apparently families of us boys, if there were any family members at all, were sometimes contacted, and permission was sought before a child was sent to places like Canada or Australia.

When we had put our names down to go to Australia, we would have had no idea that some of us would go and some wouldn't.

Fred, whose father had agreed that he, Les and Billy could go, was now destined for Australia.

SUFFER LITTLE CHILDREN

Fred Dyos
This photo was taken at Churchill House just before he was migrated to Australia - 1946

SUFFER LITTLE CHILDREN

It was quite traumatic for Fred, Baggy and me, and, to some extent, Flappers. We had now known each other ever since we were all about eight years old, and during that time had been as close as any brothers could be.

The difference between biological brothers and us, a brotherhood of orphans, was that we chose or 'adopted' our brothers and bonded closely with them, whereas natural brothers do not select their brothers; they simply have what they were given.

Natural brothers have no desire to, and nor do they necessarily ever, bond as close as we did, and in many instances may find their closest friends to be closer even than their own siblings.

Fred, Baggy, Flappers and I, had suffered the same misery and mistreatments as well as the very happy times of growing up together, through thick or thin. Now we were to say goodbye to Fred, possibly for ever, though 'for ever' was something we never really contemplated.

It took about three weeks for Fred and about fifteen of the other boys, including Fred's two brothers, to get ready to go. Fred gave Baggy and me his 'treasures' – the only things he had in the world. He wasn't allowed to take anything except the essentials with him to Australia.

He gave Baggy his rabbit and cage, and a few other things, and to me he gave his bike and a catapult. We all had catapults, but his was a very good one. I remember too that Fred gave me a carpenter's chisel. Fred and I always said we wanted to be carpenters, and he had acquired this chisel from somewhere or other.

Then the day came when Fred and his brothers and the other boys were to leave Churchill House to go to Australia. It must have been a Saturday or a Sunday, as we weren't at school.

Baggy and I, being closer friends with Fred than was Flappers, hung around Fred for several days prior to him leaving. Fred said how he would write to us after he got to Australia. He had no idea what life had in store for him or his brothers.

I recall we were comparatively quiet. Life without Fred would not be the same, and yet for Fred it was, of course, a very exciting time.

Then there was an announcement that the boys going to Australia were to assemble in the playroom with their kitbags. We understood too, that each of the boys going to Australia would eventually be receiving a

SUFFER LITTLE CHILDREN

'sea trunk', in which they would store their entire luggage for the trip. The voyage was expected to take them three to four weeks.

I remember thinking that we had made a mistake putting our names down to go to Australia. What we hadn't realised was that this would have been a point of no return. We had learned that Australia was not just around the corner, and that it would be a long time before we saw Fred again, if in fact we ever would.

Mr Fowlermott said a few words of encouragement to the boys leaving, and wished them well.

It was raining as they filed out the main entrance and onto the gravel driveway towards the waiting coach.

Baggy and I were in the playroom watching through the window as they boarded the coach. Then after a few minutes of organising, the coach started moving away and around the horseshoe driveway. We got a glimpse of Fred and waved goodbye frantically, but I don't think he could see us through the drizzle and the rain-splattered windows.

Fred, who had been Baggy's and my best friend since the day that Baggy and I had had our fight many years ago at Bayfordbury, and who had been with us at Bayford School, when we were a little more than eight years old, was now gone.

We would always remember laughing over such things as "Do you want my dumpling, Fred" and many, many other occasions, including Fred heading the wooden ball at Ware School.

Life without our 'brother' Fred was again changed. Baggy and I became even closer friends. Eventually other boys would take Fred's place, but we would never forget Fred and the good times we had together.

~o~o~

I only ever received one letter from Fred, that was a little over a year after he had left Churchill House. He was an apprentice carpenter in Sydney. He sent me a photo of himself and Leslie in Sydney, taken outside of the boarding house they lived. I still have his photo.

Some fifty years later a friend of mine (not a Dr Barnardo boy), who had immigrated to Australia in 1962 and became the librarian at the University of Queensland, tracked the Dyos boys down for me. He

SUFFER LITTLE CHILDREN

couldn't find Fred, but he located Les Dyos and sent me Les's address in Sydney.

In 1989 Leslie (Dicky) Dyos and I wrote to each other a few times and Leslie gave me Fred's address. Fred also lived in Sydney. Les told me that Fred had become a very good carpenter and had built his own house, which Les said was a great credit to his brother.

Leslie also told me that Fred was, to that day, still quite bitter towards Dr Barnardo's Homes. Fred, it seems, felt that Dr Barnardo's had never treated him well and that the cruel treatment we received at Bayfordbury at the hands of Mr Scougall, Mr Nash and, to some extent, Mr Fowlermott, had remained with him all through the years.

Leslie also mentioned in his letters that Fred would not even talk to him – his older brother – or his younger brother Billy about Dr Barnardo's Homes, even briefly. Fred apparently never spoke to his wife or the rest of his family about his life in England or Barnardo's, and didn't wish to remember any part of it.

Nevertheless, I wrote to Fred and told him a little about Baggy and myself, and how we had fared over the years, but Fred never did reply. I had thought that Fred would surely have wanted to write to me, as we had been such good childhood friends and also because Baggy and I had suffered the same treatment as him when he was in England. But unfortunately Fred couldn't even bring himself to do that.

~o~o~

Having assisted Dr Barnardo's as an 'aftercare' volunteer in Canada over a fifteen-year period, I am aware that many, many Dr Barnardo boys and girls who were brought up in the homes were very badly treated, and many have suffered lifelong psychological damage.

Even my own sister Barbara, I feel, seems to have little if anything, good to say about her upbringing in Dr Barnardo's Homes, though she bears no grudges toward Dr Barnardo's Homes.

However, not having seen enough of Barbara since we left Barnardo's, I can't really be sure exactly how she feels about her upbringing.

SUFFER LITTLE CHILDREN
~o~o~ Defiance ~o~o~

One morning at Churchill House during breakfast, Flappers and I were talking and joking around, just as Mrs Fowlermott blew her whistle to get everyone's attention. She had an announcement to make and, regrettably, Flappers and I weren't listening.

Mrs Fowlermott didn't seem to notice Flappers talking, but she noticed me. She was furious and charged towards me from the other end of the dining room. She struck at me, slapping me across the face and at the same time told me to leave the dining room and to stand in the corridor outside.

After she had made her announcement she came out into the corridor, gave me another good clout around the ear, and told me to go up to Mr Fowlermott's office.

I was about thirteen years old now, and a slap around the face from a woman was not like a beating from Mr Nash, but I didn't let her see that it didn't really hurt. What was probably most upsetting for me was the fact that she was so angry. Of course, I wouldn't have dared to answer her back.

Nevertheless, still stinging from the clout I had received, I went up to the office fully anticipating my getting the cane, which, like at Bayfordbury, was so freely given.

With Mr Castle long gone, life was now back to the days of 'the spider and its web'. If we had to 'report to the office', it was similar to a fly being asked to step into a spider's web. Mr Fowlermott, being the spider was, in many respects, feared.

After several minutes or so of my waiting outside the office door, Mr Fowlermott told me to come in.

Obediently, I did as I was told and entered, head bent submissively, trying to look sorry for myself and sorry for making Mrs Fowlermott so angry. That was about all I could do: there would be no explanation asked of me, and as usual, no appeal. All I could do was grovel and humble myself before Mr Fowlermott and hope for leniency.

Unfortunately for me, Mrs Fowlermott must have told him I had been extremely insolent to her, which wouldn't have been true, as we wouldn't have dared to be insolent. She had come into the office and

SUFFER LITTLE CHILDREN

was standing beside him.

Mr Fowlermott stood with both hands on the desk, supporting himself and at the same time glaring at me. All the time, Mrs Fowlermott was nodding her head in agreement with his indications that I was going to get a beating.

Mr Fowlermott, too, was very angry, and got angrier and angrier as the minutes passed. He was ranting on, telling me how no boy was going to be disrespectful to his wife. I didn't know how it could be considered that I was 'disrespectful' towards his wife. I wasn't aware of what exactly I had done that was so bad.

No boy would dare to cheek or answer back or show any disrespect to any member of the staff, and in particular to Mrs Fowlermott.

Then all heck broke loose. This one-legged man with the wooden leg, still holding on to the desk, came around the desk and grabbed hold of me and tried to pull my braces, which held up my short trousers, off my shoulders.

He really thought he was going to pull my trousers down in front of his miserable wife, and cane me on my bare bottom. I think I would have died first.

I pushed him as hard as I could and he staggered back against the desk, losing his balance somewhat. Then Mrs Fowlermott got into the act, and tried to grab hold of me. She, too, was trying to pull my trousers off.

I broke loose from her and scrambled under Mr Fowlermott's big office desk. Mrs Fowlermott was screaming at me to come out from under the desk, while Mr Fowlermott was trying to poke me with one of his crutches.

I was shouting "No! No! I won't. You can't do that. I won't let you." I had now abandoned all fear, and was totally and completely defiant, and virtually out of control.

They still both persisted in catching me but she was an awkward woman, and he only had one leg. They didn't stand a chance.

Because of all the noise we were making in his office they gave up trying to catch me, and spoke to me while I was still under Mr Fowlermott's desk.

Eventually I agreed to come out from under the desk and to be caned, but not with my short trousers off.

SUFFER LITTLE CHILDREN

So I was caned and it surely hurt, but it never could hurt as much as when Mr Scougall caned us at Bayfordbury.

Mrs Fowlermott must have known that lots of boys were laughing at her behind her back, because most certainly they were. Baggy, Flappers and I had told everyone about the 'fight', and how the Fowlermotts had unsuccessfully tried to pull my trousers down.

~o~o~

About a year later I was to spend Christmas in Clacton-on-Sea, where Mr and Mrs Castle had moved to from Churchill House. Actually, I was going from one Dr Barnardo's home to another Dr Barnardo's home, much like a busman's holiday.

Mr Castle had arranged for two other boys and myself to spend Christmas with him. Quite unexpectedly Mr Castle mentioned to me, with a big smile on his big bruiser face, "So Mr Fowlermott couldn't catch you, eh Reg! He couldn't get you out from under his desk."

He too, had obviously heard about my altercation with the Fowlermotts. Such news must have travelled between the staff at Dr Barnardo's Homes. I felt Mr Castle didn't like the Fowlermotts very much either.

~o~o~ Moving On ~o~o~

After much waiting and believing we would never leave Churchill House, at last the big day came. It all started when a notice was put on the notice board informing us that boys over the age of thirteen could put their names down to apply to go to the William Baker Technical School, Goldings, Hertford.

Baggy, Flappers and I immediately put our names down. We had been disappointed before, but we felt sure that eventually we would be sent somewhere. We were also aware that at thirteen, we could possibly stay at Churchill House until we were fourteen or even fifteen.

Living with Mr Nash and the Fowlermotts for two more years would, for me, be a daunting prospect.

Baggy was thirteen and a half years old at the time of us putting in

SUFFER LITTLE CHILDREN

our applications to go to Goldings. As it was, because I was no more than thirteen and about two months, and Flappers was just about the same age as me, we were both just a little too young to go.

Again I went to Bedewell School and told the teacher I was leaving to go to Goldings. All he did was wish me good luck. He didn't give me sixpence this time.

A few days later we were to again be disappointed. Four boys, including Baggy, were told they had been accepted to go to Goldings. Neither Flappers nor I, being just a little younger than Baggy, were included to go.

So now Baggy was going away, but the situation, though disappointing, was not devastating. Knowing that Baggy was that little bit older than Flappers and me, I felt sure that we would be going to Goldings with the next batch selected.

So, no doubt, I went back to Bedewell School yet again, only this time there was no surprise, and no one lost a 'tanner' (sixpence).

~o~o~ Goldings ~o~o~

About three to four months after Baggy had left to go to Goldings, another notice was posted, again inviting boys to apply to go there.

Again, Flappers and I put our names down on the piece of paper on the notice board. This time we were accepted as being old enough. We were both about thirteen and a half, physically fit, and with an acceptable level of academic education.

I went to school and told everyone I was finally leaving Bedewell School and going on to a technical school in Hertford. The impression was, it seemed, "O yes! We've heard it all before." No one acted as though they would miss me, except perhaps Miss Gardener, and even she was used to my saying goodbye by now.

I was very pleased to be leaving Churchill House. Not so much Churchill House, but rather because now I would never see Mr Nash or the Fowlermotts again.

I would sadly miss Nurse Rand and lots of the boys, including a boy named John Goodger. John Goodger and some other boys had in many ways replaced Fred and Baggy, and so naturally I would miss them also.

SUFFER LITTLE CHILDREN

So now it was my turn to leave Eastbourne and to embark on a new life. I would see Baggy again soon, and start to learn a trade.

The day came for us to leave Churchill House. We said our final goodbyes to dear Miss Rand, who, sadly, I was never to see or hear of again.

I also said goodbye to some of the other masters, and an unspoken 'good riddance' to Mr Nash and the Fowlermott's. Then we boarded our transportation to the William Baker Technical School, Goldings, Hertford.

The transportation to Goldings was a big van, which in due course we affectionately called 'the Albion'. One of the Goldings' masters, Mr Whitbread, drove the Albion. Eventually, like most boys, I was to become to know Mr Whitbread quite well.

Baggy had left Churchill House to go to Goldings about four months earlier. Four months is quite a long time in the life of a young boy, and although I'm sure we missed each other, Baggy and I would, as may be expected, be getting used to our separate ways of life and with different friends.

19

GOLDINGS – Part 1

~o~ William Baker Technical School (WBTS) ~o~

And so it was that in 1947 I was moved from Churchill House to the William Baker Technical School, Goldings, Hertford.

Goldings, as the William Baker Technical School (WBTS) was most usually called, was another of Dr Barnardo's Homes' orphanages, located in the tiny village of Waterford, near Hertford. I was now to be known as a Goldings boy. Goldings would become my home and the last orphanage I was to be housed in. Eventually, after I left Goldings, I would go out into the outsiders' world to earn a living in the trade of my choice.

On the day of my departure from Churchill House, Flappers and myself, together with two other boys, Bloor and Marsden, got up earlier than usual. We had an early breakfast, and with our kitbags packed, waited for our transport to arrive to take us to Goldings.

Once again I was on the move to yet another orphanage, where there would be lots of 'new' boys, among whom I would have to have to establish my 'pecking order'. The big difference between my moving to Goldings, as compared with the other moves I had made, was that at least I wasn't alone in my moving.

There were a few boys I would know at Goldings, including my special friend Baggy, who had been there for about four months by now. There would also be other boys who Flappers and I had been 'homed' with at Bayfordbury and Eastbourne who we would both know.

The other boys – Marsden and Bloor – although they came to Goldings with Flappers and myself, weren't particular friends of ours at Churchill House. They were just other boys who we knew reasonably well, but who we didn't 'knock around' with.

Most of the boys who live together in the same orphanage generally know each other, but are not all special friends. In fact, some of the boys just didn't get along with each other, and so there would be cliques or even gangs, though they weren't actually called 'gangs'.

SUFFER LITTLE CHILDREN

~o~o~

We travelled through London, and on the way we stopped to pick up about a hundred or more loaves of bread. This was a regular trip for Mr Whitbread on Tuesdays and Fridays. Other days he would go to Woodford Bridge, Barkingside and other Dr Barnardo's Homes in the greater London area, and pick up boots and shoes. The boots and shoes, which required repairs, belonged to other Dr Barnardo boys and girls in other Dr Barnardo's homes. I will explain more about shoe repairing later.

As we approached Goldings we were aware that we were in familiar territory. Goldings is situated just outside of Hertford, but in the opposite direction from Bayfordbury. The two Dr Barnardo's Homes institutions were about five to six miles apart. When we lived at Bayfordbury, even though Goldings was such a short distance away we had no idea that Goldings even existed, and likewise, those boys at Goldings were not aware of Bayfordbury.

We passed through the middle of Hertford and past the Hart statue (male red deer) in the centre of the town, the Castle cinema – which had now been restored after being damaged by the doodle bug – also Woolworths where we used to do our 'free' shopping, and past the Corn Exchange, where we would go for Christmas parties. It was nice to see these familiar places again, including the common, where we would enter the outsiders' athletic sports.

Almost forgotten were the troublesome times we had at Bayfordbury: the Scougall regime with their constant bullying, and the horrible food. In many other ways though, it was like coming home again.

Goldings was a well-appointed piece of property consisting of several hundred acres. There were two rivers running through the grounds, with roach, pike, trout and other types of fish in them.

A private narrow road, treed on both sides much of the way, looped through the property, entering on the one side at Mr Whitbread's gatehouse, and leaving at the other side into the centre of the little village of Waterford, the road being about two miles long in total.

A pair of humpback bridges crossed over the rivers in two different locations. In places the winding rivers would join together, forming

SUFFER LITTLE CHILDREN

small islands with trees and shrubs on them. The Goldings estate also included beautifully hedged fields and several acres of woods. The woods were very old, dense and dark, consisting of huge old oak, beech, ash and sycamore trees.

The huge domicile of Goldings was much, much bigger than Bayfordbury and Churchill House put together. It was three or, in some places, four storeys high, and had many wings to it. Construction on this rambling and uniquely beautiful old building started in the early 1700s. Eventually, in 1922, it was bought by Dr Barnardo's, and became the William Baker Technical School.

There is much to be said about Goldings with its classic architecture, and Flemish bond red brickwork and huge corbelled chimneys. The numerous bay windows and its many sculptured stone inlays make the domicile a majestic picture, and a wonderful monument to its architects.

In front of the Goldings mansion there were beautiful yew trees and several rhododendron bushes the size of big trees – about twenty to thirty feet tall.

Goldings, which was now to be our new home for the next three and a half years, was a huge, exciting looking place full of mystery, and like everywhere else in those days, a new beginning to my future.

~o~o~

In visiting Goldings with my wife Donna some fifty years in the future, I was to be astounded by its overwhelming architectural beauty, and the grandeur of the domicile I had called home. The beautiful trees were all still there, just as I had first seen them, only bigger, of course.

~o~o~ Goldings Orientation ~o~o~

On our arrival at Goldings the Albion travelled up one of the two roads within the estate.

Mr Whitbread ushered us, together with our kitbags, into the main reception hall. The school captain came to meet us and after taking our particulars, names, etc and other documents we were given to travel

SUFFER LITTLE CHILDREN

with, he gave us our school numbers and assigned us to our 'houses'.

My number, the number which I was to be identified with for the rest of my time at Goldings, was number 7. Flappers had the distinction of being given the number 1.

There were 250 boys at Goldings, ranging from the age of thirteen and a half to seventeen and a few even eighteen. Like most boys when they first arrived at Goldings, both Flappers and I were just thirteen and a half years old.

Besides the school captain being in charge of our orientation, it was one of his duties to inform 'new boys' of the way the school was run, and its principal rules. He told us briefly to listen to and learn the school bugle calls, and to respond to the instructions they carried. Every boy, upon arriving at Goldings, went through this initial and absolutely essential basic orientation process.

The four of us, along with any other new boys who arrived from other orphanages, or boys who had until now been fostered or 'boarded out', would, upon their arrival at Goldings, automatically be called 'spares' or 'weeds'. The term was a derogatory term given to new boys basically to let them know their social status in the school i.e. that they were at the lowest level in the 'pecking order'.

At one time the term 'spare' was given to a new boy entering Goldings and waiting for a place to become vacant in a trade shop, which he could then enter. And so, until he was assigned a place in a shop, he was called a 'spare'. The term 'weed' was simply a degrading indication of a boy's status upon arrival at Goldings.

As such, spares or weeds were given the worst skivvies (jobs) to do. They also slept on the worst beds (those with broken supports etc), had the most worn out mattresses, and also, they were given the least-wanted locations in the dormitories. When we ate we would have to sit at the furthest end of the dining room table, with the other weeds as our principal companions.

Weeds would also be picked on by the other boys still trying to establish themselves. This struggle would go on until there were other new boys arriving to be picked on, or until we managed to establish ourselves by fighting and becoming known as 'fighters', or by looking out for ourselves.

SUFFER LITTLE CHILDREN

Goldings would best be described as being much like a British public school. The same sort of order among peers existed, where weeds knew their place and one worked his way up the pecking order.

The main difference, however, between a British public school and Goldings, was that for a boy to enter a public school huge fees had to be paid, which for the most part only wealthy families could afford; whereas we at Goldings were primarily orphans without means. Another big difference was that unlike with the public schools, there were no academic entrance exams.

As in a public school, an orphanage like Goldings had terminologies such as prep school, tuck shop, and the likes. There was also a unique colloquial language that we conversed in, and it was important that new boys, just as soon as they arrived at Goldings, learned it quickly.

~o~o~ Goldings Slang ~o~o~

I can't recall all of the slang words that were commonly used at Goldings. Many, but not all of them are listed here:

Baccy baron	One who sells cigarettes
Bags's	I'm next, I choose this one
Bags your core	I want your apple core
Bags a chew	I want your chewing gum
Beetle crushers	Boots
Bungy	Cheese
Copped	To be caught
Coggie set	Crystal set, with headphones
Colonel Bogey	A master or boy who tells tall stories
Crusties	Underpants
Deuce	Tuppence, two one penny pieces – old English money
Dicky boy	Barnardo Boy
Diggy eye	Keeping a lookout
Diggs	Someone's coming, look out
Digs	Lodgings
Dobbed	Drop someone in it

SUFFER LITTLE CHILDREN

Doing a bunk	Running away
Doorstep	A slice of bread, one inch thick or thicker
Dykes	The ablution block, gone to the dykes
Fatigue	Punishment, not serious
Frogspawn	Sago pudding
Fruitcake	A nutter, a mad person
Gander	To have a look
Ginner	Slice of bread
Ginner and marg	Slice of bread and a pat of margarine
Gnats Hiss	Orange drink made from powder, normally quite weak
Goldings doughnut	Fried bread
Gobbing	Spitting
Gritty greens	Green cabbage
Grog	Tea that has been made in one pot, with milk and sugar
Hard bake	Bread pudding, but overcooked
Half Dead	Hertford town centre
In Dock	In sick bay
Jankers	Not allowed out of Goldings' grounds
Joey	A thre'penny piece – old English money
Legger	A boy who tells tales
Licker	Someone who creeps around the masters
Miggy	Tennis ball
Newbie	A new boy
On the book	On report, in trouble
Pinhead	Mr Wheatley, the headmaster
Plonk	Bread pudding (see hard bake)
Pongy	Porridge
Prep	Evening school
Richard the Third	To move one's bowels
Shreddies	Underwear
Skanky	Dirty/unclean
Skeet	Out of bounds
Skinnies	Not a fair share
Skive	Get out of doing a chore or your daily work

SUFFER LITTLE CHILDREN

Slog .... A fight
Snout .... Tobacco, a cigarette, or a roll-up
Spare .... A new boy
Spot cash .... Money now, on the dot
Stever .... One-penny piece – old English money
Tea leaf .... A thief, person who steals other people's property
The bogs .... The ablution block
The cuts .... The cane
Trashy .... A child's paper comic e.g. Dandy, Beano
Todd, 'on his todd' .. A loner, a person who is always on his own
Topper .... The crust ends on a loaf of bread
Two's up .... Share a fag or comic etc
Weed .... New boy (see spare)

~о~о~ Long Trousers ~о~о~

Almost on the same day that we arrived at Goldings we were fitted out with our new grey-flannelled suits with long trousers. They were the first pair of long trousers I had ever worn, and I was now thirteen and a half.

The grey flannel suits were our 'best suits' – the suits we went to church in. Also, we each received a Dr Barnardo's tie – but as well, we were allowed to wear other ties.

Our school uniform consisted of grey flannels (long trousers) and green blazers which displayed our school crest, much like a public schoolboy's uniform might.

The Goldings School crest, located on our blazer breast pocket, illustrated the various trades taught at the William Baker Technical School.

Inscribed on the crest was the school motto, *FINIS CORONET OPUS*. Our Latin motto, we were soon to learn, meant 'The End Crowns the Work'. I still have my school crest.

We wore grey shirts and typical Dr Barnardo's grey socks with green rings on the tops. To complete our attire, we always wore black boots with steel heel and toe caps as well as steel studs in the soles.

SUFFER LITTLE CHILDREN

Whenever we left the school grounds to go into Hertford or almost any other place we, unless we were required to wear our 'best suits', wore our grey flannel long trousers and our green school blazers. The grey flannel suits were mostly worn on Sundays to church, or on special occasions.

However, until the day I actually left Dr Barnardo's Homes, at the age of almost seventeen, we still wore short trousers – summer and winter – all of the time we were on the school grounds.

For the first time in our lives we were now allowed to wear belts to hold our trousers up. Gone for ever were the braces (suspenders) and the underpants which sagged or even fell down if the loops were broken, or if the buttons came off our shorts.

We still wore the same type of heavy, cotton, rather long-legged underpants, but if we had our belts tight enough this would help to hold them up and stop them sagging. Even so, when we were wearing shorts we could often be seen with our underpants tops showing over the top edge of our shorts.

~o~o~

The two hundred and fifty boys at Goldings were divided into six houses. The houses were called:

Somerset House   Cairns House
Buxton House   Aberdeen House
Mt Stephen House   McCall House

Upon arrival, each boy would be assigned to one of these houses. As it was, Flappers, Bloor and I were all put into Somerset House, while Marsden was put into Cairns House.

The term 'house' was just symbolic, or a team arrangement. Each house consisted of forty to forty-five boys of varying ages, and occupied its own section on one of the dormitory floors. Somerset House, like all of the other five houses, had its own area in the dining room, and its own position on the parade ground.

As boys completed their term of academic and trade training at Goldings, which generally ran for about three and a half years, they

SUFFER LITTLE CHILDREN

would be sufficiently prepared so that they could leave Goldings and the Dr Barnardo's Homes system, to go out into the world to earn a living on what was called a 'situation'. When each boy eventually left Goldings, new boys, otherwise spares or weeds, would replace them.

Each house had its own housemaster and support masters, including a selected senior boy who became the house captain. The house captain was usually a boy over sixteen years old. The masters didn't interfere much with the day-to-day discipline in their houses, but they were there for assistance if their house wasn't running itself properly.

Three prefects, also senior boys, supported the house captain. The prefects were thought to be somewhat level headed, and who had accomplished some sort of distinction, one way or another, in the school. Even by constant good behaviour.

The house captains and the prefects were expected to run their respective houses in an orderly manner. Also, being older and, more often than not, bigger boys, they were usually physically able to 'beat up' their younger peers if necessary, to keep order, which they did from time to time, though generally speaking they weren't bullies.

~o~o~

There were, needless to say, a few bullies at Goldings, as is normal in any institution. Such bullies as there were, would make life pretty miserable for the more timid boys, or the weeds. There would sometimes be surprises, of course. From time to time a weed or timid boy could possibly have a bigger boy or a fighter for a friend. They might even have a big brother who would come to their rescue, and very often the would-be bully would come off second best.

Like in most institutions, the entire social structure of Goldings was still, without a doubt, a type of class level structure, based on our ages, size, and fighting ability. Age would be a factor in many ways, but big boys or boys known to be fighters would, mostly as the result of their reputation and posturing, get their own way.

The bigger boys, bullies, or fighters would choose the positions they wanted to play on their house football or cricket teams, for instance. Even the prefects would sometimes think twice about challenging a

SUFFER LITTLE CHILDREN

fighter for some things. If a fighter didn't want to do one thing or another it could be a problem for a prefect, unless the prefect could convince another friend to help him maintain his stature. That, simply speaking, is the way it was in an orphanage.

~o~o~ Describing Goldings ~o~o~

The house dormitories at Goldings were huge. The school captain and the house captains had their own exclusive dormitory, while the prefects had the best locations within their respective dormitories, which they chose for themselves.

Somerset House's dormitory was divided into three adjoining areas, almost like three huge rooms, with about fifteen boys in each. There were no doors, but rather arches into each dormitory area. The youngest boys or juniors were in the first part, intermediates in the second, and the seniors in the third part.

As new boys came to the school and senior boys left, boys moved up into more senior dorms and chose better positions within each new dorm. In each section there was a prefect, the most senior prefect being in the senior section.

The beds were still of the same institutional cast-iron rail head-and-foot design, all of which were painted black – typical of all the orphanages I was ever brought up in.

Outside the window, in the part of the dormitory I was first assigned to, were several big sixty-foot high oak trees. The trees were beautiful, but there was a reason that us weeds got to have this particular or otherwise choice location in the dormitory, the reason being: rooks.

High up in the tall old oak trees, just outside of our window, was a huge rookery – a nesting site in which a large concentration of about a hundred or so rooks lived.

At about five thirty in the morning, or perhaps even earlier in the spring and at the first glimmer of light, the rooks would start hawking and hawking, the noise being almost deafening. It was just about impossible to sleep.

As it was, I had a slight advantage, being deaf in my left ear as the result of my childhood ear operation. I could lie on my right ear and

SUFFER LITTLE CHILDREN

by doing so could block out much of the rooks' squawking. However, for many of the other boys the noise would have been unreasonable.

Each house had toilets on their respective floors, but the showers and ablutions were in another part of the building, on the ground floor, and were used by the entire school. In order to get to the ablutions during the frosty winter mornings, we had to trek outside in the cold, sometimes freezing, early morning air, to get to them. Sometimes there would even be snow on the ground.

The showers were constructed the same way as those in Bayfordbury, consisting of several horizontal pipes running parallel to each other, about seven feet above the floor, with holes in them. The holes were about four feet apart, allowing water to simply spill out by means of gravity. There were no shower heads.

The same problem with the showers still existed, just like it did in the other institutional showers, with the most, and hottest, water coming out of the holes at one end of the pipe, and cool or even cold water dribbling out at the other end.

~o~o~ Cabinet Making with Mr Dunning ~o~o~

Within a few days after arriving at Goldings, I was sent over to the junior cabinet making shop to meet my new teacher. His name, to my surprise, was Mr Dunning. To surprise me even further, I was soon to find out that he was the husband of Mrs Dunning, my dear 'old' teacher at Bayford School.

Mr Dunning was a little older than Mrs Dunning. He was not very tall and wore half-oval wire-type glasses, making him look a little like Pinocchio's dad, Geppetto, though perhaps a little more gruff. Nevertheless, he was a nice, but most important, patient man and, I believe, a good teacher.

Mr Dunning was a very skilled cabinet maker, and had been working at Goldings teaching boys in his trade for many years.

I had first arrived and met Mrs Dunning at Bayford School about four and a half years ago, which to me seemed like an eternity in those days. I would marvel at the realisation that Mr Dunning had been working at Goldings all those many years while I was at Bayford School.

SUFFER LITTLE CHILDREN

Time moves so slowly when one is young and waiting to grow up, yet so quickly as one gets older. It felt to me like it was many years ago that I had attended Mrs Dunning's village school. I would from time to time ask Mr Dunning about Mrs Dunning, and on at least one occasion he suggested I go and visit her.

He said that he and Mrs Dunning would speak of us Bayfordbury boys on occasion. He also said that Mrs Dunning had asked him to tell me that she would like to see Baggy and myself again, and that we should come for tea one day. I told Mr Dunning we would, and some time later, we did.

Mr Dunning taught me the fundamentals of cabinet making and how to use tools properly, how to sharpen them and care for them. He also taught us how to recognise the various hardwoods and the character in the woods.

The workbenches in the cabinet making shop were about seven feet long and four feet wide. Two boys worked at each bench and were positioned diagonally at opposite corners, which each had a big wooden vice. I shared a bench with another weed called Dickenson.

Dickenson seemed like an 'all right' chap, and although I didn't really get to know him very well, we got along just fine.

Unknown to me in those early days, Dickenson was to have a profound effect on me a few months after I was to become more acquainted with him.

One might even say that Dickenson became perhaps a fearful character, not just to me, but to many of the other boys, as I am going to tell you later in my story.

~o~o~

I was to be under Mr Dunning's tuition for about six months. During that time I realised that I enjoyed the trade of cabinet making and I believe that I subconsciously intended to be a cabinet maker for the rest of my life.

Mr Dunning's cabinet making shop was filled with a sweet, yet pungent smell of the constant boiling, bubbling wood glue, made from the bones of horses and other animals.

SUFFER LITTLE CHILDREN

Combined with the smell of the wood glue and the fragrance of the exotic woods that we worked with, the shop had a distinctive smell of its own.

We learned that to make anything, there was always the preparation time, the planning of the article we were to make, the 'reading' of the grain in the wood, and the studying of the wood itself. All this before one cut is made, or one shaving is taken off the wood.

A motto that Mr Dunning had carved in a large piece of hardwood many years before I came to Goldings, and which hung up over his teaching bench, read:

MEASURE TWICE, CUT ONCE

It was a saying I often quoted to others when I was working with them, including my sons. Unbeknown to them I would quite often remember Mr Dunning when I was telling them this, one of his fundamental 'shop rules'.

Baggy was also in the cabinet making shop, but he was in the senior shop now. He had started with Mr Dunning but after about four months or just before I arrived at Goldings, he had moved up to the senior shop, under the tuition of Mr 'Stormy' Tempest.

~o~o~ Friends and Nicknames ~o~o~

I saw a lot of Baggy shortly after I first arrived at Goldings, but the situation was to change. Having arrived at Goldings just three or four months before me, Baggy was now my senior.

Seniors didn't want to be identified with weeds or spares and so Baggy, as well as being my senior, was also in Cairns House, which resulted in us being in competing houses.

And so, as time passed, Baggy and I drifted apart somewhat. Although we always remained good friends, we were friends from a distance, somewhat like older brothers finding other friends their own age. We simply didn't 'knock around' together like we did at Bayfordbury and Churchill House, but that didn't change the fact that we were, and always would be, the best of friends.

SUFFER LITTLE CHILDREN

From time to time nevertheless, Baggy and I would reminisce about the miserable and yet frequently happy times we had at Bayfordbury. We would remember our good old friend Fred and talk about those hateful men, Scougall and Nash, and what we would like to do to Nash when we were grown up.

Although we always had good times to remember, as time passed we spoke less and less about those memorable times, and lived those now early teenage years with different interests, and with different friends.

~o~o~

For most of my life at Goldings my closest friends other than my life-long friends Baggy and Flappers, were John 'Goodg' Goodger (34), Victor 'Fuzz' Foley (24), Stan 'Dizzy' Dean (66), Dicky Moore and John 'Fanny' Noble. There were many more, of course, but those I have just mentioned all stuck together in a sort of clique and all became special friends until, having completed our trade training, we one by one eventually left Goldings to go out into the world at the age of almost seventeen.

Many of my friends had nicknames. Such nicknames often came as the result of reasons such as Stan 'Dizzy' Dean, who got his because he was a particularly good football player, just like the professional footballer 'Dizzy' Dean, known for his clever 'dribbling' with a football. 'Fuzz' Foley got his as the result of his crinkly and wavy hair. Flappers got his when he was about eight years old, as I have already explained. Why 'Fanny' Noble got his girlish nickname, I have no idea. He certainly was no sissy, and in fact he did his military National Service in the Paratroop Regiment.

~o~o~ Back to Bayfordbury ~o~o~

Several weeks after Mr Dunning had suggested I visit Mrs Dunning, we decided to go to Bayford School to see her.

So, eventually I told Mr Dunning that Baggy, Flappers, and I were going to walk to Bayford and visit Mrs Dunning. He thought it was a long way to walk but said he would tell her, and that they would expect us.

SUFFER LITTLE CHILDREN

The following Sunday after chapel and having had dinner, we set out to walk the five or maybe six miles to Bayford. Our walk took us through the centre of Hertford, past the river where we had caught minnows and collected frogspawn, and under the familiar viaducts we knew so well.

We also saw the places in the River Lee where we had pulled out watercress directly from the river to eat while on the way back to Bayfordbury on Saturdays after a wicked day of shoplifting.

Then we came to the entrance gates to Bayfordbury. We walked through the big gates and past the gatehouse, which appeared to be empty, and up the long driveway to the Bayfordbury mansion.

There was a big sign at the entrance gate informing everyone that an agricultural firm called John Innis now owned the Bayfordbury estate, and that they were in the process of planting an orchard of specialty apple trees.

We walked past the main entrance steps to the mansion. Being Sunday, there seemed to be no one on the premises, not even a watchman. No one challenged us, and so we walked around the outside of the mansion, remembering mostly the good times we spent there. It seemed wonderful to be there now, especially because Mr Scougall and Mr Nash weren't.

Continuing on, through the fields and the woods where the doodlebug had crashed, we arrived in Bayford.

There, with its Sunday look, was the little St Mary's Church. Down the narrow lane into Bayford were the fields where we, as children, would stop and talk to the Italian prisoners of war while they were in the fields, doing the heavy menial farm work to keep them occupied and to help the farmers. Everything seemed to look absolutely unchanged.

When we finally arrived at Mrs Dunning's house she was so pleased to see us. She still had Bonzo, her black Scottish terrier dog. Mrs Dunning told us how her little two-roomed school had become so empty and felt so big after Bayfordbury had closed and the orphanage had moved to Eastbourne. She told us how much she had loved having all of us perky little boys in her school.

Mr Dunning didn't come into the house to talk with us; after all, he saw enough of us at Goldings. Before we left to walk back to Goldings

SUFFER LITTLE CHILDREN

though, he did eventually come and have a cup of tea while we had lemonade. Mrs Dunning also told us how she heard all about her 'little boys' – though we were now fourteen going on fifteen – from Mr Dunning, and what trouble we got into.

Then we said goodbye to Mr and Mrs Dunning and walked all the way back to Goldings. When we were a little less than a mile away from the Goldings estate we could hear the bugler playing the 'five-minute warning' call, ahead of the 'cookhouse' (tea time) call, so we had to run the rest of the way back to Goldings, or miss tea.

The now-familiar bugle calls would drift or echo through the trees and over the fields. Many months ago we had learned and knew the meaning of all the bugle calls, and would run as fast as we could in order not to be late for parades or miss our meals altogether.

To be late for a meal meant that the dining room doors would be shut and locked automatically by the duty master. The doors couldn't be opened from the outside, so if one of our friends couldn't let us in when the masters weren't looking, then we went without whatever the meal was, until the next meal. In such circumstances, which happened quite often, there was no other way to get anything to eat unless one of your friends saved something for you from his meal, and brought it out to you later.

Mr Dunning died a short while after we visited Mrs Dunning. After his death, I never saw Mrs Dunning again. But I will always remember her as being a very gentle and lovely natured woman who, being one of the exceptions, cared about us orphans.

~∘~ The Headmaster, Mr Wheatley (Pinhead) ~∘~

Our headmaster, Mr R F 'Pinhead' Wheatley BSc, was a scholar by degree and a man with a distinctively sophisticated character. I remember well that he had 'BSc' after his name but I had no idea at the time what it meant. Without a doubt, I sincerely believe that every boy in the school, even though we called him 'Pinhead', all admired him for his integrity and fairness in his dealing with us.

He was a rather tall man of about six feet one or two inches, slight of build, perhaps even a little too thin, with a distinctive bald head. His

SUFFER LITTLE CHILDREN

rather small bald head, on top of his lean tall body and long neck, led to him being nicknamed Pinhead many years before I came to Goldings.

We only referred to Mr Wheatley as Pinhead amongst ourselves, but most certainly not if he or the other masters could hear us. He, like everyone, knew the boys called him Pinhead, but seemed to regard the nickname with some sort of affection. On several occasions, much to our amusement, he would from time to time refer to himself as Pinhead during his address to the school assembly, which always drew huge bouts of laughter.

My friends and I, together with hundreds of boys who had passed through Mr Wheatley's administration, always regarded and spoke of Mr Wheatley with the greatest of respect. He, like Mr Castle, earned our admiration and respect not by the rod, but by his fairness and integrity. Although he could look severe at times, I cannot remember ever seeing Pinhead remotely angry.

Of course, he was a moderately strict man – something which his position demanded. He was the overseer of our many teachers and the large number of staff which it took to run Goldings. Primarily Pinhead had the overall responsibility for the well-being of the more than two hundred and fifty boys constantly in his charge, and whom he had to guide, counsel, and to be accountable for.

He and his wife Mrs Wheatley, their son David and daughter Celia, lived in their own quarters apart from us and the other staff members. Celia Wheatley was about the same age as my age group, while David was a few years younger.

Celia attended a grammar school in Hertford, while David was enrolled into a public school somewhere near London. We didn't see much of David, but Celia lived with her parents at Goldings.

The Wheatleys also had a dog called 'Paddy'. Paddy was a type of terrier, and would chase us if we made barking sounds at it. We would run and jump up onto the high stone corridor windowsills to get out of Paddy's reach. Paddy, would, if it got the chance, bite or rather nip at us if it caught up with us, and it quite often did. It was only a medium-sized dog, but seemed to have a large-sized mouth.

We were constantly being warned to leave the dog alone, but I was deaf in one ear – that's my excuse.

SUFFER LITTLE CHILDREN
~o~o~ Bugle Calls ~o~o~

Coming to an orphanage the size of Goldings was a little overwhelming, maybe even confusing. Besides having to get to understand our way around this huge domicile with its many, many huge and small rooms, corridors and flights of stairs, we still had to learn the masters' names. We also had to learn the rules as well as the routine and how the school was run.

There was also the daunting effort needed to learn and remember two hundred and fifty more new faces and names of the boys already at Goldings. Among them there were several boys from other orphanages that Flappers and I already knew, and who knew us. However, if they were just a little older than us they might not acknowledge us because we were, after all, only weeds. Nevertheless, we still had to remember their names, as well as learning all the other boys' names.

It would be important to know who all the boys in the school were in respect of seniority, and their position in the 'pecking order', so that we, being weeds, would not have to find out the hard way. To make mistakes relative to position, or to fail to show due respect to other boys appropriate to their position, could result in our being beaten or severely chastised.

~o~o~

There were no whistles or bells to direct us to do anything, or even verbal orders like, for instance: "Dinner's ready", "Go to your shops", "Go to bed", or "Get out of bed" in the morning. Goldings operated and functioned entirely on bugle calls.

Five minutes before any bugle call order was sounded, a special five-minute warning call was played by the duty bugler, informing us and the staff to listen for the next bugle-call announcement.

Each and every call, including the five-minute warning call, was preceded by the 'school call', the school call being unique to Goldings.

The first bugle call of the day was played at five minutes to six in the morning, the first part of this bugle call being the school call. This was followed by the five-minute warning call.

SUFFER LITTLE CHILDREN

All of the bugle calls, starting with Reveille from when we got up in the morning until the last call at night, would be played a total of twice on each floor of the three floors that our dormitories occupied. The bugle calls, and the echoes following the calls as they travelled down the long corridors and up the many stairwells, were almost deafening, particularly if one were less than twenty-five feet from the bugler. During the daytime the bugle calls would also be played in the front and the back entrances to the school. There would be absolutely no excuse not to hear them.

Bugle calls would be sounded throughout the day. The routine for the bugle calls were:

- 5.55 a.m. .... Five-minute warning for 'Reveille' (Always, all calls were preceded by the school call.)
- 6.00 a.m. .... 'Reveille'
- 7.25 a.m. .... Five-minute warning for cookhouse (breakfast)
- 7.30 a.m. .... Cookhouse (breakfast)
- 8.10 a.m. .... Five-minute warning to Salute
- 8.15 a.m. .... Salute (raising the flag – the Union Jack)
- 8.55 a.m. .... Five-minute warning to assemble on the parade
- 9.00 a.m. .... Assemble for academic school or trade shop
- 11.55 a.m. ..... Five-minute warning to finish school or shop
- 12.00 noon..... Leave academic school or trade shop
- 12.10 p.m. ..... Five-minute warning for cookhouse (dinner)
- 12.15 p.m. ..... Cookhouse (dinner)
- 01.25 p.m. ..... Five-minute warning to assemble on the parade
- 01.30 p.m. ..... Assemble for academic school or trade shop
- 04.25 p.m. ..... Five-minute warning to finish school or shop
- 04.30 p.m. ..... Leave academic school or trade shop
- 04.55 p.m. ..... Five minute warning to Retreat
- 05.00 p.m. ..... Retreat (lowering the flag – the Union Jack)
- 05.55 p.m. ..... Five-minute warning for cookhouse (tea)
- 06.00 p.m. ..... Cookhouse (tea)
- 06.55 p.m. ..... Five-minute warning for prep (winter only)
- 07.00 p.m. ..... Prep (We only had prep in the winter.)
- 07.55 p.m. ..... Five-minute warning to finish prep

SUFFER LITTLE CHILDREN

- 08.00 p.m. ..... Leave prep
- 08.55 p.m. ..... Five minutes to 'Last Post' (to be in our dormitories)
- 09.00 p.m. ..... 'Last Post' (everyone to be in their beds)
- 09.25 p.m. ..... Five-minute warning to lights out
- 09.30 p.m. ..... Lights out

Throughout the winter months we always went to bed at 9.00 p.m. and lights out was at 9.30. In the summer we stayed up until 9.30 p.m. and lights out was at 10.00. House captains and prefects could stay up half an hour later.

This then was the standard bugle call roster, and our daily routine would follow it. The only exceptions would be if we were involved in a special event such as Wimbledon or on a movie set in which we were the 'extras'. I will write more about this later.

~°~°~ Dormitory Floor Polishing ~°~°~

Each morning after 'Reveille' was sounded, we would, after no more than a minute or two, get out of bed and get fully dressed except for putting our shirts on. One of the two masters who were on duty that week would constantly tour all of the dormitories and make sure everyone was out of bed and getting dressed.

We would take our towels, toothbrushes etc, and go to the ablutions, which meant going outside, with only our towels draped around our bare shoulders, across the parade ground to the ablution block. Needless to say, this could be pretty uncomfortable in the rain or in the winter, especially when one considers we didn't have our shirts on. However, this was our usual routine – summer, and winter.

In the ablutions we would brush our teeth using the pink, carbolic tooth powder from big pound tins, which were spaced between the many washbasins on a communal counter top. Then we would wash with carbolic soap and head back to our dormitories to finish dressing.

After we got back to our dormitories we would have to sweep and polish the floors. This we did every single day except for Sundays and Christmas day, throughout the year.

First the steel beds and any other furniture, though there wasn't

SUFFER LITTLE CHILDREN

very much of it, had to be lifted so that nothing would scratch the highly polished floors, and be moved in a systematic way to one end or side of the dormitory.

Then one of the boys, perhaps the biggest, oldest, or again, maybe a fighter, would do the 'ronucking', because being the ronucker was the easiest job. The ronucker would have a two-pound or three-pound tin of 'Ronuck' (pink-coloured floor polish), which he would either hold or slide along the floor with his foot. With a piece of wood used as a ladle, or by sometimes just using his hand, he would literally scoop a big blob of Ronuck out of the tin and flip it with a 'plop' onto the wooden floor in front of him.

Then about five to eight boys in each section of the dormitories would get a piece of 'kneeling' material – a folded piece of an old blanket – and, on their hands and knees, would, in an organised line, spread the Ronuck with a large piece of rag. The heavy pieces of rag would become saturated with Ronuck as the result of the material having been used for several weeks, if not months.

Then the rest, or most of the boys in their respective dormitories other than the prefects would, after getting the best kneeling pads that they could, also get on their bare knees, in a line parallel with the joints in the pine floor boards, and follow the ronuckers.

We would start with all of our hands to the right, and then, with one boy calling "left, right, left, right" we would move backwards together on our knees in a continual manner, polishing the floor for the length or width of the dormitory, parallel with the direction of the floorboards.

When the prefect or the house captain was satisfied with the polishing of the floors, we would put the beds and other furniture back in their place, and then we were finished until we repeated the floor polishing again the next morning.

If the floor didn't shine satisfactorily, then the house captain would, if he wished, have us all come back after school or shop, and polish the entire floor all over again.

This polishing of the floors ritual had been going on for at least twenty-five years before I arrived at Goldings. As the result of this hard work the floors shone so well we really could see our reflections in the rose-coloured floorboards. Each house was proud of its own dormitory

SUFFER LITTLE CHILDREN

floor, in a very competitive way.

Then, before we were able to go into the dining room for breakfast, we had to clean our boots. There was a special place for 'blackening' and polishing them. This was a location beside the huge recreational 'rec' hut.

Here, there were big, two-pound tins of black boot polish. We would grab a shoe brush – any brush when it became free – and then dig into the soft creamy black polish and brush it on our boots.

Because several boys were trying to brush their boots at the same time, brushes were hard to get hold of so we would, after brushing the polish onto our boots, use the same brush to shine our boots.

This meant us first rubbing the brush, with polish on it, on the brick wall right in front of us, until most of the polish came off the brush and onto the wall. Then we would use the same brush to shine our boots.

As a result of this common practice, which we all did every morning when we cleaned our boots, the brick wall, some twenty feet long, was so burnished black that it shone beautifully, so much so that we could almost see to comb our hair in it as though it was a mirror.

~o~o~

Some fifty years later, long after I had departed Goldings, I took my wife Donna to visit what remained of the Goldings I knew as a boy, and there, to my surprise, I saw, almost with tears in my eyes, the wall still showing clearly the preserved, gleaming 'blackening' signs of our boot polishing.

~o~o~ 'Spud Bashing' ~o~o~

If any of us were put 'on the book' or, as it was also called, 'on report' for doing something or other wrong like being late for shop, fighting, being out of bounds and other misdemeanours, then we would have to come before Mr Wheatley to be punished.

Mr Wheatley would assess our 'default': as a punishable offence was called, and determine a fair punishment. Only serious or capital offences were punishable by caning, and even then Mr Wheatley, in

SUFFER LITTLE CHILDREN

the presence of the Revd Corbett, was the only person to administer caning.

A common punishment for maybe two or three boys who were on 'default' was to have to peel potatoes (spud bashing) for a week. We would have to peel potatoes for the entire school, including the staff – a task which could take well in excess of two hours to do.

Believe me, I did more spud bashing than I would care to remember. It wasn't a terrible punishment as we even got extra food just by being in the kitchen. The biggest problem with doing spud bashing was basically knowing that we could have been doing something better, like playing football or 'rec' hockey. Rec hockey was played in the rec hut, with a stick with a knurled knob on the end, and a tennis ball.

The procedure for peeling potatoes was quite simple. First we would wash with a hose about twenty to thirty pounds of potatoes to get the mud off them, and sort out and remove any stones or obviously bad potatoes.

Then we were expected to put the potatoes – about ten to twenty, depending on their size – into the potato peeler. After we had taken the spuds out of the peeler, we were then expected to remove any eyes or damaged portions, and put them in water, ready for boiling.

However, we didn't really do the job quite like that.

How the potato peeling machine worked wasn't a bit like it sounds. Inside the potato peeling machine was a drum, which after being turned on, spun at a very fast speed, sending the potatoes hurtling and banging against the insides of the drum. The inside of the drum was lined with a very rough type of sharp pumice stone.

As a result of the centrifugal action of the drum and the potatoes hurtling around inside, the rough texture inside the drum would simply grind the skin right off the potatoes.

The intent, as I have mentioned, was then to take the potatoes out of the machine and remove the 'eyes' by hand, with a small knife.

As it was, the potatoes would be quite large when we put them into the machine. However, we would leave them in the machine until all the eyes as well as the peel was ground off. Doing the job our way, there were no 'eyes' or anything else to be removed.

The end result was, that potatoes would come out of the spud

SUFFER LITTLE CHILDREN

machine no bigger than large marbles, clean as a whistle with absolutely no eyes in them at all. So for the most part, we wouldn't have to take out many, if any eyes at all and the task was much easier. This, we knew, wasn't the right idea because it meant doing three times as many potatoes to fill the required number of cooking pots.

After the potatoes were boiled they would commonly be mashed with milk, and so no one else could see how big the potatoes were anyway.

We knew too of course, that we would get into trouble if we were caught wasting the potatoes, which too, would result in a further default punishment.

Some boys would do the job properly to some extent, but to take out all of the eyes would result in the task taking far more time than it took us.

Ironically, their problem, the boys trying to do a proper job, was that they, being more conscientious than us about peeling potatoes, would leave many of the small eyes in the potatoes, the end result being that there were too many eyes left in the potatoes, and this, too, could result in a further default.

~o~o~ Sexual Confusion ~o~o~

My first Christmas at Goldings was really quite eventful. It was 1947, and it all started with my writing a letter to Mr Castle, who, having been in Clacton-on-Sea for about a year, would by now be well established as the headmaster of the Dr Barnardo's Home there.

As I recall, I wrote to Mr Castle and asked him if I and two other boys could come and spend Christmas with him in Clacton.

Mr Castle, having checked with the powers-that-be, informed me that he and Mrs Castle would welcome having us spend Christmas at their orphanage.

The chaps who would be coming with me were Brian Winter and Derrick Morgan, both of whom had been at Churchill House with Mr Castle at the same time as I was there.

Everything was going fine, and arrangements were finalised for us to go. Then the confusing problem occurred.

One night, just a week or so prior to the three of us leaving to go

SUFFER LITTLE CHILDREN

to Clacton, Brian Winter, who, like Morgan and I, was about fourteen years old and no more than a junior, was found in bed with a more senior boy by the master on duty.

The master told Winter to return to his bed and subsequently put Winter on report. The next morning at breakfast Pinhead called out Winter's name and told him to report to his study.

We still didn't realise the seriousness of Winter's default, but waited to find out what exactly had happened. As it was, Winter got the cane for being in the other boy's bed, but what was worse, his Christmas holiday to Clacton was cancelled.

The boys talked among themselves about what happened, but just couldn't understand what Winter had done that was so wrong. Mr Wheatley, for what ever the reason, never did explain or inform the rest of the school exactly what the problem had been.

Nothing regarding Winter's default was ever discussed with us. Our ignorance and naivety was a further handicap, so we simply didn't understand.

Unknown to us at the time, Pinhead again proved himself to have been a very fair and wise man. Brian Winter, as far as I know, was never singled out for any such problem again.

Of course today, at the time of my writing this story, we do understand what the seriousness of the problem could have been, but at the time we simply had no idea.

Just before Christmas in 1947, Derrick Morgan and I travelled by train to Clacton-on-Sea without Winter and met Mr Castle there. I remember he was very pleased to see us, but didn't mention Brian Winter.

~o~o~ Mr Castle, Clacton-on-Sea ~o~o~

Our Christmas holiday at Clacton-on-Sea, with Mr Castle and his wife and daughters, was wonderful. They made us feel like their prodigal sons coming home. Mr Castle – this big burly man who had never ever laid a bare hand on any of us in anger, though I had been introduced to his huge slipper several times – was very kind to us, and really made us feel we had come to his family's home for Christmas, even though

SUFFER LITTLE CHILDREN

it was really just another orphanage.

The Dr Barnardo's home at Clacton-on-Sea consisted of several small cottages, much the same as at Barkingside in Ilford. Each cottage housed several – perhaps twelve or up to maybe fifteen boys – all mostly under the age of thirteen and a half.

Mr Castle ran his orphanage in a very informal way, and yet it was as disciplined, and ran as well as any orphanage in the Dr Barnardo's Homes system.

From time to time, Mr Castle even had fish and chips brought into the orphanage for all the boys, which was a great treat.

No doubt, as a result of his good relationship with the local businessmen and the surrounding community, Mr Castle managed to persuade the local merchants to 'help out' and provide treats for those in his charge, which in turn helped integrate his sixty to eighty Dr Barnardo boys into the community.

The Clacton-on-Sea orphanage was a nice, pleasant, homely place. The several individual houses were in many, many ways much nicer to house children in than the huge mansions, like Bayfordbury and Churchill House were. Such homes as Clacton would make life seem and feel more like the outsiders' family homes.

Derrick Morgan and I were put in one of the houses, in which I reacquainted myself with a boy who later became one of my best and closest friends. His name was John Goodger.

~o~o~

I had known John 'Goodg' Goodger before he had come to Clacton. He had even been at Bayfordbury and had moved to Churchill House at the same time as I did, although Goodg wasn't a special friend at the time.

Goodg was a few months younger than me, and so we just hadn't become so well acquainted until I met up with him again in Clacton.

A few weeks or so after Mr Castle had established the Dr Barnardo's home in Clacton-on-Sea, he was able to bring several boys from Churchill House to Clacton to join him there. One of those boys was John Goodger.

Goodg, because he was just a few months younger than me, hadn't

SUFFER LITTLE CHILDREN

been old enough to apply to go to Goldings at the same time that Flappers and I did. Now he was.

At thirteen and a half at least, 'Goodg' was now reaching the age when he would have to leave an ordinary orphanage like the one at Clacton-on-Sea. There were several options open to him. He would either have to go to a Sea School, a technical trade school like Goldings, or plan to eventually go 'out to work' doing, quite possibly, farming. But one way or another he would, within a year or two at the very most, have to leave Clacton-on-Sea.

I told Goodg as much as I could about Goldings, and he decided he would like to go there. He spoke to Mr Castle about the whole idea and Mr Castle in turn, spoke to Derrick Morgan and myself. Subsequently, Mr Castle made arrangements for Goodg to go to Goldings.

~o~o~

Just before we left Clacton-on-Sea to return to Goldings, Mr and Mrs Castle invited Morgan and me into their quarters for tea one afternoon, with their daughters. It was on this occasion that Mr Castle told me that he and Mrs Castle had heard the story of my ordeal with Mr and Mrs Fowlermott.

He mentioned that many of his peers in Dr Barnardo's had found it quite amusing and laughed at the image of the Fowlermotts trying to catch me, with Mr Fowlermott waving his wooden leg around and Mrs Fowlermott screaming at me in anger, and me taking refuge under Mr Castle's old desk. It certainly would have – though not for me at the time – conjured up a funny scene.

I explained to Mr Castle how it all came about, and that the biggest concern I had had was when Mr Fowlermott had tried to take my trousers off to cane me. I remember too, Mr Castle's daughters, as well as Morgan and me, being embarrassed as the story was being told.

Derrick Morgan and I said goodbye to Mr Castle shortly after New Year's Day 1948, and caught the train back to Goldings.

John Goodger came to Goldings about a month or so later, in early February 1948.

~o~o~

SUFFER LITTLE CHILDREN

I was to see Mr Castle just once more. That was in 1956, several years after I had left Dr Barnardo's Homes and was on holiday in Clacton with my still very good outsider friends Ron Heenan, Eddy Parr and Merv Oaten from Taunton.

Merv and I visited the Dr Barnardo's home in Clacton. Merv was to hear Mr Castle and myself reminisce about our times in Eastbourne and the incident with Mr Fowlermott.

A short while later, in 1958, after I had immigrated to Canada, Mr Castle died. I will always remember him for his fairness and his keeping Mr Nash at bay.

SUFFER LITTLE CHILDREN

William Baker Technical School (WBTS)
Goldings, Hertford

A view from the side

View of Main Entrance where horse driven coaches would bring new boys to the school many years ago

Rear view

SUFFER LITTLE CHILDREN

Pinhead, shaking hands with Princess Margaret

Rev. Corbett
'Lay not up for yourselves'

The Headmaster,
Mr Wheatley 'Pinhead'
'Now what am I going to do with Longman, Foley and Goodger?'

'Snowy', 'Tech' White
Thursday night pictures

20

GOLDINGS – Part 2

~o~o~ Flappers 'The Gardener' ~o~o~

Flappers had chosen to learn the professional trade of gardening. The gardening school was a very extensive course at Goldings. They had award-winning teachers in their department, one of whom was credited with a unique grafting technique which was used extensively throughout Britain. Goldings was very proud of this recognition.

I didn't see much of what Flappers was doing during the actual school day. In fact, whenever I did see him, I really only saw him from a distance, mostly raking leaves and doing the 'weeding', which he had to do constantly. There would also be lots of digging the gardens by hand with forks and spades. I must say that at that time of my life, gardening wouldn't have been for me.

There were no machines or horses to plough with. Everything was done by hand, with muscle and sweat and simply, just 'boy power'. Flappers would say he was training to be a donkey. I once told him some time earlier, that he had ears big enough for any donkey to proud of.

Many, or most of the vegetables we ate came from our school's gardening department. The gardening department would enter their best produce, including flowers and vegetables, into the local agricultural shows, where they won their share of trophies.

Flappers wasn't too happy with his choice of the trade he was learning, and it didn't take long for him to apply and to change his vocation to that of being a cook.

Shortly after we had come to Goldings, George 'Mother' Pickens, about three years earlier, had changed his trade training from shoemaking to training to become a chef. When he became of age he was sent out to complete his training at a London hotel.

So fortunately for Flappers, the opportunity for him to fill the void and take over from 'Mother' became his. Flappers worked at everything in the kitchen, from pan scrubbing to porridge making, carrot scraping,

SUFFER LITTLE CHILDREN

and even scrubbing and hosing the kitchen floor.

Eventually, under the direction and scrutiny of the cook, he took up serious cooking, which included the preparing and cooking of the masters' and headmaster's meals. He liked his new profession, and eventually left Goldings to go into a 'situation' as a practising 'grade 4' chef.

I was to see lots of Flappers over the next few years, and during this time we became even closer friends. We never shoplifted together again, but Flappers still had a low level of larceny lurking in his character waiting to come out if the opportunity arose, which it did from time to time.

~°~°~ Learning to Play the Bugle ~°~°~

Goldings had a good competitive-class bugle band. It played all over Hertfordshire and adjoining counties in competitions, also at garden fetes and annual parades in many small towns and villages.

The band had two distinct functions. First and foremost, it was the school band, but almost as important, it was the army cadet band.

In order to be in the band one had to join the army cadets also. The army cadets was organised and run by Captain 'Skip' Culver.

Of the fifteen to perhaps twenty buglers, the best ten bugle players would be called upon to play the school calls. These ten would rotate and play in pairs for a period of two weeks at a time.

I would listen to the bugle calls and, like many boys, could easily hear the difference between a good bugler and a bad bugler. Most boys, as did the masters, appreciate hearing a good bugler play the school calls.

I thought that I, too, after being at Goldings for about a year, would like to be a bugler. So when one of the buglers left Goldings to go on a 'situation' I applied for the opportunity to learn to play.

I remember well, seeing the brightly polished copper bugles, with just one distinctive silver bugle in the centre, lined up on the school's trophy display shelf in the main hall. I hoped that one day I could have the opportunity to learn to play one of those bugles.

The best bugler in the school had the distinction of being the 'silver bugler'. It never, in those early days, ever occurred to me that I could become that silver bugler.

After being accepted by Skip Culver, I was told that I would be

SUFFER LITTLE CHILDREN

allowed to practise and learn to play the bugle. I was also told that I could, when I had any spare time, take a bugle from off the display shelf when they weren't being used, and that I could take the bugle up to the 'top fields' and practise.

Bugle playing, like playing a mouth organ or any other wind instrument, is hard to teach, and is primarily learned by diligently practising as much as possible and at every opportunity one can get. It was also absolutely necessary to obtain a bugle mouthpiece to suit the individual's lips.

After weeks and weeks of practice and learning to reach the high notes, and 'hold' them, and also being able to play most, if not all, of the school calls, I applied to the silver bugler to join the bugle section of the school band.

So, I approached 'Skip' Culver. Captain Culver was the instructor who taught the army cadets how to be soldiers. There was no hesitation in enrolling me, or any boy for that matter, in the school's army cadet corps.

~o~o~

It was the result of our being in the school's army cadets, and Captain Culver's training, no doubt, that gave us a distinct advantage in later years.

All, or most boys in those days were, upon reaching the age of eighteen, required to enlist and serve two years in the British armed services. It was called National Service

Jumping ahead in my story a little, I will tell the reader that as the result of the training I received from Captain Skip Culver, I 'passed out' (graduated) as the best recruit in my battalion of the Royal Signals, in Catterick Camp, Yorkshire. A battalion consists of five hundred men. To be the best recruit at our 'pass out' was quite an honour for me and a real credit to Captain Culver, who I sent my award certificate to.

~o~o~

Back to my story. After joining the band we practised our marching and bugle playing constantly. We were eventually entered into several

SUFFER LITTLE CHILDREN

competitions and could see ourselves, through various forms of recognition, getting better and better. I, too, was becoming a better and more accomplished bugler.

Our drum major, Reg Howitt, was a strapping lad and carried the rather heavy five-foot-six-inch mace easily.

Reg had joined the band about the same time as I had, and he too practised the various juggling-type moves which made drum majors appear proud and majestic.

A year or so later I was chosen to be one of the ten school buglers and as such, was required to play the bugle calls which announced the day-to-day activity times to the other boys in the school, just as I mentioned earlier.

I was very proud of my position as a school bugler; this was probably one of the first major responsibilities bestowed upon me up to this point in my life.

Every Sunday – morning and evening – the entire school, led by the band, marched from the parade ground to the architecturally beautiful old Goldings chapel, for our routine church services. After the service we marched back again. The march, about a half a mile each way, was through a part of the school grounds, directly in front of the Goldings mansion.

Playing the bugle came fairly easy to me, and before long I was one of the better buglers in the band. The silver bugler, who without a doubt was the best bugler by far, was a boy named Parks.

Parks could make the bugle sound so melodic, with an abundance of feeling. For him to play 'Reveille' in the morning was an absolute treat to hear, which in turn helped start the day off well. Not one of us boys ever played a bugle as well as Parks.

The Goldings band or otherwise the army cadet band, depending on what we were doing when we were performing, was quite impressive. Goldings constantly received complimentary reviews for our performances by the local media.

While we would be marching to chapel or in a parade, Parks would play a solo as part of the marching tune. Then we would join in, playing loud and strong, to raise the volume of the band.

There were about thirty boys in the band, consisting of fifteen to eighteen buglers, four tub drummers, two tenor drummers, a bass

SUFFER LITTLE CHILDREN

drummer, and a kettle drummer. Out front, leading the band with his five-foot-six ornate mace, was our impressive drum major, Reg Howitt.

The only kettle drummer was a boy my size and about the same age as myself. His name was Victor 'Fuzz' Foley. Fuzz became one of my very special friends, about whom I will tell the reader more later.

Eventually, over the next year and a half or so, I became, I must modestly admit, a very good bugler and eventually, after Parks left Goldings to go out on a situation, I reached my ambition of becoming the silver bugler. But I would never say that I, or any other boy, could play a bugle as well as Parks.

~o~o~ The Grub ~o~o~

The 'grub' at Goldings, like in most institutions, was understandably not really to our liking, particularly at that time of my life. All food: meat, sugar, margarine and butter, including most of the staple foods, was still on ration, and so our providers were limited as to what they could give us to eat. But, having been brought up in institutions most of our lives, we didn't bother to complain. After all, we hardly knew anything better, and so we simply just ate it.

Porridge, for instance – a common staple food that we often had for breakfast – was either lumpy or watery. The boys, including Flappers, under the supervision of an adult cook, who prepared and cooked our food, were commonly all in training to become chefs (of sorts), and they were in many instances simply careless in their efforts.

Many times these trainees must have been told by the 'on staff' chef or cook, something to the effect that "This porridge isn't very good. It's lumpy and not acceptable. You must do better next time", and then basically add, "Go ahead and serve it up." And that's about all that would be said. So much for lessons in cooking, and how not to cook!

It was all well and good telling the boys in training to be chefs and that their cooking wasn't good enough, but we still had to eat it. When we grumbled and told Flappers about his crummy cooking he would just laugh, and before long we would be laughing too.

Although the food at Goldings wasn't ever particularly bad, it often left much to be desired. Actually, the only real problem was that there

SUFFER LITTLE CHILDREN

simply wasn't sufficient care taken to cook it properly. Nor was there enough of it for growing boys.

Several times the boiled eggs we had for breakfast on Sundays would be addled. Many times the eggs, after being boiled and ready to eat, were opened up, and we would find the texture of the egg rubbery, or we could even see signs of a young chick that had started to develop. Sometimes there would be red blood streaks in the yoke, and the shape of a beak or even a small developing eye would be showing.

I remember on several occasions, before Flappers was training to be a cook, that the boiled eggs would smell terrible. But Flappers, being in Somerset house and at my table, would say, "I'll 'ave it." Flappers would eat just about everything he could get, or anything anyone else didn't want.

Flappers would also eat mouldy cheese, including the cheesecloth rind found on the edge of the cheese which was often served to us at tea time. He never, as far as I know, ever got sick from eating any of the food we considered was bad. Regardless of the food he ate, Flappers was a very healthy, solidly well-built boy.

A typical breakfast would consist of porridge, or fried eggs, 'ginner and marg' (a slice of bread and a pat of margarine), jam or marmalade, and a cup of 'grog' (tea). On Sundays we would often have boiled eggs.

Our main meal of the day (dinner) would be at twelve thirty each day, except for Sundays, when the meal was supposedly special, and that would be half an hour after church, at one o'clock.

Typically, a main dinner course item might be 'dog meat' – a type of sausage meat made into patties, which was quite popular with us boys. On another day we would get tripe (the lining of a cow's stomach), which we also liked. It was always cooked with onions.

Quite regularly we would have stew made from beef or lamb, with lots of horrible fat. Once a week we would have liver, which we didn't particularly like, and also faggots (two-inch balls of meat made from offal). Occasionally we would have sausages, which was one of my favourites, as well as shepherds pie and other things like that. Almost every Friday we would either have fish cakes or boiled cod. We would always have plenty of vegetables like potatoes, carrots, swede, cabbage, or peas with our main items.

SUFFER LITTLE CHILDREN

As in most institutions, our meals were routinely scheduled. Every Monday we would have, say, 'dog meat'; Tuesday perhaps tripe; and Wednesdays, cheese pie; and so on. There were never choices for us to make; we simply ate what was being offered, or we went without.

A very common food served to us was fish. Fish, particularly cod, was caught in abundance all around the coast of Britain, and therefore easily available. I don't believe fish was rationed, the reason being because, like rabbit, being so easily available it would have been hard to keep track of.

The fish served to us was most often baked or simply boiled, occasionally even in milk. The thing I didn't like most about this meal was that the boiled fish was always served with boiled potatoes. The water or fishy milk from the boiled fish would soak into the potatoes, making the potatoes taste horrible. Flappers would have a big potato meal on those days.

We would have cheese pie maybe once a week. Cheese pie was basically mashed potatoes with shredded cheese in it, then simply baked. The only problem with this meal was that the boys who had been put on 'default' were often the boys responsible for peeling the potatoes, and they didn't do a very good job, resulting in them some times leaving the eyes and other black spots in the potatoes.

Although several of the main courses weren't always wonderful at Goldings, the puddings or sweets were, or at least we thought so.

Every day after our main dinner course, we always had pudding, or 'sweet' as it was called. These were usually quite good. The most common sweet or puddings were bread and butter pudding, suet pudding with molasses, jam tart, macaroni pudding, rice pudding, ginger pudding, and several other quite memorable desserts including bread pudding, which we called 'plonk' or 'hardbake'. For the reader's sake, bread pudding is not to be confused with bread and butter pudding; they are quite different.

But even then, there was a most detestable pudding most of us really disliked: sago pudding, which we commonly called 'snot bubbles' or 'frogspawn'. Fortunately for me, Flappers would eat the lot.

For the most part, although the food was called strange names, we ravenously hungry boys always ate it with gusto and, generally

SUFFER LITTLE CHILDREN

speaking, no one complained. Our food, as in most institutions, was probably nutritious and supposedly good for us growing boys, which to our keepers was the prime objective.

~°~°~ Selling Food ~°~°~

Before and after every meal, Grace was said by the master on duty, during which none of the boys spoke or moved.

Meals were served in much the same order as they were at Bayfordbury, except that instead of in age order, it was in the order of houses. The house order, with regard to who would go up first for their serving, would rotate. The method of serving was organised by the house captains, with the master on duty watching over everything.

But even then, first the prefects would go up to the serving tables, followed by the senior boys in their respective houses. Then the next seniors and finally the spares or weeds would go up.

Then after the first house, say Somerset House, had been served, the second house, Cairns House, would follow. At the next mealtime, Somerset would be last.

We were told that no one was to sell their food. Many boys did, however, including me. When the master wasn't looking, we would raise a hand and call out, just loud enough so that only the boys around us would hear, "Ginner and Marg, Deuce spot, thre'pence Friday."

This simple statement said it all, and was a condition of sale. It simply meant that the boy selling his food had a slice of bread and a pat of margarine for sale for deuce spot (tuppence right now), or thre'pence on Friday, which was the day our weekly pocket money was given to us.

There was never a shortage of takers. We only received two slices of bread each at a meal and it wasn't really enough. Everyone got the same, young and older boys, big or small. Age, size, or whether a boy was a senior or junior, made no difference.

Not being a very big boy, I was able to get by without much to eat, so I often sold 'a ginner and marg' and other parts of my meals.

~°~°~

SUFFER LITTLE CHILDREN

One day, for whatever reason, I don't remember exactly why, I decided to buy a wristwatch. Watches were very expensive in the 1940s and for us boys, almost unobtainable. There might only have been one or two boys in the entire school who had a wristwatch.

Those fortunate ones that did have a watch would have received their watches from possibly a parent or relative, but being an orphan like so many others at Goldings, there was no chance that I would ever be given one. So I decided to save up any money I could, and buy a watch for myself.

In order to increase my saving account I, like several other boys, would often sell much of my food and then put the money – tuppence or thre'pence at a time – into the savings ledger which the school bookkeeper, Mr Maslin, kept.

One should still remember that although we were teenage boys living in much better conditions (a bit like, as I have mentioned, a poor man's public school) and receiving a technical school education, it was still an orphanage. Luxuries in 1948 such as buying a watch, which could almost be taken for granted in the outsiders' world, was quite an undertaking for a Dr Barnardo boy. I never knew another boy at Goldings who actually saved up enough money to be able to buy himself a watch.

Selling our food, or buying other boys' food for that matter, was a serious offence, punishable by caning, but was nevertheless one of the few ways we could make a few pennies. However, we didn't seem to worry about the consequences of breaking the rule, or perhaps selling food was so simple and low risk, we didn't care – no one seemed to get caught. So I, like several other boys, as I have mentioned, often sold some of my food.

Usually most of a boy's pocket money, which was received on Fridays, would be gone by the following Monday, and so he would have to wait until the following Friday before he could pay his debts.

The principle of 'tuppence spot or thre'pence Friday' worked well for me, I didn't need the money right away; I was simply saving any money I could get for the watch, and time – excuse the pun – was not of the essence.

The boys always paid their debts. At Goldings, as in other orphanages, there was an unwritten honour system and all boys abided by

SUFFER LITTLE CHILDREN

it. If a boy didn't pay a debt it would quickly get around the school, and the boy would be 'blacklisted'. No one would trust him, and other boys wouldn't lend or loan him anything any more. Trust, honour, and dependability in each other were most important to boys being brought up like we were.

I would, after collecting my dues from selling food, go to the office window at the regularly scheduled time of day to put my pennies into Mr Maslin's ledger.

I would tap on his sliding window. Mr Maslin would then open a large bookkeeper's ledger, look up my name and school number, then proceed to enter the tuppence or thre'pence or even, once in a while, ninepence or more, depending on how much food I had sold.

Gradually my savings grew and eventually, after seven or more months, I had about twenty-five shillings in my savings, which was an enormous amount of money in those days. It might even have been close to a week's wages for any of the masters.

By the time I could just about see the light at the end of the tunnel and perhaps had saved enough money, that was when the trouble started.

Mr Maslin noticed that I was bringing small amounts of money quite often to his window to be put into my savings account, and must have wondered where I was getting it. Mr Maslin was a very nice chap but he had a job to do, and seeing me come to his window almost every few days with a copper or two must have made him curious, so he mentioned it to Pinhead.

Mr Wheatley called me into his office and questioned me about where I was getting the money and why I was so obviously saving it and so regularly. Perhaps he may have thought I was planning to do a bunk or something, though no one to my knowledge ever ran away from Goldings.

He must have been nice to me because, like the honest chap I was – forgetting the shoplifting etc – I couldn't help but confess to him that I had been selling my food and saving the money to buy a watch. He was quite interested in my buying a watch and seemed encouraging.

At the same time he also got out of 'Loose Lips Longman' the names of the boys who I had been selling my food to. Giving him the names didn't seem too bad to me, because the crime was for selling the food and not buying it, I thought.

SUFFER LITTLE CHILDREN

The next morning at breakfast, when all of the boys' names who were on report were called out, he called out the names of the boys I had been selling my food to.

The ones called out were mostly 'big' kids, who could have given me a good hiding. But for some reason, although they were caned and I wasn't, they didn't do anything to me. But, having been caught, I didn't sell my food anymore.

~o~o~ My First Watch ~o~o~

A short while later Mr Wheatley summoned me to his study regarding the purchase of my new watch. I remember everything about that day very well. Mr Wheatley seemed to be as enthused as I was. He showed me an advertisement in a magazine for a watch. The black-faced watch had white numerals and looked just beautiful. It was called a 'Service' watch.

Mr Wheatley told me the watch would cost exactly twenty-five shillings – the exact amount I had saved – and asked me if this was the watch I would like to buy. Mr Wheatley then wrote a letter to the watch company selling Service watches, and ordered one for me.

Pinhead almost always said the prayers in the mornings before breakfast and then called out the names of the boys who had been put on report. Following these announcements, it was also part of the routine for him to call out the names of boys who had received letters and parcels from relatives.

On this particular morning in November, he called out my name along with a few other boys receiving letters or parcels, informing me that I too had received a parcel.

The staff always opened all of our parcels and letters before we received them. For whatever the reason, this was a Dr Barnardo's policy in all of the homes.

After going to the office and collecting my parcel, I found that my parcel contained the 'Service' watch Mr Wheatley had sent away for. I remember too that Mr Wheatley was very complimentary about my endeavour to save and get the watch, adding that such ambition was most important in life.

SUFFER LITTLE CHILDREN

It was a real treasure. I couldn't stop looking at the watch and, of course, showed it to everyone. All the masters knew about the watch and would constantly ask me the time, just to make me feel proud of my acquisition.

~o~o~

I had the watch – my first watch – for at least five or six years. Eventually it stopped working, and after having had it repaired a couple of times I dropped it down a cavity wall in Lane Estate, which is a council house estate in Taunton. It's probably still there to this day.

~o~o~ Homosexuality ~o~o~

Since leaving Dr Barnardo's Homes, something that I have often spoken about regarding my childhood years in the orphanages, which of course includes Goldings, is homosexuality. During my childhood and adolescent years while in the care of Dr Barnardo's Homes, I never did at any time, and I mean any time, ever experience, hear, or be aware of any sexual assaults on boys either by the masters, or by other boys.

There was to my knowledge, no homosexual activity in any form, and no boys were thought to be 'gay', as such sexual orientation is referred to today. Goldings' boys, young or old, did not, as far as I know, ever get involved in any such homosexual activities.

Some – just a few, I might add – were a little less aggressive than others and therefore thought to be 'poofs' or 'nancy boys', but much of their problem could simply have been temperament – being too timid or even shy.

These boys, the so-called nancy boys, were often jibed or teased, but I don't believe they would ever have been involved in anything sexually with other boys. Such boys would never have survived the shame imposed on them by the rest of the boys.

In those days, during the time that I was brought up, because of our type of peerage and social behaviour, boys so different would have been outcasts and may even have been sent to another facility for special treatment.

SUFFER LITTLE CHILDREN

Of course, we were young boys and often expressed ourselves sexually in certain ways which I'm sure outsiders, and most certainly adults, would frown on. It is with much thought and deliberation that I have decided to tell the reader of what, shall I say, was a dubious 'honour' related to such activities.

However, none of this had anything to do with homosexuality, sexual orientation, assault or homosexual acts between the boys.

Having said that so emphatically, I have to admit that there was the incident, the one regarding Brian Winter, which I have mentioned previously, and which even to this day still leaves me a little puzzled, but at that time most certainly confused.

~o~o~ A Dubious Honour ~o~o~

As I have mentioned: after much thought and with perhaps some trepidation and a little embarrassment, I would not be completely forthright if I didn't tell the reader of one of our sexual oddities, which happened on at least two occasions that I can recall at Goldings, though for all I know it could have possibly have happened more often than that.

One could rationalise that when two hundred and fifty healthy, sexually curious boys are growing up together under one roof, there is, naturally, sexual activity going on, but not with each other, as far as I was ever aware.

Even though it would have been most certainly a caning offence if they were caught, most boys would without any doubt, have masturbated from time to time. Such activity, I believe, would be quite normal amongst sexually developing young boys, and really nothing to be ashamed of.

Boys would easily become aroused purely by reading books by Hank Jenson, or characters like Mickey Spillane and the likes, or seeing pictures of girls in various forms of undress. Words like 'breasts', 'knickers', or even 'stocking tops' would be enough to start our imaginations running wild.

From time to time, as may be expected, sexual oddities did occur. One such occasion was the masturbation or, as it was called, 'shooting competition'.

SUFFER LITTLE CHILDREN

On this particular occasion, an occasion that I find easy to recall, a few boys were openly bragging about their ability to masturbate and to be able to ejaculate, or what was commonly called 'shoot', further than the other.

So, with one bragging comment leading to another, and others joining in, a competition was spontaneously set up for the following evening. Needless to say, the word got around and, as scheduled, Somerset dorm became full of joking, taunting boys supporting one boy or another. I suppose any boy who wanted to could participate. Certainly anyone could come and watch, but only the boys, of course.

To become the champion 'shooter', a boy, with the rest of the boys watching, would have to stand with his toes on the edge of a floorboard line, and then masturbate in an effort to eject or 'shoot' as far as he could.

Each effort was marked by a piece of sticky paper with the boy's name written on it. Then the next boy would attempt to beat it. There would be lots of joking and cheering, as one would expect, but one boy would become the champion of this dubious activity.

I vaguely recall that the winner of this somewhat shameful event could 'shoot' across eight to ten floorboards.

As it was, the champion shooter from another competition in perhaps Buxton or McCall House challenged the winner from Somerset House. Surprisingly, none of us thought very much about it one way or another. It was all simply fun.

Shooting competitions weren't common, but I would have to suppose that such goings on in one form or another did happen from time to time, even though I may not have been aware of it.

Although I can't recollect any of the boys ever getting caught in the act of masturbating, or shooting, such activities or 'rudeness' would have been, to say the very least, frowned on by the masters and most certainly would have been a caning offence if any of the boys were caught.

I honestly can't remember who won the shooting competition in Somerset House. Regardless, the winner's name didn't make it onto the school's Honour Scroll in our main hall – that I'm quite sure of.

This was simply our way of life in a boy's orphanage. I don't believe or think any or many of us became perverse or perverted as the result of these odd types of behaviour.

SUFFER LITTLE CHILDREN

From 'Bread of Heaven'
~o~o~ to ~o~o~
'Spuds and Beetroot'

During the chapel services, morning prayers and evening song, we would sing the same hymns from the Goldings' hymn book time after time, to the point that even to this day I can still remember many of them off by heart, just like one remembers Christmas carols.

I still have and cherish one of the Goldings' hymn books that we used while I was at Goldings.

Many of the hymns selected were beautiful tunes and often I would close my eyes and merely listen to the organist playing them.

Generally, except for a few hymns, the boys would only half-heartedly attempt to sing them. Boys, I believe, don't like to have other boys hear them sing. The Revd Corbett would try to get us to sing, but most boys would only pretend to sing, or mumble the words until the hymn was over. Then, all together, they loudly sang "AMEN".

The boys in the choir, and a few of the other boys, would sing, as would the staff and their families, but it still sounded like a half-hearted attempt.

Certain hymns though, we all liked, primarily because at some point over the years the words had been changed and so we all sang them at the top of our voices, just as loud as we could.

On several occasions, the Revd Corbett would tell the entire congregation to stop singing. Then he would have us start the hymn over again, making us, under threat of punishment, sing the proper words.

One such hymn, which I remember well, was called *Guide Me O Thou Great Redeemer*. The words of the hymn had been changed in fun and in keeping with a regular meal we often had served to us.

During the summer months we often received potatoes and beetroot as well as something else like spam or corned beef for dinner. Often, for periods of time we received 'spuds and beetroot' as much as twice a week, and so, needless to say, we would get rather fed up with this monotonous meal. And so, instead of the proper chorus:

SUFFER LITTLE CHILDREN

Bread of Heaven, bread of Heaven,
Feed me till I want no more,
Feed me till I want no more.

We would change the words and instead, sing in full voice, and as loud as we could, thus drowning out anyone singing the correct words:

Spuds and beetroot, spuds and beetroot,
Feed me till I want no more,
Feed me till I want no more.

Many of the words to the Christmas carols too were also changed, but at Christmas time our fooling around was often overlooked somewhat.

~o~o~ Mr 'Stormy' Tempest ~o~o~

After almost four months of being in Mr Dunning's junior cabinet making class, I moved across the driveway into another building, which housed the senior cabinet making shop.

The senior cabinet making shop was under the direction of Mr Tempest. Mr Tempest was nicknamed 'Stormy' because, as his name inferred, he had a 'short fuse'. He was a rather impatient man and so for obvious reasons, we didn't fool around, certainly not while he was watching. We always took Mr Tempest seriously and did our best to learn the details of cabinet making skilfully and just as he taught us.

There's no doubt that Stormy was a good teacher and a very clever craftsman. He had worked at Goldings for over twenty years by the time I had arrived there.

The boys in Stormy's class quickly learned that we must always pay attention when he was teaching us something. If we didn't he would, without warning, throw a piece of wood at us, or hit us with any piece he would be holding in his hand, to simply get our attention. Nevertheless, in spite of his quick temper, most of us in the senior cabinet making class liked and respected Stormy.

Stormy continued on with our trade training where Mr Dunning had left off. He taught us the 'tricks of the trade' relative to cabinet-making,

SUFFER LITTLE CHILDREN

which helped me in many of the projects I was to undertake in later years. I have, over the years, made acceptable quality furniture and three noteworthy mantle clocks and while doing so, remembering at the same time, Stormy Tempest and his wise teachings.

Most woods, which were still not easily available for us to use even though the war was over, required a permit to obtain. It was emphasised right from the beginning when I had first entered Mr Dunning's class, that we could not, because it was 'rationed', waste wood, either as the result of poor workmanship or making silly things to take out of the shop.

Although I never did actually work in the field of cabinet making during my working career after eventually leaving Goldings, Stormy's primary teachings, which included my understanding of exotic veneers, 'reading' the grain of various types of woods, and French polishing, were all useful to me during my working life.

Among the other things that he taught us was geometry and drafting. Our advanced understanding of drawings or, as they were called at the time, 'blueprints', was extremely useful to me and also helped me advance quickly in my future professional occupation of architecture.

~o~o~

Between the cabinet making shop and the adjoining carpenters shop, where Goodg was being schooled in carpentry, were the glue pots.

Pieces of solid clear brown slabs, which looked a little like peanut brittle, were put into four one-gallon cast-iron pots as soon as we arrived for class in the mornings, and gas burners were turned on. Then the raw glue slabs were heated and melted down into a thick liquid form, making it look like molten toffee. The glue pots boiled all day long.

Wood glue in those days was made primarily from rendered down horse bones, salvaged from the knacker's yard and processed to be used exclusively as wood glue.

The smell in the woodworking shops, dominated by the boiling 'bone glue' throughout the day, was very strong and to some, somewhat sickening, but after a while we just got used to it.

SUFFER LITTLE CHILDREN

Baggy was located on the bench next to me. On the opposite corner from him, on the same bench, was a boy named Chick.

'Clucky', as Chick was nicknamed, was a nice fellow and a clever craftsman. When Clucky eventually left Goldings to go out on a situation and eventually into the Army, he was made to join the infantry and sent to Korea where, after being there for just a short time, he unfortunately lost a leg.

~o~o~

Several of our Goldings' boys were sent to Korea, an active war zone, while doing their compulsory National Service. There were in those days three major campaigns (war zones) they could be sent to. One was Palestine; another, Malaya; and the other, Korea.

Pinhead, during our morning prayers, would from time to time mention several of our Goldings boys after they had been seriously injured or killed in action.

On such occasions we always had a prayer, followed by a two-minute silence to remember the boys who had been killed in action, and a prayer for those injured. Sadly, in the three and a half years I was at Goldings I can remember at least four of our boys who I had known in the school, being killed or seriously injured in Korea, all of them just eighteen to nineteen years old.

~o~o~ Cabinet Making ~o~o~

Baggy's bench, being next to mine in the cabinet making shop as I have mentioned, was much like it could have been planned. We had lots of fun in those years, and many laughs.

Although we were still good friends, Baggy, as I have previously mentioned, was always ahead of me in seniority, and so we both had other friends now. But, like in the 'old' days, we still shared a sincere friendship and loyalty towards each other.

We would quite often reminisce about the old times at Bayfordbury and Eastbourne, and wonder if Fred Dyos had become a carpenter's apprentice in Australia like all three of us had said we would.

SUFFER LITTLE CHILDREN

As it was, both Baggy and I were training to become cabinet makers, which, though not carpentry, was still working with wood.

While under Stormy Tempest's tuition we would make small furniture items such as tables, desks, classic-looking chairs, clock cases, and many other such things.

I remember one project in particular, which for a short while put me out of favour with Stormy.

It happened because after about five days of making an 'occasional', or coffee table, with an inlaid top, Baggy looked at it and scoffed. I had to admit it looked terrible. The wood had been planed badly, leaving the grain torn, and the joints were poorly made. Also the inlays were crooked, and generally the whole thing was a mess.

Jokingly, Baggy called me a 'wood butcher' and told everyone. He said the table looked like someone in the gardening department had made it with a scythe.

We both laughed at my miserable effort, even though I knew I would get into trouble from Stormy and no doubt, receive a clip around the ear if he saw it, if for no other reason than I had wasted wood.

So, I cut the entire table into small pieces and hid them underneath the shaving pile. The shaving pile was swept up and removed about every third or forth day after shop.

Expecting Stormy to come to look at my project at any time, like teachers do, I worked as quickly as I could to catch up on it. I didn't spend any time talking to anyone or fooling around. Baggy even did some of my planing work to save some time. But still I couldn't catch up; after all, I had spent almost a week working on the other table, which I had now completely demolished.

There were lots of jokes made about the other table by the other boys.

One of the jokes was that if Stormy saw the table I was now making and if he said, "That's very badly done, I've thrown away better tables than that", I could say "So have I, Sir! Just look under the shaving pile".

As it was, Stormy came to look at my work and even though I had made every effort to catch up, I was still a long way behind on the project. He was somewhat angry and shouted at me, saying that I was wasting his time as well as my own.

SUFFER LITTLE CHILDREN

So after a good lecturing and some unfriendly words to say the least, he told me that I had to work something like three Saturdays to catch up, instead of going out into Hertford or playing football.

21

GOLDINGS – Part 3

~o~o~ Longman, Foley and Goodger ~o~o~

John Goodger came to Goldings during the winter of 1948, about four or five months after me, and was put into Cairns House. His school number was 34 and, even to me, he was a 'spare' or 'weed'.

It was at about that same time I became closer friends with another boy who I have already mentioned: 'Fuzz' Foley. Victor 'Fuzz' Foley was also in Somerset House. In a very short time, the three of us became inseparable friends, with Flappers ever looming in the background.

When we were in trouble we were generally all in trouble at the same time because, of course, we went everywhere and did everything together.

Invariably, if something had gone wrong or boys had been caught or perhaps only been seen scrumping, we would often hear other boys say, "I bet it was Longman, Foley and Goodger." Our names, it seemed, were synonymous with trouble.

When Pinhead called out the names of boys who had been put on report or 'on the book' for having done something or other wrong, and that these boys had to report for punishment, he very often said, "Longman, Foley and Goodger report to my study" all in one breath and at the same time raising his eyebrows.

There was always a chuckle in the dining room at the announcement of our names, partly to do with Mr Wheatley's eyebrows and lots to do with hearing Longman, Foley and Goodger's names called out again and again. We were so often in trouble, it seemed, and always together.

We did almost everything we did together. All three of us joined the school band, although Fuzz and Goodg joined a little after I did. Like me, Goodg became a bugler, while Fuzz Foley taught himself to play the kettle drum and was very good at it. He could do a 'roll' on his drum as fast as the rattle on a rattlesnake's tail.

SUFFER LITTLE CHILDREN

> Longman, Foley and Goodger
> Good Friends
> Always in trouble together

Reg Longman

Victor 'Fuzz' Foley

John 'Goodg' Goodger

SUFFER LITTLE CHILDREN
~o~o~ Chapel ~o~o~

The school band would lead the entire school on a march to the chapel twice each Sunday, playing the Goldings traditional marches. The marches we played were our own versions of *Anchors Away, Echo and Carry on, You're in the Army Now*, and several more. The same marches were played at competitions and on the army cadet parades.

After filing into the chapel, we would sit in the pews in our respective houses. The Revd Corbett, besides being the school chaplain, was also the school's assistant headmaster.

Mr Wheatley would sit opposite the Revd Corbett in the chapel. Sitting beside them, four members each side, were the chapel's choir. I don't think any of the boys were chosen to be in the choir because of their singing abilities. In all probability they joined because they received an extra tuppence a week in their pocket money just for being in the choir.

It used to be that boys randomly picked from the school roster, would read the two 'lessons' during the Sunday morning service. However, because of the many mistakes they would make while reading the lessons, and because the entire congregation of us boys and often the staff would laugh at their stumbling and mispronunciation of words, this practice was eventually discontinued and Pinhead read the lessons.

~o~o~ "Lay Not up for Yourselves…" ~o~o~

The Reverend Corbett was the first person ever to tell me that my birthday was on December 28th. Until he told me I had always thought it was on December 26th (Boxing Day). I never, until many years after leaving Goldings, ever received a birthday card or birthday present and I missed neither of them.

He was also the first person ever to tell me that I was born in Hong Kong. Up to this point in my life I didn't know and nor did I really care where I had been born or when my birthday was. I had had no previous knowledge of the fact that I was actually born in China.

When my friends Flappers, Fuzz, Goodg, Baggy and several others found out that I had been born in Hong Kong, they would make slits of

SUFFER LITTLE CHILDREN

their eyes with their fingers and would speak a 'mock' Chinese to me and chant a tune from the opera *The Mikado*.

~o~o~

One day, after being at Goldings for about three years and after I had become a prefect, I got into a spot of trouble with Revd Corbett. Revd Corbett, although he was a theologian and for the most part a gentle person, could under certain circumstances become quite angry, as was the case late one evening just before lights out.

It was after the duty bugler had played the 'Last Post' and everyone was in bed, waiting for the bugler to play 'Lights Out', that the problem occurred.

I, being a prefect and thus responsible for the boys in my house dormitory, had, as was my duty, made sure all of the boys were in bed.

Not having to be in bed myself, because prefects could stay up a half an hour longer than the other boys, I was standing in the middle of the Somerset senior dormitory, fooling around.

With my white bath towel draped around my neck, much like the white 'sash' a clergyman wears during a church service, I had the attention of the other boys in the dormitory, who were now lying in their beds watching me and laughing.

Resting on my open hands, I held a big book about the size of a bible, which I had opened up and was pretending to read and speak like the Revd Corbett. Actually, I was quoting from the bible some of the verses I had learned during my school days with Mrs Blackwell at Ware School.

The verses that I was quoting off by heart were from the book of St Matthew, Chapter 6, verses 19 to 23. I was speaking loudly in an exaggerated, mournful, kind of monotone voice, much like the Reverend Corbett and other clergymen do.

I was reciting or saying:

SUFFER LITTLE CHILDREN

"Lay not up for yourselves, treasures on earth, where moth and rust doth corrupt, and where thieves break through and steal:

But lay up for yourselves treasures in heaven, where neither moth nor rust doth corrupt, and where thieves do not break through and steal:

For where your treasure is, there will your heart be also."

I think I was about half way through reciting this rather significant lesson, when the Revd Corbett came quietly into the dormitory behind me, and was listening to me.

As it was, most of the boys in the senior dormitory could see the Revd Corbett standing there, just a few feet behind me, but they couldn't say anything; they could only watch in anticipation of what was about to happen.

They just knew I was in trouble. Making fun of the Bible, or religion in any way for that matter, was just not done in Dr Barnardo's Homes, and especially so in front of the Revd Corbett.

To me it simply seemed that I must have been doing a great job entertaining the other boys, because no one was interrupting me and I had their full attention, though what I didn't realise was that they weren't laughing at my joke any more, as I would have expected.

Of course, it wasn't my performance at all that they were interested in. They were just waiting to see what was going to happen when the Revd Corbett decided he had had enough of me mocking him and the Bible.

Eventually, and probably because no one was laughing at me, I must have guessed something was wrong and, turning around, I saw the Revd Corbett glaring at me. He was, as adults may have said, "not amused".

Embarrassed, I closed the book and with a sheepish grin took the white towel from around my neck.

Until this moment I had never seen Revd Corbett angry. He certainly wasn't laughing; in fact he looked serious and rather stone faced.

Then he stepped forward, grabbed hold of my left earlobe with his

SUFFER LITTLE CHILDREN

finger and thumb, and led me out of the dormitory. I must say the lobe of my ear hurt quite a bit, but not seriously. Still, it made me wince.

Revd Corbett gave me a good talking-to but didn't put me on report. A punishment a prefect could receive for a serious offence would be to be demoted and lose their prefect's privileges. Prefects received an extra sixpence for their pocket money just for being prefects, and I didn't want to lose that.

Over the years that I knew the Revd Corbett, I found him to be a fair man and a good religious teacher, and I, like many other boys, had a great deal of respect for him. It wouldn't be his fault that I was not a more devout Christian.

~°~°~ Pocket Money ~°~°~

Our pocket money, when we first arrived at Goldings, started at thre'pence. We would get a deuce (two pence) raise every year, which was the standard pocket money increase. We would also get tuppence extra a week for being in the army cadets.

In time, I would receive an additional thre'pence for being a duty bugler and a further sixpence for being a prefect.

With all that, I would receive, during my last year at Goldings, about one shilling and sixpence or perhaps just a little more a week pocket money.

The pocket money we were entitled to was taxed by 'fines'. The fines resulted from punishments, as well as the standard breakage costs for the various things we collectively broke, such as dishes, windows; loss of knives and forks etc; and other property damage; all of which we would have to pay for.

The standard weekly breakage cost that all of us boys had deducted from our pocket money was about a penny or sometimes a penny-ha'penny a week. A penny was not much, but nevertheless a penny was a penny and not to be entirely sneezed at.

The worst loss we could suffer out of our pocket money would be as the result of being fined for doing something or other wrong. Punishments such as fines were not given for serious offences and were only levied against us for minor misdemeanours. We would often prefer a small fine to a 'weekend default'.

SUFFER LITTLE CHILDREN

Punishments resulting in pocket money deductions included defaults like not being in bed by 8.30 p.m., being late for parade, not standing still when the salute (flag raising) was being played, or talking in chapel and things like that. On such occasions and for such defaults, we could get a fine of '2-6' or '3-6' or more.

Every fine was based on increments of one sixth of a shilling, a shilling being twelve pence.

1-6th of a shilling being tuppence (two pence), 2-6 would be four pence, and so on. To further clarify:

One shilling is worth 6 x 2 pence = 12 pence.

Therefore:
Each shilling was divided into 1/6th of a shilling, which in turn equals 2 pence.

Hence:
4-6 = 4 x 2 pence = 8 pence
And 6-6 = 6 x 2 pence = 12 pence (one shilling)

Although this is all very simple to understand now, it was a little tricky when we were so young, and when all that Pinhead would say was something like, "You are fined 5-6; don't do it again."

If a boy received a '6-6' fine, the result would be that he would lose one full shilling from his pocket money. If the fine were '7-6', the fine would amount to one shilling and tuppence, and so on.

For a boy like me, for instance, receiving one shilling and seven pence a week, which I was in my last year, the total reduction of '6-6' from my weekly pocket money would result in my only receiving sevenpence for the week, less any breakage fines.

In actual fact we rarely received a fine of '6-6', as such punishments equalling '6-6' would most likely result in a weekend default or possibly the cane.

In my early days at Goldings, when I was a little more reckless and got into more trouble, my fines, together with breakage deductions, would result in my having very little pocket money, if any at all, some weeks.

SUFFER LITTLE CHILDREN

Most of the time while I was at Goldings, I didn't feel I was really hard done by, and never felt particularly deprived of money. We didn't have much but, on the other hand, we had little or no expectations in terms of buying or owning anything.

~o~o~ Confirmation ~o~o~

The Revd Corbett, being about forty years old at the time we were at Goldings, was an energetic Church of England minister, full of physical vitality and who could run as fast as most of us boys. He came from somewhere in Wales and often talked rugby, although rugby wasn't a sport we played at Goldings.

Revd Corbett taught us Christian science and gave us religious instruction during our academic days, and was ultimately responsible for many of us boys being confirmed, by the Bishop of St Albans.

The boys who put their names down to be confirmed included Longman, Foley and Goodger, though I don't really know why, as we didn't really understand or believe much about Jesus Christ, the Virgin Mary (we had no idea what a virgin was), and nor did we even like attending chapel. Even though we learned the scriptures, as I have explained, we never really understood them.

However, in order to become confirmed, we were required to attend prep school one evening a week for a month or so. This is where we learned what Holy Communion was all about.

I also learned, or perhaps I should say, refreshed my memory regarding the Catechism all over again. Father Brown at St Mary's Church in Bayford had taught me much of the Catechism, in what seemed like such a long time ago now.

Then on one particular day, the Bishop of St Albans came to Goldings and about thirty of us became confirmed Christians.

Dressed in our grey flannel suits, we all, two boys at a time, approached the altar rail. Then, as I recall, the bishop placed both of his hands on top of one boy's head, at the same time saying amongst other ritual things, "Bless this thy servant." Then placing both hands on the other boy's head, he would continue "And this thy servant..."

After several other words confirming that we were now followers of

SUFFER LITTLE CHILDREN

Christ, each pair of boys would receive a small thin wafer (body of Christ), and a sip of wine (blood of Christ). Following that, we went back to our pews and then the next two boys would go up to be confirmed and receive their wafer and wine.

There was a lot more to our being confirmed, of course, than just that but, like most of the other boys not being overly interested in religion or religious instruction, I can't remember much more about it.

The wine – port, I believe – we received that day, was the first alcoholic drink I had ever tasted up to this point in my life and, as I recall, I didn't really like it. As we returned to our pews, carefully watching that the bishop or the Revd Corbett weren't watching, we rolled our eyes and pretended that we were 'under the weather', so to speak.

Although I liked to sing many of the hymns, I hadn't ever liked going to church. However, now that I was confirmed, I was expected to attend Holy Communion once a month, which meant my getting out of bed at five thirty in the morning to attend the six o'clock Holy Communion service. So, instead of my only having to attend chapel twice each Sunday, being confirmed meant that now I would be required to attend chapel three times on Sundays once a month, as well as all the Holy Sundays throughout the holy year.

~o~o~ Punishments in General ~o~o~

Punishments at Goldings were never barbaric, cruel or unreasonably carried out like they were at Bayfordbury under the administration of Mr Scougall, or at Churchill House under Mr Fowlermott's rule, and there was absolutely none of the likes of Mr Nash for us to be concerned about.

I'm sure most boys felt that Mr Wheatley was an extremely fair and reasonable man. He always dressed in a suit, complete with collar and tie, and always wore clean, shiny shoes. Although he had a good sense of humour and often proved it in a dignified way, he didn't allow us boys to become overly familiar with him. However, he was always friendly and never ever did I see him angry.

He didn't seem to converse or joke around much with the masters in the presence of the boys, and always discussed anything he had to say to them regarding the running of the school in private.

SUFFER LITTLE CHILDREN

As Headmaster and principle administrator of Goldings, Mr Wheatley often conducted our morning prayers and attended chapel with us. He was rarely absent at our inter-house sporting events and always officiated during the presentation of 'house' or individual sporting event winners awards. As well, he was a captain and the commanding officer in the school's army cadets.

Although the Revd Corbett was the deputy headmaster, he rarely came into the boys' dining room and seldom ever did routine master's duties. However, he always had a presence in the school, and we saw quite a bit of him.

There were punishable offences in the school that were more serious than others, of course. The biggest deterrent, when we considered undertaking doing anything we knew could result in punishment, was always the cane.

Some of the more serious offences at Goldings were smoking, stealing, truancy from our workshops, insolence, being cheeky to masters, and vandalism.

The most common punishments handed out were:
- One day default – Saturday or Sunday.
- Weekend default – Saturday and Sunday. Sometimes two, or even three weekend defaults.
- Fines – (1–6, 2–6 or more)
- Kitchen duties – washing pots and pans, or potato peeling for a week.
- Caning – this was the capital punishment, consisting of two, four, or six strokes (cuts) of the cane.

When any of us had to do fatigues as the result of a default, whether a one-day or a weekend default, it entailed doing 'skivvies' or fatigues for the day or even days. Such 'skivvies' would quite frequently include reporting to a prefect or a master at a given time and location and doing whatever chore had been planned.

Some of the most common fatigues or 'skivvies' included:
- Sweeping, and then scrubbing the gymnasium pine wood floor on our hands and knees, with a bucket of water, soap, and scrubbing brush. This was a four-hour fatigue, at least.
- Sweeping the parade ground with yard brooms. The parade ground,

SUFFER LITTLE CHILDREN

being a little more than a quarter of an acre in size, meant that this fatigue was at least a four-or five-hour fatigue, depending on how many boys (eight to twelve) were being punished.
- Extensive cleaning of the ablutions (toilets, shower floors and walls) – approximately a three-hour fatigue.
- Scrubbing the flagstone dining room floor, or any of the numerous corridor floors. This was approximately a four-hour fatigue.
- Cleaning the swimming pool (only done in the summer months). This was no fun. I will explain more about this chore later. This task was a six-hour fatigue, at least.
- Sweeping up leaves with willow twig brushes. This could be anything from a two to a six-hour fatigue.

All offences had to be entered into 'The Book' by a prefect or master. Then the offenders brought before Mr Wheatley for him to judge and render an appropriate punishment.

If caning was to be administered, such caning was only carried out by Mr Wheatley, and witnessed by the Revd Corbett. Unlike with Mr Scougall, there was no anger attached to the caning. No one beat us with their fists or slapped us around with their hands any more.

Ultimately I don't think any of us ever felt abused physically and, to my knowledge, no one ever was.

The most serious offences any one of us could commit were absolute disobedience, swearing, blatant insolence, stealing, fighting, and smoking. But again, the most serious offence of all would be smoking in the dormitories.

For most of the offences, Pinhead would give us a fair hearing and if we were deemed guilty, we would generally be punished in one form or another.

The cane was almost always administered as though it was a ritual. Pinhead, with the Revd Corbett present, would, after discussing the offence we had committed with us, and establishing our guilt, calmly, without raising his voice, tell us that we were going to be caned.

He would always ask, "Do you accept your punishment?"

We would invariably answer, "Yes, Sir!"

With the Reverend Corbett witnessing our caning, we would be

SUFFER LITTLE CHILDREN

required to bend over a big armchair in Mr Wheatley's study, and then be given the predetermined number of strokes with the cane.

Have no doubt about it, the cane always hurt, but never was it as severe as at Bayfordbury. There was no brutality associated with the caning. After a caning, severe or not, we didn't think any the less of Pinhead.

~o~o~ Good Friends ~o~o~

Both Goodger and I were in the school boxing team. Goodger was a few pounds heavier than I and was therefore in a different weight classification. As the result of our weight differences, we never fought each other.

Weight classes for amateur boxing were categorised in divisions of seven pounds. I was about eight stone (112 pounds), whilst Goodger would have been approximately eight stone seven pounds, or perhaps even slightly more – a 'stone' is fourteen pounds.

There was only one representative of each weight category in the school boxing team. Baggy, too was in the team. Being about nine and a half stone, Baggy was now quite a bit heavier than either Goodger or I, and so we never met him in the ring. I will tell more about the school boxing later.

Fuzz, Goodg and I all taught ourselves how to play the mouth organ and the harmonica, the mouth organ being very similar to the harmonica. I could play these instruments fairly well, but both Goodg and Fuzz could, I believe, play a little better than me.

Goodg would often come to Somerset dorm, and all three of us would practise playing our mouth organs for hours and hours. Sometimes we would play them while we were out walking in the fields.

We commonly played our Dr Barnardo's Homes songs and many others, such as *'Swanee River', 'Danny Boy'* and *'Beautiful Dreamer'*.

As I sit here writing my story, all these many years later, I close my eyes and remember those carefree, happy days; and while remembering, I see three young 'best friends' walking through the fields or down those narrow English country lanes playing our mouth organs. At the same time our eyes would be constantly scanning the hedgerows, looking for something to eat.

They're all such nice memories to look back on now.

SUFFER LITTLE CHILDREN
~o~o~ Supplementary Cooking ~o~o~

As well as Fuzz and Goodg and myself being such good friends, Flappers and I too were still especially good friends and did lots of things together. Often the pair of us went off together looking for chestnuts, hazelnuts, and even the tiny beechnuts.

Many times in the spring, Flappers and myself would find pheasant eggs in the grass, and duck and moorhen eggs at the edge of the many rivers near Goldings. We would bring the eggs back to the pet area – where boys were allowed to look after pets – light a fire, and boil the eggs to eat.

Sometimes, before Flappers was training to become a chef, we would make stews from vegetables we had foraged. After bringing home a cabbage or kale, some potatoes, carrots and anything else we could find in the farmers' fields, we would make a fire and in any old can we could find, make a stew. We never had any meat to put in it; we weren't aware that meat was so important in a stew.

We would let all the vegetables boil until we couldn't watch them boil any longer, which wouldn't be very long. Then we would put our fingers into the hot, watery vegetable only stew, and eat the half-cooked vegetables. This we called 'stew'.

There was, for a short time, a practice of inviting other boys to share our stew, so that they would ask us to share theirs. We actually thought our stew was pretty good but really the gravy was just boiled water.

~o~o~ Indoor Hockey ~o~o~

Sometimes on rainy days in the summer, and many, many times in the winter, we would play an indoor hockey game, with crudely made hockey sticks and a tennis ball. This hockey, the only hockey we would play now, we would play in the recreation hut. The 'rec hut', as it was known, was a huge wooden hut about eighty feet long and forty-five feet wide. There were just a few wire-reinforced glass windows, but plenty of other lighting.

Indoor hockey was a great game. All we needed was a tennis ball, lines marked on the walls – like goal posts – a stick about three feet

SUFFER LITTLE CHILDREN

long and with a natural knurled knob on the end, which we used as hockey sticks. I don't remember there being any particular rules, but nevertheless there were the unwritten rules and as well, we all followed the intent of the game.

Then sides were picked with as many boys on each side as came to play, the tennis ball was tossed up in the air amongst the players, and that was it. There was no body protection except for shin pads, which we made out of newspapers, cardboard, or magazines, if we were fortunate enough to have any.

After the ball had been tossed, we did nothing more than run up and down the rec hut, dribbling the ball or playing the rebounds off the walls and swinging at the ball, trying to score a goal between the two posts marked on the wall. The score, after maybe a two-hour game of constantly running and running, may well have been something like 28 to 36 or even 65 to 78.

~o~o~ Smoking ~o~o~

Although smoking was a risky habit to get into at Goldings, many boys still did. Where the boys who smoked got their cigarettes, I have no idea. Although cigarettes in those days weren't very expensive, they would still have cost too much money for most of us boys to be able to pay for.

Boys that smoked usually hung around together and shared cigarettes. It would often be that when a boy produced a cigarette, five other boys would make claim to a drag of it. There would commonly be an entitlement for other boys to ask for a drag, because the current cigarette owner had received a drag from one or all of the other boys in their group on a previous occasion.

Even matches were not so easy to come by if one couldn't afford to buy any. So, to save money by not buying matches, many, if not most of the smokers, used a unique way of getting a light for their cigarette.

The smokers would get an ordinary lead pencil and break it in half. Then they would sharpen both ends of both pieces of pencil. Now they had two small pencils about two to three inches long, sharpened at each end.

Then, without any of the staff seeing them, they would unscrew the cover on the light switch in the rec hut, exposing the live connection

SUFFER LITTLE CHILDREN

terminals. The idea then, was to put one end of one of the pencils on the positive post and the end of the other pencil on the negative terminal. By touching the other ends of the pencils together, it creates an arc. With a piece of paper at the arc location, the paper would easily catch fire.

Although this practice was really quite dangerous, it was easy and often done.

Whereas the electric power in Canada in any residence is 120 volts, the power in a duplex outlet or light switch in Britain was, and still is, 240 volts – enough to kill a boy, or to certainly give him a serious burn, though I don't remember any of the smokers ever getting hurt.

I personally never did smoke at Goldings and I can't, except for one occasion, remember Goodger or Foley smoking either. But Flappers smoked quite a bit, and I would often see him getting a light from the rec hut light switch.

I don't know where Flappers obtained his money for buying cigarettes, though I think he used to sell food from the kitchen, as he always seemed to have more money than the rest of us.

22

GOLDINGS – Part 4

~○~○~ Armistice Day 1949 ~○~○~

There was one day in particular at Goldings which I shall always remember. It all happened on the 11th of November, 1949. This was the day that Longman, Foley and Goodger, and later in the day, Flappers, could have been in real serious trouble with Mr Wheatley.

We were all involved, in different ways, in making this day a day which none of us could, or will, ever forget for the rest of our lives.

There was no planned mischief or disrespect intended, and although to us it was funny in some ways, to others, what we did was most certainly and without doubt, disrespectful and unforgivable.

As was usual on this national holiday – Armistice Day – most people all over Great Britain and the Commonwealth went to their respective churches or place of worship to remember those men and women who had given their lives for their countries.

The war had ended just four years earlier. Armistice Day, or as some people called it, Remembrance Day, services would be going on all over the British Empire. Every city, town, village or hamlet in England had lost someone in the war, including me. The memory of those who had died for Britain and to keep the world free, was still fresh in people's minds.

On this particular day all church services everywhere were very sad and full of memories for most people, not just in Britain and the Commonwealth, but also throughout the world.

Many men and women would cry openly in church, in utter despair and sorrow, even four years after the war was over, remembering their husbands, wives, other relatives and for many, even their own children who had been killed.

Although the Canadians, Australians, Indians, New Zealanders and other Commonwealth members, plus the Americans and other allied forces who had fought in the war, had left England a couple of years

SUFFER LITTLE CHILDREN

earlier, many had become great friends with the British people while stationed in Britain. They too, particularly those who had fallen, were still remembered.

War had brought such sorrow to our entire country, the Commonwealth, and much of the world. But at the same time a union of solidarity and pride existed in the people's accomplishment of beating the overwhelming odds in having defeated the German menace.

Every year since the war had ended, several churches in the area asked Goldings to provide buglers to come to their village churches, to play the 'Last Post' and 'Reveille' during their Armistice services.

This would be the second year that I had been asked to attend and play my bugle at a Remembrance Day service. The previous year, I had played my bugle with another bugler from the school and it had all gone well. We had simply played the 'Last Post' and then 'Reveille' at the point in the service when we were directed to.

This time, the church we were to play our bugles in was in Stapleford, a small village just a few miles from Goldings.

As it was I, being the silver bugler, helped to select the buglers to go to the various village churches. So I chose to take John Goodger with me. Goodg was a very good bugler and as I have mentioned, one of my best friends.

Unknown to me, and as the devil would have it, Skip Culver told Fuzz Foley to go with us. Fuzz would play a roll on his kettle drum, whilst we played our bugles. Hopefully, it was going to be a premium performance.

However, why Skip Culver would allow Longman, Foley and Goodger out together on such an event, I don't know. He should have known something would go wrong, and that we could well get into trouble.

Because Armistice Day is primarily a military event, the three of us were dressed in our army cadet uniforms. Our boots were 'spit and polished', the creases in our long army cadet trousers had been pressed under our mattresses, and our brasses cleaned. We had blankoed our webbing belts and spats, which were a stark white. No doubt, our appearances would have been a credit to Dr Barnardo's and the cadets.

My silver bugle and Goodger's copper bugle, and also Fuzz's kettle drum, were all polished, and shone brilliantly.

SUFFER LITTLE CHILDREN

The only difference in appearance between Goodg, Fuzz and me was that instead of Fuzz having a bugle, he had a small kettle drum swinging at his hip. As I have mentioned, there's no doubt but that we would have looked quite impressive.

Then upon our arrival at the church and as was expected, we would stand to attention at the back of the quaint little country church, looking straight ahead as the parishioners filed in. Our bugles were held in our right hands, resting on our hips, and Fuzz's kettle drum attached to his waist.

I'm quite sure the minister would feel he had done everything right and that he would have a good and dignified performance from us.

~o~o~

At this point I must tell the reader that for a long time now both Goodg and I, when reaching a particular top note while playing our bugles, would both experience a very sharp pain in the back of our heads, and for both of us, the sharp pain was quite intense. Believe me, the pain really did hurt, to the point that it would actually make us wince.

I don't know if this pain occurs with other buglers or trumpeters, or if in fact the pain, which we experienced in the crown of our heads, is common or not, but whether it is or isn't, both Goodger and I would get this pain, and there was absolutely nothing we could do about it except to basically suffer it.

~o~o~

So here we were – Longman, Foley and Goodger – all in the responsible position of being asked to add the 'trimmings' to the Armistice Day service in this tiny little village church in the heartland of England, which, like so many other towns and villages, contributed many young men and women who had given their lives for their country.

The solemn service proceeded just as it should have, with the vicar conducting it, and preaching from the pulpit.

During his sermon the vicar would naturally have made reference to the sadness of the occasion, and many people would remember their

SUFFER LITTLE CHILDREN

lost ones, and weep openly.

As scheduled, an adult – perhaps a churchwarden at the back of the church who was standing near us – gave us the signal that it was time for us to play the 'Last Post'.

The procedure was really quite simple for us. At the appropriate moment during the service we were to play the 'Last Post', and then there would be a two-minute silence. Following the two-minute silence we would play 'Reveille'.

Almost routinely, both Goodg and I brought our bugles up to our lips and started to play. Fuzz, as was expected, started his rolls on the kettle drum, and all was going fine. Both Goodger and I played our bugles well and with Foley's rolls, it must have sounded quite effective.

Then it happened. Well into our playing of the 'Last Post', and trying to reach and hold a very high note towards the end of this tune, we both got 'the pain' in the top of our heads. The pain, as was often the case, was extremely sharp and, as it often did, made of us both wince. Believe me, the pain really hurt.

Still keeping my head absolutely erect and looking straight ahead in a military fashion, I rolled my eyes and happened to glance sideways at Goodger at the exact same moment that, with only his eyes moving, he glanced at me.

As it was, we were both trying to hold the top 'painful' note and were both at the same time wincing from the pain. Unfortunately, at that very moment our eyes met, we both burst out laughing.

In order to play an instrument like a trumpet, bugle, or almost any brass or wind instrument, it's imperative that one keeps their lips tight to the mouthpiece in order to make any sort of sound at all, let alone be able to play it well. If one was to laugh, then it would be almost impossible to be able to play such instruments.

Even knowing what the consequences might be, we still couldn't stop laughing. We started and tried to continue playing, but each time we tried, we just 'blurted' out notes and then burst out laughing again; we just couldn't get it together. This shameful laughing went on for perhaps a minute or so, which is an awful long time under such circumstances.

Foley meanwhile, continued playing his rolls on his kettle drum, standing there like 'the little drummer boy'. On its own, a kettle drum,

SUFFER LITTLE CHILDREN

particularly in church, doesn't sound much like music, but more like someone beating a tin can.

So here we were, both Goodger and I, desperately trying to get ourselves under control in order to be able to play our bugles but we just couldn't, for laughing.

Foley, still drumming away on his kettle drum, was at the same time whispering to us, telling us to stop laughing, and how we would get into real trouble when we got back to Goldings.

People were turning around to look at us. A few people were actually smiling, our laughing being infectious.

Eventually we composed ourselves and got through it. We knew we had made a mess of everything, but just couldn't help it.

The vicar patiently waited for us to finish playing, then carried on with the service.

Following the service the congregation filed out of the church, passing us as we stood sheepishly at the door beside the vicar. No one spoke to us; they just looked at us and smiled, locked up in their own thoughts.

After the congregation had left, the minister invited all three of us back to the vicarage. His wife, who had been at the service, had prepared a nice tea for us. There was no mention of our performance; they were just very kind people.

We spent the best part of the day with them. They took us for a drive in their car and talked to us about our life at Goldings, and spoke of the many years they had been associated with Goldings in one way or another.

They apparently knew Mr Wheatley and a few of the staff but they never, as far as I know, ever told any of them about our disgraceful performance.

Later the minister, who perhaps gave us a shilling each for playing our bugles and drum at his service, drove us back to Goldings.

That's when the second part of this unforgettable day happened. This was to become a very troublesome day, and a day that Longman, Foley, and Goodger will always remember.

As fate would have it, I was still to be punished, but not for what happened in Stapleford Church.

SUFFER LITTLE CHILDREN
~o~o~ Smoking in the Dormitory ~o~o~

We arrived back from Stapleford Church shortly after dark. The minister said goodbye and left. It would have been about six o'clock in the evening when we had got back to Goldings. The rest of the school had gone to the chapel for evening song, which meant that the three of us boys were all alone in the Somerset dormitory.

There were no other boys around and the entire mansion seemed empty. Being Armistice Day everyone, including the staff, would have gone to the chapel.

A short while after we had arrived back Flappers, who had been helping to prepare the staff supper (a 9.30 p.m. light meal for the staff), came up to Somerset dormitory and, fishing in his pocket, pulled out a cigarette.

I know that I have mentioned the seriousness of getting caught smoking in the dormitories several times now, but Flappers never changed. He always lived on the 'edge'.

Quite possibly, we talked about how risky it was to smoke in the dorm but Flappers wouldn't listen, and lit up his cigarette anyway.

I, being in the school boxing team, had never even tried to smoke, although I believe Fuzz and Goodger did from time to time. We were told, even at that time, how bad it was to smoke, the main reason being was that it affected our breathing, and the other reason being that we wouldn't grow.

However, as I have mentioned before, Flappers was not only a bad influence on me; he was on others too.

So, Goodger and Foley shared the cigarette with him, each taking a couple of drags and then passing the 'butt' on to the next boy. I didn't take even one puff.

When they had finished the cigarette, one of them threw the very small cigarette butt, now no more than about a quarter of an inch long, out of the window.

Somerset dormitory, being on the second floor and in full view of the parade ground, was probably the worst window for any boy to throw a cigarette butt out of, because it could easily be seen by a passing prefect or master. This is exactly what happened.

SUFFER LITTLE CHILDREN

Mr Cartwright, who had been Flappers' gardening teacher until Flappers had transferred to the cookhouse, was on duty at the time, and it was Mr Cartwright who saw the glowing butt fly out of the window that dark November evening.

Surprising us, Mr Cartwright came up to the Somerset House dormitory, and saw the four of us sitting on our beds talking.

Mr Cartwright was a tall, rather lean man with a thick dark moustache. I remember him fairly well as being a quiet, laid-back, slow-talking man. Generally speaking, most of the boys including us, liked Mr Cartwright.

Nevertheless, he had a job to do and so, entering our dorm, he asked, "Who's been smoking in here?"

At first none of us answered. We knew we were in serious trouble. So he asked again, assuring us that he had seen the cigarette end come out of our window, and pointed out that the dormitory smelled of cigarette smoke.

We all emphatically denied we had been smoking, so he simply said that he was going to put us all on report and left.

We discussed our situation, with me saying it was them who had been smoking, not me, so I was out of it and that they would have to figure out what they were going to do, or how they would deny they had been smoking, which I felt they wouldn't get away with.

They started arguing between themselves about how they were going to convince Mr Wheatley that they hadn't been smoking. They also recognised that Mr Wheatley would take Mr Cartwright's word, which meant that we would all be caned.

The caning that they would receive would undoubtedly be 'six of the best', which is the most severe punishment Mr Wheatley would administer. Caning was always given, so as to maintain an example and a warning for others not to smoke in the dormitories.

Already having discounted myself, I thought about the situation for a moment, and suggested, why should all of them have to be caned? There was only one cigarette butt seen coming out of the window. Mr Cartwright couldn't have known if it was all four or just one boy who had been smoking.

With the situation for them seeming hopeless, and with me in the

SUFFER LITTLE CHILDREN

clear, there was no point in all of the rest of them saying they were smoking, because obviously they would all be caned.

So, I suggested that the three of them would toss a penny each, the odd man losing. The one who lost would, naturally, take the blame and so be caned.

After agreeing with the plan, they tossed a coin each. As it turned out Flappers was the odd man, and therefore had lost.

Flappers, realising that he was going to have to be the one to be caned, argued, rather emphatically, that it should be best of three tosses, with Fuzz and Goodg saying it was a one-toss deal, and that Flappers had lost and that he should take the blame. Eventually, after lots of arguing, they agreed on the best of three tosses, the loser being the first to lose two tosses.

As bad luck, or otherwise as fair play, would have it, Flappers lost again, and then wanted it to be the best of five. So, they argued again.

This went on for a while and they just couldn't agree, so I got involved again, and said that I had another idea.

Of course they knew I hadn't been smoking and therefore wasn't really part of the decision regarding who should take the blame, but my suggestion appealed to them and they accepted it.

Now I too, didn't like the idea of getting the cane, particularly 'six of the best' any more than they did, but I told them I would own up and tell Pinhead that I was the one who had been smoking, and that it was I who had thrown the cigarette butt out of the window. I would also say that the rest of them hadn't been smoking at all.

For this confession and for me taking the blame, they would each have to pay me a shilling on Friday, after they received their pocket money.

They all quickly agreed, and that was all there was to it.

That night in bed, as I well remember, I stewed and stewed, thinking about the prospect of getting the inevitable cane, and a full dose at that. Then, after more deliberation, I wouldn't feel so bad again, because on Friday I would be in pocket an extra three shillings, which seemed to make my concerns and anxiety more bearable.

The next morning, after Pinhead had said the morning prayers, he told the entire school that four boys had been found smoking in Somerset dormitory. He didn't need to say how serious this was; everyone knew.

SUFFER LITTLE CHILDREN

He also went on to say he was going punish them to the full extent of 'The Book'.

He then called out our names – Longman, Foley, Goodger and Foot – and told us to go straight to his study after breakfast.

I remember Baggy coming to me and saying how I didn't smoke and what was I thinking of, being caught smoking in the dorms. I told Baggy the story and what was going on, and that I hadn't been smoking.

He said he wouldn't have taken the cane, even for three shillings. I argued that I knew it would hurt, but it would all be over in just a few minutes. Baggy laughed and said something like, "I know, just like hanging."

Still, the die was cast. I had agreed to be caned, and that was that.

After we had finished our breakfast we went to Mr Wheatley's study and stood, nervously waiting to be called in. After a short while, Revd Corbett came out and beckoned us to come in. Sitting at his desk, Mr Wheatley looked quite stern as the four of us filed in and stood in a line, facing him.

Revd Corbett stood beside Mr Wheatley, on his right-hand side. Being the deputy headmaster, Revd Corbett, if possible, was always present when any of the boys were to be caned.

Pinhead again told us of the seriousness of anyone smoking in the dormitories, the dangers of fire in this centuries-old building, and the possibility of lives being lost. He also confirmed that a severe caning was the prescribed punishment for such an offence.

I happened to be the first one in line coming into Mr Wheatley's study, and therefore the first one to be questioned.

"Well, Longman, do you admit to having been smoking in the dormitory?" Pinhead asked.

"Yes, Sir!" I replied nervously.

Pinhead then asked Goodger, "And you, Goodger, do you admit to having been smoking in the dormitory?"

"No, Sir!" replied Goodger. "I wasn't smoking, Sir!"

Pinhead then asked Flappers, "Do you accept being caught smoking in the dormitory, Foot?"

"No, Sir!"

Pinhead, looking a little surprised, then asked Fuzz, "Were you smoking in the dormitory, Foley?"

SUFFER LITTLE CHILDREN

"No, Sir!" he too replied.

Mr Wheatley looked down at his desk and spent a few long seconds scribbling something on a piece of paper and, looking over the top of his glasses, said, "Now I'll give you all just one more chance. I am going to ask you all once more, and if I find you are telling me lies, you will be punished again for telling lies, as well as for smoking in the dormitory. Is that clear?"

We all agreed that we understood, and only hoped that no one would be honest and tell the truth.

And so, he asked us all the same question again; and again, with the exception of myself, they all said no, they hadn't been smoking.

Then Pinhead told me to stay and told the others that they were dismissed, and that they should go to their 'shops'.

After they had left, Mr Wheatley relaxed a little and said he didn't believe I had been smoking, but that if I insisted that I was he was going to cane me, and asked, as he always did when a boy was about to be caned, "Will you accept your punishment?"

I again told him I had been smoking and that I would accept the punishment. Pinhead always asked, "Will you accept your punishment?" which on reflection, seems so civilised. Such was the integrity of Goldings and its administration under Mr Wheatley's authority, as headmaster.

I was told to come around to the other end of the room, and then the big chair was rolled out. I felt I knew the procedure pretty well. I had been caned several times before, but not 'six of the best'.

I then bent over the chair, holding on to the arms, and waited. The Revd Corbett stood beside me on the opposite side to Mr Wheatley. He hadn't said a word all through the proceedings.

Pinhead gave me six good heavy strokes with his cane and on each stroke I jumped back with a shout. As only boys receiving such punishment would know, it really does hurt.

We would all shout. Only in movies, I believe, do you ever see a boy receive strokes of the cane without uttering any noise or displaying any stressful emotion.

Mr Wheatley, not really believing Flappers, Foley or Goodger, as I was to find out later, told me, while I was still jumping around with my hands comforting my bum, to tell the others of the importance of

SUFFER LITTLE CHILDREN

not smoking in the dormitories, and then he dismissed me.

Fuzz, Goodg and Flappers each gave me the 'bob' they owed me. The story went around the school in no time, and for a short while I was something of a hero, but only for a couple of days, and then it was all forgotten.

A few days later, as I was going into one of our scripture classes, Revd Corbett winked at me, and with a knowing smile asked,

"How much did they pay you, Reg?"

He knew, as did Pinhead, he said, that I wasn't the one smoking and that the others couldn't have bullied me into saying I was, so I must have been paid.

I don't remember Goodger or Foley ever smoking again, but Flappers did. He probably smoked in the dormitories too if he thought no one would see him but, to the best of my knowledge, he never got caught smoking again.

~o~o~ State Fair ~o~o~

The picture, *State Fair*: the 1945 version, starring Jeanne Crain and Dana Andrews, was a favourite picture of mine. I think I had first seen it with Baggy and Fred, when we lived in Eastbourne. Now that State Fair was showing here in Hertford, at the Castle cinema, I wanted to see it again and I wanted Fuzz and Goodg to see it too. So, I told Goodger and Foley about the picture and said I would 'treat' them both to see it.

To me, Jeanne Crain was so beautiful. I think I fell in love with her. I even sent away to the J. Arthur Rank studios for a photograph of her.

As I recall, someone from the J. Arthur Rank Organisation wrote back to me and told me they hadn't made the picture, but they obtained a photo of her, had it signed, and sent it to me anyway. Perhaps it was because they saw that I was a Dr Barnardo boy that they went to the extra trouble.

We were only allowed to go to the pictures on Saturdays or Wednesday evenings, never on Sundays. On Sundays we could go into Hertford, but never to the pictures.

Fuzz and Goodg were particularly nice to me following my telling them I was going to treat them to the pictures. After all, they were going to see "one of the best pictures I have ever seen", I had said.

SUFFER LITTLE CHILDREN

Anyway, after we had arrived at the entrance to the Castle cinema, I broke the news to them that I didn't actually have enough money to pay for them to go in, but that I had a plan.

Immediately their faces became sort of 'cloudy' or should I say 'cheesed off' and so, of course, they gave me the gears and argued, saying that I said I was "going to treat them", and me, the lying hound, arguing that I had said that I was going to take them to the pictures, not actually pay for them.

They really weren't too happy with me. The silly chaps actually thought that I was going to pay for them to go into the cinema the proper way. I remember we argued for quite a while.

Eventually I told these two ungrateful little sods what my plan really was, and that they should listen carefully. The plan was that I would pay for myself to go into the cinema, and that they should go around the back and hide behind the bush that was there. After a little while I would come and let them in the back door, so they should be waiting and watching for me.

They countered with: all I was doing was inviting them to dodge in, like we did most times we went to the pictures.

Anyway, after pointing out to them that this was still a treat, they agreed to go around the back of the cinema, and wait behind the bushes outside of the emergency exit doors, for me to let them in.

They knew where the bush was that I was talking about. After all, they had hidden behind it several times before. Then they left, so that I could pay and go into the cinema. They had got over their immediate disappointment, and were now happy about the idea. After all, they were going to the pictures, and they were being 'treated'.

I paid my sixpence and was taken down to the front of the cinema to the cheapest seats. The picture had already started. I watched it for a few minutes, and then I went through the doors into the vestibule where the 'gents' toilets were. In the same vestibule were the emergency exit doors to the outside.

We had dodged into the Castle cinema many times just the way we were going to do it now, there just couldn't be a problem!

Opening the exit door I looked out, but there was no one there. I quietly called "Fuzz! Fuzz!" and then "Goodg!" a couple of times, but still

SUFFER LITTLE CHILDREN

there was no answer. So I went back to my seat and sat down again. I watched the picture for another few minutes and then I went back and looked out of the exit door again.

Still there was no sign of them. I looked and looked, and called out quietly to them again, but still there was no response. I believe I tried once more to 'treat' them, but still had no response, so I went back to my seat and sat down. I even stayed in the cinema and saw the picture all the way through twice, giving no more thought to Fuzz or Goodg.

When we went to the pictures in those days, we would always see two full-length feature pictures, which meant we would miss tea.

It was late when I got back to Goldings and, as was often the case, I wouldn't expect to get any tea.

Later, when I saw Fuzz and Goodg, they were pretty angry with me. They said they had waited for me to let them in for at least an hour or more, and I didn't come out to get them, or at least I didn't try hard enough. I told them how I had opened the door twice or even three times, and they weren't there.

They said they had seen me, but that the man in the projectionist's room had the window open and was standing there looking down, smoking. The projectionist's window happened to face directly in their direction, and the projectionist seemed to be looking down each time I had opened the exit door, and so they couldn't move.

We had, over the years that we had lived in Bayfordbury and Goldings, often dodged into the Castle cinema. Usually the biggest problem would be after we had actually dodged into the cinema, and whether the usherette noticed us or not.

~o~o~

Even to this day I don't know if Goodger or Foley ever went to see the 1945 version of *State Fair*, with Jeanne Crain and Dana Andrews. However, if they ever did, they would quite possibly have told their dates or even their wives perhaps, about how they were almost 'treated' to see *State Fair* by their rotten ole friend Reg, at the Castle cinema, when they were about fifteen years old.

SUFFER LITTLE CHILDREN
~o~o~ Mr Joe Patch ~o~o~

Joe Patch. I could never forget Joe. Joe was our gym master or physical training instructor. He was a short, stocky man with sparse whitish-grey hair, and somewhere between fifty-five to sixty years old I would think, when I was at Goldngs. Joe was a no-nonsense man and as fit as any man his age could be. What's more, he was as tough as nails.

Everyone, with very few exceptions, liked Mr Patch. Unlike the other masters, he insisted we call him by his first name, Joe. I don't know why we liked Joe so much. Even though he had a rather pleasant, round, ruddy face, he was often grumpy and didn't seem to laugh much, and yet I can't help but remember Joe as always having a twinkle in his eye. I must say though, that when he did laugh, his face was absolutely radiant and full of warmth.

I know that my description of Joe sounds rather contradictory, seeing that I have just mentioned that Joe often seemed quite grumpy. But that's just it. That's how he was and how I remember him. I believe most of us old Goldings boys would remember Joe much the same way too.

We would never see Joe without his Alsatian dog 'Wolf'. As well, Joe always carried a walking stick wherever he went. He didn't really need a stick, except it seemed, to give himself an air of authority, or perhaps to control Wolf.

The aptly named Wolf was getting on in years. He would, I believe, have been about six, or even seven years old, which is a fair age for a big Alsatian dog.

We always walked softly when Wolf was around even if he was on his lead, and particularly so if he wasn't.

We were constantly wary of Wolf, for we knew only too well that the darn thing could nip or even snap at us, for what would seem like no apparent reason.

Even so, he wasn't really a vicious dog 'chomping at the bit', waiting to get at us. No one, as far as I know, ever actually received a serious bite from Wolf. Nevertheless, it was a serious challenge to our bravery to go into Joe's little office if we had to go there for any reason, because Wolf would always be tied up to Joe's chair leg. Wolf could easily have pulled the chair with him to get at us, if he was so inclined.

SUFFER LITTLE CHILDREN

Joe would ride his bike slowly, from the village of Waterford where he lived – about a mile and a half away – because Wolf would be on its lead and tied to Joe's bike.

When Joe was the duty master and on patrol going from dormitory to dormitory, Wolf would always be there. Joe simply wouldn't be Joe without Wolf being with him.

During the war Joe served in the Army and had excelled as a boxer, as well as being a DI (drill instructor). Because of his army training maybe, he would really put us through our paces in the gym.

He liked to make us 'work out' on apparatuses such as the horse, the box, the parallel bars, the beam, wall bars, and wrestling mats. We also exercised using medicine balls, which were big, 14 to 15 inch diameter, heavy leather-covered balls, weighing in the range of eight to ten pounds each.

When we used the gym equipment, which was at least twice or even three times a week, we used it vigorously, a little like proper gymnasts do. We were made to run and vault over the horse or the box, and before our feet touched the ground we would 'dive and roll' and stand up on our feet, all in one continuous motion.

All of the boys, without exception, had to attend gym classes and try to do whatever Joe instructed us to do. The tasks or exercises expected of us would often look quite difficult, or even dangerous, but Joe wouldn't listen to our concerns. From time to time we would be concerned as to whether we could do the exercise safely or not. But Joe wouldn't allow any of us not to do, or certainly not try to do, the gymnastic feats he expected us to perform.

Joe was also our boxing instructor. When he was in the Army, Joe was a regimental boxing champion in about the ten or eleven-stone class. Boxing instruction was where Joe's no-nonsense reputation was most evident.

If during a boxing lesson demonstration, Joe said to a boy "Lead with your left at my chin", indicating his own chin, and if the boy punched and stopped short with his punch, afraid of hitting Joe, Joe would tell him again, "I'll tell you once more: lead and hit me, hard."

Joe, just as before, would have his right glove up, 'blocking', as though to defend himself.

SUFFER LITTLE CHILDREN

At the full extent of the boy's punch, Joe would deliberately drop his gloves, or guard, completely. If the boy's punch was too short, as was often the case – the boy, being fearful that he would actually hit Joe – then the boy would be in trouble. Joe, to show the boy that he must pay attention and do exactly what he was told, would say to the boy, "Defend yourself." Then Joe, who as well as being short and stocky was also very fast, would lead a fast and straight, solid 'left'.

A boy would rarely be fast enough to block a punch from Joe, if Joe wanted to make a point. As a result, sometimes the boy would actually get hit in the face, but not particularly hard. This way, we all learned to do just as Joe said. In his own almost 'joking' way, Joe would make it clear to a boy that he must box aggressively, but most importantly, skilfully.

But I wouldn't want the reader to begin to think that Joe was a bully; he simply wasn't. In fact, I would go as far as saying that Joe was, in my opinion, probably the most popular master at Goldings. I liked him very much. During the following years at Goldings I would have a lot to do with Joe, as I will explain later.

~o~o~

Regarding Joe and to digress just a little, I recall something that Joe once said regarding a question I once put to him.

For a short while, Flappers and I would work for Joe in Joe's garden. He would pay us about sixpence for an evening's work, or perhaps even a shilling for a full day's work on a Saturday. We mostly did weeding and digging. Mrs Patch would give us a piece of her home-made fruit cake and a glass of lemonade when we were hot and thirsty.

Once I said to Joe, "Aren't you worried, Joe, that someone will come and steal your Loganberries?" thinking of us boys and the scrumping we still did.

Joe replied, justifiably confident, "No, I don't think so. No one would steal my berries. I don't have to worry about that."

He was quite right, not just because of Wolf or even Joe catching them. They just wouldn't; the other boys at the school would see to that. Joe, even though he could be quite grumpy sometimes, was basically too popular with the boys.

SUFFER LITTLE CHILDREN

There's much more I will tell the reader later about Joe when I mention the Goldings' boxing team, and the vigorous standard of training we went through under Joe's training programme.

~o~o~ Gwendolyn Easy ~o~o~

One day Mr Wheatley sent for me, with instructions that I come to his study. When I arrived, I knocked on the door and was told to "Come in".

In the room with Mr Wheatley was a young, rather attractive woman in her very early twenties – perhaps between twenty-one and twenty-three. I can only guess she was about that age because I was to find out shortly that she was attending Balls Park Teachers College, in Hertford.

Actually, she didn't really seem particularly young to me at the time, probably because I was just a little more than fourteen years old and to me, she looked rather sophisticated and mature.

Mr Wheatley introduced me to her and said, "This is Reginald Longman, the boy I have been speaking about."

To me he said something to the effect that "This young lady is Miss Gwendolyn Easy, who would like to become your friend, and would like to take you out to tea with her from time to time."

He went on to tell me that Gwendolyn would like to make arrangements for me to meet her in Hertford sometimes, and that perhaps we could get to know each other.

I remember that I was very shy and surprised at being introduced to her, but at the same time delighted that this lovely lady was interested in me, and that she would like to be my friend.

Gwen, as she asked me to call her, smiled and came over to me and shook my hand. Immediately I liked her. She was soft spoken and there were no authoritarian attitudes about her. In fact, much like I, she was rather a shy person herself.

I believe now, when thinking back to what perhaps was happening at the time: that Gwendolyn just wanted to get to know a young boy simply because she knew nothing about boys. And as she was training to be a schoolteacher she thought, or had been advised, that because of her shyness, getting to know a boy would be an advantage to her in her career.

SUFFER LITTLE CHILDREN

If I'm not correct regarding the intent of her wanting to be nice to me, or any young boy, then maybe it was basically because she wanted to be nice to a Dr Barnardo boy. I really don't know.

It never at the time ever occurred to me that she wanted to merely be nice to an orphan. If I had thought that, I probably wouldn't have wanted to let her 'take me out'. We Dr Barnardo kids wouldn't have liked to have been pitied, or even thought of as being poor or underprivileged, even though, of course, we were.

Gwendolyn Easy was a bit taller than me, but not by very much. She had a slight build and, compared to myself, spoke with an almost cultured or 'posh' accent.

As I have mentioned, besides being quite attractive she was particularly nice. Everyone at Balls Park seemed to like her.

There were no romantic approaches or anything remotely like that in our association. She was, I'm quite sure, simply interested in knowing how a boy my age 'ticks', and how she could best understand my thinking.

Eventually she, like she might with a younger brother perhaps, took me back to her student quarters at Balls Park Teachers Training College, which was a college exclusively for young ladies.

Balls Park Teachers Training College at the time, was a very prestigious and renowned college in Hertford. There were several buildings, with as many as two thousand or so students in attendance there.

Gwendolyn introduced me as her "William Baker Technical School friend from Dr Barnardo's". She wouldn't have known it, but we boys still didn't want to be known as Dr Barnardo boys. But as there was no emphasis on the 'Dr Barnardo's Homes' reference, I don't remember this being of any great concern to me.

She often talked to me about my upbringing in Dr Barnardo's Homes, and how I came to be in the homes in the first place. We talked about Bayfordbury and Churchill House, and how it was, living at Goldings.

I remember her telling me that her home was in Hitchin, in Hertfordshire, which, unknown to me, was only about fifteen miles from Goldings. She also told me that she had a five-year-old brother, but we didn't talk very much about her family at all.

She would take me to the games room in Balls Park, where we would play table tennis with several other young ladies, who were her friends.

SUFFER LITTLE CHILDREN

There were students of various ages in the college, but the ones we had anything to do with were about the same age as Gwendolyn. I was a better table tennis player than most of them, and they made a fuss over how good a player I was.

Gwendolyn would take me into the cafeteria in Balls Park for dinner sometimes, and I would be on my best behaviour and "practise good manners", as we had often been told. The food there was much better than ours at Goldings.

As time passed, I got to know several of her friends. They were all quite interested in Goldings. One of the young ladies mentioned once that she would like to take out one of the boys, much like Gwendolyn was taking me out. For a while, I was trying to get her to take out Fuzz Foley. However, for one reason or another, it never happened.

From time to time I would meet Gwendolyn outside the Castle cinema and she would take me to the pictures, and then afterwards we would go for tea at a little café. There we would have bread, butter and jam, small cakes, and tea. On one occasion she bought me a pair of knitted woollen gloves as a present. We didn't have gloves in the orphanage, so these were a rather special present.

During the time that I was to know Gwendolyn, there was one event that I well remember, and she would too, for as long as she lives. It was all to do with a murder trial, in which I was a witness, and which I am about to write about.

~º~º~ Murder/Dickenson ~º~º~

Several months before I had been introduced to Gwendolyn Easy, and while I had still been in the junior cabinet making shop under the tutoring of Mr Dunning, a very serious event occurred.

As I had mentioned earlier in my story, there was a boy on the opposite corner of my workbench in Mr Dunning's class, whose name was Dickenson.

I suppose I saw quite a bit of Dickenson in my earlier days at Goldings, but only during the shop day. After shop I didn't really see much of him at all, he wasn't a particular good friend of mine.

Dickenson seemed to be just like any other boy to me at the time.

SUFFER LITTLE CHILDREN

Although we weren't special friends, like most boys, we got along just fine.

Then one day Dickenson actually committed a murder. It wasn't a sinister or a frightening murder, but it was murder nevertheless and, as would be expected, it put the school in a state of serious concern for a while.

It all started with Dickenson going into Hertford one day, breaking into the army ordnance store and stealing several weapons. Among the weapons he took were two 22 ga. rifles and a revolver, plus a few boxes of ammunition. In addition, he stole several 'thunderflashes'.

Thunderflashes are like very powerful fireworks, only these are much more dangerous, particularly so in the wrong hands. They were used in army 'field' exercises to simulate bombs or hand grenades. There is no shrapnel, nor are there any craters caused by thunderflashes, but still they were quite dangerous and therefore not available to the public.

Even though there must have been quite a lot of stolen items to carry, Dickenson nevertheless managed to bring the lot back to Goldings, perhaps even in two trips. Regardless, shortly after bringing the weapons back to Goldings, Dickenson and a few of his friends set off a couple of the thunderflashes in our 'top fields.'

To set off a thunderflash, all that had to be done was to simply remove a paper safety cap, and then strike the fuse end or cap of the thunderflash on an abrasive surface, much like a match is ignited. Then, just as one would throw a hand grenade, throw the thunderflash.

The explosion from the thunderflashes could be heard throughout the Goldings estate, but no one really paid much attention to them as the noise could quite possibly have come from one of the quarries in the area, or perhaps could even have sounded like a farmer or gamekeeper shooting a pheasant or perhaps at a fox.

As it was, no one investigated the sound of the explosions, and I can only surmise now that it was because such sounds were quite common.

Regardless, on the day that the murder took place, Dickenson didn't show up in the shop. Because he worked at the same bench as I did, naturally I would notice he wasn't present. Unless they were sick, which was pretty rare, boys seldom would be absent from their shop classes for no apparent reason.

Anyway, on that particularly memorable day Dickenson went on

SUFFER LITTLE CHILDREN

some sort of rampage. He took at least one of the rifles he had stolen, and waded across one of the two rivers that ran through the Goldings estate, and onto one of the small islands. The island was covered with rushes, some small trees and long grass.

There, Dickenson positioned himself so that he had a view of our mile-long entrance driveway, and actually fired the rifle at the Goldings Albion van. The shocked Mr Whitbread immediately reported the incident to the office or duty master, who in turn phoned the police. For whatever reason, perhaps because they were village policemen stationed in Waterford, they had to come on their bicycles, which took them a little while getting to Goldings.

The next thing that happened, we were to learn later, was that Dickenson left our grounds and went onto the main road just outside of the Goldings estate. The road, although still not a major road these days, runs between the town of Hertford and north London.

There he stopped a motorist, and told the driver that he wanted a lift. Then, just as the infamous highwayman Dick Turpin might have done, Dickenson pointed the rifle at the motorist and told him to take him into London, which is between ten and twenty miles away.

The motorist told Dickenson that he didn't have enough petrol to get to London. So Dickenson naively told the motorist to go and get some, and then come back. He would be waiting for him.

After the motorist had left, Dickenson, perhaps coming to his senses, realised the man wouldn't come back, so he returned to the Goldings estate.

As the story goes, and as it was described in court eventually, it was then that the serious trouble really started.

Turning a bend in one of the rivers on our estate, Dickenson saw a man fishing from the bank on the opposite side of the river. As he approached the man, he saw that the man was eating a sandwich, so Dickenson asked him for one of his sandwiches, or perhaps it was something else, to eat.

Not taking Dickenson seriously, the man told Dickenson that he wouldn't give him anything to eat and so there was something of an altercation. Dickenson supposedly got very angry and pointed the rifle at the man. Still the man refused to give Dickenson a sandwich. It was

SUFFER LITTLE CHILDREN

then that Dickenson, quite coldly it seems, shot the man, who had simply been fishing, dead.

Whether it was as the result of Dickenson shooting at the Albion, or because the motorist who Dickenson had stopped earlier had contacted the police, I really don't know, but the police were called nevertheless.

While all this was happening, we were up at the school, speculating as to what was going on, or talking amongst ourselves. Lots of us boys, including some of the masters, were outside their shops, listening to the muffled sound of gun shots, not too far from the school. Certainly what was going on had our attention.

We had heard the distinctive sound of someone firing a rifle, though we certainly didn't have any idea that it was Dickenson doing the shooting, or even that one of our boys was involved at all. We knew that something rather seriously wrong was happening, but we didn't know exactly what. All that we had heard to this point was that someone had been shooting at the Albion.

~o~o~

What happened next was that the two policeman, as the result of being informed, came on their bicycles from the village of Waterford to where Dickenson was, and saw him on an island located in one of the two rivers, and told him to give himself up. Dickenson fired his rifle at the policemen, but fortunately he didn't hit either of them.

I don't know if the policemen knew at that point in time, that Dickenson had already killed the fisherman. If so, I feel sure that they would have been far more cautious.

Eventually, however, while one policeman kept Dickenson's attention, the other one waded across the river behind Dickenson, and surprising him, wrestled the rifle out of his hands and arrested him.

A short while – perhaps an hour or so – later, several police cars arrived at the school. They searched everywhere for the weapons Dickenson had admitted he had stolen.

We could see Dickenson from a distance showing the police where he had hidden some of the weapons. He gave them, or the police otherwise found, several thunderflashes and a revolver. They also found

SUFFER LITTLE CHILDREN

ammunition under a holly bush, which was right beside our parade ground.

Then Dickenson was taken away in a police car and we didn't actually see him again for several months. In fact, the next time I was to see him was in court.

For the next few weeks there were several policeman on our grounds looking for additional weapons, which, if there were any, were apparently never found.

During the next week or so, the police interviewed boys who knew Dickenson and who had witnessed him with the thunderflashes.

It was then that they spoke to me. I would presume that Mr Dunning had told the police that I shared my workbench with Dickenson in the junior cabinet making shop. So, the police naturally wanted to interview me.

Eventually I was called into Mr Wheatley's study.

There were two police inspectors plus Mr Wheatley and another man present – probably a lawyer representing Dr Barnardo's Homes – during my interview.

One of the police inspectors asked me whether Dickenson had indicated anything unusual to me, or if he had told me anything that could assist them in their inquiries.

I told the police inspector that Dickenson had asked me, "How old do you have to be before you can be hanged?"

I then told the inspector that I had told Dickenson, "You have to be eighteen before they can hang you."

The police inspectors also asked me if there was anything else that might be relevant that Dickenson and I talked about, and I told them there was. I then told them that Dickenson asked me if I thought he was mad.

"And what did you tell him?" the inspector asked.

"'Yes!' I said. 'I think you are mad'," I told the inspector, and in the same breath added, "I didn't really think he was. It was just a joke. I had no reason to think he was mad."

Throughout the interview the police inspector took notes. I thought that was all there was to it and that I wouldn't hear any more about it.

A few other boys were interviewed in a similar manner to the way

SUFFER LITTLE CHILDREN

I was. Later I spoke to one of the boys who had also been questioned. He was an older boy, who was about to go out on a 'situation'.

~o~o~

To go out on a 'situation' meant to leaving Goldings (though the boy would still be a ward of Dr Barnardo's Homes until he became twenty-one years old) and go out into the outsiders' world to work in the trade that the boy had been trained in while at Goldings. A boy could be situated or sent almost anywhere in Britain.

~o~o~

The older boy apparently had, a week or so before the murder event had actually taken place, known that Dickenson had stolen the rifles etc from the armoury, and was being investigated by the police as being an 'accessory after the fact'. As it was, he could have been in very serious trouble.

The entire Dickenson event was the talk of Goldings for several weeks. We, the entire school, were told not to talk to any outsiders (probably the media) regarding Dickenson or the murder case.

It was all quite disturbing and hard to believe. One of our boys had actually murdered a man, and just because the man hadn't given him a sandwich.

Gradually, as the days and weeks passed, Dickenson and the entire event was beginning to be forgotten.

Then one day, several months later, I was again summoned to Mr Wheatley's study. He told me that I was to appear at the county assizes (court) to be held at the Corn Exchange in Hertford at the end of the month.

~o~o~

When I saw Gwendolyn shortly after I had been told that I was to have to appear as a witness in Dickenson's murder trial, she told me that she was aware of the whole Dickenson case. She told me that she had heard or had read that the 'Crown versus Dickenson' case was to he held shortly. She had also told me that she couldn't attend the court

SUFFER LITTLE CHILDREN

case for one reason or another, and so one of her friends was going to come and watch me when I was on the 'stand'.

On the day of the trial I dressed up in my Sunday grey flannel suit, grey shirt, grey socks, black boots, and I presume that I wore my Dr Barnardo's Homes tie. Mr Wheatley drove me and another boy down to the assizes.

The other boy in the car was the boy who had known that Dickenson had had the weapons prior to the murder taking place. He, too, was to be a witness in the case.

The other boy had, since the murder, gone out on a 'situation' somewhat under a cloud. Being about seventeen, he was older and because he had witnessed the thunderflashes having been set off, should supposedly have reported Dickenson. He might even have known that Dickenson had also stolen the rifle that had murdered a man, and not reported it.

However, I believe the court was advised by Dr Barnardo's lawyer defending Dickenson, or perhaps by Mr Wheatley, that under the unwritten 'code of conduct' which prevailed in orphanages, actions like 'snitching' or 'ratting' by boys, under any circumstances, just wasn't done.

I don't remember any further discussion regarding the other boy, so I presume there was a measure of understanding given, and that he was perhaps cautioned and dismissed. Whatever happened, I never heard any more or anything further about him again.

~o~o~ The Murder Trial ~o~o~

As it was, I waited with the other boy in what I suppose was the court's witness waiting room for several hours it seemed. There were probably other witnesses, but none of them were boys from Goldings.

I must have been quite relaxed, sitting in the waiting room before actually going into the court, as I clearly remember studying the detail of the beautiful wall panelling in the room. This type of fine woodworking was what we were learning in our cabinet making shop at Goldings. I could see how the veneers had been 'book matched', how the joints in the panels were made, and how well the French polishing had been applied.

SUFFER LITTLE CHILDREN

After quite a long time of waiting in the witness waiting room – it could have been even a day or so – I was eventually ushered into the courtroom and shown into the witness box.

I was 'sworn in' and the judge explained the need for me to tell the truth. The judge was either very wise or may even have known a little about us Dr Barnardo boys. I believe, even though it was one of us Dr Barnardo boys who was on trial for murder, that he clearly knew the difference between the borstal boys and us.

Mr Wheatley was in the courtroom and gave me a reassuring nod.

I wasn't to know at the time how important my testimony was. It never occurred to me, and nor did I have any idea, if I was getting Dickenson into trouble or not. I simply told the court what I had told the police inspector several months or even a year earlier in Pinhead's study.

The judge asked me if I knew Dickenson. I looked at Dickenson, who in turn was sitting quietly in the prisoner's dock looking at me. He didn't look threatening; nor did he look like a murderer. I certainly didn't feel concerned about him.

I answered the judge and told him that I knew Dickenson, and that I had shared the same bench with him in Mr Dunning's class.

Gwendolyn's friend told Gwendolyn that she thought I spoke very confidently and clearly. She also told Gwendolyn that she thought I spoke quite a lot, even though perhaps I shouldn't have at times.

The judge asked me if I had had any previously conversations with Dickenson that would be of interest to the court – or something to that effect. I told the judge, who seemed to be speaking just to me, that "Dickenson asked me if I thought he was mad."

The judge then asked me, "And what did you tell him? Did you tell him you thought he was mad?"

"Yes, your honour," I replied, and then very quickly added, "But I didn't really…" and then I rationalised my answer by adding, "But I didn't really think he was mad, your honour, because you wouldn't tell a madman he was mad, would you, your honour?"

I remember there was a lot of chuckling at that point. Even the judge smiled, which made me look around the court, grinning shyly, no doubt. I suppose I had unknowingly asked the judge a question.

SUFFER LITTLE CHILDREN

After the court had settled down again, the judge asked me if there was anything else that was said between Dickenson and myself.

Then I told the judge the other thing Dickenson had asked me and said, "Dickenson asked me how old he would have to be before he could be hanged."

The judge asked me how I had replied. My next response also brought a chuckle from the court because I spoke so positively. "I told him 'eighteen' your honour, because I knew."

After the normal formalities the judge dismissed me, and I returned to the waiting room.

When I saw Gwendolyn next, she told me that her friend had told her that I was funny in court. She asked me about Dickenson, basically out of interest, but unfortunately I couldn't tell her very much about him. I couldn't because he had always seemed somewhat mysterious to me, and I realised that I didn't really know him very well.

Dickenson, being just fourteen years old at the time of the murder, was sentenced to 'imprisonment to the King's pleasure', which we understood meant that the authorities could keep him in prison for as long as they wanted to, in order to rehabilitate him back into society.

There was no time limit as to how long Dickenson could be in prison, as is the case with anyone who is sentenced to 'the King's pleasure'.

A few months later, after being sent to a prison in Cambridge, Dickenson escaped. We at Goldings were told to report any sightings of him to a master, and were also told how it was an offence not to report him if we did see him.

Most of us were aware of the other boy, who almost got into serious trouble for purely knowing Dickenson had stolen the rifles and thunderflashes and hadn't reported it. We were made to understand the seriousness of not reporting such a situation.

Fortunate as it was, we didn't need to have given too much thought about reporting Dickenson, as the unspoken code regarding 'snitching' didn't have to be tested, because, to the best of my knowledge, no one at Goldings ever saw Dickenson again.

A short while later, because Dickenson was so young and had no knowledge about the outsiders' world or where to get food, much like when we used to 'do a bunk'; he was caught and sent back to prison

SUFFER LITTLE CHILDREN

again. I was never to hear anything more about Dickenson again.

I must admit that it had crossed my mind that Dickenson might have come looking for me, because he had seen me in court and maybe thought I had something to do with him being sent to prison. But a short while later I, like most of the other boys, apart from remembering the entire incident, forgot all about Dickenson completely.

Apart from the murder trial, there isn't much more to tell about Gwendolyn. We were simply good friends for a while. One day, possibly because she graduated or for whatever other reason, she left Balls Park and, sadly, I never saw or heard from her again.

~o~o~

Many years later, after I had immigrated to Canada in 1957, I wrote to Mr Wheatley asking him the whereabouts of a boy who had come to Canada directly from Goldings, named 'Kit' Carson.

Pinhead wrote back to me and sent me Carson's address. The address in Montreal was no longer in existence for some reason or other, so I never did get in contact with 'Kit' Carson.

However, Pinhead seemed pleased to have heard from me and asked me several questions regarding how well I was doing in Canada. In the same letter, he recalled and wrote about my appearance as a witness in the 'Dickenson case'.

He said words to the effect that I had been very forthright and outgoing in court, which was quite the opposite of my normally shy character.

~o~o~ The Old Man and Flappers ~o~o~

I, as far as I know, was the only boy at Goldings, except one, to have, in Gwendolyn, a fleeting benefactor and a friend from the outsiders' world wanting to befriend one of us orphans on a personal basis. Strange as it may seem, the one exception was Flappers. Really, apart from myself, I don't know of any other boy at Goldings or any other Dr Barnardo's home for that matter, who had an outsider come to take them into their homes or to the pictures, give them small treats or in other ways be interested in them, like Gwendolyn was to me. Perhaps there were

SUFFER LITTLE CHILDREN

others but I wasn't aware of them.

Right now, while remembering him and just how he was, I could almost imagine that that sly old Flappers had found his 'benefactor' himself, but, of course, he couldn't have done, and nor would he be allowed to.

Regardless, how Flappers was chosen to have an outsider friend, I really don't know.

For whatever reason, Flappers was very fortunate to have been selected. Maybe it was because Pinhead knew that Flappers, as I have explained earlier, had no family or anyone in the entire world who had any interest in him. Perhaps it was for that reason, and for that reason alone, that he was chosen.

Somehow, there was quite a difference though, between his new 'adult friend' and my Gwendolyn. Gwendolyn was a pretty, young lady with lots of class, whereas Flappers' friend was an elderly man with one leg, who walked with the aid of a walking stick.

As it was, one day Flappers told me that a man was coming to take him out to the pictures. A short while later an older man, in his late seventies or early eighties, came to visit him at Goldings.

The man was no doubt a very nice chap. Unfortunately he had lost one of his legs and now had a wooden one. It could have been that he had lost his leg as the result of something that had happened during one of the wars, like on the battlefield or during an air raid or almost anything like that. He always used a thick walking stick with a fox's head carved in the handle.

It was also quite possible too that the old man had lost his son during the war, and found some solace in being able to give some affection to a boy like Flappers.

The man would often bring Flappers boxes of chocolates – something that we in orphanages would otherwise never get or even see. We would buy ourselves chocolate bars with our pocket money and sweet coupon, but never a box of chocolates. The old chap quite possibly used his entire sweet ration on Flappers. I don't think I ever knew the old chap's name.

One day Flappers' new friend took Flappers and me out to the pictures. We saw what was at the time a rather scary film, and even to this

SUFFER LITTLE CHILDREN

day I can still remember what it was about, though I don't remember what it was called.

Why I remember the old man and why I am writing about him, is because of something very good and heart-warming that happened to both Flappers and the old chap during our school's inter-house annual swimming competition. As it turned out, it left me with a lasting impression, which I have often thought about from time to time.

~o~o~

Each year, Goldings would have an inter-house swimming competition, which was held in our school's swimming pool.

The swimming pool was fairly big, being about sixty feet long and thirty feet wide. It was about eight to nine feet deep at the deep end, and no less than three feet six inches deep at the shallow end. We also had a 'springboard'.

About once a month or perhaps every six weeks, the pool had to be drained and cleaned because the water would become so murky that when a boy dived into the pool he would become immediately invisible beneath the water, and another boy could easily dive on top of him.

There was no water circulation or filtering system for the pool, and so the pool would become stagnant and alive with literally millions of little red worms. When we touched the sides or the bottom of the pool, we would feel these slimy little worms everywhere. To clean the pool required all the boys from the entire house, almost a full day to complete the task.

~o~o~

Anyway, back to Flappers. Flappers was not thought to be, and nor was he, a particularly good swimmer, but during this year's inter-house swimming competition I was to be completely surprised and taught a very interesting lesson.

One of the boys – a boy named Simmons – was a very good 'over arm' sprint swimmer. He could beat anyone in the school in a freestyle race, save for maybe one other boy. We said that Simmons swam like our hero, Johnny Weissmuller – Tarzan.

SUFFER LITTLE CHILDREN

The other very good swimmer was Derick Morgan. Morgan, too, could swim 'over arm' exceptionally well. There wasn't much between Simmons and Morgan, they were without doubt, the best two swimmers at Goldings.

Well, as was expected, all of us in Somerset House, just as they did in the other houses, entered most races.

Flappers' gentleman friend came to see 'his boy' Flappers in the races, and was given a guest chair beside the pool. Just as it was every year, there were a few relatives of some of the boys present to see the competition.

After several heats between the boys in each house, Flappers found he was doing quite well. In fact, he was doing so well he actually found himself representing Somerset House in the 'sprint' final.

Like the rest of the boys in Somerset House, I was emphatically shouting encouragement, and in particular to my friend Flappers.

Unfortunately, poor old Flappers was up against Simmons and Morgan, and three other finalists in the freestyle race, the sprint being the climax of the entire swimming tournament.

It was absolutely remarkable to see Flappers in this, the final of the fastest race of the competition, between the best swimmers in the school. I, like many others, could hardly believe it.

The six finalists all lined up at the end of the pool, ready to start. With Flappers' 'old man' cheering, and all of the Somerset House boys and masters shouting encouragement to Flappers, the big race was about to start.

Above the cheering, the starter blew his whistle and the finalists dived in to race one length of the sixty-foot pool.

Flappers, right from the start, swam like a torpedo, except not quite so smoothly. Even though he didn't look like a good smooth swimmer, because he splashed and splashed, creating huge waves in the water, he nevertheless swam fast.

Being the underdog, everyone cheered him on. He forced himself on and on, never giving up for a second and, to absolutely everyone's surprise, he came in first, with Simmons and Morgan right behind him.

Flappers turned around to look for the old man, his face beaming. The old man was standing up perilously close to the edge of the pool, cheering

SUFFER LITTLE CHILDREN

'his boy' non-stop. I, too, was very proud of my friend Flappers.

He had actually beaten Morgan and even Simmons, and had won the points for Somerset House and, of course, made his 'benefactor' so proud.

The freestyle sprint is comparable to running the hundred-yard dash in the track event, both being the climax of their sport.

Flappers' friend was overjoyed. I remember him hobbling over to Flappers and hugging him. It was so good for Flappers; there was no one in the entire world that could have cared more. It was almost like Flappers had found a father and that Flappers was the old man's real son. I always thought, and still do think, that Flappers performed for his adopted 'father' that day.

The lesson I learned on that special day was the power of support. Flappers did what I would have said was the impossible, just for that dear old man.

A few weeks later the old man died and Flappers, as I well remember, was very quiet and rather upset for several days after. Still, their association was nevertheless a very good experience for the both of them; they had both brought some happiness into each other's lives.

On reflection, I have often thought, did our headmaster, the wise Mr Wheatley, know what he was doing, finding this old man for Flappers? Now I believe, of course he did.

~o~o~ Silver Bugler ~o~o~

About two years after I had first learned to play the bugle, Parks, the silver bugler and sergeant in the band, left Goldings to go on a 'situation'. And so, as the result of there now being no silver bugler, there had to be a competition between a boy named Hodges and myself to see who was the best bugler and therefore the new silver bugler.

The band's drum major; Captain Skip Culver; and Mr Leroy, a semi-professional cornet player; carried out the judging to decide who would become the school's new silver bugler.

Mr Leroy was one of our masters who, besides teaching shoemaking, taught the brass band during the winter 'prep' season. In some circles Mr Leroy was known as a very accomplished cornet player. Besides

SUFFER LITTLE CHILDREN

teaching, he played his cornet in a well-established orchestra in London somewhere.

On the day of our competition, Hodges and myself were required to go up to the top fields, which was almost a quarter of a mile away from where the judging was to take place, and play several of the school calls.

Hodges was no doubt a good bugler, though to me personally, I felt that there was no feeling or melody in his playing. His playing of the bugle, I always thought, was harsh, and what I would call forced.

Several boys, including Goodg, said that they thought that I was by far the better bugler, but then, of course, Goodg, being one of my best friends, was no doubt a little biased.

So, as I have mentioned, Hodges and myself were told to go up to the top fields with the drum major, and play all of the school bugle calls individually, beginning with 'Reveille', then many daily calls commonly required of us, and then, finally, the 'Last Post'.

I remember that I played my bugle well, and when we came down from the top fields to meet up with Skip Culver and Mr Leroy, who had been listening and judging at the school's main entrance doors, both Hodges and I were informed that I had won.

The following morning after breakfast Mr Wheatley presented me with the silver bugle. It was a proud moment for me.

From that day on and for perhaps the next year or until the day I left Goldings, I had the distinction of being the school's, and the band's, silver bugler.

Skip Culver, as was expected, promoted me to the rank of sergeant of the band. I must say I was also very proud of my promotion, but I never doubted the fact that Parks was by far the best bugler that I had ever known, certainly up to that point in my life.

A short while later, probably as the result of some influence on my part, Goodger became a corporal in the band. Although he too was a fairly good bugler, Goodg never became the silver bugler. Fuzz was a very good kettle drummer, but never advanced further than being a lance corporal in the army cadets.

~o~o~

SUFFER LITTLE CHILDREN

Several years later, in about 1985 when our family owned a farm, I saw a bugle for sale in a local sale, and bought it. I still have the bugle, but can't blow a worthy note on it.

~o~o~ The Royal Tournament ~o~o~

During my time as the silver bugler, Goldings were fortunate enough to acquire Mr Walker, who had been a drum major in the Army, to come and train our band. Mr Walker had, just a few years earlier, been demobbed from the Army after serving in the Grenadier Guards. Immediately, Mr Walker was given the rank of lieutenant in the cadets.

Mr Walker had been a drum major and conductor for most of his army career, which probably accounted for much of his desire for teaching us boys how to perform as a disciplined band, and for us to become a top-performing bugle band.

At the time that we knew him, Mr Walker owned and operated a milk dairy in Ware. On certain days he would come to Goldings to teach us the finer art of performing as a band, including 'Display and Figure' marching.

After several months under Lieutenant Walker's direction, the band became more and more disciplined, and eventually we became quite an accomplished band. One organisation even sponsored us and bought us several new pieces of equipment, including a new leopard skin apron for the bass drummer and a new mace for our drum major.

Then, after all the hard work, our band was entered into competitions in several parts of southern and eastern England.

In one particular 'open' competition in a place called Hornchurch, in Essex, our band played and performed so well that out of perhaps fifteen to twenty bands, we came third.

This was a huge honour considering it was an 'open' competition, and entries came from all over the southern and eastern counties of England.

Our drum major, being an excellent showman was, as I have mentioned, Reg Howitt. At the competition he was awarded the first prize for mace-bearers for his performance.

Reg could throw the five-pound mace, which was about five feet

SUFFER LITTLE CHILDREN

long, twelve to fifteen feet into the air, and after it had twirled a couple of times he would catch it again, while at the same time he would be marching majestically in step and ahead, leading the band.

As the result of our coming third in the Hornchurch competition, we were selected to play at the Royal Tournament. The Royal Tournament is a command performance dating back many, many years, and is held each year at Earl's Court in London. Usually there is a member of the Royal Family present on such an occasion, and there was at the one we were performing in.

I played the marching solos on my silver bugle at the performance. It was quite an occasion, and obviously an extreme honour for our band to have been chosen to perform at Earl's Court, representing both Dr Barnardo's Homes and Goldings.

In contrast to other times, when we were so often in trouble, Longman, Foley, and Goodger were, this time, in good standing with the school and, together with the rest of the band, were recognised for our efforts. We took our school band very seriously and loved it.

SUFFER LITTLE CHILDREN

'Baggy' – Aged 15

Sgt. Reg (Silver Bugler) & Corp. Goodg
(REFER TO PAGE 433)

'Flappers' – Aged 15

Reg – Aged 15

SUFFER LITTLE CHILDREN

Army Cadet Bugle Band – Goldings
(REFER TO PAGE 435)

23

GOLDINGS – PART 5

~°~°~ Thursday Night Pictures ~°~°~

On Thursday evenings throughout the winter we would have 'pictures' shown to us in our gymnasium. Mr 'Snowy' White would be in charge of this activity, as well as being the projectionist.

Mr White, who looked a little like the puppet maker Geppetto in Walt Disney's *Pinocchio*, was 'getting on' in years. His hair was a brilliant snow white, and so he got the very appropriate nickname of 'Snowy' White. Mr White was primarily our science teacher, and so he was also nicknamed 'Tech' White as well.

The term or nickname 'Tech' was derived from 'detective', which was most appropriate because during our lessons Tech White always seemed to teach us science as though he was discovering things for the very first time himself, which to us was quite funny.

However, his nickname would be Snowy White at other times, and Snowy who would change the film at the end of each reel on our regular Thursday night picture shows. One reel of film lasted about twenty minutes and there were perhaps four, or even five, 18-inch-diameter reels of film for each picture show.

It would also be Snowy who would repair the film when it broke, which it often did. Once in a while the film would actually catch on fire, and we could smell the burning celluloid fumes, but I can't recall us ever having to have to vacate the gym because of it.

Where the reels of film came from, or who provided them for us, I don't really know. They were fairly old pictures – pictures like the 1929 film *Lloyds of London; Time of Their Lives*, starring Bud Abbot and Lou Costello; Laurel and Hardy pictures, and many other older pictures like that. Sometimes there were silent pictures, which we found somewhat disappointing.

All of the pictures, although they were old, were good entertainment for us. We enjoyed watching them for more than one reason. Besides

SUFFER LITTLE CHILDREN

watching these vintage pictures, we also had the opportunity to be moderately rowdy.

When these old film rolls broke, and they did quite often, we would laugh and boo, generally making as much noise as we could. Snowy White would work feverishly to mend the film or change the reels.

Just changing the reels would take at least five minutes. It sometimes took Snowy rather a long time to repair a broken film, and even longer if the film had caught fire.

Why the celluloid film caught fire, I'm not sure. Perhaps it was because of the intense light needed to illuminate the film, projecting the pictures onto the screen.

Snowy must have been a very tolerant man. He never, as I recall, ever became upset with our jeering, booing and clapping. The prefects would go around the rows of boys and try to stop us, but many of the prefects were just as bad as the rest of the boys in their charge. It was all mostly in good fun.

~°~°~ Academic Schooling ~°~°~

Something I hadn't mentioned was that besides our attending shop, we also attended a day and a half each week in academic schooling classes. During these classes we were taught the standard lessons, including English, arithmetic, science, history, social studies, geography, religious instruction, and physical education.

Our teachers: Mr Snowy/Tech White, Mr Misty Fogg, Mr Joe Patch and the Reverend Corbett, besides being house masters were also qualified teachers, and taught us most of the subjects between them. Unfortunately we weren't really very enthusiastic students.

We would for the most part behave fairly well. We wouldn't fool around in class excessively, under threat of punishment, and under no circumstances would we ever answer our teachers back.

The big difference between our academic schooling and that of outsiders' schooling was that we had no exams. There would be no counselling if we weren't doing well in a subject, and no one seemed to really care if we understood what we were being taught or not. This was perhaps the biggest single failing at Goldings.

SUFFER LITTLE CHILDREN

Regrettably there wasn't really anyone, except for our trade shop teachers, who were interested or encouraging in relation to our individual futures.

The end result was that our academic education left us lacking in many respects. Snowy White, for instance, would tell us how to weigh the world, or maybe I should say, how heavy the entire world was. The problem was that we didn't have a clue as to what he was really trying to teach us.

He would tell us that carbolic was poisonous, and yet we brushed our teeth every day with carbolic tooth powder. The only soap we used was red carbolic soap. My question could have been, "Isn't this a contradiction?" but because we weren't encouraged to ask questions, we didn't.

The Revd Corbett conducted lessons in what was called 'religious instruction' and 'Christian science'. I tried hard to understand what was being taught, but logic and so-called 'questionable facts', prevented me from comprehending or understanding Catholicism, and accepting the Revd Corbett's teachings.

I know the Revd Corbett tried hard to get through to us but, understandably, he had huge obstacles to overcome.

Many, if not most of us boys, had suffered so many unexplainable hardships up to this time in our lives, which in turn made it very difficult for us to understand the meaning of love and kindness, and what any of this really meant. It seemed that no one had ever really wanted us, and most certainly no one, in any sense or meaning of the word, loved us.

Of course we could read and listen to such teachings as are mentioned in the New Testament, such as St Matthew, Chapter 19, verse 14:

> *But Jesus said, SUFFER LITTLE CHILDREN, and forbid them not, to come unto me: for of such is the kingdom of heaven.*

All of this was very confusing to us orphans and other Dr Barnardo boys. Were we the 'children' Jesus was referring to? God, Jesus, Jehovah, the Holy Ghost, the Virgin Mary or by any other name – none of them seemed to even know we existed, let alone wanting to nurture us, or simply to love us.

Why one would "turn the other cheek", only to be struck again, was

SUFFER LITTLE CHILDREN

absolutely beyond our understanding.

In our understanding of life up to this point, it would have been easier for us to believe that we should treat other people like we had been treated, and that we should be cruel to the weak and rob even the poor.

By example we had never, with few exceptions, until coming to Goldings experienced any kindness from most adults. Even at Goldings, where understanding of boys like us was now evident, there was still no love as any outsider child would commonly have experienced, or expected.

But the Revd Corbett, as I may have already mentioned, was a tolerant man. A few years after I had left Goldings I found out that he had left Goldings and moved on to be the chaplain of the very prestigious Trent College in Derbyshire.

Trent College is a school associated with Cambridge University, where only the very fortunate, with plenty of financial resources, could go. It seems ironic that the Revd Corbett could have been the chaplain of 'our' orphanage, and then in just a few years become the chaplain of this exclusive college.

~°~°~ Prep School ~°~°~

During the winter months all of us boys had to attend three evenings a week of prep school. Prep school consisted of normal academic schooling, plus gymnastics, cadets or the brass band, and various hobbies such as leather craft.

On Monday evenings I and several of the school's boxing team (I will mention more about the boxing team later) would go to the gymnasium during the boxing season, and train with Joe Patch.

On Tuesday evenings I played in the brass band, with Mr Leroy teaching.

Wednesday evenings was a night we were allowed out, and we could, if we wished, go into Hertford. If we went into Hertford we would just walk around the town. None of the shops would be open after five o'clock in the evening. If any of us were fortunate enough to have any money, which wasn't very often, then we could go to the pictures. However, we, except for prefects, still had to be home and in bed by 8.30 p.m.

SUFFER LITTLE CHILDREN

Thursday evenings were picture nights in the gymnasium for everyone, including the staff and their families.

Friday evenings was mostly academic schooling. If we didn't go for academic schooling on Fridays for whatever reason, we could go on Monday or Tuesday evenings, depending on one's schedule.

Sometimes, on different nights of the week, we would go and play table tennis against other teams in Hertford. I played in one of the Goldings' table tennis teams for a year or two in the winter.

Playing in one of the school's table tennis teams meant that we would walk into Hertford after our tea and play against teams such as the Post Office, Hertford Town Hall, the Utility Works Dept, or one of several other council organisations in the town. There were four or five table tennis teams from Goldings who played.

Many of the boys at Goldings were fairly good table tennis players, and I believe we always gave a good account of ourselves.

The brass band, under the tutoring of Mr Leroy, was a bit of a rabble. Although most of us could play our instruments fairly well, none of us could read music, and I don't recall Mr Leroy trying to teach us how.

I played a cornet. Generally speaking a cornet plays the same notes as a bugle, plus many more, because unlike the bugle and like the trumpet, the cornet has 'keys'.

Even without being able to read music, many of us could play almost anything by ear. All we needed to be able to do, was know the tune well, such as Christmas carols and most hymns, then we could play the tune.

Mr Leroy would often, during our brass band prep night, play for us many of the solos, which he played in concerts in London from time to time. One piece of music I particularly enjoyed listening to him play was 'The Trumpet Voluntary'.

We, as a brass band, never gave a concert or displayed our talents, even for the other boys. We simply weren't good enough.

The compulsory academic prep nights, whether on Friday or Monday, depending on one's schedule, were primarily an extension of our academic school day. Whichever night it was, we thought it to be the worst night of the week.

Throughout the three and a half years I was at Goldings, except for the summer holidays, we attended 'academic school' one and a half days

SUFFER LITTLE CHILDREN

a week. The rest of the school days were spent in our respective trade shops.

~०~०~ Coloured Boys ~०~०~

Something which I have mentioned from time to time to people, when speaking of my days as a child in orphanages, relates to black boys in the homes. Throughout my early childhood in Dr Barnardo's Homes, I believe that I only came in contact with perhaps four or maybe five coloured children, including the little coloured girl I ran away with in Barkingside.

However, at Goldings there were at least five boys who come to mind that were black. They were all, with the exception of one, older than me, and although I didn't have very much to do with them, I found them to be really nice chaps. One of the coloured boys who perhaps I had a little more to do with, was a boy named Ritchie, who I will write more about later in my story.

Whether it was because they were older or not, the black boys seemed to be much bigger and stronger boys than most of us and so, as was their right in our unique society, they demanded plenty of respect.

No one would give them trouble but they, except for perhaps one whose name I can't remember, didn't give anyone else trouble either. They weren't bullies, even though I'm sure they could have been.

However, as in all orphanages, there were always quite a few bullies, but none of them that I can recall was black.

A rather interesting thing about them though, was, how we were expected to address them. Believe me, all of them were addressed as 'Nigger'.

The term 'nigger' was given to all black boys, just as a Welsh boy would be called 'Taffy', a Scottish boy 'Jock' or an Irish boy 'Paddy'.

In actual fact, I feel quite uneasy in today's world as I write and tell the reader that the black boys, even though it meant absolutely nothing to us at the time, were all called Nigger. Unbelievable as it may seem, that is how life was at Goldings and as such, I feel committed to write it just as it was.

To this day I can remember particularly Nigger Arends, Nigger

SUFFER LITTLE CHILDREN

McKinnon, Nigger Bardon and Nigger Horton. I recall Nigger Bardon as being an outstanding school boxer. He rarely lost a bout.

Believe me, what I am telling you is absolutely true and the way it was. No offence was ever taken to this derogatory, and now unspoken address. In fact in those days the black boys would more than likely have taken issue if we hadn't have called them by the established prefix to their names.

Shortly after Nigger Bardon left Goldings to go out on a 'situation', and to be otherwise 'free', he had to report to do his National Service in the armed forces. Sadly, one morning after prayers, Mr Wheatley informed us that Nigger Bardon had been killed in Korea after being there for just four weeks.

~o~o~

There were no prejudices that I was ever aware of at Goldings, and quite possibly throughout the entire Dr Barnardo's Homes system. I, and probably most of the boys, wouldn't have known if a boy were a Jew, Catholic, Methodist, or Protestant. We all went to the same schools and attended the same church or chapel services. If we had known that a boy was of a different race or creed, we wouldn't have really understood the differences, and nor would we have cared.

Actually, I did know that Baggy, one of my best friends was a Methodist, but I must emphatically say that it meant absolutely nothing whatsoever to me or anyone else.

As far as the 'dog eat dog' saying goes, the black boys were amongst the 'top dogs' in the school. Before most, if not all of the black boys left Goldings, they all as I recall, became prefects.

~o~o~ Ritchie ~o~o~

There was as well, one coloured boy from India, whose name was Ritchie. He was the only one, who, as I recall, we didn't address as 'nigger'. I can't as I write, understand why we didn't call him nigger, like all the rest of the coloured chaps, perhaps it simply was because he wasn't an African, I really don't know.

Ritchie, although he was older, wasn't as big as the other coloured

SUFFER LITTLE CHILDREN

boys and also didn't really look like a negro. His skin was quite dark, but wasn't quite as black as the other boys we called Nigger, and he didn't have crinkly hair. However, he was a school boxer and, as it happened, was in my boxing weight class.

~o~o~

One day, as the result of a minor default, Longman, Foley and Goodger, along with several other boys, were sent to help clean up part of the cellar. Ritchie, because he too was on a default and was our senior, though not a prefect, was put in charge of us. There were perhaps eight of us on default, and we were sweeping and washing the cellar floor and walls.

On this particular occasion, Ritchie told me to do something or other and, for whatever the reason, I said I wouldn't, in a defiant and challenging way. He and I argued and even though I knew he was a school boxer, I wouldn't back down.

I, not wanting to lose face in front of my friends, challenged him to a fight, not doubting for a moment that I could beat him.

Ritchie and I fought toe to toe, like all boys did whenever we fought each other, with the other boys standing around us forming a circle. Because we were in the cellar there were no masters to stop us fighting, and so it went on for a while.

Ritchie was far from being a walkover. Of course I knew, like we all did, that Ritchie had a reputation of being a good school boxer, but I just didn't have sufficient respect for him.

At that time though, neither Goodger nor I were learning or training to box, I was already thought of by most of my peers as being a good fighter, and I wouldn't give an inch to Ritchie.

As it turned out, I was quite wrong. Eventually, with a bloody nose and bruised face, as I recall, I gave up, dropped my fists and conceded that Ritchie had won.

This was a big loss to my pride, which I don't doubt I had plenty of.

I had lost face and a certain amount of respect from the boys in the cellar including, to some extent, Goodg and Fuzz for a short while.

As was normal in an institutional environment, my defeat quickly got

SUFFER LITTLE CHILDREN

around the school.

But that was life in an orphanage. Even at Goldings there was a 'pecking order', and I had just slipped a few notches.

~o~o~ School Boxing Team ~o~o~

A few months after my scrap with Ritchie, the army cadet boxing competition was about to start, and so we were all expected to put our names down to compete.

Age wasn't a factor in who we fought, but weight was. The winners of each weight among the Goldings cadets would go on to box other outsider army cadets in Hertford and the surrounding districts, and then on to box winners in the other adjoining towns and eventually counties.

Well, who would I be drawn against in my first fight in the ring? It was none other than Ritchie.

Needless to say, I was nervous having to fight Ritchie. Ritchie was one of Joe Patch's favourite boxers. Joe, at the time, had no interest in me; I wasn't in the school boxing team. Ritchie, on the other hand, was one of his 'boys'. Joe had high hopes for Ritchie continuing on in the cadet boxing competition, and even perhaps reaching greater heights.

I believe that Ritchie was pleased that he had been drawn against me, and that in the ring, where fighting was a controlled sport, I would be a walkover. I, on the other hand, had actually been hoping to be drawn against Ritchie. This would be the rematch that would, if I beat him, re-establish myself amongst my peers.

This time I would have more respect for Ritchie. I knew he had staying power and could fight. I had found that out the hard way.

Nervous and not overly confident but nevertheless determined, I climbed through the ropes into the boxing ring to face Ritchie. In Ritchie's corner, attending him as his 'second', was Joe Patch. Joe always attended his boxers. I only had one of our senior boys as my second. I remember the fight well.

The last time, which was also my first time in the ring, had been at Bedewell School in Eastbourne. I remember that on that occasion I fought with my two gloves together and both hands punching at the same time, like a double-fisted piston, with the gym teacher almost

SUFFER LITTLE CHILDREN

laughing at me.

This time would be different. The timekeeper announced, "Seconds out", and tapped his bell, indicating that the first round was to start.

I remember well that at the first sound of the bell, it was for me to either 'do or die'. I came out of my corner in what must have looked like a whirlwind. My arms swinging wildly, I went straight at Ritchie, driving him up against the ropes and keeping him there. Poor Ritchie; he couldn't get near me.

A typical amateur boxing match consisted of two two-minute rounds and one three-minute round. Boxing is a very exhausting sport and the rounds seem very long. But I fought all of the rounds just the same way. I didn't let Ritchie hardly breath or see what was coming; I was just so fast and swinging so wildly that I didn't give him chance to think or organise himself.

I don't believe that Ritchie got in one punch that landed properly. I felt pretty good, and I wasn't getting hurt at all. I just didn't give Ritchie any opportunity of hitting me, and most certainly there was no possibility of him beating me.

At the end of the fight, because I had landed so many more punches than Ritchie and therefore scored more points, I was announced the winner. Joe Patch was disgusted. I'm sure he didn't approve of the fact that I had won, but of course, accepted that I had.

Poor Ritchie, as they say today, was history. Having lost the boxing match with me there was no comeback for him, until next year.

After perhaps one or two more boxing matches and thus winning my weight class, I was told, not asked, to report to the gym for boxing training.

That was the beginning of my being taught to box by Joe Patch. The training was quite strenuous at first, and hard to get used to the idea of. But training for the army cadet boxing got me, like the rest of the boxing team, off some of the daily or routine fatigues, which the rest of the other boys were required to do, and so it was OK.

Goodg too, had won his weight class much like I had, and was also told to attend boxing training.

My next boxing match after winning my weight class, was to fight an outsider in Hertford. This resulted in a further win, and so it went

SUFFER LITTLE CHILDREN

on. We – myself and about six or seven other boys – trained in the gym almost every evening after tea time, until prep school. Every second day we ran a couple of miles, with Joe riding his bike and setting the pace. Wolf always accompanied us.

Possibly, the most outstanding boxer in the school was a boy named Ed 'Kit' Carson. Carson was an outstanding boxer, who eventually won all of his bouts and was to be in the army cadet finals to be held at the Royal Albert Hall in London. Unfortunately, a few days before the event, he came down with the flue and had to drop out.

~o~o~

In the school's boxing team were Baggy, Nigger Bardon (who, as I have mentioned, was later killed in Korea), Goodger, Nigger Arrends, Kit Carson and myself, and a couple of other boys, all in our various weights and all with the prospect of winning our boxing matches and advancing towards the Army Cadet Eastern Counties championships.

On several occasions, possibly to raise money for charities, we would be invited to go and meet other boys in our respective weights, in towns several miles away. Goldings had a very successful boxing team, and we came back with several individual and team medals from several tournaments.

On one unforgettable occasion, Baggy and myself were taken to Hertingfordbury, where I had been a choirboy, to be the supporting bouts for a professional match between Freddy Mills, the British middleweight champion, and another boxer who's name I can't recall. The entire event was a charitable event to raise money for something or other.

As it was, some boys were good cricketers, others good footballers, and others good at other sports, like swimming and athletics. If we were particularly good at any of these sports we were virtually made to pursue them and represent the school, whether we liked playing the sport or not.

Regrettably for me, the only sport I was any good at in particular was boxing. However, there's no fun in boxing really.

When I, or any of us stepped into the ring, we never expected our

SUFFER LITTLE CHILDREN

opponents to smile or be friendly. Like us, our opponents would also be nervous. They certainly wouldn't ask, "How are you tonight? Are you having a good time and are you enjoying yourself?"

Think about it: the object generally is to punch your opponent, mostly anywhere in the face or in the body to wind or hurt him, to make his nose bleed, or give him a black eye or a fat lip, all in the name of sport.

To step into a boxing ring is not exactly my idea of a fun evening out. On the day we were to attend a boxing match I would almost always be worried all day. Fortunately, I was always able to defend myself fairly well and, for the most part, win. But I was always scared stiff every time we were scheduled to attend a tournament

I can't say that I liked boxing at all. If the truth could have been told and I would have dared to, I would have told Joe that I didn't really want to box. I would have explained to him that I was always nervous, or even scared for that matter, for up to a couple of hours before I was to have to climb into the ring. One could never be sure if, or when it would be my turn to get a beating from one of my opponents.

Although I did on one occasion during a training evening, actually dare tell Joe Patch that I didn't want to box. Joe seemed somewhat disappointed but wouldn't hear of me or any of us even thinking of quitting. His rationale was that in football one could get a broken leg, or a kick in the head with a football boot. He would also point out that in the game of cricket we could quite possibly get hit with the rock-hard cricket ball and receive a broken nose or a cracked rib. But in amateur boxing, in our weights, the worst we might get would be a bloody nose, a black eye or a cut lip.

There was, of course, some truth in what Joe told us. No one in our weights and with our limited skills could really deliver a knockout punch or cause serious injuries, though a year or so later I did get a broken nose. My nose healed within a couple of weeks or so, but it left a rather large bump in the bridge of my nose, which I can still see to this day.

During my short career in the ring I never actually knocked an opponent out, or was I ever near to being knocked out myself. Usually boys won on points, and sometimes by a 'technical knockout'.

A 'technical knockout' simply means that the referee would determine that one boxer was just too good or too overwhelming for his opponent.

SUFFER LITTLE CHILDREN

So, the referee would stop the match and award a technical knockout to the superior opponent.

My abilities to box, I believe, included for the most part my ability to 'think' in the ring. I could remember after just a few seconds into the first round of a bout, what my opponent was doing and perhaps recognise what he wasn't doing right.

But mostly I attribute my ability to box to my speed. On several occasions I won by a technical knockout, but this was the result of my being particularly fast in the ring, and merely overwhelming my opponent.

One thing I do remember hearing in several of my boxing matches, was the referee often telling me, "Longman close your glove," and again a few seconds later "Longman close your glove." Often my left hand would open when I punched and my thumb would catch on the other boy's body somewhere, resulting in my thumbs hurting and becoming swollen. An open glove was a foul in amateur boxing, and at the discretion of the referee, could result in lost points.

So, without much choice, I kept on training and boxing, but still wasn't liking it. Upon getting into the ring, however, the 'butterflies' would leave, and I would be resolved to defending myself and fighting to win.

On reflection, apart from the traditional shaking of the hands and the 'touching gloves', there were no sporting gestures in the ring. The intent was to fight the other boy and try to hurt him as much as you possibly could. Of course, that was our opponent's objective as well.

I still believe there is no sportsmanship in boxing. Apart from having to be as fit as the fittest, and trained in pugilistic skills, boxing is primarily simply a primitive survival game, and much better to watch than to participate in.

Just imagine it. If one boxer gives another boxer a good punch in the face, of course he would see bright lights or even get a bloody nose, and it would darn well hurt. The receiver of the punch doesn't smile at the deliverer or the punch, and sportingly say, "Oh! What a good punch. I enjoyed that, but please don't do it again, though if you must, please don't punch so hard!"

SUFFER LITTLE CHILDREN
~°~°~ Goodg Took a Dive ~°~°~

We didn't always go as a team to boxing tournaments. Sometimes we were taken to exhibition matches performed at charity events, and only two, or sometimes just three or four boys, would participate.

One day, after we had been boxing for about a year, Goodger and I were taken to a boxing exhibition by car to a small town in Bedfordshire called Leighton Buzzard.

There were only the two of us who went to this boxing exhibition. It was a charity event to raise money for some cause or other, possibly even Dr Barnardo's. We were selected to represent our weights against other local opponents, from Bedford.

How well I recall this occasion. The air in the drill hall, where the competition was to be held, was full of cigarette smoke. In those days it was quite normal for the spectators to smoke in such places, and with as many as a hundred spectators present there would always be lots of smokers, and the smoke would hang thick in the air.

As we fought and our eyes became scuffed and bruised, they would sting to the point that they hurt. Of course the smoke would have affected our breathing too, certainly to some extent, no doubt.

Anyway, I remember someone telling us that the boy who Goodger had come to fight had a reputation of being pretty tough and fast, and that he really hurt his opponents. I remember too, how Goodger was so worried and fretted about what may happen. He, like myself, had overheard things that were said about his opponent's reputation, to the point that he was actually already scared stiff of the boy.

Until our little group: Joe, Skip, Goodg and myself, arrived at Leighton Buzzard none of us, even Joe, had ever seen the other boy box, and nor did we know anything about him. I don't really remember, other than rumour, how we found out about this other boy's prowess in the boxing ring.

Unknown to us at the time – Goodg and myself – this was intimidation at its best. After Goodger had heard about the boy and how good he was, the match was virtually over. It completely shattered Goodger's confidence, and scared the living daylights out of him.

I wasn't to box until after Goodger, so I was able to watch his boxing

SUFFER LITTLE CHILDREN

match. Goodg got into the ring, as did the other boy. I must admit that the other boy surely did look rough and tough. But then again, that was only the way he looked. None of us knew how well he would perform against Goodger.

After the seconds left the ring, the bell sounded and the two of them squared up and started to spar, each feeling the other out.

No more than a minute into the first round the other boy, leading with his left, punched Goodger in the face, but not, as far as I could make out, particularly hard. Goodger immediately went down flat on the mat.

It wasn't a knockdown like you see in the pictures; no one in our weights could, generally speaking, deliver a knockout punch and most certainly, not with a 'leading left.'

Commonly, if a boy went down it was mostly either a stumble or he tripped. Regardless, Goodger went down and just lay there pretending that he had been knocked out or stunned, and he stayed down. The referee dramatically stood over Goodger and counted him out.

I can still remember thinking how phoney it all looked, and wondered why anyone else couldn't have seen the folly in Goodger's dive.

We found out later that Joe Patch believed that Goodg had faked his knockout, and wasn't happy about it. But Joe understood the effect that intimidation could have on an opponent, particularly in a boxing ring, and he used Goodger's fight to teach us the valued effect of intimidation.

Goodger was really a very good boxer and in my opinion, and as Joe said, had the fight gone just one round, Goodg may well have developed a measure of confidence and even won the match.

Afterwards, I said to Goodg, "You were as good as him, you might even have beat him. Why did you give up so easily?"

Goodger replied, "I waited for the right moment and then I went down. I could hear the referee counting me out, but I decided to stay down."

We often joked about the entire incident, and I never let him live it down.

~o~o~

About fifty years later, in 2000, while Donna and I were visiting England, I met my now old friend John Goodger again, and reminded him jokingly of his 'taking a dive'.

SUFFER LITTLE CHILDREN

Maybe it was because his wife Christine was present when I recalled the story – I couldn't be sure – or perhaps it simply embarrassed him: I couldn't be sure of that either. Nevertheless, he said that he couldn't remember the event. I'm sure he did remember, because he could remember almost everything else we talked about including much of which I have written about in this book.

~o~o~

On the same day that Goodger lost his fight, I too lost my boxing match.

When we had arrived at the drill hall in Leighton Buzzard, sitting on the table in the entrance to the drill hall was just one trophy – a large silver cup – and several silver and bronze medals.

We knew what the medals were for; they were quite commonly awarded to winners and losers of the individual boxing matches. But we had no idea what the large silver cup was for. We weren't there as a team, and usually only teams won cups.

Unknown to any of us at the time of my match, including Joe Patch, the big shiny silver cup was to be presented to the winner of my boxing match.

I was to find out later that the local newspaper reported said, that from the spectators' point of view, the boxing match that I was in was a good, entertaining fight, and was the match of the night. For sure, it was a toe-to-toe fight, with neither of us giving an inch. The other boy, too, was fast on his feet and had good footwork.

I remember even to this day that I had put everything I had into that fight and fought well. I felt sure that I had won the match, though it was a close fight.

Then the referee raised the other boy's arm announcing him to be the winner.

It turned out that the chap I was fighting was a local boy from Leighton Buzzard, who had won most, if not all of his fights over the past two years or so.

Joe Patch said, while he was discussing my match with Skip Culver on the way back to Goldings in the car later, that he was quite sure I had won the fight, and that he was very disappointed in the decision.

SUFFER LITTLE CHILDREN

On reflection, it seems there was no way I could have won that boxing match short of knocking the other boy out, which, as I have mentioned, due to my weight, would have been quite unlikely. The only other way would be as the result of a technical knockout, but the other boy was too good for me to be able to win this way.

The following weekend one of our old boys, 'Brocky' Brocklehurst, who had been in Somerset House with me, had left Goldings just a few months earlier, and now lived somewhere near Leighton Buzzard, came back to Goldings to visit for the weekend. He brought with him a newspaper clipping from a local Bedford or Leighton Buzzard newspaper. The paper, with reference to my boxing match, said to the effect – that it was a very unfair decision, and that Longman from Dr Barnardo's Homes was the obvious winner.

The newspaper also reported that the big silver cup had been brought to the Leighton Buzzard drill hall with full expectations that my opponent would win again, and that the trophy would therefore be presented to him after our match.

And so, I received the loser's bronze medal for this, perhaps my most memorable boxing bout. Even though I lost that match, I kept that medal for more than sixty years as a keepsake. Eventually I gave the little bronze medal to our son Shane who now knows, as the result of his reading this book, its origin.

~o~o~

During my short period of boxing, I received about eight or nine silver medals for winning my matches, as well as perhaps a couple of loser's (bronze) medals.

Several years later, after leaving Goldings, I was to give all of my medals except one to the brother of one of my best outsider friends, whose family I lived with. The then six-year-old Danny Wood in Taunton, Somerset, took the medals to school and ultimately swapped them or gave them away.

I didn't pursue boxing in later years because I basically just didn't like the sport at all. It's not a fun sport and one doesn't really make friends doing it.

SUFFER LITTLE CHILDREN

When I, too, had to do my National Service in the Army, I boxed for a short while and attained reasonable success at it. But again, I didn't box because I liked it. Boxers in training in the army, had a pretty easy time and so, following my basic training and while I was doing my trade training, I boxed for a while to get out of guard duty and other similar duties.

The best distinction I achieved was reaching the Royal Signals regimental championships, but I was 'posted' before the championships actually took place, much to my relief. That was the last time I ever boxed. From personal experience I found that having boxed and having achieved some modest success at it, that it is not a sport to speak of one's prowess about, to friends or anyone else.

If one speaks of having played cricket, football, tennis, or other such sports, then such a subject is quite acceptable. However, sports like boxing, judo, karate or wrestling and such, are not viewed in the same way. In my experience, to speak of one's ability to box, is, I have always felt, an intimidating inference to one's aggressiveness, as compared to football and cricket, which are not pugilistic or martial art type sports.

With the exception of some very special outsider friends who I grew up with in my late teens, and who have become my lifelong friends, very few other people ever knew of my shortlived boxing ability.

~o~o~ Captain / Mr 'Skip' Culver ~o~o~

One of the most colourful and unforgettable masters at Goldings was Mr Culver. We seldom called him Mr Culver; we simply called him 'Skip'.

Skip was always a friendly and fun man to be around. He was very familiar with the boys, and most boys when they were around him, were always at ease. Everything except the army cadets was a joke to him, it seemed.

As I have mentioned previously, shortly after I arrived at Goldings Baggy suggested I join the army cadets. He told me I would get an extra tuppence a week pocket money, and that as a cadet I would be able to go to army cadet camp in the summer.

So, I joined the cadets, though Flappers never did. Shortly after Goodger arrived at Goldings, he too joined. I received my uniform, and

SUFFER LITTLE CHILDREN

a book containing information about what I was going to need to know about the army cadets. It explained that I would learn map reading, arms drill, communication skills, about cleaning and shooting a rifle – though I wouldn't actually be firing it – breaking down, cleaning and reassembling Bren guns, and many other things required to survive in battle.

We would have cadet training in groups of about fifteen boys, once a week for about two hours on certain afternoons. We would, amongst other things, practise 'arms drill' with .303 rifles. These were the same type of rifles used by the British soldiers during the Second World War, and which we used in the Army whilst I did my National Service.

Captain Culver, as he was known when we were actively army cadets, would tell us stories about his experiences during the war. Many of the stories he told were no doubt true and very interesting, while other stories were obviously made up, but nevertheless related to things we would have to learn about real soldering, in due course.

One such story he told us was regarding communications, and the need for accuracy in keeping messages precisely clear, and being relayed without changing anything. As Skip Culver told it, the story went like this:

> During the First World War, communications between the 'front lines' and the military chiefs 'behind the lines' conducting the battles, were so critical. Such communications were carried by dispatch riders – men on motorcycles.
>
> The communications were not written down for fear that the enemy could possibly shoot the messenger and intercept the messages. So, front line messages were commonly passed on by word of mouth.
>
> On this particular occasion the front line troops could see an opportunity to break through the enemy lines, but needed reinforcements to do so. As was the normal procedure in those days, a dispatch rider was dispatched back to headquarters, which was about twenty to thirty miles behind the front lines. The dispatch rider was told to inform the commanding officer at headquarters of the following brief, but critical message:
>
> "SEND REINFORCEMENTS, WE'RE GOING TO ADVANCE."

SUFFER LITTLE CHILDREN

Due to the great distance to be travelled, the dispatch rider had to pass on the message to another dispatch rider some eight miles away.

"SEND REINFORCEMENTS, WE'RE GOING TO ADVANCE"

The second dispatch rider then passed on the message to yet a third dispatch rider and finally, after going through five or six different dispatch riders, the message arrived at the headquarters, sounding quite different.

Whether it was due to the roar of the motorcycle engines or because the dispatch riders were tired, or that they didn't speak clearly, the message arrived asking the commanding officer to:

"SEND THREE AND FOURPENCE, WE'RE GOING TO A DANCE"

This was the typical way Skip Culver communicated with us boys. Everything seemed to be a joke, with a learning objective. I learned a lot from good old Skip. He, too, was a very popular master.

~o~o~ Army Cadets ~o~o~

On the first Sunday of each month we would have our army cadet parade. On these days Skip Culver became almost a different man: he would become the proud Captain Culver. He took the army cadet parades very seriously.

Boys had to be in full uniform, brasses polished, boots 'spit and polished', and our webbing belts and spats properly blankoed.

I, being in the band, was dressed in the same army cadet uniform, except it was enhanced with a colourful sash and a red, yellow and gold lanyard which was attached to my bugle.

Mr Wheatley, being the headmaster, was a major in the army cadets – a rank higher than Captain Culver's. Like Captain Culver, he too, on these special Sundays dressed in an army officer's uniform.

SUFFER LITTLE CHILDREN

When the 1st Battalion of the Hertfordshire Regiment – our cadet squadron – was called to attention by our regimental sergeant major, the silver bugler played the salute. It was all very grand, with lots of pomp and ceremony.

After an inspection by our Commanding Officer, Major Wheatley, the cadets – about a hundred and fifty strong – led by the band, would march as a squadron to the Goldings chapel, and after the morning chapel service, back to the parade ground again.

I'm sure we all looked very grand and Captain Culver was in his glory.

~o~o~ Cadet Camp ~o~o~

In early summer each year, we would go to a small place in Essex called Fingringhoe. That is where the army cadet camp was. Fingringhoe is just a short way from Colchester. In Colchester, there's a big regular army barracks, and a huge military cemetery.

Although unknown to me at the time, I was to find out many years later that my father was buried at Colchester, in the military cemetery there. There's a headstone over his grave noting that he died in 1939 serving his country, and that he was just thirty-four years old. His grave is numbered – seven.

While camping at Fingringhoe, we would primarily develop our training as army cadets and also practise our band displays, but mostly we would have fun. I remember that I was the bandleader Lieutenant Walker's 'batman' one year, – a bit like being his servant – and he gave me half a crown for cleaning his boots every day and for bringing a cup of tea to his tent in the mornings. Half a crown, (thirty pennies) was enough to take myself and a friend to the pictures perhaps three times.

Skip Culver did, however, have a bit of a dark side to him, which some would say was a bad influence on us young and impressionable boys. He would tell us how when he was in the Army, if anyone lost anything, then he, the soldier who had lost it, would go and find a replacement in another billet. In other words, get it back by stealing it from someone else. He called it 'scrounging.'

During our cadet camping period one particular year, there was a borstal army cadet company behind us, in the same field. Once, as

SUFFER LITTLE CHILDREN

I recall, no doubt as the result of Skip's influence, lots of us boys, and I mean lots, raided the borstal boy's tents and swiped everything we could find.

As with ours, however, there wouldn't be much of any value in their tents, as they didn't seem to have much more of any value than we had, probably because they simply weren't allowed to own anything while they were in borstal.

Borstal boys weren't orphans though, and very likely had parents or family who would replace things we may have stolen. At least it helps my conscience a little, to think so now.

Anyway, I remember that one of the boys had stolen a tube of toothpaste during a 'raid', because we all came to look at it.

We at Goldings only brushed our teeth with pink, dry carbolic powder. Toothpaste – the paste in tubes – was a rare luxury in those days, and most of us (unless Flappers and I had shoplifted it in the old days) had never even seen it before.

There were many other things stolen at that camp from the borstal boys, as the result of, I believe, Skip's influence and stories, all in the acceptable idea of scrounging.

It's ironic that we Dr Barnardo boys, who always claimed not to be thieving borstal boys, stole from those same borstal boys. It's rather sad in a way when considering that they didn't steal from us, at least as far as I know.

~o~o~ A Lesson in Integrity ~o~o~

In many ways Mr Wheatley, Snowy White, Mr Leroy, and Misty Fogg, who were 'gentlemanly' types of people, were perhaps somewhat more refined or more cultured than Skip Culver. Skip Culver was a rough-and-tumble type of man, full of 'smutty' jokes and sayings. Skip's 'smutty' jokes weren't terribly bad, unlike the dirty jokes of today. Such jokes as told today were never told in those days.

Generally speaking, people, and most certainly we boys, didn't swear, not even words like 'sod', 'hell' or 'bloody'. To be heard saying such words would be a punishable offence.

Skip had many standard sayings. One which I remember in particular

SUFFER LITTLE CHILDREN

which he often said while wandering through the dormitories, when he was the duty master and responsible for seeing we all got out of bed in the morning, was, "Up you get; no lying in bed stinking."

And the one he was almost famous for was, "Hands off your cocks, and on with your socks!"

My sons, in later years, often heard me repeat old Skip's saying in the mornings at our family farm:

"Come on; no lying in bed stinking." – But I didn't suggest the other one.

~o~o~

I only remember getting Skip very angry on one occasion. As the result of my getting him so angry I learned a very important lesson in my life, and also about life, and I always remembered it.

It happened one morning during a week when I was the duty bugler. Skip, being the duty master that week, came to my bed in the Somerset House dormitory to wake me up so that I would go and play 'Reveille'. It would have been about ten minutes to six in the morning.

I must have been tired, and simply went back to sleep again. After about fifteen minutes or so, Skip came back and again told me to get up, and that he had already called me. He also said that it was past six o'clock and I was late playing 'Reveille'.

I answered him back, and told him that he hadn't called me, to which he replied rather angrily that he had. Like a fool, I responded to Skip much like I would have if I was talking to another boy. I said rather loudly, "You're a liar."

To make matters even worse, besides being one of Skip's sergeants in the cadets, I was also a prefect, and all the boys in my dormitory could hear me.

Skip was very angry: so angry that he put me on report. This default must have been one of the last times I was to be put on report, and I certainly deserved to be.

The next morning Pinhead called out my name and said I was to report to his study. When I appeared before Pinhead, expecting to receive the cane, or even worse, to lose my prefect status, Skip Culver was also present.

SUFFER LITTLE CHILDREN

Mr Wheatley must have had a discussion of the entire event with Skip before I came into his study. Pinhead told me of the seriousness of speaking the way I did to a master, and that my calling him a liar was almost unforgivable.

He also said that ordinarily I would be caned. He then went on to say that Skip Culver had already forgiven me, and had asked that I not be caned or otherwise punished.

Then Mr Wheatley asked Skip to leave his study, and at the same time told me that he wanted to talk to me on my own.

After Skip had left the study, Mr Wheatley told me something which saddened me, and left me with sincere regrets for the way I had acted, and at the same time taught me a profound lesson. I was to remember the lesson Mr Wheatley taught me that day for the rest of my life.

Much like a father might tell his son, he told me how Skip Culver had served as a private in the First World War and had survived the hardships of fighting in the trenches, and also of some of the many hardships Skip had experienced in doing so, including losing some of his closest friends in battle.

In the Second World War, Skip had served as a sergeant in the Beds and Herts Infantry Regiment, receiving medals for bravery and for being in many campaigns.

As a sergeant Skip had been in charge and responsible for many men's lives whilst under fire in Africa and throughout Europe.

The point Pinhead brought home to me was that this worldly man, the man who I had disrespected and even called a liar – our Mr Culver, Captain Culver, Skip Culver or whatever we wished to call him – had far more depth and courage than most men. He had experienced life to a greater degree than most men that he, Mr Wheatley, had ever known, and had also devoted much of his life to us boys.

He told me that I should, with sincerity, go and apologise to Skip, and that would be the end of it.

So I went to see Skip, who accepted my apology and simply smiled but said little more, not, as far as I know, ever knowing what Mr Wheatley had spoken to me about.

I'll always remember the talking to that our wise old headmaster Pinhead had given me. I believe in many ways that the entire incident

SUFFER LITTLE CHILDREN

left a strong and lasting impression on me.

~o~o~

A year, or perhaps a little more, after leaving Goldings, I was required to do my compulsory National Service in the 'regular' Army, just as most young men at that time had to upon reaching the age of eighteen. As it was, I was instructed to report to The Royal Corps of Signals Regiment in Catterick Camp, Yorkshire.

After completing my basic training, I was the only soldier in our troop of thirty-five to forty men to be entered into a competition to determine the most accomplished or, as the honour was called, 'the Best Recruit', in our battalion of between five to six hundred men. Sergeant Johnson was my troop sergeant.

To put my accomplishment into prospective, I should explain that there are approximately forty men in a troop and about twelve troops in a Battalion – hence five hundred or more men in a Battalion.

Chosen as being the best recruit in my troop, I was entered into a competition with the best recruits from the other twelve troops in our battalion and won the distinction of being the Best Recruit. For this accomplishment, I was awarded a certificate for being the Best Recruit, as well as five shillings to spend in the NAAFI – Navy, Army and Air Force Institutes – (camp snack bar). This was really quite an accomplishment.

As it was, two battalions passed out at the same time, thus a total of about a thousand men were on parade.

One other soldier and I, just the two of us, 'passed out' as being the best recruits in our respective battalions.

I sent my certificate to Skip Culver for him to have; I knew he would be proud of it.

Several years later Skip gave the certificate back to me, believing that one day I would be proud of it myself.

Unfortunately, during my travels throughout England and other countries during my youth, I misplaced or lost this certificate.

24

GOLDINGS – PART 6

~○~○~ Girls and Dancing ~○~○~

There were many other boys of course, who were also my friends – perhaps not my closest friends, but friends nevertheless, and who had their place in my life at Goldings. One of the boys was 'Bosky' Stuart. 'Bosky', needless to say, was his nickname. I don't think I ever knew his real Christian name; he was simply called Bosky because he was 'cross eyed'.

Even with his crossed eyes though, I can remember Bosky being in the school cricket team. Believe me, he was one of the school's best cricket bowlers. Bosky Stewart was in Somerset House, his bed in the dormitory was quite near mine, so I knew him fairly well.

Amongst my other good friends, there was one particular friend I will always remember. His name was Brynley Webb, a Welsh boy. He too was in our dormitory, and was a particularly good friend of Bosky's.

Bryn was a very good-looking boy with raven black hair, just like Flappers and me. He, at about five foot eight inches tall, was taller than me. Eventually I was to name one of my sons 'Brynley', no doubt with my old friend Brynley Webb in mind. Fortunately for my sons, they're kind of lucky that it didn't occur to me to call any of them Flappers, Fuzz, Goodg, or even Baggy, or Bosky.

One day, girls from a girl's boarding school in Hertford were invited to Goldings to a ballroom dance. None of us boys had ever danced in our lives, or had even been given the opportunity to try.

Shortly before the day of the dance, one of the ladies in the laundry department and Matron, as well as a couple of other women, gave about twenty of us senior sixteen year old boys, dance lessons.

We paired off together to learn the rudiments of the quickstep, foxtrot and waltz. I remember during the dancing lessons that I danced with Foley. We, of course fooled around, both agreeing we were simply 'lovely'.

SUFFER LITTLE CHILDREN

The girls arrived as planned, but unfortunately, except for Brynley Webb and a few others, who had more confidence than the rest of us, we were mostly too shy to dance. I don't believe the dance was a particular success, and because of that, I don't remember that we had another one.

Other than at the dance, a few, but only a few, I believe, of us boys were at ease with girls. Those with more confidence in themselves as far as girls were concerned, would go down a country lane, which we called 'the short cut', and meet girls on a little humpback bridge which crossed over one of the small tributaries that ran into the River Lee. This is the same River Lee that we went swimming in when we lived at Bayfordbury, except that where I am referring to now is about eight to ten miles further upstream.

One of the boys I would see with one of the girls when we were passing the little humpback bridge, was a boy named Bloor – the chap that Flappers and I came to Goldings with from Eastbourne, a few years earlier. I didn't really have very much to do with Bloor, even though he was in Somerset House. He was quite a friendly chap, but just wasn't in my circle of friends.

Eventually, several years into the future, I was to learn that Bloor married the girl who he was with on the bridge. At the time of him getting married he apparently had developed an eye problem and was learning Braille, expecting to go blind some time in the future. Whether he did eventually go blind, I never did know.

As with many of the other boys I was friends with at Goldings, I don't know anything more about Bosky Stewart or Brynley Webb. I never saw or heard from either of them again after we all eventually left Goldings.

~o~o~ Ball Boys – Wimbledon ~o~o~

Every year following World War II, the Goldings boys would go to Wimbledon to be the 'ball boys' at the annual Wimbledon international tennis tournament, held in June each year.

So, for two weeks each year during two of the three and a half years whilst I was at Goldings, I too, together with about sixty or so other boys, were driven by coach every day through London to Wimbledon.

SUFFER LITTLE CHILDREN

A week or so before the start of the tournament, a representative from Wimbledon would come to Goldings and train us to do the required job of being a 'ball boy'.

These 'trainers' would come to Goldings each year in order to refresh those of us who had been ball boys before, and as well, to teach those who hadn't been ball boys before and who were not familiar with the procedures or duties of being ball boys.

Every day during the tournament we would arrive at Wimbledon, all dressed in our grey flannel long trousers, open-necked light-grey shirts, and green blazers. Then we changed into blue cotton gym shorts with elastic tops. As well, we wore white tennis shoes.

To be a ball boy entailed two boys standing at each end of the court behind the players, and two boys, each kneeling on one knee, one on each side of the net. There would always be six of us on a court.

We were instructed not to move during 'play'. After each point, depending where the ball was after a play or rally, the appropriate boy either side of the net, or at one of the ends of the court, would run as fast as he could to retrieve the tennis ball. We were also taught that we must always bounce the ball when returning it to the server, or 'store' the ball if we were at the opposite end to the server.

At the end of each game, the players would quite often shake the ball boys' hands if we were close to them.

One of the American players, Gussy Moran, was quickly dubbed 'Gorgeous Gussy' by the newspapers because she was extremely attractive. Gorgeous Gussy was very popular with the press, and they photographed her more than they photographed anyone else. They paid particular attention to her frilly-laced knickers, which made lots of sporting news headlines.

How well I remember the thrill of shaking Gussy Moran's hand. Being so small and particularly shy, I must have looked to her like Bashful, one of the seven dwarfs.

During my time at Wimbledon, besides Gorgeous Gussy, I also shook hands with Drobny and Sturgess. There were many more players whose hands we shook but Drobny and Sturgess, I believe, were the big winners and Gussy Moran, although she wasn't a big winner, was simply 'gorgeous'.

SUFFER LITTLE CHILDREN

So, just remember, if you have ever shaken my hand, then you have shaken the hand that shook the hand of the lovely 'Gorgeous' Gussy Moran.

~o~o~ Distractions at Wimbledon ~o~o~

There were quite a number of distractions at Wimbledon for us young boys though, one of which in particular, was quite embarrassing for us.

In the main courts 1 and 2, as well as in Centre Court, there were wooden stands, or bleachers, all around the court. These stands, about twelve to even fifteen levels high, rose sharply up from the ground level of the tennis courts. The seats were made of wood and so people would bring or rent cushions for their seating comfort.

The Wimbledon tennis tournament was, for one particular reason, a tough time for us young boys. Being the beginning of summer, the weather during those two weeks in June was often quite warm, even hot, but this wasn't the problem.

As a result of the warmer weather, young ladies and girls came to Wimbledon in short cotton dresses or skirts, and sat in the stands.

Without much difficulty, we could easily see up these girls' and ladies' dresses or skirts, and see things we could otherwise only imagine in a boy's orphanage. We would, with only our eyes, bring each other's attention to whatever attraction caught our eyes.

The result was that we, in our light cotton gym shorts, would become quite aroused, and have to stay knelt down beside the net on one knee for as long as we could – sometimes appearing to be slow off the mark – in order to not embarrass ourselves.

Unfortunately, while in the embarrassing condition we were in when a ball was hit into the net, we boys, still with our imaginations running wild, and our young 'manhoods' announcing themselves proudly, would have to stand up. Then we would run rather awkwardly into the middle of the court to retrieve the ball, with all the spectators watching.

Need I say more? Later, amongst ourselves, we would discuss our experiences and laugh, but at the moment of it happening, well, to say the least, it wasn't really funny at all.

Every day, each of us ball boys would receive, as well as our

SUFFER LITTLE CHILDREN

sandwiches from Goldings, a marvellous 'Lyons' fruit pie and a bowlful of strawberries and cream, all of which, for us, was the height of luxury.

Wimbledon, even to this day, is famous for serving strawberries and cream at their international tennis championship event.

~o~o~

At the end of each day, while the last match on Centre Court was being played and the other courts were finished being played on for the day, and the spectators had left to go home, we would walk up and down the aisles in the stands and look under the seats for items left behind by the spectators.

We would find such items as cameras, binoculars and wallets, as well as purses and coins. Most of the valuable stuff, like purses and wallets, as well as cameras, we would hand in, but loose change and the likes, we wouldn't.

The most common things we would find were umbrellas, men's trilby hats, women's hats, and sunglasses. None of these were much good to us and so we handed these in also.

Wimbledon – Goldings 'Ball Boys' – 1948
(I am the boy 6th from right, middle row)

SUFFER LITTLE CHILDREN

The newspapers always had good reports of us in them, regarding the Dr Barnardo's Homes boys' honesty, and how a boy had handed in something or other of particular value. They also had editorials stating how well disciplined and well mannered we were.

We were paid a shilling or maybe two a day each, which was put into our Goldings saving accounts. The money we saved would be given to us for when we went on our annual holiday to Dymchurch, in Kent, or perhaps, in my case, to my grandmother's house for my summer holiday.

~o~o~ The Browning Version ~o~o~

One day, after our regular Sunday morning chapel service, a group of well-dressed men and women were on the parade ground waiting for us after we had marched back from the chapel.

We were told that they had come to Goldings to select boys to appear in a J. Arthur Rank picture, to be made at Pinewood Studios in London.

Needless to say, all of us boys wanted to be in the picture. As well as it being an interesting experience, we would also receive extra pocket money. In addition to the money we would receive, it would be like a holiday, and a period of time away from our normal school activities.

The group from the J. Arthur Rank organisation passed up and down each line in each of our houses. As they passed each of us, and if they chose to use the boy for their picture, they simply tapped the boy on the shoulder. The boy then stepped out of his line and joined the other chosen boys at a pre-selected spot on the parade ground.

I, together with Baggy, Fuzz, Goodg, Stan Dean, and many more of my good friends together with about sixty other boys, were chosen to be in the picture.

Flappers, as was often the case, was not on the parade ground at the time because he, now training to be a chef, was in the kitchen preparing our Sunday dinner.

The making of the picture at the Pinewood Studios was a most interesting time for us. We could, with some restrictions, wander throughout the studio looking at new stage set-ups for upcoming pictures, including the now abandoned sets or stage for *The Blue Lagoon.*

The 1950 picture, called *The Browning Version,* is about a prestigious

SUFFER LITTLE CHILDREN

public school, a schoolboy, a schoolmaster being forced to retire, and his adulterous wife.

We, from Goldings, were the 'extras' in the school scenes, playing the part of being the students in this very exclusive public school.

The stars in the picture were Jean Kent, Nigel Patrick, Michael Redgrave and Wilfred Hyde White. All of these movie stars were household names in those days. The director of the picture was Sir Anthony Asquith, a very well thought-of picture director in his day.

When the picture was released it received excellent reviews and was given several recognisable awards, including the best actor (Michael Redgrave) and best screenplay honours at the 1951 Cannes Film Festival.

Many years later I was given a DVD of the 1950 version of *The Browning Version*, and have watched it several times. I knew exactly where I should be in one particular scene in the picture, and can see myself quite clearly. I can also see several of my old friends, or other 'old' boys from Goldings, who I remember well.

The 1949 picture *The Blue Lagoon*, with Jean Simmons starring in it, had just been made at the Pinewood Studios shortly before we arrived.

On one occasion, Jean Simmons visited our 'set' and we all saw her. She was beautiful, and again, I, as well as several other boys, sent away to the J. Arthur Rank studios for a photo of her. Upon receiving mine, I hung it in my bedside wardrobe. It hung there for a long, long time.

Prior to us being the extras in *The Browning Version*, our Goldings boys were also the schoolboys in *The Guinea Pig*, which starred Richard Attenborough and Diana Dors. I wasn't selected to be in that one, though.

~o~o~ Pets ~o~o~

Many of the boys kept pets. The school allocated an area, well away from the school, where pets could be kept. Boys made their own rabbit hutches, birdcages and open pens, resulting in the area looking like a miniature zoo.

Some of the pets they kept included jackdaws (a small type of crow), magpies, owls, rabbits, guinea pigs, and any other small animal or bird

SUFFER LITTLE CHILDREN

they could find or catch, as well as the usual mice and rats. One boy even kept a couple of young fox cubs for a while.

The jackdaws were easily tamed, particularly if we found a nest and could manage to take a chick straight out of it. Just like old 'Blacky' the rook that Fred, Baggy and I had at Bayfordbury several years ago, the jackdaws would, after they were big enough, be set free and allowed to fly anywhere they wished. They would, unless they were set free too soon, usually come back to their owners again.

It would be common to see four or five boys with jackdaws perched on their wrists, or on their shoulders as they watched a football match on the top fields.

The jackdaws would commonly fly anywhere they wished inside the school, even in our dining room. They would brazenly perch on the dining room heating pipes, which ran overhead. We would chase them away from being over our tables, for fear they would do their 'droppings' on us, or even in our food.

Feeding some of the animals the boys kept was often a problem. Rabbits' and guinea pigs' food, such as dandelions, cabbage, and many other vegetables, were easily obtainable, as was food for jackdaws and crows, but food for owls and foxes would be a different story. How the boys fed them, I can't remember. It's quite possible that these types of animals didn't last too long.

~o~o~ Dymchurch ~o~o~

Every year, during the first week in August, the boys who didn't go away to whatever families they had, would go in coaches to Dymchurch for three weeks of our summer holidays.

Dymchurch is a seaside village on the south coast of England, in the county of Kent. It was, at the time I was there, just a small village near the Romney Marsh. This is the same place where it is reputed that a headless horseman rides a black horse at night, and is up to no good.

Romney Marsh, like many areas and small towns in England, has many stories related to smuggling and romantic villains who roamed the countryside.

Pinhead never, as far as I know, ever came to Dymchurch with us.

SUFFER LITTLE CHILDREN

He and his family would go on holiday somewhere quite apart from us.

Masters like Skip Culver and several others would come with us, to take charge of us. This trip, or holiday for us, would not be a holiday for them, and so they would take their holidays later.

For much of the holidays we would simply spend time on the beach and swim in the sea, or if the tide went out far enough we would play football or cricket on the sandy beach.

Near Dymchurch is a small town called Hythe, which has possibly, the smallest and narrowest gauge steam train service in Britain. The miniature railway as it was called, was, while we were there, used commercially for transporting passengers between Hythe and Dungeness, stopping at the little villages in between to let passengers on and off. Actually it is still in operation.

Laurel and Hardy had the distinction of opening (or reopening after the war) this railway in about 1946. It cost very little to ride on the train – maybe a 'tanner' (sixpence) or less to travel the full length of its run of about ten to twelve miles. But even sixpence was far too much for us at that time in our lives.

Flappers, Foley, Goodger and I would often run beside the rather fast-moving little trains, and jump on. We would hitch a lift for as far as we could in either direction. Before arriving at the stations we would have to jump off again, so as not to provoke the station masters too often.

There weren't any conductors on the train, but there were station masters at the little stations who, even if they could catch us, I don't think would bother to do anything about us.

The camp at Dymchurch consisted of about fifteen long, wooden, dark grey huts, spaced in rows about thirty to forty feet apart.

The huts had been barrack huts for American soldiers during the war, and had now been abandoned by the Americans and handed over to the British government.

Most of the huts were empty and had probably been so since the end of the war. As it was, we Goldings boys occupied four of them. This was where we would come to spend our summer holidays.

At the end of each hut was a gaslight on top of a fifteen-foot high pole. Gaslights were very common in those days, and at night gave off a dim light, and with it, flickering shadows.

SUFFER LITTLE CHILDREN

If we dared go outside the hut after dark, which we were not allowed to do, we would crouch down below the windowsills, dodging between the huts. In the dimly lit night and if we were out of our hut, the atmosphere resembled a German prisoner-of-war camp, and our task was to avoid being seen by the guards.

Of course, it was not, or even near to being like a prisoner-of-war camp really, but by us just being out of our huts, we were taking risks and we most certainly didn't want to be caught.

~o~o~ To Maud, Love Victor ~o~o~

A short way away from our hut was a hut occupied by girls, who were about the same age as us. They were from a girls' orphanage (probably Dr Barnardo's Homes) which also came to Dymchurch for their summer holidays. It could be that, like us, they came every year. I don't really know. Regardless, most of us Goldings boys didn't, to the best of my knowledge, want anything to do with the girls.

I only remember the girls being at Dymchurch for one particular summer, and for only one reason.

The reason being, as well may be expected, one boy did have an interest in a girl, and that was my friend Fuzz Foley. Fuzz, even though he too was quite shy, was perhaps a little more aware of girls than me or Goodg, or any of my other friends.

As it was, Fuzz met one of the girls from the girls' orphanage on the beach or somewhere like that, and immediately fell for her. Her name, old-fashioned as it was, was Maud, the same name as my grandmother.

As I recall, she was a pretty girl, with a lovely oval face and a 'pageboy' haircut, typical it seemed, of girls in orphanages at that time.

Fuzz immediately, so he said, "fell in love" with her. He constantly talked about her to me, but he wouldn't speak to her or about her if any of the other boys were around. He would only wave to her from a distance.

Unlike outsider boys, in our exclusive type of society it was felt that to even want to know a girl was to be a pansy or a sissy.

One must remember also that girls played no part in our lives. We had, for the most part, absolutely no contact with them; we only ever saw them from a distance. Personally, I had absolutely no interest in

SUFFER LITTLE CHILDREN

girls whatsoever, and had no idea if any of the other boys did either, though I would say with conviction that they didn't.

While we were on holiday in Dymchurch that year, I remember the band putting on a display at a garden fete somewhere near Dymchurch. A garden fete is a little like a sophisticated garden party, where one could play garden games for money.

Skip Culver must have prearranged the band's performance arrangements, because we took our army cadet uniforms with us that year.

We marched in our smartly pressed uniforms through the little village, with its villagers and holidaymakers standing on each side of the street to watch us.

Fuzz played his kettle drum, proudly showing off for Maud. Both Goodg and I were aware of Maud and her friends giggling, and, I suppose, flirting with us.

It was perhaps the first time I became aware of any such girls' attention since June Chalkley, when we were at Ware school, and I was just nine or ten years old. I'm sure that such attention would have made me extremely shy and very bashful.

At the fete the band was treated very special much like minor dignitaries. We were given tea, which included small delicate sandwiches and dainty little cakes. Us urchins were not used to such delicately served food, and pretended to be 'toffs' or otherwise posh. To top it off, we were each given sixpence to spend. Maud and her friends couldn't come into the fete. They, being orphans like ourselves, had no money to spend and so they watched us, and in particular Fuzz, from outside the low, white picket garden fence.

Fuzz's first love was quite serious in its adolescent way. He was, without a doubt, completely smitten.

After the lights were turned off in our huts, Fuzz and I would stuff our clothes and pillows down our beds to indicate we were in bed asleep, then clad only in our nightshirts, would go to Maud's hut to talk to her from outside of her window, making sure no one saw us. We did this several times and each time more girls would come to the window, until there were perhaps six girls who came to talk to us, trying to get us to bring more boys. But none, even Flappers or Goodg, ever did.

As I have mentioned, there were risks being out of our billet hut

SUFFER LITTLE CHILDREN

after lights out, because if we had been caught by any of the masters we would have been punished. The punishment would probably have been our being confined to the hut for a day.

When we left Dymchurch to return to Goldings, Fuzz was upset and rather moody. He had got Maud's address and I know he wrote to her a couple of times, but eventually they stopped writing.

I don't know how it came about, but to this day I still have a photo of Victor 'Fuzz' Foley, dressed in his school blazer. On the front of the photo is written: "To Maud, Love Victor".

As I have mentioned, I have no idea, and nor do I understand how it is that I have this photo. It was given to Maud, I know, because I was there. Something must have gone wrong at some time, because Fuzz obviously had it returned. Anyway, he gave it to me and I've kept it all these years.

After we left Dymchurch and returned to Goldings that year, we never saw Maud again. Perhaps she never remained in the same orphanage, or, for whatever reason, she simply didn't return to Dymchurch the following year; and Fuzz never saw her again.

As I write, remembering Dymchurch and the happy, carefree holidays we spent there, the miniature railway, Fuzz and Maud's romance, as well as the huts we stayed in, it all seems so strange now, but at the same time, nice to remember.

~o~o~ Ah! Peaches ~o~o~

Flappers, after all this time since we had moved from Eastbourne to Goldings, still hadn't changed an awful lot in his behaviour, and was still the 'Artful Dodger' at heart. He still had that same vein of larceny in him that I had always known.

Changing his trade from gardening to that of learning to be a cook didn't help much either. Many times I would see him with more money than he should have had. He unlike the rest of us, had things like a new tie from time to time, cigarettes, a sheath knife, and even a camera, as well as other things, including an air rifle, which got him into lots of trouble.

None of the rest of us had, or could afford to buy any of these things, but Flappers had them. I never really knew how he managed to be able to

SUFFER LITTLE CHILDREN

obtain such things without fiddling. Thinking back, I don't recall us ever talking about how he got them, he basically had the things, like the things I have mentioned and we just took it all for granted. That was Flappers.

I knew he sold food from the kitchen, but to what extent, I wouldn't know. He also had a flourishing business selling cigarettes. Many boys sold cigarettes, one fag at a time, even though to be caught doing so would result in being punished.

After being caught by Mr Castle shoplifting, I had learned my lesson and was never involved again in Flappers' devilish dealings like swiping food from the kitchen and selling it.

But I have to admit that on one occasion Goodger and I helped Flappers a little, in order to swipe a tin of peaches.

We most certainly would have been labelled as being 'accessories after the fact', and had we been caught we, too, would have been punished for stealing.

Peaches in those days were the epitome of luxury, and they were only for the staff. I'm not sure that I or Goodg had ever up to this point in our lives even tasted a peach, so given the opportunity, we were prepared to go along with Flappers' plan to swipe a tin of peaches.

So, on this particular day, Flappers told Goodg and me that he had a tin of peaches ready for the taking. All that we had to do after dark was to go and get them.

It all sounded so easy. So we followed Flappers to the window near our ablutions. Actually this window was the window to the headmaster's larder, or maybe it may have been the storage room window to the staff food supply.

Regardless, when Flappers had left the kitchen after tea for the day, he had deliberately left open the window lock or catch, which otherwise would have secured the wired glass window shut.

Shortly before it was time for us to go to bed we decided to have our late night snack. Flappers showed us the window, which was fairly high, but not too high above the ground, and so between us we 'bunked' him up to it.

Flappers lifted up the now unlocked window, and reached in. On the shelf, just inside the window and where he had strategically placed it, was the big commercial-sized tin of peaches.

SUFFER LITTLE CHILDREN

Eagerly he took the peaches from off the shelf, and then jumped down to the ground, unintentionally dropping the can of peaches. The can landed on a piece of wood or something, making a loud noise, just as one of the masters was passing in the dark.

We stayed completely still. Fortunately, the master didn't see us, though I'm quite sure he heard the noise. Regardless, he continued on his way.

The three of us giggling, Flappers, having been completely unfazed by the master nearly catching us, picked up the tin and placed it between his knees. Then he stabbed the top of the can with a tin opener – the type that leaves a really jagged edge when the lid is cut. Goodg and I both sat watching.

With our mouths drooling at the prospect of our devouring these delicious peaches, Flappers then proceeded to lever open the jagged, half cut tin lid.

Well, we couldn't believe our luck, or otherwise bad luck. The peaches inside the tin were totally bad, and absolutely inedible, even for Flappers. The risk we had taken, and the planning Flappers had made, was all for nothing.

If we had been caught swiping the peaches, even though they were bad, we would most certainly have been caned and Flappers, no doubt, would have been kicked out of the kitchen for good.

~o~o~ Crazy Flappers ~o~o~

But that wasn't the only thing Flappers got up to.

One day, as I have briefly mentioned, Flappers managed to obtain an air rifle from somewhere. Quite possibly he bought the rifle with money he always seemed to be able to get, by perhaps being able to sell food and cigarettes or whatever.

The air rifle only fired small pellets, and although such a rifle was not thought to be a particularly dangerous type of gun, and certainly not a weapon when used responsibly, I'm quite sure we would not have been allowed to have one.

Certainly I had never seen any other boy with a pellet gun at Goldings, or any other orphanage, other than the one that Flappers had now.

SUFFER LITTLE CHILDREN

I don't doubt that I would have shot the air gun a few times, but to be quite honest I can't remember if I did.

When the problem occurred, Flappers hadn't had the gun very long and in all probability hadn't fired it very often either, though of course, he may well have when I wasn't with him. Certainly, he wouldn't have wanted to be seen with it, or, I believe, it would have been confiscated.

Anyway, shortly after he had acquired the air rifle he managed to get himself into trouble again, which, although it turned out all right, could have been quite serious.

In the corridor, outside our Somerset dormitory, there was a master's bedroom suite, and next to it was another staff bedroom suite, this one occupied by Matron.

The entrance doors to these quarters were side by side, and about eighteen to twenty inches apart. The doors being hinged, one left, the other right, meant that the doorknobs were approximately eighteen inches apart.

The masters at Goldings were required to do shift work. Some of them would have rotating or staggered shifts between the hours of 6.00 a.m. until 9.30 p.m. and so, needless to say, they had time off at certain points during the day. Flappers, knowing that these particular staff members were resting in their quarters, thought up a great idea, like only Flappers would.

So, on this particular afternoon, while we were all in our shops and no one else was in the dormitory, Flappers, thinking it was a great joke, so he told me later, opened the door from our dormitory into the corridor where the staff quarters were, and tied the two doorknobs together with an old necktie.

Then, from our dormitory door, he fired his pellet gun at the centre of one of the doors, and then he hid just inside the Somerset dormitory to watch what would happen.

When there was no response he fired another pellet, only this time he fired at the other door, and again dodged back inside the dormitory to watch through the crack in the slightly open door.

After a couple of more shots, Matron came to see who or what was tapping on her door, and found she couldn't fully open it.

Due to Matron pulling on her door, the master's door next to hers was rattling also. So naturally he came to see who was at his door, only

SUFFER LITTLE CHILDREN

to find out that he couldn't open his door either.

They both called out repeatedly for help, hoping one of the boys might, for some reason, be in our dormitory, which normally there wouldn't be, as we would all, supposedly, be in our shops.

Flappers, acting full of surprise, answered their distress calls and like 'our hero', came to their rescue and untied the necktie.

Like anyone would, they thanked Flappers for his help and talked to him, questioning why anyone would tie the door handles together, not at that time realising there were pellet holes in their doors. Then, unfortunately for Flappers, the master followed Flappers into the Somerset dormitory.

That was when it all became clear to them. There, standing up beside Flappers' wardrobe, poorly concealed, was the air rifle. So Flappers was 'copped' (caught) and his name put in 'the book'.

Of course I didn't see first hand what Flappers had been doing – I wasn't there – but he told me all about it later. He actually seemed quite pleased with himself, and did nothing but laugh about it.

He also told all of our friends about his bravado. Eventually the entire school knew the story. I don't think Flappers really saw the seriousness of his crazy actions that day but still, it really did sound quite funny at the time.

Mr Wheatley eventually confirmed the entire story when he told us how dangerous such a prank could be. Flappers, over sixteen years old now, received 'capital' punishment, and proved it by showing us the welts on his backside.

I believe now, fortunately, that by this time in my young life I had outgrown Flappers and his larcenous and crazy ways.

Nevertheless, Flappers and I were always very good friends, and we still had many laughs together. But by now, I believe, I could tell the difference between stealing and scrumping; and what was fooling around and what was reckless and simply wayward behaviour.

~○~○~ A Goldings Boy's Funeral ~○~○~

I don't remember any of us boys in Goldings being particularly ill or ever being hospitalised except for perhaps one, and in this instance it

SUFFER LITTLE CHILDREN

was particularly serious.

The one boy that I do remember being very sick, was so sick he actually died. Naturally, the entire school was very disturbed by the boy's death.

As we understood the situation at the time, the boy visited the school's sick bay suffering from stomach pains. Within a very short time – maybe a day or even less – the boy died right in the Goldings sick bay.

I can't honestly remember much about the boy as he wasn't a particular friend of mine. All I can remember about him was that he was my junior.

Mr Wheatley announced the death of the fourteen-year-old boy at our breakfast prayer time. The boy I believe, probably died during the night.

I remember that we were all shocked and somewhat worried, the death of the boy being the talk of the school. We had never known any of us boys to actually die.

Although many of us were from families where our parents had died, we didn't really understand that young people like us could die also. The prospect of such an event actually happening to us was simply not even considered.

We were eventually told something to the effect that the boy had been in the sick bay, suffering from what was called a 'blocked bowel'. A doctor had come from Hertford to our sick bay, but unfortunately it was too late. Apparently, there was nothing that could have been done to save him.

Because the boy was in the army cadets, he was given a military type funeral.

With many of the boys dressed in their army cadet uniforms, there was a full army cadet parade, with a guard of honour. The rest of the boys in the school, were dressed in their grey flannel suits.

The band played, and we marched to the chapel like we would on any Sunday. It was all very dignified. The coffin was brought to the chapel on a small hand cart, draped with a Union Jack.

I believe it was the boy's mother, as well as his young sister, who were present in the chapel, the boy's mother weeping quietly through much of the service.

On reflection, I can't help wondering that if the woman was his

SUFFER LITTLE CHILDREN

mother, which she quite probably was, how she would feel knowing she had never mothered her son, and now he was dead.

She, all through her son's young life, quite possibly or even probably, had never ever really known her son; or him, ever even given the chance to know her, his mother.

At the appropriate time Parks being the silver bugler at the time, played the 'Last Post'.

We sang the hymn that has the words from the twenty-third Psalm: "The Lord is my shepherd, I shall not want..." It was all very moving, with the boys hushed in thought. It was most certainly a sad and memorable occasion.

The circumstances of the boy being born, and then being brought up all his life in an orphanage and dying without ever really being 'free', is almost too sad to contemplate.

As regards his mother, who knows what she would have really been going through, or how much even, she really cared. But then again, who are we to rationalise or judge, not knowing the poor woman's circumstances.

25

GOLDINGS – Part 7

~∘~∘~ The Goldonian ~∘~∘~

Twice a year, Goldings published a small twenty-page magazine called *The Goldonian*, which every boy received a copy of. We were encouraged to write articles for publication in *The Goldonian*, but, as may be expected, very few boys did or were particularly interested in doing so.

The subjects encouraged to be written about were subjects related to our own houses, accomplishments in sports, short stories, poetry, and updates about 'old boys' who, in turn, had written to friends still at Goldings about their new found families etc.

We would also read about 'old boys' who were in the Army, Navy, or Air Force, doing their National Service and stationed in Palestine, Malaya, Germany, and even Korea, 'on active duty'.

The 'house notes' for each of the houses would include items such as house captain and prefect promotions, and about boys who had left the school to embark on their various 'situations'.

From time to time special accomplishments may have been achieved in the outsiders' world by one of our own Goldings boys, which someone at Goldings felt needed to be recognised.

If a boy achieved and was awarded his 'School Honours' for athletic achievement, playing football or cricket for the school or, as I did, in boxing, then we would be awarded a special 'Honours' recognition, which was sewn into our normal William Baker Technical School crest on our green school blazers. These achievements, too, would be noted in *The Goldonian*. I still, to this day, have my Goldings blazer Honours crest.

Goldings School *'Honours' Crest*

SUFFER LITTLE CHILDREN

~o~o~

On one particular occasion, when Pinhead had asked all the boys to "Try your hand at writing an interesting item for *The Goldonian*, such as a poem," I decided to give it a go.

Interesting as it is, the only item which I ever entered for publication was a poem I had written, which, for whatever reason, Mr Fogg wouldn't publish because he wouldn't believe I had written it.

Lying on our beds one Sunday afternoon, Goodg, Fuzz and myself put our minds to work, and tried writing a piece of poetry. The other two didn't have much going for them and didn't, as I recall, write anything worth entering for publication.

But after a few attempts, I composed a verse which, I have been told since, is quite reasonable.

The poem I wrote was as follows:

In Autumn, the leaves come tumbling down,
And as they fall, they twirl around,
Like snowflakes spread upon the ground,
They form a carpet, of golden brown.

That's it. It wasn't a particularly long poem. In fact, it's rather short, but I was quite proud of it.

Unfortunately, Mr Fogg, our English teacher and the master responsible for editing *The Goldonian*, and, as well, the person who decided what should or shouldn't be published in the magazine, wouldn't believe that I had written the poem, and in a sceptical way, told me so.

I tried to convince Mr Fogg otherwise, but to no avail. So, it was never published in *The Goldonian*. As a matter of fact, it was during my conversation with Mr Fogg that I learned the word 'plagiarism', and never forgot it.

However, even though it was only four lines and just a few words, I did get some satisfaction in knowing that I did write it myself. What too, was good for my ego, was the fact that Mr Fogg thought it was too good for me to have written, and therefore he couldn't publish it for fear that I had actually plagiarised it from somewhere or other, which, of

SUFFER LITTLE CHILDREN

course, I knew I hadn't.

To some degree Mr Fogg's opinion of my poem was, in a sardonic way, rather a compliment, and I'm satisfied with just that.

~o~o~

When I, with Donna, first revisited Goldings in 1987, some thirty-seven years after I had left there in 1950, I was given two publications of *The Goldonian* by an 'old boy', Jimmy James, who was actually one of the school captains during my time there. Jimmy still lived in Hertford after all those years.

There were actually three or possibly four Goldonians issued during my time at Goldings. I couldn't obtain the others, but the ones that I received are wonderful. They mention events like my winning the backstroke in the inter-house swimming competitions but, most interestingly, Flappers winning the 'sprint', with Simmons coming second.

~o~o~ Slap-up Supper ~o~o~

Whenever annual sporting events took place, such as athletics, swimming, boxing, football, and cricket, we competed, house against house, with all six houses participating. Only one house would emerge as the winner.

The winning house would receive what we thought was a fantastic treat. At the end of the month that any sporting event had been won, the winning house would receive a slap-up meal. To top it off, the special slap-up meal would only take place at about ten o'clock at night, when all of the rest of the boys were in bed.

The only other boys that weren't in bed were the boys serving the meals and waiting, like lackeys, on the winning house. These boys would be boys in the house that had performed the worst, or had finished last.

Why the slap-up meal was scheduled so late at night, I really don't know. Perhaps it simply added to the excitement of the occasion, and the fact that the boys in the house being honoured were able to stay up so late while the rest of the school was in bed with their lights turned out.

During the dinner there would be lots of chest pounding, with the

SUFFER LITTLE CHILDREN

boys who contributed the most points being recognised, and the 'Hip! Hip! Hurrahs' being voiced boisterously.

Even with meat, sugar, margarine and many other foods still being rationed, the meal would be something extra-special, with extra helpings of 'dog meat', 'plonk' or 'hardbake', mostly prepared by – now don't laugh! – my friend Flappers and our other oddball cooks.

A special feature of the slap-up meal was that we wouldn't have to file up to the buffet-style serving tables to get our food. The humiliated lackeys, as I have mentioned, would serve up the meals to the boys being honoured, at their table.

It was all good fun and there would be lots of fooling around. The housemasters, too, would get into the spirit of the occasion and even eat with us.

~o~o~ To Go on a 'Situation' ~o~o~

Towards the end of our time at Goldings, after an average period of about three and a half years or upon reaching the age of sixteen or seventeen even, and when we were also considered educated or perhaps mature enough, we would be sent out on a 'situation.'

Businesses in London and other cities and towns throughout Britain would send in requests for boys from Goldings to come to their firms to continue their apprenticeships, or to just go to work for them.

It was during my last few months at Goldings that Baggy was sent out on a situation to Dagenham, London.

He was given a situation (job) at a piano making shop, with the prospects of completing an apprenticeship there. In those days piano making was one of the most highly skilled trades in the cabinet making field.

To be a cabinet maker in the business of piano making, one needed a large range of hand tools, including moulding planes, nests of specialty saws, and fine scrapers – tools unique to such fine cabinet making work.

The type of apprenticeship the boys in the cabinet making shop were to be situated in would determine what tools they would be required to have for their trade. Mr Tempest would go with the boys to specialty ironmonger shops to select their tools. Tools for 'high class' cabinet making such as piano making or specialty furniture making were numerous

SUFFER LITTLE CHILDREN

and very expensive. Only top-quality tools would be purchased.

With all the tools selected, a tool chest had to be made. To meet his needs, the boy going to the 'situation', would make his own tool chest.

Baggy made a beautiful tool chest, big enough to hold all of the numerous tools purchased for him. The tool chest when filled with tools was very heavy, but there was no other way to carry them. All of the tools were provided and paid for by Dr Barnardo's Homes.

Most of us, including myself eventually, didn't get situated as well as Baggy, and instead of a tool chest, I received a simple toolbag.

So it was that John Baggaridge, who I had known as a brother since I was just seven years old, left Goldings to become a cabinet maker in a piano maker's shop in London.

We said goodbye, vowing to write to each other and, depending on where I would eventually be situated, meet up again in the outsiders' world.

Fortunately, we kept in touch and when I eventually left Goldings a few months later, I was situated in Edmonton, north London. I'll tell you more about that towards the end of my story.

~o~o~ Interview for a Situation ~o~o~

It was early November 1950 when Pinhead mentioned that I wasn't to go to shop that day. He told me that I was to report to his study, while everyone else went to their respective shops.

I can still remember the excitement I felt that day. I knew what was coming and that I would soon be leaving Goldings to go out on my own situation, and that was why I was to report to Pinhead's study.

Mr Wheatley told me that a situation had been found for me, and that I would be going to Stepney Causeway, Dr Barnardo's head office, for an interview within the next day or so. As well, Mr Wheatley gave me some advice and encouragement.

On the given date I was the passenger in the front seat of the Albion van, and was driven to Stepney Causeway in London. Mr Whitbread, the same Mr Whitbread who had brought me to Goldings about three and a half years earlier, left me at the Dr Barnardo's Homes head office, telling me he would return for me later in the afternoon.

SUFFER LITTLE CHILDREN

It must have been about midday when we arrived at Stepney. A lady in the office gave me one shilling and sixpence, and told me to go across the road to a café and get something to eat for my dinner.

I was now sixteen, almost seventeen years old, and this would be one of many 'outsider' experiences I was to have to get used to. I had never ever eaten in a café on my own before and having to actually have to pay for it, so this was a very first time for me. There would be many of these 'first times' for so many things.

Being alone and believing the other customers were staring at me, which of course, they might have been, I felt very self-conscious. After all, I was dressed in my grey flannel suit and probably had on my Dr Barnardo's tie and as well, was particularly shy. I must have looked like a Dr Barnardo's 'flag' sitting there.

Also I remember that I had 'bangers and mash' in the café. There were no eyes or solid lumps in the creamy mashed potatoes, and the sausages were crisply cooked. It was absolutely delicious. I think the meal cost exactly one shilling and sixpence.

After dinner I returned to the Dr Barnardo's head office, and met a man who was to give me a good 'pep talk', and to bid me farewell from Dr Barnardo's Homes.

I remember the talk quite well, and much of the advice he gave me. He told me never to drink alcohol, and showed me a picture of a man carrying a huge steel beam on his shoulder, with just one hand helping to support it. In the other hand he held a big glass of Guinness with a delicious looking foam head on it.

It was an advertisement. Under the man carrying the huge steel beam and the glass of Guinness, the advertisement read:

Guinness is best for you.

My interviewer emphasised that it would be better for me, if I interpreted the advertisement to read:

Guinness is best LEFT ALONE.

SUFFER LITTLE CHILDREN

I always remembered his advice that day, and although none of my future outsider friends or I were ever very serious drinkers I believe that I, unintentionally, heeded his advice to some extent.

Dr Barnardo, being a rather religious man, had emphasised and insisted that every one of 'his' boys and girls, upon leaving the Dr Barnardo organisation, be given a copy of the King James version of the Holy Bible.

As was his direction, I too was given a bible, which to this day I still have.

Inside the bible is a picture of my benefactor, Dr Thomas Barnardo, and a few words saying:

Presented to
Reginald Charles Longman
on leaving the Homes
With best wishes for his future welfare
and prosperity, from
his sincere Friend,
Dudley Evans
Chairman of Committee of Management
21st of November 1950

The 'man' then told me the date I would actually leave Goldings, which was to be in just a few days, and that 'digs' (board and lodgings) would be found for me. He also explained to me that I would be taken to meet my employer at Swallows Baby Carriages in Tottenham, north London.

Later, as prearranged, Mr Whitbread returned to Stepney Causeway to pick me up and take me back to Goldings. In the back of the Albion, what seemed at the time to be quite normal, were hundreds of loaves of bread and many, many pairs of boots and shoes to be repaired, which Mr Whitbread had picked up from other Dr Barnardo's homes in the London area while I was attending my interview.

Also, sitting quietly in the back of the Albion, amid the sweet-smelling freshly baked bread, and the sour-smelling boots and shoes, were two fortunate young boys who were about to start their new lives, under Mr Wheatley's wise and careful administration, at Goldings.

SUFFER LITTLE CHILDREN
~o~o~ Goodbye Goldings ~o~o~

Within a couple of days, Mr Wheatley announced after the morning prayers that Longman would be leaving Goldings to go out into the world, to a situation in London.

There was some, but not much sadness in my saying goodbye to Flappers, Goodger and Foley, who were at that time my very best friends, as there was no such thought that I may never see any of them again. We always knew our leaving was imminent, and that they too, at any time, could be summoned to Stepney to go for a situation.

Fuzz Foley had been a special friend ever since I had arrived at Goldings, and we knew everything about each other. We had been in so much trouble together – Longman, Foley and Goodger – that another book could be written just about us three, but that wouldn't be 'just' my story. Fuzz was one of my best friends, and I knew I would miss him after I left Goldings and he was no longer part of my life.

John Goodger, I had known even longer, much longer in fact than Fuzz, but as I would with Foley, I would, as life turned out and time passed, surely miss Goodg as well.

I had been friends with Flapper Foot since those early days at Bayfordbury, when he had first been dubbed Flappers by Mr Scougall. Calling Albert Foot 'Flappers' was probably the best act Mr Scougall ever did for me, as I couldn't think of Flappers being called anything else but Flappers. Flappers had that nickname all the time I knew him, and somehow, it was most appropriate.

Flappers, like John Baggaridge and myself including John Goodger, had all suffered physical abuse at the hands of Scougall and Nash for more than three and a half years, and had come through it all without too many scars on our characters.

But we had always known that the day would come, and that we would all, one day, be leaving Goldings for ever. We had often spoken of our leaving and how we would all meet up and continue our friendship until, we believed, the day we died.

~o~o~

SUFFER LITTLE CHILDREN

Finally my big day came. I was told to go to Mr Wheatley's study. Pinhead gave me his traditional 'farewell and best wishes' talk, and at the same time told me, just as he would have told all of the other boys leaving Goldings, that I would always be welcomed back to Goldings as an 'old boy'.

Then he gave me a package containing my ration book. Even in 1950 there were many things still on war rations. He also gave me some money to see me over until my first pay day, and to pay my landlady for my first week's 'digs'.

I wandered around the school and said goodbye to the masters and teachers, including Joe Patch, Skip Culver, Stormy Tempest, Snowy (or Tech) White, and several others of the staff. None of them seemed to have aged a day since the day that I first met them three and a half years earlier. I remember that I felt a particular sadness saying goodbye to good old Joe Patch.

As it was, they all wished me well and told me to come back and visit them, as a traditional 'old boy'.

That was it: my trade training as a cabinet maker at Goldings was complete and I now felt somewhat prepared to tackle whatever the future may hold for me.

With my same old blue kitbag (I can't think of what else I could have had) packed with new clothes, and my toolbag containing the tools Mr Tempest had chosen for me, I was driven to the Hertford North railway station by Mr Whitbread.

I had now finally left Goldings, the place I had grown to love and call home, and yet still couldn't wait to get away from. Now I was 'free', no longer to live in an orphanage with its constant, though necessary, discipline and rules. I was actually on my way to a new life with the outsiders, and to imminently become an outsider myself.

~o~o~

Besides the immediate changes about to happen in my life, I couldn't help but remember a sad and lonely little six-year-old boy, who so many years ago, with tears in his eyes, had stood under the stars outside of a small church orphanage in a small village somewhere in the heart of England. After seeing the first star in the dark sky, the little boy had

SUFFER LITTLE CHILDREN

made a wish.

It seemed like so many years ago now, when that little boy had made his wish. He had, from the depth of his soul, wished to be 'free'. At last he was now beginning to see his wish come true.

~o~o~

There's no doubt, as one could well imagine, that I would be somewhat apprehensive about leaving Goldings to go out into the big and mysterious world, not knowing much, if anything, about how the outsiders lived, but anticipating the challenges anyway.

After I arrived at Kings Cross Station a Dr Barnardo's Homes representative met me, and we travelled in his car through north London to Tottenham, to a firm called Swallows Baby Carriages.

Swallows Baby Carriages' primary industry was to make baby carriages and wooden toys. I was taken in to meet the factory foreman, and shown what I would be doing there.

The work I was to do was not really the cabinet making that I had been trained for as a craftsman to do – something which to me, at the time, was a little disappointing. However, they were all nice people and I looked forward to working there.

Then the Dr Barnardo's representative took me to Edmonton, and 26 North Road, also in north London, to meet my landlady Mrs Davis. I must have arrived at Mrs Davis's house at about two or perhaps three o'clock in the afternoon.

Shortly after the Dr Barnardo's chap left, Mrs Davis made me a cup of tea and gave me something to eat. She was a dear old lady, in her mid to late seventies I would think, who told me that apart from having another lodger, she had lived alone ever since her husband had died just few years ago.

Sometime around five or six o'clock in the afternoon I heard the back door open and, to my absolute surprise, who should walk in the back door, but one of our 'old boys' from Goldings: Reg 'Scoffer' Howitt.

Reg, you might recall from having read my story, was the drum major in our band – the same chap who had won the drum major's competition at Hornchurch when the band had come third in the south and eastern Counties open competition.

SUFFER LITTLE CHILDREN

'Scoffer' had left Goldings about a month or so earlier than me, and just after Baggy had left. He had been taught the trade of shoemaking and shoe repair. Students in the shoe making trade at Goldings were called 'snobs' just as cabinet makers and carpenters were called 'chippies'. Scoffer Howitt had been put into digs at Mrs Davis when he had left Goldings, and now worked in a little shop a tuppenny bus ride away.

It was good seeing Scoffer there. Although Reg Howitt was not a particular 'best' friend of mine (we all had our little cliques), he was nevertheless a friend and someone from the band who I knew very well.

He too was very surprised but pleased to see me, as he hadn't got to know anyone or make many friends so far, since he had left Goldings.

After my contacting Goldings, Pinhead gave me Baggy and Stan 'Dizzy' Dean's addresses in London. From then on, Baggy, Dizzy Dean, Scoffer and myself would meet most Friday evenings after work and spend time together, sometimes going to the pictures. From time to time we would go to an 'old time' music hall called the Finsbury Park Empire.

Scoffer and I had a great time living at Mrs Davis's house; she treated us like her family.

Baggy wasn't too happy with his situation or work, but was quite happy in his digs.

Dizzy Dean incidentally was a 'snob'. He told us how his landlady always only gave him two slices of bread and Marmite for his lunch, and how his boss in the shoe repair shop where he worked would say, when he saw Dizzy's lunch, "Ah! Chicken again then, Stan."

~o~o~ On Reflection ~o~o~

So, there it is. I have finished my story: the story of a little boy who survived the lonely and loveless upbringing of a parentless childhood; the story of a small boy who lost his mother at the age of three, and then, with the loss of his father, was orphaned at just five.

My story is not all sad, though at times it no doubt was. The sad times, not the least of course, were the loss of my parents and what could have been a family that I would have been part of, complete with my two sisters.

SUFFER LITTLE CHILDREN

Besides the turmoil in my young life, there were many, many good times and good friends, whom I shall always remember and cherish.

However, there were other heart-aching times, much of which, with proper administration from the higher echelons at Dr Barnardo's Homes, could and should have been corrected.

Such sad times would have to include times like losing 'best friends', which happened too often due to our being moved from 'pillar to post'. As well, there were the brutal times, such as was the case during our lives at Bayfordbury, and at times even at Churchill House under the incompetent care of the Fowlermotts.

There was also the sadness at not seeing enough of my grandmother, Auntie Molly, Uncle Sid, cousin Jill, and, of course, my sisters.

But Britain was at war, and many, if not most of the men and women who would have been the best caregivers for us children, volunteered or were drafted, and so had to go to defend our country. Unfortunately this left the unqualified and possibly mentally incapable people, or even the draft dodgers, to stay behind to look after the orphans and child casualties of war, who were in need of being looked after.

However, many, or most of those people dedicated to look after us, and who sustained, fed us, and nourished our minds, no doubt did a good or even an excellent job. Those people, like the Castles, Nurse Rand and the Goldings staff, I will always remember and be thankful that they were part of my young life.

Regrettably, the most damaging or memorable moments in our lives occurred, as I have mentioned, when our heartfelt feelings or young bodies were damaged or hurt by those unthinking and incompetent custodians.

Sadly, many Dr Barnardo's Homes children will sustain for ever, the damage caused to them by those few, no doubt unqualified and brutal staff commissioned to look after them.

~o~o~

But my childhood was not all sad. Besides surviving the ordeals of being physically abused, under the 'spare the rod and spoil the child' theory, there were the good times, and the compassionate people who

SUFFER LITTLE CHILDREN

cared for us.

My memories of the better-run orphanages, like Meriden, and Churchill House under the direction of Mr Castle, and, above all others, Goldings, will always be dear to me. These orphanages were in many ways comparable, no doubt, to the best orphanages in the world, whether part of Dr Barnardo's Homes or any other orphanage organisation.

Besides my resenting those who mistreated us children, I want to remember even more so, the compassion shown us by so many people, like dear old Mrs Dunning at Bayford School and her tolerant husband, Mr Dunning.

In particular, I will always remember my time at my never-to-be-forgotten orphanage, the William Baker Technical School, Goldings, Hertford.

As well, I cannot help but remember the staff at Goldings such as Pinhead – our wise headmaster Mr Wheatley – and the likes of Joe Patch, Skip Culver, Snowy/Tech White and Stormy Tempest. Another one I will never forget was my friend Miss Gwendolyn Easy.

These are the people to whom I owe whatever is good in my character, and who I am still beholden to. I can't, nor am I likely, to ever forget them. They help make the memories of my childhood and adolescence pleasantly warm to remember.

I will endeavour not to forget the good times and the 'best friends' who I met during my growing up. Special friends like Willy, who sadly, after his leaving Meriden, I never saw or heard of again.

As well to remember were my foster parents who had lived near Tamworth, in the tiny village of Wilnecote, whose patience I quite likely taxed to the limit as the result of my behaviour, but who I don't doubt remembered me fondly. Much to my regret, I never ever saw or had contact with them again after returning to Dr Barnardo's Homes.

26

DR BARNARDO'S HOMES REVISITED

~o~o~ 1957 – Canada ~o~o~

In 1957, at the age of twenty-three, I emigrated from England, to Toronto, Canada, with three other 'outsider' friends who I had met in Taunton, Somerset. After leaving England I was not to return again until 1987, some thirty years later.

In 1963 I married Donna Irene Scott, a Canadian girl, and together we had four sons.

Since 1987, Donna and I had, up to the time of the completion of my story, in 2010, visited England more than twenty-two times, staying for more than a month each time, and on one occasion staying for five months. During these visits to England we made several special trips to visit the orphanages in which I had been raised. Much had changed.

For many years now, Dr Barnardo's Homes has no longer existed as an institution for orphans. They do exist however, as a charitable organisation now called simply: Barnardo's.

~o~o~

We were, and have been, made very welcome in Barkingside by 'Barnardo's Aftercare' several times during the past decade. As the result of our Canada–England connection, we have made several lasting friends relative to Barnardo's Aftercare.

One of those particular friends was Collette Bradford, who for many years was the head of Aftercare. As well included, and who we, Donna and I have met over the years at Barnardo's and still call friends are: Anne Newill, Karen Fletcher, Lyn Clargo, Anne Maddieson, and in particular, Edna and Brian Partridge.

Donna and I have, over the years, assisted Barnardo's in Canada as volunteers, helping to obtain personal records for Dr Barnardo's Homes children who were migrated to Canada since the year 1882, by

SUFFER LITTLE CHILDREN

Dr Barnardo's Homes.

A particularly good and helpful friend of Donna's and mine, who recently left Barnardo's Aftercare, was Anne Newill. Anne, during her time working for Barnardo's Aftercare, was, being an extremely competent and dedicated social worker, particularly helpful in my being able to contact several of my old Goldings friends from those earlier years. Anne even found out the name and address of my dear old foster mother in Wilnecote – something which I shall always be grateful for.

During our visits to England, Donna and I visited all of the orphanages mentioned in this book that I could find or otherwise remember. As well, we visited Wilnecote, the foster home that I so fondly remember.

Visiting my old orphanages so many years after leaving them, I found it all quite emotional. Sadly, the old domiciles were either gone completely or undergoing major renovations, leaving them, to some extent, almost unrecognisable.

~°~°~ Barkingside ~°~°~

In 1987 Donna and I were invited by our good friend Collette Bradford, the then head of Barnardo's Aftercare, to visit Barkingside, Ilford, which is a suburb of Greater London. Barkingside, as the reader may recall, was the place, in 1940, where my sister Barbara and I were first admitted into the Dr Barnardo's Homes orphanage system, and where I lived for a very short time.

Today, Barkingside is the head office of Barnardo's which is now the UK's leading children's charity. The organisation changed its name from 'Dr Barnardo's Homes' to simply 'Barnardo's' several years ago as it no longer runs orphanages. However, they work with more than 190,000 children, young people and their families each year in over 800 projects in communities across the UK. Just as when I was in the Dr Barnardo's Homes system, there is still no discrimination or distinction between race, colour, or creeds.

The charity's work, I believe, includes counselling for children who have been abused, fostering and adoption services, vocational training and disability inclusion groups. The charity also campaigns on important issues, such as child sexual exploitation and child poverty.

SUFFER LITTLE CHILDREN
~o~o~ Woodford Bridge – the Boys Garden City ~o~o~

During our many visits to England and our contact with Barnardo's Aftercare, we often stayed in the Prince Regent Hotel in Woodford Bridge, London.

Many years earlier, the now Barnardo's organisation sold the entire site of 'the Boys Garden City', including the church, to a developer who, in turn, turned the church where during the war, we were taken for shelter during the air raids, and several of the of the other buildings, into a five-star hotel.

Today, unknown to passers-by, the Prince Regent Hotel, or part of it, is actually all that remains of the old 'Boys Garden City', or what was also called simply Woodford Bridge. The main portion of the hotel is new and yet the church and part of the headmaster's house was to some extent, architecturally retained, and is part of the history of the famous Dr Barnardo's Homes.

I have no memories of the Boys Garden City except what I have already written about, including the air raids and my having to spend nights in the church cellars. And, how could I forget the worst cooked potatoes that I, even to this day, can remember.

~o~ My Dear Old Foster Mother, Mrs Pownell ~o~

On a very foggy day in December 2006 Donna and I, while visiting England to spend Christmas with our dear, 97-year-old Uncle Sid, took time to drive to the little village of Wilnecote, which is situated just outside of Tamworth. We drove to Wilnecote to see the place where I was fostered by Mrs Pownell during the war.

Arriving in Wilnecote and finding Quarry Hill, the street I had lived in as a very small boy of six, we asked a man who was walking along the street going to get his morning newspaper, where, because the numbering system wasn't as clear as it might be, number 23 was.

After having told the man briefly why I was in Wilnecote, and the fact that I had been fostered there during the war, he offered to show us exactly where the house I was looking for was.

As it was, the man didn't know the person who lived at number 23,

SUFFER LITTLE CHILDREN

but he did know the chap who lived at number 27, and that the person living there had lived there all his life. He also felt that the chap, being well over seventy years old, would certainly have known Mrs Pownell and her family. Without much prompting, if any, the man knocked on the door.

The lady of the house at number 27 answered, and after my telling her why we were there, invited Donna and me into her home. The man who had introduced us said a brief hello to her, and then left.

The gentleman of the house, who was perhaps in his late seventies, was about six or seven years older than me. Unfortunately he was dependant on a wheelchair to get around, but was in good spirits and told us that he certainly knew Mrs Pownell, and told us stories of her and her family.

He remembered much about the war years, including the little ironmongers where I would have taken the radio batteries for recharging because he, too, as a young boy, took his family's batteries there.

Even though he would have been about twelve or thirteen years old when I was living there, he couldn't remember me, or of my being fostered by Mrs Pownell. Of course, I wouldn't have expected that he would; after all, it was more than sixty-five years ago since I had lived there, and I would have only been about six years old at the time.

As I quite expected to hear, Mrs Pownell and her husband had passed away a long time ago. However, the school where I had sold the revolver was still there, and so we drove by it. There was nothing much for us to see, and I couldn't recognise or remember anything about it.

The village of Wilnecote had developed and expanded to the point where it was now almost a suburb of Tamworth. The field that I had set fire to and the houses which backed onto it, and also the place where my foster grandmother had lived, had been developed into a housing estate, and therefore had gone.

After a pleasant and memorable visit with the elderly neighbours of Mrs Pownell, we left the Tamworth area and returned to Uncle Sid's house in Weston-Super-Mare.

The day we had driven to Wilnecote was reported to have been the foggiest day in the west of England in fifteen years.

SUFFER LITTLE CHILDREN
~o~o~ Meriden ~o~o~

During the fall of 1999, again while visiting England and staying in Nottingham with my sister Carol, we, with the help of my nephew Mick, one of Carol's sons, took a side trip to Meriden to see if we could find the small private orphanage where I had lived for a period of time in 1942.

Being just seven, or perhaps even eight years old at the time I was living in Meriden, I couldn't now recognise anything about the tiny village at all. In fact, without anyone to actually show us, we couldn't be sure which of the beautiful old large houses on the narrow country lane, might have been the one used as an orphanage, and where I had lived.

The village of Meriden is very beautiful and, standing there in the middle of the village, is the commemorative monument to the cyclists who gave their lives serving their country during the first and second world wars.

Also, there is a large stone monument claiming that Meriden is geographically the centre of England.

My feelings for Meriden were very warm as we walked along the country lane where, it was suggested by an old lady in the local library, the orphanage might have been. Although I didn't speak much about my feelings at that point in time to either Donna, Carol, or my nephew Mick, I couldn't help but remember Willy, and our pigs Pinky and Belly, and even that silly little imp 'Gyro the Germ'.

~o~o~ Bayfordbury Revisited ~o~o~

Donna accompanied me when, in 1987, some forty-four years or so after living at Bayfordbury, I revisited Bayfordbury, Bayford village, and Hertingfordbury. For me it was a very emotional visit, so full of memories both good and bad, but nevertheless extremely interesting.

First, we visited Bayford, and the place where Bayford School had stood. I was sad to find that the school, including Mrs Dunning's house, had all been demolished. Now there were only new houses built on the property that had once been Bayford School.

While Donna and I were standing looking at the very spot where the two-roomed Bayford School had stood, and I was telling Donna all

SUFFER LITTLE CHILDREN

about my childhood there, a rather elderly lady, seeing us surveying the spot, walked up to us.

The dear old lady asked if she could help us. Finding her easy to speak to, I asked her if she had lived here in Bayford for very long. To my delight, she said she had lived here all of her life, and had even attended Bayford School herself when she was a little girl. Because of her senior age, she would have attended Bayford School long before I was even born.

I asked her if she remembered the Dr Barnardo's Homes boys, who came from Bayfordbury to attend Bayford School during the war.

"Yes I do," said this lovely, yet feisty old lady. "Those naughty, naughty little boys; they were so naughty and got into so much trouble."

Smiling, I pleasantly told her that I was one of those "naughty little boys", and how I had loved coming to her little school, and how the villagers had been so kind to us.

The dear old soul smiled too, and we carried on with our conversation. I just loved to hear her; she really did remember us Bayfordbury boys. Had she said we were anything else but naughty little boys, I think I would have been somewhat disappointed.

I told the old lady that Mrs Dunning had been our teacher, and asked her what had happened to her.

She told Donna and myself how Mr Dunning had died many years before Mrs Dunning, and how Mrs Dunning was so disappointed with the village council when they decided to demolish the quaint little old Bayford School.

We said goodbye to the old lady after she told us that the same village hall still stood, even though it wasn't used as the village hall any more. So, I took Donna to see the hall. It was, of course, the same hall where we had had our school dinners, and where I had asked Fred Dyos, "Do ya want my dumpling, Fred?"

Standing there quietly looking at this old wooden structure, I couldn't help remembering Fred, and Baggy, and the fun we had there, and wondered if Elaine Alger might still live in the village. And if she did, would she ever have thought that her little 'rabbit with red wings' might visit Bayford one day, and include her in his lasting memories of her little village.

SUFFER LITTLE CHILDREN

I was so pleased to see that St Mary's Church was still there just as I had remembered it, its gothic architecture still dominating the small village of Bayford.

While we were there, we went into the beautiful little church and read the visitors' book.

Coincidentally, in the church visitors' book, which we too signed, was an entry telling us that a woman from Scarborough, Canada had been there about two weeks before us. I couldn't help but wonder how anyone from Canada would be visiting, or could even find the tiny little village of Bayford, tucked away in the beautiful countryside of Hertfordshire.

After we returned to Canada, and because we actually lived in Scarborough ourselves, I tried to contact the woman, but for whatever reason, or because I simply didn't try hard enough, we just didn't connect, and eventually I forgot.

~o~o~

During our visit to the now empty Bayfordbury, the watchman invited us to look inside the old mansion in its present state. Surprisingly, the old mansion hadn't changed very much over all the years. Very little, if any, restoration or renovation work had taken place. The inside of this otherwise beautiful old mansion looked rather run down, but much like I remembered it.

I was able to show Donna the basement areas where I had lived as a small boy of just nine years old. The atmosphere and the way it looked, gave us both the feeling that it might have come right out of Charles Dickens's classic story, *Oliver Twist*.

Clearly evident and just as I remembered, were the dimly lit corridors, the cold dingy dormitory, and the dining room. The décor, with its whitewashed walls, flagstone floors and cement- rendered ceilings, although dusty, had hardly changed at all.

I couldn't even try to tell you, the reader, the emotion I felt while touring the Bayfordbury mansion. We saw Mr Scougall's office, and the playroom where the piano had stood and where we would sing songs and hymns on a Sunday morning before church.

We also saw the room where the huge Christmas tree had stood,

SUFFER LITTLE CHILDREN

and where I received my first ever Christmas present: a silly, stuffed plasticlike-covered fish, with buttons for its eyes and red cotton stitches for a mouth.

Leaving Bayfordbury and having taken several photos, we visited Hertingfordbury Church. On the way to the church we drove over the little humpback bridge, and stopped the car to look over it. I showed Donna where Williams had taken that almost disastrous jaunt in the kayak.

While we were in Hertingfordbury Church, besides seeing such a beautiful example of the flint pebblestone construction of this lovely church, I showed Donna the spot where at one time I was a choirboy. I even sat in the choir pew where I had sat as a little boy of no more than ten years old. Everything, some forty-five years later or more, was just as I remembered it.

In the graveyard adjoining the church, Donna and I, after much searching, eventually found Mr Scougall's neglected gravestone.

The weeds around the grave were high and the grass overgrown to such an extent that the headstone was hardly visible. The area where Mr Scougall was buried had the appearance of being almost forgotten.

After we had pulled out the longest grass, weeds and stinging nettles, and were able to distinguish the deteriorating lettering on the headstone, we managed to read the name of James Somerville Scougall and his wife Lucy Beatrice Scougall.

As well as their names, was the ironic inscription, which I feel is worth repeating.

IN A LIFETIME OF SERVICE TO YOUTH, HE REMAINED YOUNG.

Seeing Mr Scougall's gravestone brought back memories of the frightening, fearful times we spent at Bayfordbury.

But quickly the bad memories passed, and I couldn't help but recall the fond memories I have of the other times Fred, Baggy, and I had while we lived at the Bayfordbury estate.

Oh yes! I had been so happy to see that Mr Scougall was still there, but couldn't help but remember how much happier we young Bayfordbury boys had been on the day Mr Scougall died, and on the day he was buried.

SUFFER LITTLE CHILDREN

I felt a certain obligation to take a couple of photographs of Mr Scougall's grave to send to my friends Baggy and Lois in Bedford, and to John 'Goodg' Goodger who now lives in the west of England with his wife Christine.

~o~o~

On Donna's and my second visit to Hertingfordbury, a few years later, we took Goodg and Christine with us to see Mr Scougall's headstone. He too, was quite moved, in a somewhat happy way, just as it had been for me. Goodg too, revelled in once again seeing Scougall's grave. After all these years, it was to him too, like a belated moment of closure.

~o~o~ Churchill House, Eastbourne ~o~o~

In 2005 Donna and I went to visit Churchill House with Brian and Edna Partridge, friends from Barnardo's Aftercare, and found that the beautiful old mansion had been completely demolished. It had been replaced by a collection of custom-built houses.

The narrow cinder lane, Love Lane, was still there. Again, I couldn't help but remember my riding our tireless home-made bicycle, without any brakes whatsoever, down the lane, and running over the dog and for my cuts and scrapes, receiving sixpence from the concerned couple.

The playing field, which belonged to the Churchill House estate, and where Flappers and I had swindled the scouts out of money from the 'Aunt Sally' stand, had gone completely in the redevelopment of the area.

Churchill House was gone for ever but, for me, the memories of the good and bad times there will always be with me.

~o~ Revisiting Goldings as a 'Very Old Boy' ~o~

My first of several return visits to Goldings over the ensuing years was in 1987. Jimmy James, a Goldings school captain during my time, made the arrangements for our visit. There were three school captains altogether during my time at Goldings. Jimmy had graciously made arrangements with a senior official who worked for the Hertfordshire County Council,

SUFFER LITTLE CHILDREN

to take the three of us on a personalised tour through Goldings.

Until our visit to England, and subsequently Goldings, I had not been aware that Goldings had been sold in 1965, to the Hertfordshire County Council.

It was, to say the least, extremely sad for me to find that this, my most unforgettable orphanage full of so many happy and yet ghostly memories, was now being used as temporary offices by the Hertfordshire County Council.

Goldings, its name having been changed from the William Baker Technical School to the William Baker Polytechnic School, closed down completely in 1965, and the entire estate was sold.

For me it was very disturbing to see this glorious mansion's irreversible transformation from the 'William Baker Technical School', as I knew it, into a temporary, utility office building.

Nevertheless, as the result of Jimmy James's influence with the Hertfordshire County Council's senior representatives, Donna and I were fortunate enough to have the opportunity to be able to return and see Goldings.

~o~o~

It was now some thirty-seven years after my leaving Goldings, in 1950, until I was to return for this visit. As it was, I found that Goldings looked so forlorn and sad. The boys, having been the heart and soul of the domicile, were now completely gone.

Gone as well, was the boyish laughter that filled the halls, corridors and dormitories. The gleaming polished floors in the dormitories, which had been the pride of their respective houses, were now just scarred floorboards. The ablutions were closed, as was the dining room and Flappers' kitchen.

Joe Patch's gym was an empty shell and in a natural state of abandonment. Gone without a trace, as would be expected, of course, were the memorable characters of Joe and his dog Wolf, absolutely nothing to remind me of them was anywhere to be seen.

But of all the disappointments, the one that I shall never forget was the chapel.

SUFFER LITTLE CHILDREN

I will always remember, that as Donna and I approached the big arched gothic entrance doors to the chapel, I thought I heard muffled voices inside. I stopped and said quietly to Donna, "Listen. There's something going on in there. It must be a service."

Quietly, I opened one of the big solid old oak doors slightly, and peered in. To my utter disbelief, I saw that there was nothing resembling a service going on at all.

Instead, I was appalled and shocked to see that our pews were all gone, and that stained glass windows and the big pipe organ had all been removed. Even the altar, the font and the rostrum were gone. Instead, erected across the centre of our beautiful chapel, a net had been set up and a game of badminton was underway. The muffled sounds that we had heard were the grunts, laughter and the score being shouted out by the players. The players I realised, were a few of the office workers for the council.

Flooding back to me came the memories of our Sunday services, my being confirmed, the atmosphere of the Christmas services, and the singing of 'Spuds and Beetroot'.

I found the transformation from chapel to recreation hall very sad, perhaps even somewhat sacrilegious. I couldn't help but wonder how sad Mr Wheatley and the Reverend Corbett would be to see the absolute degradation of this, our beautiful chapel.

It brought a lump to my throat too, remembering the poor boy that had died, and we had had his funeral in there. The memories stirred me, such that I could almost hear the quietness of the moment just before Parks played the 'Last Post' on his bugle during the funeral.

~o~o~

It was then, while Donna and I were standing in the chapel, that I became so aware that this was now, no longer the Goldings that I, and hundreds of boys before and after me, had known it to be.

The ghostly memories of Mr Wheatley, Skip Culver, the Reverend Corbett, Joe Patch, and Stormy Tempest and the other masters seemed to be everywhere. It was as though they were rather whimsically looking and smiling at me, with Pinhead asking on behalf of all of them,

SUFFER LITTLE CHILDREN

> *"Did we teach you well, Number 7, Reg Longman? Have you suffered in life as the result of being brought up in Dr Barnardo's Homes, and in particular, Goldings?"*

And,

> *"Are you having a good life, Number 7, and did you make something worthwhile of yourself since leaving Goldings?*
> *How are the other boys you were most friendly with? You know who we mean, don't you? – your closest friends, like Number 68 'Baggy' Baggaridge, who you were friends with since the age of seven, and Number 1 'Flapper' Foot, Number 34 'Goodg' Goodger and 24 'Fuzz' Foley?"*

~o~o~

As I have mentioned, Donna and I have visited Goldings on several occasions over the past fifteen years or more. The last time we visited, part of Goldings was in transformation and being turned into a movie set for the making of scenes for the Steven Speilberg and Tom Hanks movie, *The Band of Brothers*.

Because of its age and its architectural character, Goldings lent itself well as an appropriate setting for the Harry Potter movies, and parts of the earlier Harry Potter films, we were told were made here.

Now the entire estate has been turned into condominiums, which cost a minimum of one million pounds each. Sadly, the Dr Barnardo or 'Dicky' boys, but as we would rather be called, 'Goldings boys', are no longer allowed past the estate gatehouses. Now a pass is needed to enter the estate, which even to this day, is still called Goldings.

~o~o~ Childhood 'Brothers' Update ~o~o~

After more than sixty years of my leaving Dr Barnardo's Homes, I have been reacquainted with a few of my old Dr Barnardo 'brothers'. As I have previously mentioned, these were the boys who, – unlike natural born brothers – living together in orphanages throughout

SUFFER LITTLE CHILDREN

our childhood, were as close as any brothers can be.

I can only thank the 'powers-that-were' for the good fortune for my having met, and known my adopted 'brothers', and for being with them throughout my childhood and adolescent years of growing up.

Interestingly, I can add the following conclusions to my story:

~o~o~ Fred Dyos ~o~o~

A good friend of mine, Eddy Parr (not a Dr Barnardo boy) from my late teenage years and early twenties while I was living in Taunton, immigrated to Australia in 1963. There he became a scholar at Queensland University. In 1998 Eddy visited Donna and myself in Canada. I asked Ed if he could track down Fred Dyos, who had been migrated to Sydney, Australia in 1946 by Dr Barnardo's Homes.

I gave Ed as much information as I could, and after some diligent investigation he put me in touch with Les Dyos, Fred's older brother. Eddy wasn't able to find Fred.

I wrote to Les, who in turn wrote back. He told me that Fred had apprenticed and had become a very good carpenter, just as Fred, Baggy, and I had planned to do as young boys in the orphanages.

Fred, I was to learn, had built his own house, and that he was married and had a nice family. Les also informed me that Fred was very happy in his life in Australia.

At the same time, Les cautioned me not to expect a reply from Fred if I wrote to him. Les said that neither he nor his younger brother Billy heard from Fred very often.

Les also told me that Fred had been emotionally affected by having been brought up in Dr Barnardo's Homes, and wanted nothing more to do with his past, or those who had formed any part of it.

I had asked Les for Fred's telephone number, but he told me that Fred was not listed in the Sydney phone system. However, he gave me Fred's address, and suggested I write to him.

Regardless of whatever the disappointment that may follow, I couldn't be deterred. I was sure Fred would want to hear from me, so I wrote to him and told him briefly how our old friend Baggy and I had fared in life over the years since he had left us at Churchill House to be migrated

SUFFER LITTLE CHILDREN

to Australia.

I told Fred how much I would like to hear from him, and that I would write and tell him more about Baggy, and the other boys we knew at Bayfordbury and Churchill House. But, much to my disappointment, Fred never replied.

During our time of writing, Les told me that he and his brother Billy seemed to hear less and less of Fred, and now hardly ever heard from him at all.

Apparently, due to his treatment at Bayfordbury and for other reasons Fred, as Les had forewarned me, didn't ever reply to me. I heard from Les a few more times, and then our correspondence ceased.

~o~o~

While Donna and I were helping as volunteers for Barnardo's Aftercare in Canada, we were to learn that many children – boys and girls – often, after reaching adulthood, became disillusioned with their upbringing and life in general. They, to some extent, became antisocial and did not mix well. There are apparently many suicides among the orphans who cannot cope with the turmoil of their childhood.

I have often said myself that most psychologists would have a 'field day' having an orphan, including myself no doubt, for a patient to study.

~o~o~

Mr and Mrs Castle have, as would be expected, both passed away now, as have most of the names I have mentioned in my story, including Mr Wheatley (Pinhead); Skip Culver; Joe Patch; Mr and Mrs Dunning; Snowy White; and Mr Fogg.

At the time of writing this book, Miss, or Nurse Rand would be in her late eighties should she still be alive today. As it is, I still think of Miss Rand fondly from time to time, but have absolutely no idea how I can find her.

SUFFER LITTLE CHILDREN
~o~o~ John 'Baggy' Baggaridge ~o~o~

Baggy made a career in the Army, serving in the Beds and Herts Regiment – the same regiment that Captain Skip Culver served in during the two world wars.

After a full term in the Army, Baggy retired, having reached the distinguished rank of sergeant major, a very senior non-commissioned rank in the Army. He could have gone no further in his career without becoming an officer, but without the necessary academic education this would have been a very difficult endeavour.

When he retired, after serving in several parts of the world and in several campaigns, he and his wife Lois bought a lovely little house in Bedford.

Donna and Lois often heard Baggy and me speak of our lives together at Bayfordbury, of Mr Scougall and Mr Nash and the way we were treated, as well as the hardships we were forced to endure.

Donna and Lois would listen and hear the experiences Baggy and I would reminisce about.

We spoke of the fun we had at Bayford School, of the gentle Mrs Dunning, and our happy and more organised lives at Goldings. We would also speak of the people we had known throughout our childhood, including the good and the bad masters. But in particular we would remember the Goldings staff, many of whom are mentioned in this book.

Baggy, just like I have, had a remarkably good memory, and remembered well our good old friend Fred Dyos. Of course, he also remembered Flappers, Foley and Goodger. Although they weren't particularly his friends, he knew them well.

Baggy easily remembered the many other boys who had lived at Bayfordbury and Churchill House, and the fearsome Mr Scougall, Mr Nash, and the miserable Mr Fowlermott and his shrewish wife.

Like myself, Baggy could never forget the big yet fatherly Mr Castle and as well Mrs Castle and dear Nurse Rand – or the other Churchill House staff – who between them had made life for us much happier, than ever it was when we were at Bayfordbury.

Of Goldings, we remembered and spoke much about Joe Patch and the school boxing team, the competitive house sports, Wimbledon, and

SUFFER LITTLE CHILDREN

the good times we had during those youthful, almost carefree days.

Those were the days when our characters were being moulded, for better or for worse. Fortunately, the harsh treatment we received at Bayfordbury was greatly outweighed by the much happier life we had lived at Goldings.

I was still in touch with my old lifelong friend Baggy until in December 2007 – just a little over a year prior to my completing the writing of this book – when John 'Baggy' Baggaridge died. He was seventy-four years old. I will never forget Baggy, and will always remember him as being one of my best, lifelong friends.

~o~o~

Just as I found Donna, John found the love that had been missing in his earlier life when he found Lois. They had four lovely daughters, and, as once was described of my parents and their children, they too lived "the wandering life of a soldier's family" and as such, travelled the world happily together.

Donna and I are still in touch with Lois, who is in reasonable health. Needless for me to say, she misses Baggy every single day of her life.

~o~o~ Number 1 – Albert 'Flappers' Foot ~o~o~

In 1998 I wrote to Barnardo's Aftercare and inquired after Flappers, hoping that they may have some knowledge as to his whereabouts. I had had hopes of being able to meet up with Flappers again after having said goodbye to him almost fifty years earlier.

I asked Lyn Clargo, the lady I wrote to in Barnardo's Aftercare, if there had been any contact with Albert Foot since he left Goldings, in what would have been in the early part of 1951.

I had mentioned to Lyn that Flappers had trained as a cook at Goldings, and that perhaps he had been situated somewhere in the London area, and that maybe he worked as a chef in a hotel.

I also told Lyn that I wouldn't think Flappers would have been qualified to work in a particularly good hotel, as he had primarily only learned how to cook 'hardbake', 'plonk', 'dogmeat', cheese pie and the likes.

SUFFER LITTLE CHILDREN

Lyn wrote back and mentioned, to my regret, that unfortunately Barnardo's had never heard from him since the day that he had left Goldings. She also added in her comical reply to me that,

> *If Flappers had been situated as a chef in a reasonably-classed hotel, she hoped his repertoire relative to his professional cooking abilities would have expanded by now, and that his culinary skills would include, for his sake, better or perhaps more dignified dishes than those I had mentioned.*

~o~o~

Eventually, Anne Newill, who had been a conscientious and a very diligent worker for Barnardo's, doggedly tracked Flappers down for me. In doing so she was to learn that his name, Albert Foot, was not the name he was born with.

Anne found out that for some reason, probably as a result of an error, Dr Barnardo's Homes had changed his name to Albert Foot when he entered the homes. Upon his leaving Dr Barnardo's Homes, the mistake had been discovered, and Flappers' name was changed back to his rightful name.

Anne was also to inform me that unfortunately my childhood friend Albert 'Flappers' Foot, as I had always known him and wished to remember him, had passed away several years earlier.

Poor ole Flappers had died at a fairly young age, apparently. He had lived all of his remaining years since leaving Goldings, in London, and eventually died of a drug overdose.

Sad as I was to hear it, I can't say that I was overly surprised. Flappers was a good, loyal, and very special friend to me. But right from our childhood days, he always walked a 'tightrope' between good and bad, and at some point, like so many others, he fell off.

And so it turned out that after my leaving Goldings, I never saw or heard anything about Flappers again, except for what I have mentioned. Nevertheless, for better or for worse, I will always remember and cherish the memories of my good ole 'Artful Dodger' friend, Flappers.

SUFFER LITTLE CHILDREN
~o~o~ Number 24 – Victor 'Fuzz' Foley ~o~o~

I was sorry to learn, upon our first visit to England in 1987, that another of my special friends, Fuzz Foley, had also died several years earlier. He had stayed and lived in Hertford for the rest of his life, having first served in the Parachute Regiment in Africa while completing his National Service.

As with Flappers, I was never to see Fuzz again from the day I left Goldings in 1950, but I will always remember him for the good and special friend that he was.

~o~o~ Number 34 – John 'Goodg' Goodger ~o~o~

Through Barnardo's Aftercare, I discovered the whereabouts of John Goodger and visited him in 1999 at his home near Sidmouth, Dorset, England. Goodg was fine. He too, remembered most, if not all, of the good and bad times we had during our 'growing up'.

We laughed when remembering the pain in the back of our heads when we reached the top notes playing our bugles, and certainly remembered the terrible mess we made of playing the 'Last Post' during the Armistice service in 1948 at Stapleford Church.

To my amusement, however, he wasn't overly enthusiastic about remembering 'taking a dive' during his boxing match at Leighton Buzzard, or at least he wouldn't let his wife Christine even believe the story, which I know that he knows is absolutely true.

I was sorry to have to tell Goodg that our old friends Fuzz Foley and Flappers had passed away several years ago. He, like me, remembered them with fondness, as brothers would.

Unfortunately John Goodger and I have little in common today, and so we have lost touch again. However, it's nice to know that he fared well in life and is happily married to a lovely girl and has a fine son.

SUFFER LITTLE CHILDREN

CONCLUSION

To conclude my story, the story of a small boy who was orphaned at the age of almost five, and who had been brought up or raised under the guardianship of Dr Barnardo's Homes, I would simply say that although life for me had many ups and downs, it was not, as it ultimately turned out, to be such a bad beginning in life.

For the likes of myself, life, without the help and sanctuary of Dr Barnardo's Homes, could have taken a much different turn. Who could know what any child could suffer, without parents or proper guardianship in their young and impressionable years.

Dr Barnardo's Homes gave me the benefit of many satisfactory attributes and with them, my start in life. I believe that, as the result of my benefactor's guidance, I fared reasonably well in life.

SUFFER LITTLE CHILDREN

POSTSCRIPT

For a short period of time after leaving Goldings I, together with Reg Howitt, would meet regularly with Baggy and Stan Dean on Friday evenings in Tottenham, London, and we would spend time together exploring London, gradually acclimatising and blending into the outsiders' world and its way of life.

Just before Christmas in 1950, I said goodbye to Reg Howitt and Stan Dean. At the same time I said a somewhat sad goodbye to Baggy, and left London to move to Taunton and live with my grandparents.

Except for one very brief meeting, just before I left to come to Canada in 1957, I wasn't to see or hear of Baggy again for the next forty-four years.

In the spring of 2001 Donna and I, with the help of Anne Newill of Barnardo's Aftercare, managed to find and get in touch with John and Lois Baggaridge, and later in the year we went to Bedford in Bedfordshire to see them.

We stayed with John and Lois for three days. John and I constantly, with Donna and Lois listening intently, recalled the good and the bad times in our lives at the three major orphanages we were together at: Bayfordbury, Churchill House, and Goldings. Lois was already familiar with many of our stories, but liked to hear them again anyway.

On another visit to England a year or so later, John, Lois, Donna, and I attended a Goldings' reunion together. There were not many old boys of our time present. However, our old friend Reg Howitt, who has lived in Ware for most of his life, was there. Needless to say, we had lots to talk and reminisce about.

I end my story by proudly quoting our Goldings motto:

FINIS CORONET OPUS
(The End Crowns the Work)

SUFFER LITTLE CHILDREN

CHAPTER INDEX

CHAPTER 1 – PRIMARY MEMORIES
~o~o~Longman – My Father's Family
~o~o~Pinfold – My Mother's Family
~o~o~Queenie Eastland (Pinfold)
~o~o~Carol Muir (Pinfold)

CHAPTER 2 – THE BEGINNING OF A TURBULENT CHILDHOOD
~o~o~Arrival in Hong Kong
~o~o~Stepmother, Beatrice Snell
~o~o~The Millbank Barracks, London
~o~o~Feeding the Birds and Us
~o~o~World War II – Evacuation to Brighton
~o~o~The Big Red Rooster

CHAPTER 3 – DR BARNARDO'S HOMES
~o~o~Orphaned
~o~o~Entering Dr Barnardo's Homes
~o~o~Goodbye Stepmother Beat and Half-sister Betty
~o~o~Thomas Barnardo
~o~o~Goodbye Barbara
~o~o~The Boys Garden City – Woodford Bridge
~o~o~Air Raids over London
~o~o~Running Away

CHAPTER 4 – ON THE MOVE AGAIN
~o~o~Pillar to Post
~o~o~Adventure
~o~o~A Village Orphanage
~o~o~Frogspawn
~o~o~My Childish Wish
~o~o~I'll Walk Beside You
~o~o~The Soldier in Church
~o~o~Sad Goodbyes

SUFFER LITTLE CHILDREN

CHAPTER 5 – TAMWORTH – FOSTER HOME
~○~○~A Real Home
~○~○~Mrs Pownell, My Foster Mother
~○~○~Ration Books
~○~○~A Good Old-Fashioned Spanking
~○~○~The Revolver
~○~○~Return to Mrs Pownell
~○~○~The Big Fire
~○~○~One More Chance

CHAPTER 6 – HAPPY DAYS AT MERIDEN
~○~○~My Friend Willy
~○~○~Pinky and Belly
~○~○~Parcels from Canada
~○~○~'Giro the Germ'
~○~○~'How Do You Make Glass?'
~○~○~Chickenpox
~○~○~Gas Masks
~○~○~Orchestral Concert Outings
~○~○~Goodbye Willy
~○~○~The China Plate

CHAPTER 7 – BAYFORDBURY – PART 1
~○~○~Mr Scougall
~○~○~Bayfordbury, The Mansion
~○~○~Institutions, Borstals, Dr Barnardo's Homes
~○~○~Dicky Boys
~○~○~Lady Clinton Baker
~○~○~John 'Baggy' Baggaridge and Fred Dyos
~○~○~The Gamekeeper
~○~○~The Bucket
~○~○~'Spinning Up'
~○~○~Brutal Caning
~○~○~A Reason for Caning?

SUFFER LITTLE CHILDREN

CHAPTER 8 – BAYFORDBURY – PART 2
~o~o~Bayford School
~o~o~The Rabbit with Red Wings
~o~o~The Outhouse Toilet
~o~o~Here's to Bayford School
~o~o~Fred and the Fat Ball
~o~o~Gleaning
~o~o~Potato Picking
~o~o~Bayford Church
~o~o~Incendiary Bombs and Shrapnel
~o~o~Brick Fights
~o~o~Goodbye Mrs Dunning and Bayford School

CHAPTER 9 – BAYFORDBURY – PART 3
~o~o~Daily Routine
~o~o~Cheating for Survival
~o~o~Ware School
~o~o~Mrs Blackwell
~o~o~Girls
~o~o~The Chinese Auction
~o~o~Vegetarian
~o~o~Reciting the Bible
~o~o~Mr Tustin, Our Music Teacher
~o~o~Heading the Wooden Ball
~o~o~Feeding Little Birdie
~o~o~'Trashy' or 'Span it'

CHAPTER 10 – BAYFORDBURY – PART 4
~o~o~How Well We Remember
~o~o~Loyalty to Each Other
~o~o~Fighting
~o~o~Bayfordbury Staff
~o~o~Punishment to the Extreme
~o~o~Out of Bounds
~o~o~Foraging
~o~o~Hertingfordbury Choirboy

SUFFER LITTLE CHILDREN

~o~o~Williams 'Kayaking'
~o~o~Hertingfordbury Village
~o~o~Bayfordbury Food
~o~o~Food Servings
~o~o~Sunday Teatime
~o~o~Bread Slicing
~o~o~Bed Wetting
~o~o~A Beating from Mr Nash

Chapter 11 – Bayfordbury – Part 5
~o~o~Albert 'Flappers' Foot
~o~o~The Sport of Shoplifting
~o~o~Flappers, Our Leader
~o~o~Special Outings
~o~o~My First Christmas
~o~o~My Christmas 'Fish'
~o~o~'Blacky' the Rook
~o~o~Making Butter
~o~o~Doodlebugs
~o~o~John Thomas and the Mouse
~o~o~Mr Scougall's Humour
~o~o~Organised Unfair Sharing
~o~o~Conkers

Chapter 12 – Bayfordbury – Part 6
~o~o~Chilblains and Chaps
~o~o~Beating (for Hunters)
~o~o~Summer Living at Bayfordbury
~o~o~Outdoor Dining
~o~o~Raiding Wasp and Hornet's Nests
~o~o~Swimming in the River Lee
~o~o~Bayfordbury and Dr Barnardo Songs
~o~o~American Soldiers
~o~o~Bird Nesting
~o~o~The Owl's Nest
~o~o~Bicycle Wheel Hoops

SUFFER LITTLE CHILDREN

~o~o~Crude Field Hockey
~o~o~Picking Wild Mushrooms
~o~o~Exploited

CHAPTER 13 – BAYFORDBURY – PART 7
~o~o~Holiday with Gran and Granddad
~o~o~Meeting My Sisters
~o~o~Meeting Aunty Molly and Cousin Jill
~o~o~Blue Anchor
~o~o~Sister Carol
~o~o~Flowers for Aunty Molly

CHAPTER 14 – BAYFORDBURY – PART 8
~o~o~Back to Bayfordbury
~o~o~Approaching D-Day
~o~o~VE Day
~o~o~One of the Happiest Days of My Life
~o~o~'Good Riddance to Bad Rubbish' (As the Saying Goes)
~o~o~Enter Mr Castle
~o~o~Closing Bayfordbury
~o~o~On the Move

CHAPTER 15 – CHURCHILL HOUSE – PART 1
~o~o~Moving to Eastbourne
~o~o~Churchill House
~o~o~Bedewell School
~o~o~Mr Castle in the Sudan
~o~o~Miss (Nurse) Rand
~o~o~Sea Scouts
~o~o~The Scouts International Jamboree
~o~o~Scouts Paper Drive
~o~o~Scouts Garden Fete
~o~o~Paid a Penny

SUFFER LITTLE CHILDREN

Chapter 16 – Churchill House – Part 2
~o~o~Fatigues
~o~o~Poor Ole Flappers
~o~o~Love Lane
~o~o~Cheeky Beggars
~o~o~Dodging in
~o~o~Staff Qualification
~o~o~Fox in the Henhouse
~o~o~Angora the Rabbit
~o~o~The Handcuffs
~o~o~Chocolates in the Window
~o~o~The Day of Reckoning

Chapter 17 – Churchill House – Part 3
~o~o~Back to Taunton
~o~o~Blue Anchor
~o~o~Making a Kite
~o~o~VE Day Anniversary
~o~o~Carol – Torquay
~o~o~Sad Goodbyes Again

Chapter 18 – Churchill House – Part 4
~o~o~Traditional Begging
~o~o~Carol Singing
~o~o~For Better or for Worse
~o~o~Poetic Justice
~o~o~Making up Plays
~o~o~Sad Announcement
~o~o~A Turn for the Worse
~o~o~Mr Nash, My Childhood Nemesis
~o~o~Plans to Move
~o~o~Goodbye Fred
~o~o~Defiance
~o~o~Moving On
~o~o~Goldings

SUFFER LITTLE CHILDREN

Chapter 19 – Goldings – Part 1
~o~o~William Baker Technical School (WBTS)
~o~o~Goldings Orientation
~o~o~Goldings Slang
~o~o~Long Trousers
~o~o~ Describing Goldings
~o~o~Cabinet Making with Mr Dunning
~o~o~Friends and Nicknames
~o~o~Back to Bayfordbury
~o~o~The Headmaster, Mr Wheatley (Pinhead)
~o~o~Bugle Calls
~o~o~Dormitory Floor Polishing
~o~o~'Spud Bashing'
~o~o~Sexual Confusion
~o~o~Mr Castle, Clacton-on-Sea

Chapter 20 – Goldings – Part 2
~o~o~Flappers 'The Gardener'
~o~o~Learning to Play the Bugle
~o~o~The Grub
~o~o~Selling Food
~o~o~My First Watch
~o~o~Homosexuality
~o~o~A Dubious Honour
~o~o~From 'Bread of Heaven' to 'Spuds and Beetroot'
~o~o~Mr 'Stormy' Tempest
~o~o~Cabinet Making

Chapter 21 – Goldings – Part 3
~o~o~Longman, Foley and Goodger
~o~o~Chapel
~o~o~"Lay Not up for Yourselves..."
~o~o~Pocket Money
~o~o~Confirmation
~o~o~Punishments in General
~o~o~Good Friends

SUFFER LITTLE CHILDREN

~o~o~Supplementary Cooking
~o~o~Indoor Hockey
~o~o~Smoking

Chapter 22 – Goldings – Part 4
~o~o~Armistice Day 1949
~o~o~Smoking in the Dormitory
~o~o~State Fair
~o~o~Mr Joe Patch
~o~o~Gwendolyn Easy
~o~o~Murder / Dickenson
~o~o~The Murder Trial
~o~o~The Old Man and Flappers
~o~o~Silver Bugler
~o~o~The Royal Tournament

Chapter 23 – Goldings – Part 5
~o~o~Thursday Night Pictures
~o~o~Academic Schooling
~o~o~Prep School
~o~o~Coloured Boys
~o~o~Ritchie
~o~o~School Boxing Team
~o~o~Goodg Took a Dive
~o~o~Captain / Mr 'Skip' Culver
~o~o~Army Cadets
~o~o~Cadet Camp
~o~o~A Lesson in Integrity

Chapter 24 – Goldings – Part 6
~o~o~Girls and Dancing
~o~o~Ball Boys – Wimbledon
~o~o~Distractions at Wimbledon
~o~o~The Browning Version
~o~o~Pets
~o~o~Dymchurch

SUFFER LITTLE CHILDREN

~○~○~To Maud, Love Victor
~○~○~Ah! Peaches
~○~○~Crazy Flappers
~○~○~A Goldings Boy's Funeral

CHAPTER 25 – GOLDINGS – PART 7
~○~○~The Goldonian
~○~○~Slap-up Supper
~○~○~To Go on a 'Situation'
~○~○~Interview for a Situation
~○~○~Goodbye Goldings
~○~○~On Reflection

CHAPTER 26 – DR BARNARDO'S HOMES – REVISITED
~○~○~1957 – Canada
~○~○~Barkingside
~○~○~Woodford Bridge – the Boys Garden City
~○~○~My Dear Old Foster Mother, Mrs Pownell
~○~○~Meriden
~○~○~Bayfordbury Revisited
~○~○~Churchill House, Eastbourne
~○~○~Revisiting Goldings as a 'Very Old Boy'
~○~○~Childhood 'Brothers' Update
~○~○~Fred Dyos
~○~○~John 'Baggy' Baggaridge
~○~○~Number 1 – Albert 'Flappers' Foot
~○~○~Number 24 – Victor 'Fuzz' Foley
~○~○~Number 34 – John 'Goodg' Goodger

SUFFER LITTLE CHILDREN

AFTERMATH

Shortly after leaving Goldings, I studied for my National Certificate in Building Science and Technology at Bristol University.

In 1957, I immigrated to Toronto, Canada. Shortly after arriving, even though I wasn't qualified under Canadian standards as an architect, I was examined and qualified as a certified architectural technologist, and worked as an architect for the rest of my working career.

In 1963, I became happily married to Donna Irene Scott. Together we have had, in every respect, a good life together. We were, as is said, blessed with four sons.

In 1968, I first joined Bregman and Hamann Architects and Engineers, which even today, is still one of the largest and most prestigious firms of architects in Canada.

Eventually, in 1998, I retired from B & H Architects, having achieved the position of being the firm's Director of Contract Administration and, as well, an Associate in the firm.

Donna and I have been retired for the past fourteen years, in the beautiful country setting of Roseneath, near Cobourg, Ontario, Canada and are very content and happy here.

IN RETROSPECT

The welfare of children in many orphanages during the Second World War, as compared to the relatively compassionate world of today, was extremely different in Britain. There were no 'watch dogs' or others, to officially monitor, inspect, or observe the way in which institutionalised children, orphans or otherwise, were looked after. And so, in many instances, children were abused physically and mentally, as well as being carelessly nurtured.

Life, until perhaps the latter part of the twentieth century, was very hard for the majority of orphans of the day.

Many, if not most caregivers, employed by Dr Barnardo's Homes, as well as other orphanage systems no doubt, to look after the children in their charge, particularly during the Second World War, were simply not qualified to do so.

Because of the inabilities of the staff, due to their lack of understanding of children, and insufficient training, if any training was even given at all, the children to some extent, suffered, and in certain 'Homes' in particular, lived to some extent, a life of stress and misery